DRIVEN

DRIVEN

RUSH IN THE '90s AND "IN THE END"

MARTIN POPOFF

Published by ECW Press
665 Gerrard Street East
Toronto, Ontario, Canada M4M 1Y2
416-694-3348 / info@ecwpress.com

Editor for the Press: Michael Holmes
Cover design: David A. Gee
Front cover photograph © John Arrowsmith

LIBRARY AND ARCHIVES CANADA CATALOGUING IN PUBLICATION

Title: Driven : Rush in the '90s and "in the end" / Martin Popoff.

Other titles: Rush in the '90s and "in the end" | Rush in the nineties and "in the end"

Names: Popoff, Martin, 1963- author.

Identifiers: Canadiana (print) 20200404431 | Canadiana (ebook) 20200404490

ISBN 978-1-77041-537-9 (HARDCOVER)
ISBN 978-1-77305-669-2 (EPUB)
ISBN 978-1-77305-670-8 (PDF)
ISBN 978-1-77305-671-5 (KINDLE)

Subjects: LCSH: Rush (Musical group) | LCSH: Rock musicians—Canada—Biography. | LCGFT: Biographies.

Classification: LCC ML421.R95 P84 2021 | DDC 782.42166092/2—dc23

The publication of *Driven* has been generously supported by the Canada Council for the Arts and is funded in part by the Government of Canada. *Nous remercions le Conseil des arts du Canada de son soutien. Ce livre est financé en partie par le gouvernement du Canada.* We acknowledge the support of the Ontario Arts Council (OAC), an agency of the Government of Ontario, which last year funded 1,965 individual artists and 1,152 organizations in 197 communities across Ontario for a total of $51.9 million. We also acknowledge the contribution of the Government of Ontario through the Ontario Book Publishing Tax Credit, and through Ontario Creates for the marketing of this book.

ONTARIO ARTS COUNCIL
CONSEIL DES ARTS DE L'ONTARIO
an Ontario government agency
un organisme du gouvernement de l'Ontario

Canada Council   Conseil des arts
for the Arts   du Canada

Canadä

PRINTED AND BOUND IN CANADA

PRINTING: FRIESENS   5 4 3 2 1

MIX
Paper from responsible sources
FSC   FSC® C016245
www.fsc.org

TABLE OF CONTENTS

INTRODUCTION

The book you now hold in your hands marks the conclusion of a trilogy, a long journey down the path of progressive metal greatness. It started with *Anthem: Rush in the '70s* and was perpetuated and provoked by *Limelight: Rush in the '80s*, and it concludes now, beyond bittersweet, after the death of Neil Peart from brain cancer on January 7, 2020.

The dark news came to light near the end of the production process for *Anthem* and *Limelight*, so in those books Neil remains forever alive and disseminating his wisdoms as "the Professor." But the tragic end to one of rock's towering greats can't be avoided any longer, and so it is part of this story.

For now, however, some background for you, on the subject of this book. If you are wondering why — or indeed *how* — this book exists, let me explain, quoting more or less verbatim from the intro of the first book from way, way back, *Anthem*, if I may.

There I wrote:

> As you may be aware, this is my fourth Rush book, following *Contents Under Pressure: 30 Years of Rush at Home & Away*, *Rush: The Illustrated History* and *Rush: Album by Album*. And since those, there have been a number of interesting developments that made me want to write this one. To start, only one of those three books, *Contents*, was a traditional biography — an authorized one at that — but it was quite short, and given that it came out in 2004 before Rush was officially retired, it was in need of an update. I thought about it, but I wasn't feeling it, not without some vigorous additions.
>
> That, fortunately, took care of itself. In the early 2010s, I found myself working with Sam Dunn and Scot McFadyen at Banger Films on the award-winning documentary *Rush: Beyond the Lighted Stage*. Anybody who works in docs will tell you that between the different speakers and non-talk footage that has to get into what might end up a ninety-minute film, only a tiny percentage of the interview footage ever gets used, the rest just sits in archive, rarely seen or heard by anyone. Long and short of it, I arranged to use that archive, along with more interviews I'd done over the years, plus the odd quote from the available press, to get this book to the point where I felt it was bringing something new and significant to the table of Rush books.
>
> So there you have it, thanks in large part to those guys — as well as the kind consent of Pegi Cecconi at the Rush office — the book you hold in your hands more than ably supplants *Contents Under Pressure* and stands as the most strident and detailed analysis of the Rush catalogue in existence.

Now, to the present tome, what to make of Rush in the '90s and "in the end," so to speak, the 2000s and the 2010s, right up until the band's retirement in 2015 and the great loss to family and friends resulting from Neil's being taken from us in 2020?

Obviously, we'll get to that, but this is the place for a spot of personal reflection, so here goes. As an angry metalhead more excited by what Pantera was doing to music now that they had Phil and a major label deal, the twee tones of *Roll the Bones* had me casting that record aside pretty quick. Sure, there's always excitement around a Rush album, and this one for some reason generated a bit more than usual, but still, I wasn't happy.

When *Counterparts* launched, to my mind, Rush was back — the music was full-bodied, the writing not appreciably different, but it wasn't hobbled by a lightness that brought the already underpopulated trio down to what seemed like 2.5 or 2.25 members. I loved the record, loved the resonance of the bass, the boom of the drums, the authority howling out of the guitars. *Test for Echo* left me cold, like the album cover, and then right after, we all had to deal with the shock of the horror that was Neil's personal life after the death of his daughter, Selena, and then his common-law wife, Jackie. Maybe it was the end of Rush: Alex and Geddy both had solo albums (that sounded like Rush in the '90s), and there were a hundred other flavors. Yes, maybe this was the end.

Fortunately, it was not to be. Neil mended as best as could be expected under the circumstances, and the band returned with a masterful new record, *Vapor Trails*. I don't know what it is about this record, but putting aside the dark wisdom of its lyrics, it's arguably the best of a top-shelf canon thus far. I felt like this was the first time since *Grace Under Pressure* that the band had created a whole new style of music, and it was art at the same time.

I loved the record — still do — old mix, remix. I've always got time for *Vapor Trails*.

So then a weird thing happens. I do the *Contents Under Pressure* book and then work at Banger on the movie. Add another couple of Rush books later on, get interviewed for a couple of Rush docs, and suddenly, Rush reminds me of work. I imagine that's where I am any time I even think to put a Rush record on (this reticence fades, fortunately). But yes, here I am living in Toronto, and it's all Rush all the time and I'm full up. But then — God love the guys — *Snakes & Arrows* is issued, and it's all fresh again. Something has shifted since *Vapor Trails*. Whether it's new producer Nick Raskulinecz or just the band's typical rapid growth, suddenly there's a new sound, if I can generalize, one characterized by warmth along with acoustic guitars massaged in with electrics.

Next came *Clockwork Angels* and little did we know it would be the last. Not only was this a record that lived lively like its predecessor, but there was an additional heaviness due to the subtraction of the acoustics. What's more, Rush delivered their first concept album proper after stopping at a full side in the past. Here they barreled on through a somewhat befuddling plot, but one brimming with rich imagery with the addition of steampunk to the stew, which was stressed more through the stage sets of the tour.

Then it was all over with a languid goodbye, the band touring the record proper and then embarking on something called R40, a fortieth anniversary tour that found the band playing songs from their catalogue in reverse chronological order, making progressively modest their stage set in tandem, until there they were, three kids rocking songs from 1974.

Four years and five months after the band's last show, the shocking news reverberated through the rock community that

Neil had died, and it was horribly clear to all that the soft retirement of Rush was final. More, unfortunately, on this later, but there you go. That's where Rush ends and that's where we can end this set of three books, this particular tome celebrating the biggest expanse of years and the worst news imaginable, but on the happy side, there is a raft of records similar to those covered in both *Anthem* and *Limelight*. In any event, thanks for reading along. Whether you parachuted in here with modern Rush or have been following the bouncing ball since the first book, I'm glad to share my deep appreciation of Rush with you. Without further ado, in the immortal words of the Professor, "Why are we here? Because we're here. Roll the bones."

MARTIN POPOFF

CHAPTER 1

ROLL THE BONES

"We keep looking for the better version of Rush."

Here's how the '90s started for Rush.

One week after Geddy, Alex and Neil would propose an austere something-or-other called *Roll the Bones*, Guns N' Roses would drop two near-double albums, *Use Your Illusion I* and *Use Your Illusion II*.

Another week goes by and on September 24, 1991, Nirvana offered for your consideration their second album, *Nevermind*, led by a little something called "Smells Like Teen Spirit."

Roll the Bones did not sound like Guns N' Roses or Nirvana, nor did it sound like really anything out there (and that's not necessarily a good thing), other than *Presto*, Rush's similarly thin, mild and modest record from two years previous when the band was facing the same realities: hair metal, grunge and thrash at the fore, Rush's brand of progressive bonsai tree and origami pop — a curious thing — but let's go see Rush anyway.

But credit to the guys in one sense: they were believing in the stark and odd and oddball evolutionary path they were on and damn the torpedoes. Rupert Hine returned as producer, signifying that they thought they got it right on *Presto*. Rupert was in a sort of fourth member role in the Rush cabal, which helps underscore the identity of any given project.

"We felt we were missing something," figures Geddy, on the importance of these strong outside voices. "We felt we weren't learning enough. It's like going into a fantastic restaurant and seeing all these great dishes and wanting to try all of them; that's how we were. We felt like we had this great start. We had this great upbringing, and we learned a hell of a lot about making records. We were born into this rock world, and we had some tools and we wanted to refine those tools. And the only way to do that was to work with more people, different people.

"Because of the style of music we played, there was a real bias against kind of progressive heavy metal, and we found it difficult to work with all the producers we wanted to work with. And so every time out, we had a new list of people. We came into this whole mode of unearthing producers that maybe would be unlikely people for us to work with, but we felt had some real heart as producers. And that started the whole thing. It's like, when it's time to make a record, let's dig up the names, let's pick up the lists. Who can we find? Who is out there? Who is just coming into his own as a producer? And can we grab some of that excitement?

"In the early days of doing that, it was experience we were after. I think now, and especially with Nick, it's youthful energy and a different attitude toward making records, and that's a way for us to stay current. We can't help being who we are, and we're not going to work with anybody else. There's the three of us, and we're dedicated to that, so what's the easiest thing to change?

It's the people around you when you make a record. That's the easiest way — and for me the smartest way — of bringing new energy, new ideas, into an old idea — Rush — you know? A forty-year-old idea."

Reflects Rupert: "At the time, because of the urge to keep things fresh, you are looking for all kinds of ways of moving the parts around, and some input, some random input. That just marks them as wanting to stay in the world of making records together, because they could have split up, they could have formed three independent bands based on each other and done a million things with the kind of fan base they had, and still had a pretty good living. But they were never tempted to do that, and the odd solo record is always very much a sidebar project.

"There's the absolute will to stay together and find out just how far these three people in each other's pockets can travel. And I don't think it's ever a scramble, I don't think it's ever desperate, I think it's always willful, it's always thought about in advance, it's always to a degree calculated, in terms of the moment they ask this random input to come into their world. It's a calculated decision about a point that's been well thought out by them. They're in masterful control of their lives and the band's direction. That in itself is so unique — it's one of the many truly unique things about this band."

Typical of the civilized men of letters that they were, Rush went on a writing retreat in advance of making the new record, holing up at Chalet Studio in Claremont, Ontario, for two and a half months to write, each in their longstanding roles. When not birdwatching and repairing birdfeeders, Geddy and Alex would put music to Alex's rudimentary drum machine patterns, the two convening with Neil in the evening to see what they could cook up together. As with *Presto*, writing centered around guitar, bass and drums and not keyboards, with a heavy emphasis on vocal melodies as well — common parlance would eventually position the Rupert Hine years as the singing era, where Geddy would shift the attention he was placing on keyboards over to the making of memorable vocal melodies, or melodies that played a stronger role in the song, almost as a fourth instrumental narrative.

"It felt to me very much like a part two," agrees Rupert. "But the second part built on how they felt about part one, meaning Geddy liked that his voice was in these different registers. He understood why I thought it had made a difference, and he liked it. And I think they were encouraged by the three-piece idea again and minimalizing the keyboards. We carried on doing that, and so there's probably even less keyboards on that record, and there weren't many on *Presto*, certainly not compared with the previous two albums.

"But I find it hard not to think of them as one piece. I'm not sure I went into the second album with anything like the objectives we had for the first because it had seemed like the objectives had made sufficient change — and the band had themselves compounded on that change. I would say things were amplified. There was no real 'Well, the one thing we got wrong with *Presto* was blah, blah, blah, so this time we'll try this.' I think everything was compounded, which was encouraging from my perspective. It seemed to be starting off with an enthusiastic kick up the bum."

In other words, the guys were happy with what they had done on *Presto*. Even if there were less keyboards, no one at this time was concerned with heavy, rocking Rush. Alex was exploring texture, color, atmosphere, funk and acoustic guitar, and all five of those descriptives tend to put the guitar in a supportive role. In support of what? Well, vocals, and thus almost automatically, lyrics. Bass would and could be moderately busy in that wee and twee box, drums slightly less so, pretty much on par with guitar. All of this adds up to a hermetically sealed bubble of Rush's own making, a contrivance even, albeit one that moves along an evolutionary path. Forget what's happening with surging wider tidal musical gyres; there's this thing we are doing, and we'd like you to hear it.

"I don't recall ever having a discussion with individual Rush members about any other band or music," muses Rupert. "Of course I was only too happy to keep any sonic interference out of the way and just look at the purity of what the band can do. That's not strictly true, because you've just rung a bell: I do remember talking to Neil about Living Colour, but I imagine with respect to some relatively ideological stance, nothing directly affecting the band. I mean, I delighted in the fact that not once did Alex ever say to me, 'You know for this track, I sort of thought the sound of the guitar could be a bit like . . .' Never went there.

"And almost every band, it's like, 'You know that sound of that part on so-and-so's track? When they do that?' And you work from there. I always love the idea that you have an absolutely blank page for everything, for every song, for every album, for every part. You just start with, 'Well, I wonder what we could do to make this part really sing, really work, you know?' And not to jump outside of any frame of reference, other than your own, so you can dig into some mad little demo that you did on a matchbox ten years ago and say, 'Here, look, I love this' and, 'Oh, yeah, let's take that.' That will just be more intensely them. Just borrow from your own oeuvre.

"I can't say that *Roll the Bones* is part of the era when the Seattle sound was out. It feels to me like we were in absolute isolation of it, but I wouldn't really encourage them in any other way than to be aware. You can't not be aware if you're musical. I'm not suggesting people go and live on an island and listen to nothing — you've got to soak in the musicality of the planet without a doubt — but you're going to do that anyway, if your eyes are open and you're musical."

"I don't think I've ever known where Rush is in the musical landscape, to be quite honest," chuckles Geddy. "I don't think any of us do. And that's a blessing because we go in and do what we think is fun to do and what is cool to do. Yeah, we listen to other things and we try to bring new things in. At that time, it was kind of the beginning of rap and hip-hop and all this, and Neil wrote this really funny kind of piss-take on this whole thing, and we thought, why don't we throw that in the song? And that's how that whole middle section of 'Roll the Bones' came to be. It was just us having fun playing this goofy background kind of rhythmic track and then rapping on it.

"So we basically have no plan. I think a lot of bands do have a grand plan, master plan, and we don't really have that. At the start of a record, we just don't know what's going to happen. We just let it happen. Certainly, I wanted to improve the songwriting on the *Roll the Bones* album, because I had that feeling we were more style than content on *Presto*. That was kind of the residue that was left with me from *Presto*. 'The Pass' was really strong, but a lot of the other songs on that album didn't really stay with me from a song resonance point of view. And so we really focused on the songwriting, and I think we nailed that. I think a lot of the songs on *Roll the Bones* are really strong.

"But we're always experimenting," continues Geddy. "I mean, just because we got successful doesn't mean we're going to stop. That's the way I look at it. We could've gone in and done *Moving Pictures* all over again, but we're not really well built for that. We're too curious; we're too dissatisfied with where we're at, so we feel we have to keep moving. We have to find the better Rush, you know. We keep looking for the better version of Rush.

"And even though we've got this great success — oh, that's great, we've got success, we can do headline shows, we can spend more money on productions — it afforded us a hell of a lot of latitude, but it didn't change that feeling when we get together to work on our music: 'Okay, what will make us better? What will make us better writers, better producers, better players?' That's the motivation. Maybe it seems like we just started experimenting after that time, but if you look at the first Rush album and then listen to *Fly by Night*, they're completely different records. What does 'By-Tor & the Snow Dog' have to do with 'Finding My Way'? Worlds apart. That's when the experimenting started. And then look at *Caress of Steel*. That's an experiment in hash oil! We've always experimented.

"We've also always been pigeonholed and categorized. Most bands are, I guess. But I felt there was always more to us than the labels that were attached to us. I felt there was more going on, and we were easily written off as a three-piece metal band, or a prog band, or a sword-and-sorcery band. Maybe that's a motivator for us, in a way. Keep trying to shuffle those labels off of us, you know? At the end of the day though, we're a hard rock band — I've said that many times. I identify with that, and I think we would all agree about that — if we had to be labeled anything, it would be a hard rock band."

The guys were so prepared coming out of the writing sessions for *Roll the Bones* that the performances and arrangements on the demos were referenced quite closely, with Neil nailing his meticulously mapped drum parts with ruthless efficiency. The album was recorded between February and May of '91, using the idyllic and storied Le Studio in Morin Heights as well as McClear Place back home in Toronto. Thanks in the album's liner notes would go to the birds, reflecting Geddy's new hobby, and CNN, which the guys watched a lot, staying abreast of the news. Things went so smoothly — drums and bass put down in four days, guitars in eight — the guys finished two months early, moving the release date three months forward from the initially proposed January of 1992.

"We sort of do that," mused Alex, on using Rupert Hine for a second time. "We like to give a producer a couple of chances. The experience was positive, everything seemed to go well, the album did well, and I don't think we had any fears of working with him again. We thought that would be a good thing, so we just continued. Rupert has a great sense of musicality, arrangement, songwriting. That's really what he brought to the whole project. We're pretty set in our ways. We know what we want to achieve. It's nice that we have somebody there to guide it along and make some of the decisions that we don't wanna make. And I think that record got a little more meat on it. It was a little heavier, or harder. Good songs and some good arrangements.

"But it's a funny thing with us, working with producers at least a couple of times. Maybe once you haven't realized the depth of the relationship and how far you can go. I mean, we always learn from everybody we work with — that's always key. I wonder now if we should just do it once and move on and go with the unknown. That's exciting and challenging. With Terry, during those first few years, we were recording two albums a year, so it was a different environment. We hadn't reached the stage where we incorporated other instruments; the band was simpler in its form and very comfortable with Terry. But after nine records, it was really time for us to move on and work with other people.

"You don't want to stay in the same place, ever," continues Lifeson. "It's boring and you get itchy and antsy and you want to move on. And that's always been the thing with us. It's easy to do something over and over and over and over, like some current bands that are very popular, that have a particular sound and a very identifiable singer's voice. They just create the same album over and over. It's a great success, and that's fine, but eventually that ends and it's over and there is no growth, there's no development. You can look back and say, well, I made a lot of money, and that's all fine and good, but really what does it do for you? It's always been key for us to change and to move forward. We experimented a lot. We've taken some chances and we tried some things, and we haven't always been successful. And our fans have been vocal about those things, what they like and what they don't like. And I'm kind of proud of the stuff I don't like, because we learned from it, and we're always moving forward. We're always thinking about how to approach something in a different way.

"Well, not albums," laughs Alex, not willing to say whole records failed. "Some songs are certainly weaker. And of course, you feel this once you get more distance from the album. They can't be helped. We never started with twenty songs and burned it down to the best twelve. We always work on those twelve, and that's all you get. So it's do them all one hundred percent. Invariably there are some weaker songs than others. There's a lot of information, a lot of music to work on. That's why we have producers, someone to bounce ideas off of and help you feel a little more focused. There are some arrangements that haven't worked, some songs that haven't worked, sounds at times, little things that just don't get me to one hundred percent satisfaction."

That restlessness, again, is something Rupert Hine greatly appreciated in the band. He recalls: "I do remember having a chat — mainly with Neil, although the whole band were there — about how much we admired David Bowie for being the finest example of an artist who will risk losing half his fans — and he often did — on each new album. But he always picked up the same amount of fans who'd never bought a record of his before, album after album after album, all the way through the

'70s and half of the '80s, at least. I would speak to so many people who said, 'I've never liked a David Bowie record before, but this new one's fantastic — I actually went out and bought it.' And you know there's one just like him who's not bought it for the first time. And Bowie would continue this process, which kept him fresh and at the absolute top of his game for like fifteen to eighteen years.

"Neil loved that idea," continues Rupert. "With a band, it's much, much harder to do, some would say almost impossible, certainly to do it to the degree that David Bowie did it. Rush have done it, I think, probably more than any other band, in trying that idea out, to keep themselves fresh. To make their writing have new purpose. Neil particularly, who after all is the textual voice of the band. He's the one the responsibility falls on each time to make sense of each individual song and the whole album. It's a contextual and very much textual parallel route.

"I'm not saying that Geddy and Alex haven't contributed to a lyric, but Neil often writes these completed lyrics, and they're presented to the band as a complete idea, which in and of itself is unusual and really good. From a producer's point of view, that is the best, because right from the get-go you know exactly what you're trying to do with this song, what's being communicated. I hate when you're working with a band that haven't gotten the lyrics together yet — 'We've got a line and the chorus, which is going to go blah, blah, blah.' So we're recording arbitrary parts to a song that's not yet saying anything."

Given his bond with Neil over lyrics, Rupert figures it might have been Peart who wanted him as the band's producer more than anybody else.

"Thinking about it now, yes. I know the idea originated with Neil. Often the most conceptual discussions about the album and its music — as opposed to its arrangement and production

— would always come from Neil. I would assume that's because he's the man in charge of the words that come out of Geddy's mouth. The voice piece of Rush — the horn if you like — is Geddy's voice, but the motor is Neil. I feel that he is often driving the band, the band's ideology. It's collective of course; sooner or later, it's collective. But I feel that the essences of change probably start with Neil. They certainly felt like they did in the two albums I worked on, but I'm imagining that's probably always true."

If Neil is the engine that drives the ideology of Rush, Hine figures that "Geddy is the M.D. of the band, the musical director. He's involved in everything, even guitar solos and what have you — always lovingly, never unpleasant or provocative in a bad way. He would be the organizer, the equivalent of a tour manager. That's the pragmatic side. But to me it's always, 'What are we trying to do with this record that I've been invited to be a big part of? What's the point of doing this record, apart from it being #14 in your lifelong story? What are we going to do that's going to make this chapter really significant? What is it that you guys want to say?' And as soon as you use a word like *say* — and I would all the time — you feel everyone's looking toward Neil. The voice of Rush is Neil. He was always at the epicenter.

"On the day-to-day stuff, it was Geddy, and Geddy is such a lovely chap, a fantastic man to work with, bright-minded, sparkly, very funny. I carry with me all the time his Jewish grandmother voice, which is just to die for. And I'd say Alex has more fun making a Rush record than the other two put together. He just seems to be in the sandpit playing. That's when he's at his best. I wanted to see him in the sandpit the whole time, you know, not being watched over by his parents."

The artwork Hugh Syme pulled off on the cover of *Roll the Bones* is a stunner. It's visually appealing, with the bold band name front and center — as is tradition, no distinctive typography for the band's name is brought forward from the past, hence there's no attempt at establishing a logo. Still, *Rush* in mixed upper- and lowercase letters built from black dice makes quite the impression. Note also top to bottom, the dice get "darker" as the number of white dots on each die decreases from six to two. This is set within a wall of white dice, or "bones," in slang parlance, named because dice were originally made from ivory but also because of their visual similarity to a skull. And, of course, there is a skull on the cover: Hugh is always up for an extra joke for the eyes and brain. The boy in Syme's realist painting recalls young men pondering their lot in life through Rush's discography, including the figure on the *Power Windows* cover and the protagonist in the song (and video for) "Subdivisions" — as well as the vignettes drawn up for "Tom Sawyer" and "New World Man." Our young Dennis the Menace type is booting a skull along a thin stretch of sidewalk next to a waterway, which is rendered in the exact same colors as the dice wall, reflective of it. The skull is one of the most rollable bones, and it's also the bone most laden with meaning. It is in itself a *memento mori*, an object that serves as a reminder of death, as is the entire scene, from the young boy courageously flaunting death, to the weeds struggling to grow in concrete, to the evocations of chance and randomness one can derive from the dice.

Neil's inspiration for the title was a Fritz Leiber sci-fi story called "Gonna Roll the Bones," which he had read back in the '70s; there's no direct influence of the story on Peart's concept or lyrics, but Neil had liked the phrase, so he jotted it down for future reference.

Unsurprisingly, the opening track on *Roll the Bones* is one of the album's fastest rockers, and it's quick to get rocking. "Dreamline" also finds Neil almost immediately getting down to the deep tissue and exploring the themes suggested in the record's title and cover art. He's already leapt from the platform and is examining the appeal of geographical exploration: the road trip, the restlessness, the vitality slaked from getting out in the world. Remarks about the fleeting nature of time and therefore life are reinforced by Alex's guitar picking, which sounds like the ticking of a clock. Even Neil's title, a made-up word, is laden with enough meaning to serve as a microcosm for the song as a whole, as well as the wider album.

"They have different satisfactions," muses Peart. "'Dreamline' I really liked because I was able to write verses that were imagistic and non-rhyming, freeing myself from my usual neatness habits. *Roll the Bones* still remains really satisfying; it's just a good selection of songs." The opening lines have Neil referencing astronomy, which he was prompted to write about after watching a PBS *NOVA* episode on satellite imagery after one of his famed long stretches of cycling between gigs, this time between Cincinnati and Columbus. The CD single artwork for the song features three floating wishbones (one for each member of the band?) over an ocean and sunset scene. So there's bones, a yearning, and a sense of the possibilities one gets from open vistas. A wishbone is called that because two people are to grasp the ends with their pinkies, make a wish and break it. Whoever winds up with the largest piece gets his wish. Here again, there's the element of chance, rolling the dice.

"Dreamline" became a live favorite of the band's for years to come — the song was strong enough to serve as opener on the *Different Stages* live album — as well as hitting #1 on the U.S. Mainstream Rock Tracks charts. Indeed, even if Rush had no ability to rock out at this juncture, "Dreamline" is built for live execution, given its pause for the verses and attack come chorus time. Again, even across this "heavy" part of the album, Alex's chords are behaved and tightly wound, Neil's drums troubled and trebly, and Geddy is playing a Wal bass. All three performers are further emasculated by a similarly timid sound, that of braying keyboard stabs, which, through lack of competition from Rush, become the signature of the chorus, the highlight of the song that is to be the highlight of *Roll the Bones*.

"'Bravado' is a song where I just loved how the music and the words married," says Neil of the record's next track, a hypnotic and measured dark pop song framed by Neil's two-handed hi-hat pattern. "That's one of our more successful overall compositions — arrangement, performance, all of that wedded together."

Alex loves that his guitar solo on the track was a late-night one-taker: laden with emotion, performed in solitude on his Telecaster direct to tape, all the more perfect to go with Neil's serious lyric about people doing the right thing, personal heroism from often unsung heroes, and Geddy's steady and slow delivery thereof.

Rupert thinks of this song with respect to the album's sense of emotion and fragility. "I suppose if you really are keeping things as fresh as possible that means danger — it's got to. I mean, to be truly fresh is to go somewhere new and pushing that one foot forward inch by inch or leaping a little in the way that Rush have done, more than a little. So yes, there is a danger that probably makes some of the moments have a certain fragility. I certainly felt there was some emotional stuff that came out. I just referred to the playing around in the sandpit side of Alex, which I found quite emotional. There was a joy to that.

"People are a bit on the fence about Rush. They respect them a lot, but they think they're too technical, you know, not emotional enough. And often Neil is somewhat narrative, with the objective view rather than creating a cry from the inside. Those aspects of Rush can keep them feeling like they're a little distant in the way they communicate. I thought we got through some of that on 'Bravado,' which is still my favorite track of all the tracks I did with them. It's one of the least 'Rush-like' tracks. It's sort of a ballad, nothing terribly tricky. I get chills listening to that track. I do. I love it; it's gorgeously harmonic, melodic, expressive, simple, but with meaningful text. That's a set of skills that perhaps showed some of that fragility."

Hine was particularly impressed with Neil's busy playing late in the song, where he stretches out against yet another round of the hypnotic, almost haunting chorus refrain.

"Yes, there were a couple of points, one in particular, where I was listening in the control room. They were all playing together, and Stephen Tayler, the engineer I was working with on both those albums, I turned to him and said, 'Are you checking out what Neil's playing? Can you figure out how many limbs he's got? Can you work out what's playing what there? And it was 'Bravado' actually. It was impossible for just four limbs to play this part if you check it out. My count was six limbs he needed, not just five but six.

"So in the end we soloed everything to figure out how. Now we're not even checking out sounds or anything — we're obsessed by working out how on earth he was playing what he was playing. And in the end, I had to get out . . . they were still playing, and I had to go into the studio, I had to walk in front of him, I had to stand in front of his drum kit and I had to watch. And I'm staring at him, and that's when I realized I still couldn't tell. That's only happened once in my life — it was completely weird. It's a trick. He does these amazing, amazing trick things, that even when you're looking at him, it's a sleight of hand, it's magic."

"I spent days on that drum part," explained Neil, speaking with *Powerkick* magazine. "Just over and over again. And that's what I'm saying about time being a luxury . . . we finished songwriting and everything early, so I had time to rehearse my drum parts for two weeks after that. I had a demo work tape that I would play a song over and over until I was burnt out on it, and then I would start on the next one. So I spent a couple of hours every day on each song for like two weeks. 'Bravado' is a great example of that because I orchestrated every section of it so carefully, but I also left a lot of it free. A lot of the key things, a lot of the drum fills, for instance, I didn't allow myself to work out. Every time they came, I just closed my eyes and let it happen. I didn't want that to become too big a part of the recording, because you can over-rehearse, and a part that's played the same way too many times can become stale. I wanted to leave a little bit of it feeling on edge.

"Over time, I think you learn that you want both, not just a well-worked drum part and not just spontaneity, but both. It shouldn't be an either/or situation. I want to be both orchestrated and improvised. It's the way I start working on a song. I think of everything that will fit in the song and try it out once, and everything that I don't like, gradually I will eliminate. And then sometimes you do end up with less, because ultimately that's what the song requires and thus I'm satisfied by it.

"'Bravado,' for example, satisfies me to listen to and to play as well," continues Peart. "It's deceptively simple perhaps to someone who is not sitting down and trying to play it. It may sound easy enough, but from my point of view on the level of refinements — and the technical level too — it is demanding. To juggle all those different approaches to verses and keep the tempo smooth and all those other elements — including sequencers when we play it live — makes it challenging. The consistency of tempo during something like that becomes critical. Overall, I don't think it's a question of 'less is more' but 'better is more.' You keep searching for the best way to do it."

Neil's part was kept, but much else about the song was cut. For this one, the guys had an embarrassment of riches, so many quality parts, but in the end it was pared back to the sober and resolute final product. Geddy calls "Bravado" one of his favorite Rush songs ever, for its texture, for its emotion and for Neil's lyric, which he found poignant for its idea of paying the price eventually, but in the present, not counting the cost.

As Neil explains in the *Roll the Bones* tourbook, this sentiment was inspired by "a line from John Barth's *The Tidewater Tales* (he said I could use it), which echoed around inside me for a long time after I read that book. To me, it just means go for it. There are no failures of talent, only failures of character. I think that's often true too. Sure there are a lot of talented people who don't achieve artistic or worldly success, but I think there's usually a reason — a failure inside them. The important thing is: if you fail once, or if your luck is bad this time, the dream is still there. A dream is only over if you give it up — or if it comes true. That is called irony. We have to remember the oracle's words, from Nike, the Greek goddess of victory and lumpy athletic shoes: Just do it. No excuses."

Next up is the album's title track, a song destined to linger in the collective consciousness of Rush fans as long as or longer than "Dreamline" and "Bravado." Curiously, this record's most famed songs all come at the very beginning, although fully six songs from the album would be floated as single proposals in various territories, as the album would mark a moderately unexpected uptick in sales over the previous two.

"'Roll the Bones' I really liked," says Neil. "It's from an ongoing series of songs that is our attempt to weld together diverse styles into the same song. Sometimes it works, sometimes it doesn't, but it's obviously something that interests all of us as an ongoing pattern of song construction. And I had a lot of fun doing the rap section in the middle of that tune. This was out in '91 or so, so yeah, rap was just starting to become increasingly prevalent then. So I just did a kind of tongue-in-cheek thing that I really like."

"Fun — pure, unadulterated Rush fun," says Rupert when asked about the rudimentary and not very funky rap wedged into the song with a foot-long shoehorn. "They knew that Geddy wouldn't be able to really pull it off because it would be just too preposterous. I don't mean Geddy the individual, but Geddy's vocal style. He was singing on the ceiling almost all the time, and at least I brought it down a little bit. But it seemed ridiculous that you would pull him down any further and stick it into a spoken, rhythmical rap-like quality, or something I often refer to as 'talking blues,' which to me was kind of the original rap of the '50s.

"Very early on in the conversation they wanted to get John Cleese to do it," continues Hine. "Now if you think of John Cleese doing that rap, that gives you a really clear perspective as to how they were thinking about the whole song, right? And if John Cleese had done it, it would have clearly been an even madder Rush moment. Which would have in some ways been less divisive because it would have been clearly a novelty, a spoofy bit of madness. My argument with them was, that was the problem — it would be seen to be a novelty. I was getting ahold of John Cleese; we were having a dialogue about it and I was following it through. But at the same time, I was getting the feeling he probably wasn't going to do it anyway. You know, I'm not sure this is a great idea because, do you really want a novelty track? What if this actually became a hit with John Cleese on it? I mean, what a mess we've got. Maybe, maybe not. It became a discussed point. There were quite a few people considered, none of them rappers. All of them were personalities outside the music world, so we were still looking at something that would be seen to be a novelty unless we were smart about it.

"At one point they said, 'Why don't you do it, Rupert?' Because I've got these sort of raps on my own albums; I had these very fast spoken parts. And my only top three single was this song I did when I had a band called Quantum Jump in the '70s, which had the longest word in the world on it — ninety-six letters long — and it was sung very fast, a rapid machine gun–like rap. So they said, 'You do it.'

"So I did a pass at it and we all liked it. I mean, I don't know whether Al liked it or not, but the rest of the band liked it. And then out of the blue I said, 'Geddy, why don't you have a go? But do it down at that level.' And he's like, 'I can't sing that deep.' And I said, 'Don't worry; we'll take it down. You just sing as deep as you can, and we'll smudge it down electronically.' Which is what we did. That was just a tester, just to see if worse came to worse and none of these ideas came about, whether we could get away with it within ourselves. For me to do it would still be an outsider. I thought it's just more fun if it stays within Rush. And if Geddy did a vocal that most people wouldn't believe was Geddy, that was also fun. The cheating is relatively slight; it's just to push it a bit further down to make it feel a little unnatural.

"And it was hysterical," continues Rupert. "He had great fun doing it. We were just rolling about laughing. As with so much on a Rush record, there's a lot of laughter. The music is often so intense, one somehow imagines that the mood must be intense while doing it. I'm glad to say they're one of the most playful bands I've ever recorded with. They had super amounts of fun. I can remember being absolutely tearful with laughter on many occasions with the band, and that was one of them."

"I don't know, lack of sense of humor, I guess," laughs Geddy, on why the "Roll the Bones" rap tended to upset so many Rush fans. "I mean, we're kind of a serious band in their eyes, and to go out on a limb and do something like that, which was, I think, completely appropriate in the context of the song, but completely inappropriate in the context of Rush; it is polarizing. You're going to get some fans that get it and like it, and some fans that think it's a rap part. But if you listen to rap, and then listen to that, it's not the same thing.

"And we had the same problem with radio stations," continues Ged. "Some rock radio stations would not play that song because it had the rap in it, and they didn't want to be associated with rap. And we're like, 'Dude, this is a rock band, and this is just a weird part of the song. It's not rap.' There's no rapper on earth who would think that's genuine rap. But maybe I don't have the necessary objectivity to realize how that part is received by other people. I'm always inside looking out. The polarizing is probably a combination of all those different things. Some fans, I guess, saw it as a rap thing, and what does that have to do with Rush? But we've used every imaginable rhythm in our songs, every imaginable keyboard noise, guitar noise, all kinds of vocalizing. This to me is just the same thing, another musical thing that we throw into our stew, the stew that's Rush. It's no different from having a middle section that suddenly goes all jazz. That's more acceptable, I suppose, because it doesn't have that connection with another less popular style of music."

But with hip-hop surging at the time, Geddy says, "You listen to it, and you have to. Every musician listens to all kinds of stuff and tries to figure it out. Do I like rap and hip-hop music? Not too much, but I appreciate it when it's done really well. I appreciate a good arrangement, regardless of what style it is. It comes on and you listen to it and you go, 'Wow, that's well done; that's a good arrangement.' Like if you listen to something by Kanye West, the way he uses orchestration in some of his stuff, it's very clever, very well designed.

"As an artist you have to listen to everything, you have to analyze everything from your own perspective and see if there's something you can learn. Is there something useful there? And when that section of the song comes up in 'Roll the Bones' and that rhythm starts, I love that. I love that shift of gears, that change of reality, where you've got this kind of grooving section. We're a band that's not really known to groove for longer than a minute at a time, but the vocal part and the rap part were to me pure satire."

"If they think of it generically like it's rap, then they've got a problem," figures Rupert, further on the subject of fan reaction. "Because, sure, they're going to say, well, it's rap, meaning the whole world of rap, essentially what people call urban now, which is a polite word for Black music. But if you're going back to other forms of what I call talking blues, which has been around forever, and rapid-fire poetry, the beats in the early '60s, all kinds of spoken rhythmical work has been out there. So to call it a rap is in itself, I don't know, it's like calling a bit of slide guitar that Alex would do once in a blue moon country. 'See, they're doing country music now.' You wouldn't say that, so why say a bit of spoken word like that was rap? I mean, sure it was spoofing rap a little, but it was playful and fun. Rush certainly tests their fans regularly, so let's just call that a test. It was probably just the dread that, oh my God, if they're moving into rap, where are they going to go to next?!"

Rap aside, "Roll the Bones" is one of the band's most successful experiments in this progressive pop mode no one else was doing. Forget the screechy, dated keyboards, forget Alex being obtuse, Rupert and the guys get a fulsome sound through use of rich acoustic guitars, sensible and organic tones all round, creating a bed for the song's angular parts and transitions not to come off too angular. As bonus, there's a chorus that is instantly and effortlessly memorable, and then if one's appreciation to hook extends to novel and slightly mathematical rhythms, there are those hooks to digest and master as well.

Indeed, Geddy professed around the time an appreciation for the Red Hot Chili Peppers and Faith No More, and he went so far as to opine that the band was getting a little funkier in their old age. The rap is a red herring — and everybody seems to miss this elephant in the room here: it's embarrassingly un-funky, more like the guys in their famed *Leave It to Beaver* prank mode of the '70s trying to rap — just sort of white and not funny. But the rest of the song is indeed kind of funky, underscored by Alex's funk guitar and Geddy's cool bass lope. It's math rock to be sure, but it's funky math rock.

As Neil told Willebrord Elsing from *Dutch* magazine, "Basically at the start of *Roll the Bones* I decided that I wanted to get away from familiar patterns. So I physically changed my drum setup around pretty radically and put the drum which used to be here over there, the one which used to be there is now over here. Whatever I did, if it was the same move, it would sound different. And also with drums in different places it would encourage me to do different things which worked great too. So the actual number and choice of drums is the same; they're just all switched around. And electronically, ironically on the *Roll the Bones* record there is almost no drum sampling at all, except for in the rap section of 'Roll the Bones,' which are electronic drums just for the character of being what it is. But when we were setting up in the studio for *Roll the Bones*, it was pretty much just a little drum kit and that was nice to do that."

Asked about moving away from science fiction–inspired lyrics, Neil says, "I used it so little, for how much attention that gets paid to it, and it was always just a vehicle. There are really maybe thirty minutes of music that had anything to do with science fiction at all: '2112' and 'Cygnus X-1' I suppose. But in both cases it was a phase that I was going through of using allegory and characters as symbols, which I seemed to grow out of, because I wanted to write about people as people and not as symbols.

"Nobody is a hero, nobody is a villain, everybody is a lot of each," continues Peart. "At one point I was interested in clarifying my thoughts on things and thinking about the difference between reason and passion. So I used symbols for them and put them in a speculative world. But as in most cases, as with Isaac Asimov, Frank Herbert or Ray Bradbury, they are not writing about science and they are not writing about symbols or robots, they are writing about people in extraordinary circumstances. Which is what good lyrics are always about. The drama of it, of someone you can relate to as a person getting caught up in something that is difficult to deal with.

"For me, that was just a period I went through, and I learned from it and grew out from it. It was a long time ago and it wasn't very much work to begin with. I was never a science fiction writer at all; it was just a vehicle for a while. The same as before when I was all caught up in fantasy because of the decorative aspects of words, and truly in the Gothic sense of architecture with lots of curlicues and architraves and stuff. But at a certain point you strip it down, and all you want is walls and a roof."

More specifically on the "Roll the Bones" concept and lyric, Neil told Roger Catlin, "The idea of chance and randomness on the album came out of one incidental image — the wild card. I thought of that image more and more: how randomness affects us as a band, and people at large. There are so many different areas. There are things for which there is no explanation. The only answer I can come up with is: it happens because it happens. And if things occur, what can we do about them? That's what kept driving me deeper and deeper. These are the kind of intellectual questions I throw around with my friends, one of whom said, "'Because they happen" sounds like something my dad would say.' Things on earth are not futile but random. I had to juggle everything to see if I could say anything. I readily confess to being didactic sometimes and not expressing myself as clearly as I should. But one time Geddy pointed out to me that I was just giving my idea, saying what I thought and asking 'What do you think?' I'm not saying something is black or white. I'm just saying, 'Maybe this is something you'd like to think about.'"

But Neil has also emphasized the productive positive around this concept: even though it's a random world and anything can happen, you can bend chance to your will through trying and trying hard, through perspiration over inspiration, through preparation, through enthusiastic participation in the world. In other words, it's not so much about going with the flow, but confidently wading into the flow and figuring out how to paddle to the ideal spot. As he's pointed out, "Hope for the best and prepare for the worst."

"'Face Up' is one of the songs we didn't think lived up to the potential hope we had for it," says Neil, concerning this driving rocker turned almost invisible, not so much by the performance but by the record's curiously powerless production knob job. It's not that the song is "played" pop (other than Geddy's sober vocal); rather, it's that the sounds chosen for application to Alex's guitar, Geddy's bass and all of Neil's drums and cymbals are thin, cloistered, hysterical — three wedgies applied to a power trio, the deluxe kind that has the victim howling as he hangs from the high school locker door.

The "sober" singing was a deliberate thing, hearkening back to preferences expressed by both Geddy and Rupert while record-ing *Presto*. "It wasn't so much a moment as a series of moments," recalls Hine, "but I was listening to Geddy singing in this lower range and I was actually hearing Geddy, the man. I mean, it's exactly what I wanted to hear, rather than Geddy the impressive singer doing all this high shrieky stuff. I remember feeling that I could hear and feel, at times, much more emotion coming through Geddy, but it not being remotely theatrical. It's not like playing to the crowd at all, just quite the opposite. But now his voice was down here and contained. It was more inside the text, and I was getting it more and I was feeling it more and he was feeling it more. Those moments often felt emotional in a way that when you're singing in this crazy acrobatic way, you can't. They're skills, they're impressive talents, but there's no emotional connection, not to me anyway."

Fragility is a word that comes to mind, but then again, given the accomplishing personality of Geddy, along with the same sort of fatherly authority in the words he's given to sing, it's more a sense of resolute and sanguine reflection from inside the driver's seat.

"Through these changes that happened during *Presto* particularly, perhaps there was a tenderizing process, a sort of bashing-of-meat element," describes Rupert. "When you're tenderized, obviously you're much closer to being immediately open to things you might have had a wall up against. I didn't feel there were any walls at all on that record. Nobody really had any walls. Now, there were a couple of habits that we broke out of, but they weren't really walls. It was just things they hadn't noticed, and as soon as I commented, they go, 'Oh, okay, you know, we don't have to do that.' It was immediate if you suggested something, a change. It was never really defensive. It's another really great thing in all three of them — they're so open to change. I've not really come across a band like that — how are all three so open to possibility? Because if you say 'open to change,' people could read that wrong and say, 'Well, so do you mean it was not focused?' Not at all, no — the train is solidly on Rush tracks. But at any point there was a possibility of going in a new direction. Your tracks veer off there; well, let's go down there and see how that feels."

Lyrically, "Face Up" finds Neil striking a nice balance between a relationship-type narrative and the injection of the wild card imagery, which plays to the record's chance and gambling themes. Still, there's a vague dissatisfaction with verb choices and a sort of befuddled motion, as if there are a few mixed metaphors, except you're not so sure they are metaphors, but you are sure they are mixed — or mixed up.

In the *Roll the Bones* tourbook, Peart explains that a line from "Face Up" ("Turn it up — or turn that wild card down") started it all. "On a rainy day in late summer, cool enough to draw me close to the fire, I sat on the floor of my cottage with a pile of papers around me — notes from the previous two years, lines and phrases collected on the road or in that dreamlike moment before sleep. I began playing with the phrases, 'turn it up' and 'turn it down,' thought about turning a card down. I started to think more about the 'wild card' idea. I guess that's called inspiration. So many wild cards we are dealt in life — where we're born, the genes we wear, the people we meet along the way and the circumstances of the world around us.

"Sometimes we even choose a wild card; faith is like that and so is trust. One of the biggest chances you can take in life is trusting somebody, and yet most of us take that chance at least once or twice. Some of us pursue ambitions where the odds against success are great (and where we might have to stay adolescents all our lives). That is called bravado. There is truth in homilies like 'the harder I work, the luckier I get' and 'luck is when preparation meets opportunity' but they are only tendencies not laws. The best-laid plans etc. No matter how intelligent, talented and beautiful we might be, we still don't know what the hell's going to happen next. But we can improve the odds by the choices we make. I am not an existentialist; I am a free man!"

At the record's halfway point, "Where's My Thing?" serves as another selection supporting Geddy's assertion around the band's becoming funky. Again, if Neil is the whitest drummer on the planet, and if Rupert Hine is a very white producer, Alex and Geddy counter gamely with funk parts against the rigid snap-grid built by Rupert and Neil. As for the song's subtitle, "Part IV, 'Gangster of Boats' Trilogy," this was an inside joke where Geddy and Alex threatened to name one of their albums *Gangster of Boats* if Neil couldn't come up with a better title. The song was deliberately kept simple by Geddy and Alex, having somewhat of a standard verse/chorus structure.

As Geddy explained to Dan Neer from WNEW, Neil very deliberately abstained from putting a lyric up for consideration so that Geddy and Alex would be forced to write an instrumental.

"Well, normally most people don't write the fourth part of a trilogy, so we thought we would," cracked Alex, with Geddy helpfully adding that "most people don't realize you can have a fourth part to a trilogy. But it's so much fun to do too. We tried to do one on *Presto*, and every time we started writing it, you know, we played this piece of music and would be like, 'Oh, this lyric fits perfectly with it.' So we'd go off, we'd steal from the instrumental, and it would become another song. And it kept happening over and over again. And finally, Neil said, 'Okay, you keep promising to do this instrumental, and I'm not giving you any more lyrics until you write the thing.' So we sat down and wrote it."

Chuckles Alex, "Actually this whole album is an instrumental album. But then we added some words." When Dan compares the beginning of the song to James Brown, Geddy agrees that it's "as funky as Canadians can get, I suppose."

On a promo interview CD put out by Anthem, Neil expressed his pleasure that "Where's My Thing?" saw issue as a single, albeit low-key. "I was really proud of our record company, that they released 'Dreamline' as the first track and then they put out 'Where's My Thing?' for alternative stations or basically anyone who had the nerve to play it. And it made a great alternative for college radio in the States or alternative radio anywhere that exists. But at the same time it was a creative thing for a record company to do, I thought. Not just to be worried, 'Okay, here's our marketing strategy,' but they would say, 'Let's do this because it would be fun and unusual, and the song is there.' So I thought that was really a good thing to do. A friend of ours says that it's just another version of 'Telstar' like all instrumentals are, which is funny. And very true!"

"The Big Wheel" contributes to the questionable narrative that the album is looser and more guitary than the last record with Rupert and the preceding two with Peter Collins as producer. Alex's guitar is fairly distorted, and the song is simple and chord-dominant, a bit like the Who. Also, Neil grooves in part with hi-hat open, while elsewhere he's hitting lots of cymbals, riding his ride, executing his fills casually and rocking.

Noted Peart, speaking with John Derringer: "I'm not very self-referential in lyrics, and when I do write about that innocence/experience dichotomy, or about childhood or something, it's usually from a character point of view. 'The Big Wheel' is a good example on this album, where it seems to be autobiographical, but it's really not. It's where I've looked for a universal of that trade-off between innocence and experience, and that song certainly addresses that. Not in the circumstances of my own life so much, or if it is, it's not important that it be autobiographical — that's just by the by, really. Very much I want to find universal things that others can relate to, and that's a thing that's part of everyone's life. I think that's probably one reason why I'm drawn to it. And so much of it is drawn from observing people around me too, so that becomes a factor: how they responded to life and how they take to it. How they adapt to that innocence and experience thing."

Next up is "Heresy," which has a bit of a Celtic/Big Country/U2 vibe to it. With the synth and snappy drums, with the quiet yet pulsating and tribal verse, this one's a bit of a throwback to *Power Windows* and *Hold Your Fire*.

Noted Geddy, speaking with Dan Neer from WNEW: "It just seemed that a lot of stuff was going down where it was hard to leave the television set during the writing. A couple of the songs on the record were, I guess, kind of worldly in what they were describing. It seemed like they fit in some weird way." Specifically on "Heresy," Geddy framed the subject of the song, the fall of communism, as "that horrible and wonderful moment all mixed into one when somebody realizes that they've had their freedom removed for so many years, and they finally get it back. It must be such a bittersweet moment. All those years, all those lives that were lost and all the struggle, all the people that were fighting. All the years and suddenly it's all over. And what do they do about all the people that did not survive, who were not lucky enough to be around when the wall fell down? It's an unanswerable question, but it's certainly one to think about. It's very topical, obviously, because of what is going on right now. That's a culmination of that whole movement."

With "Ghost of a Chance" we're back to that fairly consistent narrative proposed by the band, the one that says *Roll the Bones* is essentially a dialogue between guitar, bass and drums. Again, the song is only held back from hard rock by the deliberate production choices. Otherwise, the band is playing fairly loose here, evoking a bit of an up-tempo Police vibe, complete with dark or at least "mischievous" Andy Summers guitar chromatics.

"'Ghost of a Chance' is one of our all-time good ones," says Neil. "I like to think it's more gaining technique really; it's ten more years of practice and learning. I've always shied away from love songs and even mentioning the word in songs because it's so cliché. And until I thought that I'd found a new way to approach it, or a new nuance of it to express, I was not going to write one of those songs. 'Ghost of a Chance' fit right in with my overall theme of randomness and contingency and so on. But at the same time, it was a chance for me to write about love in a different way, of saying, 'Here are all these things that we go through in life and the people we meet — it's all by chance. And the corners we turn and the places we go and the people we meet there.' All those things are so random and yet through all of that, people do meet each other, and if they work at it they can make that encounter last. So I'm saying there's a ghost of a chance it can happen. The odds are pretty much against it, but at the same time that ghost of a chance sometimes does come through and people do find each other and stay together.

"Some greater guitar stuff in this song, I think, but don't tell Alex I said so," joked Neil in the tourbook (of note, Alex plays a PRS on this one). "This is the kind of song that we always think ought to be a massive hit single, but by this time we've learned that it won't be, because we're too weird."

Previously in pop culture, *Neurotica* was a beat-era magazine and "Neurotica" was a song on King Crimson's album *Beat*, which loosely celebrates beat-era writers. But Rush's "Neurotica" is none of that. Neil explained: "Some people can't deal with the world as it is, or themselves as they are, and feel powerless to change things, so they get all crazy. They waste away their lives in delusions, paranoia, aimless rage, and neuroses, and in the process, they often make those around them miserable too. Strained friendships, broken couples, warped children. I think they should all stop it. That is called wishful thinking."

On a musical tack, this is another Rush song isolated in a hard pop place to which only Rush has the keys. Guitar, bass, drums, recorded politely and played pop-proggy, "Neurotica" also supports the narrative that Geddy is singing in a comfortable range, a bonus being what one might call back-up vocals.

Finishing off *Roll the Bones* is "You Bet Your Life," which opens starkly post-punk before settling into something Fixx- or INXS-like. With all of these songs, pumping away in the background is Neil, in a way, conspicuous. As we've revisited in widening gyres, there's nothing muscular about the sounds, but there's also nothing muscular about the playing — except from Neil. Is he rocking out to an imagined rock-out song in his head? Perhaps so, because he's getting busy when no one else is. One nice touch, however, is the way the delay applied to Alex's guitar creates an effect not unlike the Edge from U2. Lifeson credits engineer and right-hand man to Rupert, Stephen Tayler, with coming up with the delay pattern that breathes life into the track.

"I particularly like the lyrics in that one," muses Neil. "I wove together all the different religions and musical styles and everything. Those kinds of things are really fun and satisfying. Yeah, I like that one." Of note, Geddy had called "You Bet Your Life" one of the most difficult tracks to assemble on the album, specifically in the mixing stage, because of the density of the chorus.

"No matter what kind of song you choose to play, you're betting your life on it, for good or ill, and what you believe is what you are," wrote Neil in the tourbook for the album — these documents were increasingly serving as the definitive vehicle in which Neil could say his piece on these songs, leaving Al and Ged to handle things on the press trail.

"So there. However you slice it, you're taking a chance, and you *might* not be right (just this once). No one can ever be *sure*, in this best of all possible random universes. That's why the essence of these songs is: if there's a chance, you might as well take it. So what if some parts of life are a crapshoot? Get out there and shoot the crap. A random universe doesn't have to be *futile*; we can change the odds, load the dice and roll again. And there's no escaping the dice. Even if you try to take the sting out of a random universe by embracing the prefab structure of faith, you still have to gamble that it's the *right* one. Say the secret word and win a hundred dollars. For anyone who hasn't seen Groucho Marx's game show *You Bet Your Life*, I mean that no one but Groucho knows the secret word, and one guess is as good as another. You might have lived a good long life as an exemplary Christian only to be met at the gates of Heaven by *Mohammed*. Anything can happen. That is called fate."

And so ends *Roll the Bones*. With twenty more years of perspective, where does it fit in the Rush catalogue? Well, according to Peart, "*Roll the Bones* I love for its variety of things and so many good songs on it that have come back to us. 'Bravado' was always a great one to play. 'Dreamline' stays with us now. We just brought back 'Ghost of a Chance' after not playing it for many years — oh, that's really a good song. Like anyone, you put your past work aside and you tend to think less of it over time. And then just before we came out for the second run of the *Snakes & Arrows* tour we were exchanging ideas for other older songs that we might like to change. We knew we wanted to change up about four of the older songs and Geddy suggested 'Ghost of a Chance,' and I was like, oh yeah that would be great. And there was another one from that *Roll the Bones* album, which kind of falls between the cracks, I think, in any estimation of people's favorite Rush albums. It's a little brittle sonically and all, but again, that you learn."

"Brittle." A perfect description, and a recognition.

"We realized after time that there was a core of our fan base that was as curious as to where we were going as we were," laughs Ged, thinking about this era, one in which Rush concocted the stark and monumental antithesis of a grunge album. "And those are the ones who have sustained us through all these years. There is a part of the audience that comes and goes, depending on the style of each particular album. I think that's true. *Moving Pictures* got us into a much broader world of rock fans, but there were some rock fans that just wanted to hear us doing that. And then we came out with *Signals*; there was a shift and we lost some of those people, but other people picked up. But it's an evolving thing, our audience. They are evolving like we evolve. It's nice. I mean, I like looking out there and seeing a complete variety of human life in front of the stage, from little kids to guys as old as us, or older.

"You're always looking for reasons to explain why this tour, you know, you were selling out, and then the next tour you had seventy percent full houses," continues Geddy. "What is it? And so you analyze what you think is going on. And I think that's what it was — we just keep shifting our style a little bit, and it doesn't click with everybody. There are certain periods of Rush that are more universal than other periods. Certain albums that resonate. Now, you can say that on one hand, they're better records — maybe that's the best Rush, the more popular ones. But our fans would tend to differ. I think it's just a stylistic thing. Certain albums have a broader appeal than other albums. Why that is, I can't really put my finger on. They'll tell you. They'll fill you in."

Geddy goes on to express a hint of regret with the band's sound picture circa *Roll the Bones*. "I think there were a couple of issues. Sonically, I think we felt it could've sounded better. I think we all agreed that the record could've sounded bigger. It had a small-ish sound and we wanted a bold sound. We loved the songs, as I said, and we loved the performances — no problem with any of that. But in the end, you know, Rupert and Stephen are kind of a team. You get one, you get them both, and they have a sound that travels with them. And we wanted a different sound, and that's why we moved on. But if I had to pick five of the best Rush albums, *Roll the Bones* would be one of them, absolutely. I think it's one of our more successful albums — I mean, creatively successful."

Widening the scope, Geddy adds that "Peter Collins and Rupert Hine are both what I would call classic, or classical, producers — maybe traditional is a better word: traditional producers. In the sense that they are all about making your songs better. And I love that. As a writer, as a singer, I learned so much from working with those two guys, about putting a song together, about the dynamics of the song, about taking consideration for the singer's role. And it doesn't matter if you have a great piece of music, if it's the wrong key or the wrong tempo, you can lose the impact of what the vocalist does. The songs can be sold or not sold by the singer. And I learned a lot about that from those two guys.

"I would work with either of them again for that reason, because they are so sound fundamentally. But they both have their own way of doing things, and being Rush, we just feel the need to keep moving. I think there's a part of us that never wants to get into that comfortable situation of working with the same producer for ten years again, like we did with Terry. We were just always on the lookout that we didn't slip into complacency."

As for Alex, he says, "We never changed the core of what Rush was all about and what we wanted to do, and that was to make music that was engaging and exciting and challenging and always changing. Around the time of *2112*, or just after *2112*, I guess, *Farewell to Kings*, we really started to fool around with keyboards and bass pedals and things like that. That was the starting point of the whole experimental period. And perhaps it rose up to that peak with *Moving Pictures* and *Signals*, but it could've stayed there and probably not have made it through the '80s. We could've made *Rush*, the first album, over and over again. *Caress of Steel*, that was the kind of criticism we were getting at the time: 'Well, maybe you guys should just go back to what you were doing, as kind of a Led Zeppelin–y sort of rock band.'

"But we came back and sort of stopped that thinking with *2112*, and it turned out to be very successful for us. We've always maintained that over the years. We always wanted to be our own band, and *2112* was the start of that. You just kind of go with what feels right, and instinctively it was to experiment as much as possible. But still keeping the essence of what the band was about, the core three-piece hard rock band. But in lots of ways of messing around with that format and not just staying on that same narrow path.

"It's always a surprise that people followed us over the years," continues Alex, with a laugh. "I mean, wow, I guess we've gone through at least a couple generations now. We have people at our shows who are there with this guy's father, whose son is there with his son. And it's his first Rush concert — his grandson. It's pretty amazing that we've been able to do that and keep those fans for that long. It's interesting to me that people can be pretty eclectic or broad, in terms of a band like us — they accept the changes. The earlier core fans, a lot of them were disappointed at the time of *Moving Pictures*. They wanted the headbanger's kind of heavy metal, something I never thought was a very big part of our character. But they were disappointed when we went into this whole thing — but we gained a new audience. We still have a lot of those older fans, but it's something we sort of scratch our heads about."

Speculating on why fans would exercise patience through these radical changes, Lifeson says, "The fact that we've managed to exist this long, we come from this polite little country of Canada, we're only a three-piece, there's no friction between us . . . it's not a volatile relationship — we're like a very happy marriage. I think people look at those things about us, that we work well together, that we've done it on our own, that we've established ourselves earlier on, and on a particular path that we truly feel is our path. And we've managed to avoid the pitfalls of the industry, for the most part. We've never had our record company representative in the studio for a second in all our years. We've always done it on our own terms, and I think those are the elements about Rush that really touched a lot of people. I think that gives them hope that they can do things in their life that we have done in our career, and have control, and live a fruitful existence. At least that's what I read from some of the mail I get; that's my sense. I think when fans talk about Rush as an inspiration, I don't hear our music in their music, other than a couple of bands. Those bands I'm talking about, well, if these guys can do it on their own, then we must be able to do it on our own — it gives them hope."

Specifically addressing the band's status at the point of *Roll the Bones*, Alex says, "I guess we were kind of like that lone tree on the side of the hill. Because the whole grunge movement was really building steam, and that's what everybody wanted to be and wanted to sound like. But, you know, whether we were stubborn or just very individualistic, we continued in that same direction that *Presto* was. A little bit chunkier and a little bit heavier, but eventually the same, and it was down to working with pretty much the same conditions. It was a lonely place to be, but we were still very strong. Fortunately, we do pay a lot of attention to our live show, and in particular our playing, and we always manage to bring our audience to come see us play.

"But you know, getting back to our core hardness and heaviness was something that was always very important to me. Right from the mid-'80s on. There was a bit of a dilemma, wanting to get back into that hardness but in a newer, fresher way, not something that was old and done. I've always combined clean sounds with dirty sounds and tried to make something interesting in that way, but essentially I always wanted to get back to that harder side. I want to bring the power of those big, heavy chords and that big, thick, heavy sound, but in a different way.

"I think just in terms of my guitar sounds, I've always been a little restrained. So I wanted to put back a little bit, just play harder with my right hand, hit the strings harder . . . Pete Townshend was the best example of that. He can make an acoustic guitar sound so heavy and powerful. The grunge movement brought in all of these bands that were starting to de-tune and amps on a million, with a very, very heavy, thick sound. I didn't really want to be in that game. We'd sort of been there earlier, and everything sounded like that through the '90s. But I loved it! I loved it! It was dark and heavy and I loved it a lot, but it wasn't for us. We could easily have gone in that direction; we could've turned around and layered a dozen guitar tracks and gone there, but we had that melodic aspect. There was also the articulation of Neil's drumming, leaving the air and space around it. It's a real balancing act.

"You could push it in that direction," continues Alex, meaning toward guitar, "but there are many complex aspects to the way we put our records together, and how we write and what we want to come across in the presentation. The interaction between Geddy and Neil is very active — very active rhythm section. And you don't want to lose that with thick, overbearing guitar sounds, and that's not my style. Although I really enjoyed listening to it — and certainly, when I was sitting around practicing, I had my fair share of cranking it up and de-tuning — but for the band, there were other things that were more important."

Alex was certainly aware of what was happening with grunge. Hair metal — another mania Rush politely skipped over — was trundling off a cliff, and all eyes were on Seattle, with a little Smashing Pumpkins, Faith No More and Jane's Addiction thrown in.

"At that period, things were changing very quickly and quite dramatically," remembers Lifeson. "Anybody from a record company, that's all they talked about, going to Seattle and finding the next Nirvana or Pearl Jam. We've seen a lot of trends and we've lived through a lot of trends, and it's always tempting to jump on that bandwagon. In the long run it's more satisfying to stay in your own path, in your own trail, and wind your way through all this other stuff that is going on. I mean, we've talked about that. We talked about writing songs in different tuning and a heavier approach, and then we realized, you know what? We're just going to sound like somebody else. I mean, they're already sounding a little bit like us, so why would we do that?"

Keyboards were on their way out too — with grunge or alternative or hard alternative, it was all about guitars. "Yeah, that's true," Lifeson agrees. "Keyboards had sort of run their course. And increasingly, after those records with Peter, we started to downplay the keyboards whenever we used them. We would use very basic pad sounds, organ or piano. Gone were the synth-y sort of sounds. And that's been dwindling ever since. It's interesting, I had a conversation with Geddy recently about going back to work and we should get together and do some writing, and that brought up the keyboards. And I said, maybe we'll incorporate a little more keyboard stuff, just, you know, some interesting rhythmic things. And he said, 'No way! I don't want any keyboards.' Which I thought was fantastic. It took twenty years, but it happened . . .

"See, I think, for him, because those duties end up falling in his lap, I don't think he wants to be stuck behind all that stuff anymore. And I don't blame him. It's very restricting playing live, to be there triggering keyboards or playing keyboard parts. You're stuck in that one space and you want to be a little freer and move around. But it does add a nice dimension to the sound. I didn't imagine that I would ever have brought it up in a positive way.

"I don't know how I would sum that up, in terms of the developmental curve," says Alex, asked to survey the changes in the band from *Signals* to *Roll the Bones*. "You know, I think our production expertise was moving in a particular direction. I think our production sensibilities are much richer over that period of time. We had worked on more levels in terms of our production. We had heard more music in our music."

But ask Rush fans or ardent followers of music, and most would say these are some of the band's worst sounding albums — there's no one complaining about any record between *2112* and *Signals* — or for that matter the first album or *Fly by Night*. Those records sound robust, electric, timeless. When hardcore fans and music critics today put those albums under examination, no one ever raises their hand and wants to talk about the production first. But *Power Windows*, *Hold Your Fire*, *Presto* and *Roll the Bones* . . . that's the first thing anybody says: the production is weak, criticism that seems to deflect from putting down the songs, from putting down *the guys*, as if the dislike of this period can be blamed on something trivial, or at least not personal.

"I think we also became a little more sophisticated in our songwriting," continues Alex, further on the comparison. "We heard other things that would work in terms of harmony and melody and all of that. Whereas in '82, maybe it was a little more straightforward. The sounds were more straightforward and the parts, although active, were more straightforward. They were more traditional, I think, in their composition. By the time we got to *Roll the Bones*, we were really moving around in other areas. For me, the kind of chords I was playing, the kind of air I felt around things, what I wanted to fill, what I wanted to leave open, it was a pretty strong learning curve through that period. We also went from being twenty-nine years old to thirty-nine years old — there's a lot of living in that time."

And again, with respect to the keyboards, Alex says, "Where we really sunk our teeth into it was around the time of *Grace Under Pressure*. And then it peaked and started to trail with those last two records, *Presto* and *Roll the Bones*. And certainly by the time we got to *Counterparts*, we were sort of over it."

Rupert is adamant that Rush had earned the right to morph and morph rapidly, comparing them to Radiohead. "Yes, Radiohead invented a certain world that they exist in and you just can't copy it — nobody can. It's a world where they earned every single place in that chain of events that became what we know as the absolute phenomenon of Radiohead. In their own way, Rush have done the same thing over a longer career. They've earned that right, through these building blocks of success and change and unpredictability, taking their fans places they maybe didn't want to go, but always taking them there kindly, always thoughtfully.

"There's always the tracks that the fans want to hear, either side of that 'Roll the Bones' track. 'Oh, I really don't like that. Aah, but there's this nice one straight afterwards.' Because they've all got a wicked sense of humor, there's lots of playfulness in a Rush record. That constant inventiveness is absolutely at the core, as well as that absolute will to not be sucked into what was a video single syndrome, what you can always call the lust to be more commercial. As soon as you become #1 and have that big, big hit, like Peter Gabriel with 'Sledgehammer,' everything changes. It's much better, as Avis once said about Hertz in the '60s, to be proud to be #2. If you stay at the second level, sort of top of the second division, you can go on forever. As soon as you're #1, you can only go down."

On the promotional trail for *Roll the Bones*, Alex articulated that he was more than pleased that the band was able to put the album together so quickly, indeed finishing two months ahead of schedule, where previously, a day or two early was a happy circumstance. The release date for the album was subsequently moved up a couple of months, and this time out there was less talk of quitting the road. Indeed, the guys had a tight schedule worked out clear to the release of the next album. But first came what was still the usual grind, a grind that, as they say of the ocean, deserved wary respect.

The band would be up for a robust eight-month campaign, beginning down the highway in Hamilton, Ontario, on October 25, 1991, with Andy Curran from Anthem act Coney Hatch as support but for one date — years later, Andy would take a prominent role in the band's front office. *Roll the Bones* received its gold certification in the U.S. the same day as well, on the heels of opening at #3 on Billboard, the highest placement of the band's career thus far. Otherwise, the tour included a handful of other central Canadian dates, only Vancouver in the west, and then the band's usual blanket coverage of America. A typical stint of about a month in Europe included an even split between Germany and the U.K., with Rotterdam and Paris filling out the trek.

Band photographer and video director Andrew MacNaughtan (who tragically died of a heart attack while on assignment with

Rush in 2012 at the age of forty-seven) would join the band on the road on and off beginning with this tour. As he recalls, "The band insisted they stay in East Berlin, just to experience it. Because the wall had just come down two years before that. So I thought that was pretty interesting and pretty cool, and we did that — we stayed in a hotel in East Berlin."

Earlier in the tour, the guys ended up having one of their worst shows ever. "I'll never forget it," explains Andrew. "I think it was an outdoor show in Sacramento. And somehow it got past the band that it was a general admission show. The band never allows general admission shows anymore. Ever. And somehow it got through without the band knowing. So the Primus guys go on first, and sometimes fans get stupid and they throw up water bottles onto the stage, and one hits Les, and Les is the very first person to stop, right in the middle of the song, and say, 'Look, you can't do that.' He always makes a really big deal of it instead of just ignoring it. All that does is fire up the fans even more. Things really started flying, like other bottles, beach balls, shoes — everything started coming up onstage.

"So by the time Rush came out — and this is GA, so the fans are all squished up and rowdy and it tends to fire craziness — when they were up there, I think Geddy got hit with a banana at one point, or a shoe, and it landed on his panels. And so right in the middle of a song like 'Spirit of Radio' or whatever, one of the earlier songs, all of a sudden it triggered a sound from a different song. And already they were so furious when they came onstage. They were absolutely irate — so, so upset. Alex was just fuming, really, really pissed off. Because they're very insistent that they do not do general admission shows. It's not safe for anyone involved, and it gets the fans all rowdy.

"There's no point in telling the rest of the story," continues Andrew, "but, you know, I'm gay, and of course I'm sort of the brunt of their jokes. Because we're very close, good friends for many years. So Alex came offstage and he was yelling and slamming the lockers in the dressing room, really pissed off, 'Those fuckers, oh my God, and that cocksucker over there, he threw the . . . no offense, Andrew.' And as soon as he said that — 'no offense, Andrew' — the guys all started laughing. And it just changed the whole tone of the rest of the night. They were not having a good night. They were pissed off the whole time and it was not a good night, but after he said that, at my expense, they all started laughing and it was fine."

Back to business, Canadian heroes the Tragically Hip chimed in as support for a hometown show on December 16, 1991, set up as a United Way benefit, with the Daily Bread Food Bank also ending up with fifteen thousand pounds of crowd-donated food. Axe shredder Vinnie Moore supported on the tour, as did Mr. Big. After Andy's show, guitarist Eric Johnson handled the balance of the first leg of the tour, while avant-garde anti-power trio Primus jumped on for the first of their storied two terms with the band.

"Eric was one where I would go out and watch him almost every night," recalls Alex. "His playing is so articulate but still very soulful. He and I are a year and a day apart in our birthdays, so we had a Virgo thing. We jammed a couple of times in the tuning room and spent a few evenings just talking about other nonmusical things. He's quite a spiritual guy. I gave him my double-neck guitar as a gift, and about a month after I gave it to him, one of the crew guys who had a drug problem and was quite ill stole it and sold it, and that was heartbreaking. I mean, that was a special gift."

With respect to the tour's set list, *Grace Under Pressure*'s "Distant Early Warning" was dropped in time for the European leg, replaced by "Red Sector A." "Subdivisions" was replaced by "Vital Signs" at the same time, "The Pass" replaced by "The Analog Kid." Late in the tour, the band added a "Cygnus X-1" teaser at the close of the show, with "The Trees" added for the American dates after the European tour, the third leg as it were if the second leg could be called the appendage, starting January 18, 1992, after nearly a month's break. For the encore, there was a medley that took in "The Spirit of Radio," "Overture" from "2112," "Finding My Way," "La Villa Strangiato," "Anthem," "Red Barchetta" and then finally back to "Spirit" again. From *Roll the Bones*, "Ghost of a Chance" was a late arrival, joining clear choices "Dreamline," "Bravado," "Where's My Thing?" and "Roll the Bones."

"The film was a big one with that, the skull singing the rap section," says Neil, when asked about other distinguishing features on the *Roll the Bones* tour, Rush lifting the footage from the amusing and successful video. "I don't think there was anything else, particularly, production-wise, that I remember. We still had the bunnies on that tour, I think; we hadn't retired them yet."

Geddy, ever the film guy, points out an additional dimension. "That's when we got into the whole computer thing; that was the whole CGI revolution, with the computer graphics. And the great thing with being involved in the visual production is that you learn so much about different animation techniques. We experimented with some different kinds of animators over the years. Even going back to the early, early stuff, through the *Power Windows* and *Hold Your Fire* period, we used all kinds of different young animators in Toronto to do things. For 'Manhattan Project,' there was a really great animated piece done. Even 'Red Lenses' we had this wacky, wacky cartoon done for it. That's something that really intrigued me.

"So when it came time to do something for *Roll the Bones*, I can't remember where the idea came from, but the whole talking skull idea popped up. It was a major production coming up with the people that could animate the skull in the right way, do computer graphics plus real-time animation. So we used three or four different styles of animation in the film. But also it forced us to perform songs in a different way. In order for the animation to come on at the right time and for the skeleton to do the rap, we had to play to a click, just so the timing all worked, which was kind of nightmare-ish for Neil. But that began that whole thing where we would do that. We had done that a little bit in the past, when we played 'Time Stand Still,' and that's how Amy's voice used to appear nightly, as magic, while she appeared on the film."

One thing the guys recall fondly is their time spent with Primus, Les Claypool and company providing mind expansion on both the *Roll the Bones* and subsequent *Counterparts* tours. "Les is amazing, a great stylist," notes Geddy. "I like the way he plays and I like his inventiveness. He's not a traditional riff guy and I usually adore the riff guys. But he brings a whole different, incredibly inventive style to playing bass."

"The deal was, you had to go out and get an instrument or instruments that you don't know how to play," chuckles Alex, giving his account of the legendary Rush/Primus jam sessions from the road. "That's what we would do. So after our soundcheck, we'd come back and have dinner. They would do their soundcheck; they'd come back. And from six to seven, we would jam. We bought a flute, a harmonica, a clarinet, some weird drums, all just cheap stuff from pawnshops. And we would jam for this hour. We did it every day; it was just a riot. It was the most bizarre music you could imagine. And we started recording some of it. I don't know where those tapes ended up. But I know there are these tapes kicking around with probably twenty hours of these crazy jams, from Berlin, from America. They're probably sitting somewhere at the bottom of a case. You don't think about it at the time . . ."

"We had a little practice drum kit for that," adds Neil. "Alex would go to pawn shops and come in with a flute or a violin. And there'd be bicycles, pipes; everybody was playing something. And pretty well every day we just had that kind of free-form blowout."

MacNaughtan was witness to some of this, in the course of performing his unofficial duties of keeping the band entertained. "It became the habit that they would jam every night together in one of the shower stalls or something. And the thing was each guy could not play the instrument he normally would play. There are photos I shot of Geddy playing drums, Alex playing accordion. Geddy would play acoustic guitar, Neil would play his bongos, Alex had another stupid instrument, like a triangle or something. He would find anything. Like if it was in the shower stall, he would play the pipes. Whatever made a sound, he would goof around on. He bought a flute."

"I didn't really catch on to Rush until my freshman year in high school," explains Les Claypool, who would become one of the key figures in the '90s promoting bass playing as an art form, and doing so in front of often confused alternative rock audiences, at some sun-dappled festival gig populated by much more accessible and digestible acts. In essence, Les was to the '90s what Geddy was to the '70s, and what Billy Sheehan or perhaps Steve Harris was to the '80s. "What converted me was, I joined the RCA record club, where you get six records for a penny or ten records for a dime, and one of them was *All the World's a Stage*, which I proceeded to wear out — and wear my parents out with. Besides the power of the music and the drums and whatnot — I wasn't a bass player at the time — those lyrics were compelling because it was this space and dungeons and dragons kind of thing, which as a young fellow you are very much drawn toward.

"And then eventually, becoming a bass player, well, Geddy Lee was my hero when I was fourteen. There were only a handful of guys who were playing bass that were really in the forefront in rock. I was just learning Zeppelin and Aerosmith, and then along comes Rush, and the bass was very prominent in the mix, and he had a distinct tone. His tone was as compelling as his playing, and for a good many years I tried very hard to replicate that tone. Unfortunately being a young fellow of limited means, I had no idea how you got those tones. I just kept trying to crank up my crappy little amp. And I had a bass that had flat-wound strings on it. It was just the strings it came with, and there was no way I was getting anything close to a Geddy Lee tone on it. It was just a flappy, flumpy thing.

"I remember seeing those guys," continues Claypool. "It was my very first concert, and it was Pat Travers opening for Rush at the Cow Palace in San Francisco. And I remember scalping a ticket, even though it wasn't sold out, but I didn't know that driving down. I figured it was sold out. So I had a scalped ticket at probably twice as much as I should've paid for it. I drank three beers and threw up in the parking lot. And I went in and saw Pat Travers, which was amazing, because Mars Cowling is a phenomenal bass player, and then Tommy Aldridge doing his drum solo. And here comes Rush. And I remember seeing the black Rickenbacker. I used to draw pictures of Rickenbackers . . . I would look in magazines. I wanted a Rickenbacker more than anybody, but I didn't have any money. And there was this guy next to me. He was another bass player in my school, and he had money and a big fancy amp, and he had just gotten one, a Rick. And before they came onstage, there was the bass sitting there, and there were the roadies setting up. He's like, 'Mine's just like that, the black!' And I'm sitting there going, 'You bastard.'

"Anyway, that show was a religious experience for a fourteen-year-old kid, however the hell old I was. It was phenomenal. It was *Hemispheres* tour, so they had 'Cygnus' and the ships going through the black hole and the two hemispheres, the brain was coming at you — it was mind-blowing, unbelievable. So from that point on, there was nobody that could beat Geddy. I had friends that had big record collections — I didn't — who were always trying to turn me onto other things like Larry Graham and Stanley Clarke. And I'm like, 'No, Geddy Lee is the best bass player on the planet.' I just wasn't hearing it, until I got a little older, that there were these other guys. But Geddy and Chris Squire were the two guys who were able to take the bass and give it a distinct tone that cut through. Even John Entwistle, who was fabulous and had a fabulous tone; it wasn't as present as Geddy's tone. And of course, years later, I picked Geddy's brain to find out how he did it. I got some secrets. I don't think he gave me all the secrets."

Further on, what makes Geddy special, Claypool explains that "his phrasing is very unique and he's very melodic, and you just didn't hear things like that back then. A little bit here and there — Paul McCartney is a very melodic player, but not as aggressive as Geddy. And of course Chris Squire. But the interaction between Neil and Geddy was so intense, it seemed like every low note that Geddy hit, it was accented by Neil's kick drum and vice versa. So between the two of them, and with everybody in the audience air drumming and playing air bass, it was a pretty spectacular thing. And I think a lot of Neil's and Geddy's presence also contributed to the textural playing of Alex. You know, Alex is not a riff rocker. He plays these very textural, layered, full guitar parts, and that lends itself to having this movement underneath it that is really cool and very distinctive. It's like there is the cupcake, and Alex is the icing on the cupcake.

"And Geddy's definitely much more than just a bass player. The thing about Geddy's singing, it was always the thing that repelled all the girls that I would play Rush to. Any girlfriend I even came close to having wasn't so keen on Rush. And a lot of it was that Geddy's voice back then was very distinctive and very piercing. It's a love/hate thing. And I myself, as a performer, have learned there is also a love/hate relationship with people who either listen to what I do or avoid listening to what I do. So I understand. But my wife actually grew up in Iowa, and both she and her sister listened to Rush. And I knew I had stumbled onto a unique woman when I met her."

Flash forward from Les's early intense study of Ged to when Primus is traipsing around America and Europe with Rush. Les says, "When we went on tour with Rush, we were all very excited. And in fact, that was one of the reasons we got Tim Alexander as a drummer; we started auditioning and we just started jamming on Rush tunes, and it was like whoa, we've got something to connect on. But when we toured with those guys, especially when we toured with them in Europe, we kind of got shit for it from the cool bands at the time, the Nirvanas and the alternative bands. And some of the British press were like, oh, Primus is supposed to be this young hip band; why are they going with Rush? There was a stigma attached to that. Which I've now watched slowly devolve. I remember Nirvana was supposed to tour with them. It was talked about, and they couldn't believe we would tour with them. And it's like, well, Rush was my favorite band in high school. Why wouldn't I take the opportunity to do this? It was a great thing. It was a great thing musically, and it was a great thing to meet and befriend these guys.

"I mean, here were guys that in my youth, when I was in high school, they were my world, they were my band. So to meet these guys . . . I think Alex was the first guy I met, walking down a hallway backstage. And they had some tour manager back at the time who was a real hard-ass, and he wasn't very nice or very friendly — until all of a sudden we became friends with the guys, and he came to get a little brown-nosy. But he went along the wayside. But I don't know, they warmed right up to us for some reason. We just hit it off. I don't remember exactly when we first kind of sat down and started hanging out with them, but it was somewhat surreal, because they were such a big part of my teen-age years."

As for his recollections of the jam sessions with the guys, Les says, "Oh yeah, we had some amazing memories of jamming with the Rush guys backstage. We had a little drum kit, and either Tim would be on the drum kit or sometimes I would be on the drum kit, and I remember Neil banging on the lockers, and Geddy's playing bass and I'm playing bass, and I'm watching what Geddy's doing. And I'm going, 'Holy shit, this guy has still got it,' just effortlessly playing this amazing stuff. And this was a daily occurrence. And Alex coming in and grabbing a guitar and playing it with a tortilla chip for a pick. Unfortunately, I was very high that day, so some of it's a bit of a blur, but I remember thinking to myself, hey, if I were sixteen and I was able to look forward to see this, I would literally shit in my pants.

"All three of them were very friendly to us," continues Les. "We became good friends. You know, Neil kept to himself a little more. He would kind of do his own thing. But there were some times where he would just bike from somewhere in Florida to another gig, and Larry and our road manager did the same.

"Geddy, he's just kind of Geddy. He's pretty mellow, got a dry sense of humor. We were hanging out in Berlin at some out-door café and had a nice dinner, and I remember just sitting there after having a few drinks. 'You guys have got to play "By-Tor," gotta play "Cygnus," you know?' Because it was the *Roll the Bones* era and they were stepping away from some of those old tunes. And I can relate; some of my own tunes, it's like your high school haircut. You go, what was I thinking? But we were really egging them on to bust out some of those old Dungeons & Dragons–type tunes. And they started playing them eventually. I don't know if we influenced them on that, but we were definitely egging them on.

"Alex is just Alex. Sometimes he's just Big Al, but he's just an incredibly humorous guy. He would be a good character actor. He's got that persona. He's got multiple personas. One of the drunkest times in my entire life was at his house. We were in town for Lollapalooza '93. Alex had invited us out to his house for dinner. They had all this food prepared and he busted out these really nice wines. None of us gave a shit about wine back then, and so we're drinking this wine, having a good ol' time. And we finished dinner and next thing you know, he busts out these frozen vodkas from his freezer. And we're doing shots and everybody is getting a little loopy, and somehow it came up that Ler, Larry, needed a haircut, our guitar player from Primus. And he's like, 'Oh, we just need a bowl!' So we get a bowl out, we put the bowl on his head, and Alex is trying to cut his hair. And it's a glass bowl and it slips off his head onto the ground and it shatters and cuts Alex's foot.

"So they end up finishing it with a different bowl. At this point, Ler is just a wreck, and Alex had turned on . . . he had this remote control with the hot tub, and the hot tub was going with this waterfall, and next thing you know we're out in the hot tub, with the floating champagne glasses. And I'm wearing Alex's wife's favorite hat, unbeknownst to me, and I'm completely ruining it by hanging out in the waterfalls, drunken bastards.

"Ler comes out, he's trying to put his swim trunks on, he's rolling around on the concrete, completely nude, just oblivious, trying to put the damn swim trunks on, and Alex is a standing there with champagne going, 'Damn, Ler.' We have our evening in the hot tub, Ler ends up somewhere passed out, various people have fallen to the wayside. I don't know what time it was in the morning. I ended up out in the studio with Alex, Tim "Herb" Alexander, our drummer, who didn't drink at our party at all, and we're trying to record some stuff. And I was so drunk, I couldn't play the bass. I've never been so drunk that I couldn't at least play something.

"Next thing I remember, I wake up, I hear this voice, 'Trous, Trous,' and that's our road manager's name. So I look around and I'm sitting on some couch in some room. I walk out of the room to the stairwell, and there's Ler at the bottom, completely naked, holding a towel to his crotch. And he just kind of looks up at me, doesn't even acknowledge me, and turns back around. 'Trous, Trous.' He's calling our road manager. 'Where's my clothes? And who cut my hair?' And then we played Lollapalooza that night in Toronto, and we were damaged goods."

Les has passed on his appreciation for Rush to the next generation. "Yes, the thing is now, my son, who is twelve, he has been playing upright bass in school, in the orchestra for the past three years, and I just recently bought him an electric bass guitar, and he had no interest in it prior. He still prefers playing the upright bass, and he's always had pretty eclectic tastes. His favorite band, if you asked me a year ago, it was Parliament, and he's playing 'Flashlight' and 'Atomic Dog.' He was a pretty heavy kid, and he was learning about astronomy in school, and he starts talking about black holes, and I asked him, 'Do you know about Cygnus?' 'Oh yeah, Cygnus the black hole that is closest to our solar system.' He's rattling off all this information.

"I said, 'Check this out,' and busted out *Farewell to Kings* and played him 'Cygnus X-1.' And he's reading all the lyrics, and then

I showed him the intro, the beginning part to 'Cygnus X-1,' on the bass, and he's really getting into Rush now. Which is a phenomenal thing. He's into Rush, the Residents and Parliament. That's amazing! And I'm seeing way more young kids who are getting into bands who have musicians that are a little more technically proficient than some of the popular musicians of the past fifteen years or so; they're getting into Rush, Yes, old King Crimson, and it's an encouraging thing."

Did this mean Rush were cool again? Were they ever cool?

Says Les, "I don't remember *Rush* and the word *cool* ever being in the same sentence, growing up. But then again, we were the guys who weren't looking for those types of things. What was cool back when this was going around? It was like Eddie Money, shit like that. Who gives a shit? It's all subjective.

"To me, this is amazingly cool," continues Les, pointing to the band shot on the back of *2112*. "I wish they would still come out with this. That's phenomenal; that's unbelievable. That's a statement. Look at the bulge! Look at Alex — he's got the bulge going! It's phenomenal. I would go for this look. I would do it in a heartbeat. I may not pull off the bulge though.

"The thing is — and I tell my kids this all the time — the people who are truly cool are the people that don't know they are cool and don't try. To me, that's the definition of true coolness. It's being comfortable in your own skin, which is what you're wearing on your skin, how you're wearing your hair, how you look, how you smell, all of it. It's being comfortable with yourself. And I've always tried to project that. You look at pictures of the Grateful Dead. Were they cool? To their fans they were extremely cool and well loved. But there are a lot of people who would not think they are cool. I remember hearing comments by the Beastie Boys, who did not think Rush was cool at all. And here's the Beastie Boys, a lot of people think they're pretty cool.

But there are a lot of people who don't think they're very cool either. So it depends on your perspective.

"I think if you spend your life trying to be cool, you're just going to be this insecure wreck. Because it's all subjective. And there are many elements to that subjectiveness: where it's being perceived, what time it's being perceived, by which age group, by which demographic, by which gender. I tell my kids this all the time: just be yourself and be comfortable with it. That's the way to be a happy human being. And for these guys, they make music they believe in, and they've made music they believe in for a long time.

"I'm sure like all of us, they have different periods where they are less enthused by what they did. Because at the time we're telling them, 'You gotta play "By-Tor," you gotta play "Cygnus."' And they're going, 'Yeah right, Claypool, right.' They thought we were nuts. Why would they want to go back and play that dungeons and dragons stuff? Well, it's your high school haircut again. You look at your high school haircut at a certain point in time, you go whoa, what the hell was I thinking? Then it kind of comes around. I have my high school haircut again. And for these guys, they are selling out sheds all over the place, they are revered . . . they have a revered hunk of music history. Last year they had their first big piece in *Rolling Stone*; I was blown away. It was like holy shit. And it took about thirty years. But I don't have a subscription to *Rolling Stone* — it's obviously not too cool to me."

CHAPTER 2

COUNTERPARTS

"What is genuine enthusiasm and what is ego
and what is territory?"

I f there's one thing Geddy, Alex and Neil were to bring forward
from their experience on *Roll the Bones*, it was that rare and
yet magical "when it happened" sense of spontaneity — creativity on the fly. It's not something one associates with Rush,
and indeed not even something that is all too detectable by the
listener, but it is of no mind; if it sparked the guys, if it made
record-making more enjoyable, then it was going to happen.

For two reasons: (1) the band were quite sure it made the
music better and (2) at this point in their career, they damn well
needed reasons to keep doing it. Might be an exaggeration, but
imperceptibly, invisibly, as we enter the '90s watching Rush, we
increasingly got the sense that if the band ended for one reason
or another, nobody was going to go off the deep end. Canadian
to the core, no doubt a large part of keep on keeping on at this
point was the responsibility the guys felt to their immediate
family and their extended business families to keep the franchise

operating at peak size. No inflamed desire or obsession to grow it, but more like, wouldn't it be nice if we could keep doing this? And if not, there's golf, baseball, biking, solo records, art, wine, planes, archery, learning French, travel, family, Canada.

Music was a favorite hobby, just not the only hobby. And for indulging that hobby, it was back to Chalet Studio in rural Ontario for writing sessions, same demarcated duties, trucking home on the weekends for family visits, this time somewhat inspired by their fun times with Primus — pure creativity if not exactly functional — as well as the heavier sounds coming out of Seattle.

"We made that record at home," says Geddy, "That was nice, because if you can make a record at home, you can go home every night. And some days you don't have to come in and you get to be with your family. And that's all good for keeping the family together."

About the music, says Ged, "It was starting to move into a jazzier, softer tonal area that was less satisfying for me, because I'm a rocker in my heart and I want to make rock music. This was getting a bit soft and a bit . . . the wrong color, basically. That's why *Counterparts* became such an important record because it was back to the past in a way. And also back to the future — a lot of that coincided with what was happening in Seattle at the time, where rock bands were thriving again. That was such a delicious thing to see happen, to suddenly go from such a weird period to rock bands all over the place. I loved it; it was great. Soundgarden and all these great bands were inspiring. That's an example of listening to what's around you and saying, you know, we've lost the plot a little bit here; we're drifting off into this other color. I mean, we struggled to get any keyboards on that record."

The two months in Claremont were plagued by technical hiccups, but they managed to get a decent amount of material down on eight-track, working digitally, using Cubase Audio to capture and manipulate their rehearsal ideas. The guys butted heads over the usual bugbear, keyboards, and struck an uneasy truce over the idea that guitar would be much more prominent in the mix. Meanwhile Neil was off writing lyrics, working not so conceptually this time. Though he soon discovered the theme of duality in some of the songs, which led to their naming the band's fifteenth album *Counterparts* (but not until after the record was finished).

Given the premise, and given past patterns, it makes little sense that the band would go back to Peter Collins — man of the hour on *Power Windows* and *Hold Your Fire* — to produce the new record. But in his time away — and let's not forget, the first time, Peter essentially fired himself — Collins had produced Alice Cooper's *Hey Stoopid* (heavy hair metal), Gary Moore's *After the War* (his last heavy one before going blues), and Queensryche's platinum-selling prog metal masterpiece from 1988, *Operation: Mindcrime*. Collins also produced the band's next record, *Empire*, which sold triple platinum, making Queensryche the first band to break commercially, building upon what Rush did back in the '70s. They were more of a commercial juggernaut than the elders.

Even more impressive in terms of heaviness as well as unexpected street cred, Collins worked on Suicidal Tendencies' most accessible and stadium-rocking record, 1992's *The Art of Rebellion*, which continued the band's improbable gold run. All of a sudden, "Mr. Big" was hot again, which was important to Collins, who was shaken that *Hold Your Fire* was the first Rush record in a long time to not make platinum.

The guys had stayed in touch with Collins, and a conversation proved that both camps were on the same page moving forward. Peter didn't like the sonics of the band's last couple of records, and he had put in place a procedure that would help make a difference, namely working with a new engineer, Kevin "Caveman" Shirley, who would be instrumental in helping the band and Collins work toward their stated mandate — not wuss out on it.

"All of our experiments have been riddled with failures," admits Neil. "When can they not be? Things can go too far in one direction, and then we correct ourselves. Eventually you go whoa, we tried to go along this way, but it's too much. And the guitar/keyboard thing became that, increasingly through the '80s, first sonically, and then I would say textually and creatively, because Andy Richards and Peter Collins had some ideas, and all of us loved what that brought to our sound. I still really like those records for what they are, but I understand Alex too, coming back to reclaim the sound.

"Drummers suffer from that too, getting soaked up in a huge guitar sound. Add that to a huge keyboard sound and sonically it could make drums lack the intensity and dynamics that they have. Geddy and I always say when we do the basic tracks, just the bass and drums together, 'They will never sound that good again.' It's something all of us have. And I remember there was one album in the '90s, and we were going through the mixes and the assistant engineer just said to Alex and me, 'I just want to get you boys two hats — more guitars and more drums.' So everybody is jealous of their territory sonically. And it is just sonically. It's not that your part should be louder, it's just the nuances of the tom resonance and the ride cymbal that you hate to surrender.

"It's not a massive ego thing that drums should be louder or guitar should be louder. It becomes that sonic loss, a sense of . . . guitarists like a guitar. I like drums! If I would be mixing an album, I would mix the drums loud because I love that. Not because it's me but because it's drums. I love drums that much. I love to hear the drums. And I love to hear a record where the drums are mixed loud. So that is all woven in it too. That's why you had to be careful in a partnership, seeing what is genuine enthusiasm and what is ego and what is territory.

"What I'm trying to get at with all those anecdotes is that over the years those are little corrections you make to solve problems. So yes, that time existed, but it existed over several albums, and over several stages, all of which have their nice moments musically, I think. So that was inevitable and right, and it worked out at the right time the way it should. The guitars did become more predominant in the way Alex wanted them to. And the keyboards kept serving us in a MIDI sense, as background and as texture and enriching the sound."

Neil sidesteps the issue when asked about Alex and Geddy butting heads over this. "Well sure, how could there be a creative partnership without disagreements? It's how you handle those disagreements that matters. Everybody has creative differences. You can't come at each other with rage, or outrage — 'How dare you?' There's no way any partnership of any kind is going to survive. So of course there was friction and disagreements, and finding an acceptable solution to what everybody wants. That's what the mix is after all, more drums, more guitar, more vocal! It's a contest, in a sense. And there is competition involved and there will be friction involved. Part of what makes a relationship last is handling the friction."

"I found it really, really difficult to work around the way the keyboards were developing, particularly with *Power Windows* and *Hold Your Fire*," says Alex. "I mean, they were so layered on, and the keyboards were done before the guitars were done, so I had to find areas to poke in and out of, by separating the guitar parts. I was never comfortable with doing that. It almost felt like the guitar was becoming a secondary instrument to what all the keyboards were doing, and I think Geddy recognized that too.

"In *Hold Your Fire* we tried to tone the keyboards down quite a bit. I went for the much cleaner, wiry, trebly sound just to cut through the massive layers of keys that occupied the same frequencies as those thicker guitar tones. So it was very challenging, and I don't know if it's entirely satisfying. I have nothing against those records and how they sound. I think they sound great. And there are songs on those two records that are among my favorites that we've ever done, and I think from a production standpoint there's a lot of interesting dynamics on those records. But when I see where we've gone and the kind of effort we made to go back to the core, it's far more gratifying."

When asked whether there was friction between him and Ged over the issue, Alex, like Neil, is reticent to go there, leaning toward the diplomatic answer. "I had my fill, really, by the end of the '80s. It became like a weeding process, a little less with each consecutive record."

Lifeson stresses that Geddy was also on board with the changes. "And Ged started to feel that way too. I don't think he enjoyed much the pressure of playing keyboards, playing them live. He wanted to feel freer. Playing keyboards, playing the bass, singing, it's a lot of work. And most of all, we just wanted to get that core sound back. We'd gone and done all this stuff, and now was sort of the time to regroup and come back to it. It was a natural thing for him. He had sort of turned off the keyboards, so it's not even something he gave thought to.

"I slapped him around a little bit, and he got over it," kids Alex, again downplaying the disagreement. "No, I think Ged realized I was unhappy. And it wasn't that I was terribly unhappy; it was just frustrating more than anything. But you know what? At the end of the day, if you feel that way, you stand up and do something about it. And previously I don't think I really did. I went with the flow rather than disrupt anything. And I just thought, well, I'll learn to work around it.

"And you know, maybe that makes me the musician I am today. It was a greater challenge, to fit in with what I felt were all these obstacles at the time. It gave me more of a sense as a rhythm guitarist, certainly. And I think that's a strength of mine. It's an area in guitar playing that I've really worked on over the years. And perhaps without that attention, I don't know if I would've gone to that place.

"I felt more confident with myself and with my playing through the '90s, and I think I made a bolder statement for myself, within the context of the band, more recently. It's a lot to do with trust and respect for each other. And both Ged and I have a great deal of respect and trust for each other, and we worked on that over the years, as you would in any relationship. I think now what we write, when we record, we feel a hundred percent sense of security in what's happening with the album. We know we can leave the room and it's all going to be great.

"For me, by that point, I heard guitar parts in my head that could've been keyboard parts in the past. Why not do that, instead of using keyboards? Because the technology had moved into the sample world. Why not write the part on guitar, play it, record it? If we want to play live, we can trigger that part while I'm playing the main part. Use it the same way we would be using a keyboard or sampler, but having the part organically recorded, more naturally. And later on, we really dove into that. And that helped Geddy and me develop this whole vocal and guitar relationship, in terms of replacing keyboard parts, over the years. That was really the key.

"It felt like enough," continues Alex, on why the guys moved on from Rupert Hine. "I don't think we felt we could learn any more from him, and that was no longer the direction we wanted to go in. We view those records as being a little softer than what we intended. They were entirely acceptable, and it seemed to work at the time, but we were definitely moving in a much heavier three-piece way. We really wanted to get back to those roots; that was a conscious effort at that time. And that was why we worked with Kevin, because he had a reputation of being quite a strong, heavy engineer. And Peter, we loved. Our experiences with Peter had always been great. We really wanted to bring him back at that point. Peter is always growing, and he always had such good basic instincts about music, coupled with Kevin, who was a little wild or rougher at the time. We thought we had a really good team.

"Peter is a very, very smart producer — and he feels it. It doesn't matter if the song is a pop song or a metal song, he feels it, and he has great instincts. And he's such a comfort and joy to work with. There is so much stability in his presence in the studio, in the control room. He's always there, never touches a thing on the console, except to move his ashtray when he's smoking his big cigars. It's just great to have him there, very comforting. He's on top of it, he keeps notes, he's very organized, and that takes a lot of pressure off you when you are working.

"Quite different," says Alex, comparing the nuts and bolts of recording *Counterparts* versus *Roll the Bones*. "Neil set his drums up in a big room and recorded, as he always does. Geddy might have an amp setup that is direct, but he's sitting in the control room, and there is immediate contact and communication, and that's a good way to work. Generally, I work the same way. I set up a rack in the control room, I sit behind the engineer, and I play all my parts, overdub my parts, from the control room, with a long cable going into the studio with all the amps."

"Kevin wanted me to go in the studio and play in front of my amps, being in the room so the guitar would vibrate with the volume of the speakers. And it's hard because it's loud, and you just have these headphones on and you're trying to really hear everything, to play precisely. And communication is difficult because you are in this room and you are looking through a little window in the distance. But you know, he was right. There's a resonance in the guitar when you're in there, and it adds to the sustain and to the character of the guitar sound. We didn't do it all like that, but we did most of it with me in the studio. It was fun to get back in there and feel it and to be surrounded by these big sizzling and humming amplifiers.

"I do remember we had our differing opinions. I felt like Kevin came from a particular school, and perhaps it was a little narrower than where I came from, or the sort of things I heard. But because this record was going in a heavier direction, we deferred to him. I understood what he was getting at and he was right. We had a lot of drinks together and sorted it out. With Kevin, again, it was that time when all the recordings were bone dry. You'd gone through the '80s when there were lots of reverbs and stuff happening, and I always loved a natural reverb, particularly on the guitar sound, if it suits the song. But Kevin was a no reverb sound on anything guy. He didn't want any reverb on vocals, drums, nothing, and I like that little bit of sheen on the mix. But it was not a big deal. And he's a very, very confident guy."

As for Geddy, "Kevin wanted him to get an old Ampeg amp, and he managed to find one, in somebody's garbage bin in the studio warehouse or something, and the thing was rattling and buzzing. But he wanted Geddy to use an amp as well, because Geddy had quite a bright, active sort of sound, very direct, less amp. And I know what Kevin was going through. He just wants that crunch out of the speakers, and that oomph, that air moving into the microphone, and he's right. It's just a question of taste. For the record, it was the right thing to do.

"This amp helped Geddy get more power out of the bottom end, but so did the fact that he used a Fender Jazz bass versus the Wal and worked with heavier strings. The amp rescued from the garbage was subject to some repairs, and it was used to drive Geddy's Trace Elliot cabinets, with lots of overdrive. Sometimes it was this, sometimes it was back to direct, bypassing cabinets, using the Palmer Speaker Simulator the same way it had been done in the demo stages."

"I got the call from Geddy, asking me if I would be interested in working with them again, and I said, 'Absolutely,'" begins Peter "Mr. Big" Collins, on renewing his collaboration with Rush, one that would ultimately carry on into a fourth record, 1996's *Test for Echo*. "And we talked about how rock music had changed, with Nirvana coming in, the Seattle sound. And while we were definitely not going to chase that sound, both he and I were interested in pursuing a more organic sound for the band. More natural sounds, less hyped-up sounds, less super-compressed snare drums, less reverb, thicker sounds, less multi-track guitars, which is perhaps a simpler sound, less layered. And to that end, we agreed to work together again and look for an engineer.

"I might have led the charge there a little bit. Because I felt looking at their last four records that it was time to move in that more organic direction, and Geddy was totally receptive to that. We talked about how that might be done, and it was definitely going to start with the engineer, and the engineering sensibility. I had heard a record produced by Mike Chapman, by the Baby Animals, an Australian band, and I really liked the sound. It had a woody sort of sound to it. And Kevin Shirley, I guess he heard that I liked the record. And he called me and I talked to him a little bit."

Shirley, a South African, had begun his career in South Africa but then moved to Australia in 1986 and worked on all sorts of acts from there. Shirley engineered the self-titled debut from Baby Animals, which went eight times platinum in Australia, becoming the biggest-selling debut album ever by an Australian band until Jet's *Get Born* album of 2003.

Continues Collins: "He was looking for work, and I told him how much I liked the record and I got his details. Then I went up to Toronto to talk to the band about engineers, and I said, 'I spoke to this guy, Kevin Shirley, and I think he's worth talking to.' I played them the Baby Animals record and they liked it — they didn't love it, but they kind of saw why I might like it. They agreed to fly him up to Toronto for a meeting. And I was there at the meeting, and we played some old Rush stuff, some of the stuff that I had done and Rupert had done. And he goes, 'Well, the snare drum sounds very thin, and I don't like all that reverb.' You know, he was just saying what he didn't like.

"And of course for any potential engineer or producer working with Rush, if you are being interviewed by Rush and you tell them you don't like what they've done, you're probably going to get the gig. Because they're fascinated to know what it is you're going to do differently, how it could be better. When I had met them, I said I think the vocals could be better, the whole sound of the record could be better, and I got the gig. Caveman got the gig by basically dissing Rush's sound. And he also told Neil that he could get a drum sound from Neil in twenty minutes. Which, you know, the gauntlet had been thrown down, and Neil loved the idea of that possibility. And I think, in truth, it took him half an hour, forty minutes, to get a basic drum sound on Neil."

"I was broke and impoverished, living in New York, and I was sending out tapes to all sorts of people to try to get any work," explains Kevin. "And I sent one to Peter Collins and he said, 'Come see the band.' So I flew up to Toronto, met with the band. I tried to go back home to the United States, and the

United States didn't let me back in. I was stuck in Toronto, with my two-year-old baby son in New York City. So I called them up and I said, 'Do I have the job?' They said, 'We'll let you know in a couple of weeks.' And I said, 'Well, I need to know now, because I'm stuck in Toronto.' They said, 'Let us call you back in an hour.' So I stayed at the airport, had no money and no ticket anywhere, and one of the flight attendants came and said, 'You can stay at my house.' And then I called Rush, and they said, 'Okay, you got the job.'

"So I said, 'Okay, then, there's another thing: I need some money.' So they said fine. It was a Friday night and on Saturday, Pegi sent over some cash to me and I managed to get a house and was stuck in Canada for like a month before we started work on the album.

"I think they were looking for something different," continues Kevin, on the subject of why they went with him. "They had a listen to my tape, and I think Neil was very impressed with the way the drums sounded. He asked me questions. 'Why do the drums sound like that?' And I said, 'Well, you know, they're analog and we recorded on a Neve, and I like not to EQ the cymbals.' And so he said, 'I love that.' And then we went to work finally. We used an SSL console that went straight to digital and everything that I didn't do. 'That's the way I like my drums to sound.' So I was like, 'Wow, okay, sure.'"

When asked if he was surprised Rush wanted to work with him, Shirley responded, "No, I wasn't — why would you be? I didn't know anything about Rush. I knew *Power Windows*, to be honest — that's all I knew. And I knew Peter Collins from the Gary Moore stuff. Especially 'Out in the Fields,' which I was a big fan of. I thought it sounded great. But no, I was struggling too hard to even be impressed by it. I was like, anything that pays, I'll do it. I mean, I was a fan of *Power Windows* to a point.

I've always been a Led Zeppelin, Deep Purple head, so I really like that tactile rock, where you identify the performance by the style of the players. And Rush was always a little more technical than that for me, a little more progressive, so I wasn't a huge fan. But like I said, I liked *Power Windows*. I thought it was a cool record, I had the vinyl, but I wasn't really a fan — that should be said.

"*Presto* and *Roll the Bones* for me were very much indicative of what was going on in the '80s. And we were in the beginning of the '90s at that point. I thought it sounded like Flock of Seagulls, Men Without Hats, even Duran Duran and Depeche Mode — they're all kind of lumped to me. I know there are Duran Duran fans that would kill me, but I kind of lumped them all together. It wasn't something I enjoyed at all. And *Presto* and *Roll the Bones* had that very plonky keyboard-like thing about them. I didn't like that. One of the things that's a Peter Collins strength is he gets people around him who have opinions and he lets them work things out. He doesn't have the grand overview like a Mutt Lange does. Peter gets people in and he watches them work to their strengths. And so when I got in there, I was kind of hell-bent on making a heavy record. And they weren't that in tune with that, but they weren't diametrically opposed to it. There was an element they wanted to introduce into the music. They took what they could from that and from me in that regard and applied it to the album."

And according to Peter Collins, Geddy had an agenda that aligned with that too. "The bottom end was an issue with Geddy," says Peter. "He wanted a bigger bottom end. He had worked with two English producers back to back, an English and Australian engineer, and I think he was still unhappy with the way the bottom end was sounding. So that was an issue for this next record."

But as usual, these were creative issues, so there was no inter-action between Collins and Rush manager, Ray Danniels, back at the Anthem office on College Street. "No, never. I barely saw Ray," says Collins when asked if he worked much with Danniels. "Mostly at gigs. And he'd come by the studio when we were in Toronto. But he was very, very supportive."

Lyrically speaking, "They had changed," continues Collins, who goes on to chart the construction process. "There were fewer story songs coming from Neil; that's one of the things I noticed. There were more sort of abstract ideas that he was putting into song form. Slightly more mystical, perhaps relationship-based, rather than the 'Red Barchetta' type of material or 'Manhattan Project.' The process would be, the band would work on their own until they got the songs into some sort of shape where they could play them to me. And then I would come in for a week, usu-ally, a week to ten days, and they would have some basic demos to play to me, and I'd sit and listen to them and make notes — both rehearsal facilities had studios — and we'd work on them, adjust and fine-tune and make changes and come up with something we could track to. We'd have all the tempos established, keys, all the basic changes."

Material-wise, "It seemed like a natural progression. I didn't think, oh my goodness, this is a complete change. I took the material as it came and worked with it and tried to maximize it. I didn't notice any huge difference in direction in songwriting. I'd noticed that gradual difference, from moving away from story songs. And something like 'Stick It Out,' I suppose it went with the whole direction of using the Caveman and a more organic sound and a little bit more classic rock."

As for the attendant heaviness, "A lot of it was encouraged by Kevin," figures Peter. "It was coming from the band, but it was heavily supported by Kevin. He was a huge Zeppelin fan, he was a fan of recording everything very simply, of having Alex go and play out in the room as opposed to in the control room, which Alex was not happy about at all initially, and then he grew to love it. And the whole concept of the drums being more of a mono item, where you could see the drums as one instrument, rather than drums spread out over the stereo picture."

Fleshing out this concept of Alex freed from the confines of the control room, Peter figures, "Kevin just believed the guitar needed to be in the room where the instruments were playing, because not only would the guitar player be more in touch with the sound, he also believed the sound of the drums and the leakage going into the guitar pickup was an important part of the guitar sound. I had never heard that philosophy before, but I liked it. I guess Alex liked it as well. We certainly bought into it. Because normally in the control room, after he had played something, there would be the discussion about, you know, was that good, what do we need to redo and blah blah blah. But if he's out in the studio, he wasn't party to all the discussions about his performance. He could just read a book, wait until he was asked to play again. And he didn't have to deal with all the critiquing of his work. It was difficult initially, but he grew to really enjoy it, and certainly on *Test for Echo* we did it that way as well, even though Kevin wasn't engineering."

Peter says the guys were a bit taken aback by Kevin's forthrightness, his confidence and directness. "Yes. I think they were. They're not used to that, that cavalier sort of attitude. They are used to very, very detailed engineers, very detail-oriented, which Kevin's not. He wants the big picture and he wants it to hit him. He'll make that decision fairly quickly, and it's kind of written on Kevin's face whether it's happening or not. I love that about him, but it was a bit of an adjustment for the band. I'm not sure whether Neil seemed happy with his drum sound at the time. He might have questioned it, because on the next record we went back to more of the individual miking of each element of his kit."

As for ditching the keyboards, "I was supportive of them going as well," notes Collins. "I like to think of myself as a commercial producer, and in the amount of time that lapsed between finishing *Hold Your Fire* and working on *Counterparts*, my sensibility changed, and I was totally aware of the Seattle sound, that whole movement, and I realized it didn't particularly involve keyboards. What I understood is that an essential part of Rush's sound was keeping it in that simple analog area. We did bring John Webster in on *Counterparts*, but it was not very much." Webster, having worked with Stonebolt, Red Rider and Tom Cochrane as a solo artist (and myriad other famous sessions, along with Peter on *Hey Stoopid*), is credited with "additional keyboards," while Geddy takes a simple synthesizers credit.

This eye toward Seattle, reflects Peter, "precipitated a change of direction back to more of their roots sound from the '70s. It was just in the air. They had done the hyped-up sound and they were ready to do something else, a more organic sound, and to incorporate from time to time some of the more progressive elements of digital recording and digital sounds, combining the two."

And fortunately, says Peter, Alex and Kevin "were cut out of the same cloth. They've both got a real rock 'n' roll sensibility. Even though Alex's taste incorporates effects more than Kevin's would, they still have that very basic attitude toward rock, while both Geddy and Neil could get to more cerebral places. Alex wanted to rock. And you know he was kept . . . not kept from it, but the type of music that Rush does . . . a lot of it is quite complex. And Caveman's sensibility is not complex music. It's very rootsy, so he connected with Alex at that level. Alex really liked his guitar tones, and it was not as stressful as it had been when we worked in the '80s. We didn't multi-track guitars endlessly.

We kept one guitar, it worked, we did it. I seem to remember using more acoustic guitar as well."

After one particular war over reverb, Kevin and Alex went and got loaded at the bar that evening on "five bottles of scotch" and worked out their differences. "Yes, and then Alex was actually kind of cool with that," says Peter. "And again, he was recording not in the control room for the first time in a long time. We set him up with amplifiers in the studio, he had a stool and he had headphones, he was removed from all the conversation going on in the studio. There was Geddy talking to Peter — Neil wasn't in the studio a lot — and Alex didn't have to listen to them going, 'Was that good?' He would get in there and he'd play. And he gave up his PRS guitars for a while. I said to him, 'They're pretty guitars; they should be like coffee tables. Why don't you play the Les Paul? Why don't you play the Telecaster again?' And so he'd pull out these old guitars and he really enjoyed it. He would take the Les Paul, plug it into a Marshall and turn it fucking loud in that room, in Quebec, and he'd play, and I think he had a blast."

"A lot of players, as they get older, tend to rely on effects to disguise some of what they see as inadequacies in their playing," says Shirley. "And I see it all the time. I shouldn't say older, but the more experienced players, they drift away from their roots, where they never had the option to disguise things with delays and choruses and reverbs and all sorts of things, and they tend to rely on it more. Especially when there's one guitar player in a band and you have to fill a void, a stadium every night, just to be able to pluck a string and have it go 'ga-zing, ga-zang, ga-zoong' is a wonderful thing. But in the studio, it all sounds like a jingle to me. And I'm still not a fan of that stuff; I fight it all the time with all the 'heritage' acts I work with.

"But I got a sense after the whiskey evening at the Four Seasons hotel in Toronto, where we just got destroyed, he kind of accepted that's where we were going to go, and that we were going to leave the past behind in terms of his guitar sound, and he just came in and he enjoyed it. Maybe initially he resigned himself to it, and then he just embraced it. It was like, I'm a kid again, I'm playing my guitar, I'm playing all my old guitars, you know, it's fun. It was creative, everything that you know it should have been. There were new parts coming out; there's 'Between Sun & Moon' when the Tele came out, 'Animate' and 'Stick It Out,' where he had the big dirty Les Pauls going on. It was exciting for him not to have the same old PRS with a bee-in-a-jar type of distortion that he'd had for the past five or six years."

And then there was Geddy, who had summarily given up using a bass for the frequency of bass a long, long time before, maybe since *Signals* back in 1982. Deliberately, of course — the choices Rush made were always highly deliberate. But that doesn't mean it always made for good music. And the guys often recognize that, expressing regrets from time to time, changing over time, varying in intensity.

"Geddy's one of the great jokesters of all time," says Kevin. "He's so much fun, really a blast. We started recording in Quebec and Geddy had his Gallien-Kruegers; he had the big black and green cone bass speakers. Never liked the sound of them — it's, you know, why did you employ me to do this job, when I'm not a big fan of what you do? But he had these big speakers, and when he hit the bass guitar, it sounded like a big low note on a piano. It went 'ding, ga-zing, ga-zing' and I thought it sounded awful. I never liked the Level 42 thumb bass.

"So we went into the back room of the studio, and there was some stuff they were throwing out. And there was an old . . . what do they call them? B2 or something? The old Ampeg where the head folds into the cabinet like that — you fold it out. And it was awful; the speaker was all cut and destroyed. And I took it and I said, 'Geddy, let's try this.' So we took it into the room and we plugged it in, and the speaker was distorting because it was all rattled and everything. And Geddy was like, 'That's useless, that's a piece of shit, I'm not —' 'Let's try it.' So we tried it. And I went to the control room and I heard it and it sounded phenomenal. It had this natural distortion on it, but it still had this warm fatness. It wasn't as loud as a big system, but it's a recording session; it's not a gig. And I could hear this big, low, thick bass in there, and I said, 'You've got to record this amp; it just sounds phenomenal.' So we recorded the bass on this whole album with this little Ampeg amplifier that was destined for the garbage."

"Well, it was just using the old gear," recalls Geddy of the sessions, a bit dismissively. "I think I had to bring every bass I owned at one point, try everything out. Because he wanted that real rock vibe. We went through that whole thing; you know, you get snippy with engineers — it happens. Because engineers . . . I've never met an engineer who is wrong. They are all right. How are you going to argue that? But at the same time, there's always a bit of a turf war with an engineer, because he wants you to sound like this, you want to sound like this. And it may be the same sound, but if you're not speaking the same language, you're not quite sure if it's the same sound until you hear it back. So you go through that kind of arm-wrestling. I have been known to have a fair share of arguments with engineers over sound. But I don't remember anything profound with the Caveman. I remember being frustrated with some of his abilities in terms of using gear that was not analog, because he was like an analog beast. I'm sure that's changed, because there's been a revolution of sound since then. So it was a little frustrating from that point of view. And he had a terrible tooth problem at the time; he was in a lot of pain. I had to send him to someone to fix his tooth, but that's a whole other story."

"I wanted to get rid of the Wal bass," confirms Kevin. "I wanted to get rid of Alex's effects; I wanted to get rid of all of that stuff that smacked of Flock of Seagulls to me. And I was so anti-keyboards at that point in my life; I couldn't stand keyboards on records. We were coming out of the DX7 phase, and MIDI had just come in and everyone had banks and banks of keyboards in every studio in the world and I hated it, I really hated it. I mean, there was a time when there was no guitar in music. It was dying out as an instrument, kind of weird. And as a Blackmore, Page, Beck fan — all those — that was awful. I've probably mellowed a bit, but I still don't like keyboards.

"But the keyboards were not a big part of that thing. We finished all the tracks basically without keyboards, and then we got John Webster, who did all the keyboards in Aerosmith. We would send him tracks and he would send us back tracks, ear candy as Peter Collins called it, things going zing, zing, zing all over the place. But they were just sort of meant to make the rock sound classy. There were a few places he put keyboards in, but it wasn't really done as part of our sessions. He came down maybe for a day or two and just threw on bits and pieces that were previously worked out. 'We'll put keyboards in this section, in that section.'

"But they definitely were not a part of the sessions. They may have been part of the writing and part of the preproduction, but once we started recording at Le Studio, it became a hard rock project. I mean, the rough mixes were very hard, very guitar-heavy, a lot of distorted bass. The drums were very roomy and ambient, kind of the way I like things to sound. And it was sounding very tough, especially tracks like 'Stick It Out' and 'Animate' — those were sounding super-tough. They tidied them up a little bit before it was released, much to my chagrin."

Geddy was hesitant to ditch keys altogether. "I kept thinking, well, if there's a part that's just begging for it, why should you say no? I'm a big believer in rules are made to be broken. You can have a rule, no keyboards, but if there's a part in a song that you just know would be better having a little melody there, it's hard to walk away from that. We stuck a couple on in a couple little songs here and there but nothing major. And that was really good for Alex, in the sense of increasing his control over the sound of the band."

"The nature of the recording style they have is a bit pristine and anal," continues Kevin, "but I said to Geddy, wait until you hear this amongst guitars. You'll hear it bites through. Your bass is so easy to hear through the guitars without making it louder than everything else. You can get a really deep groove through this thing and still hear all the notes. And so when we did a few tests on the first recording, he saw that, and he was like, 'You know, this is really working well,' and he got very comfortable with it. In the studio Geddy was a lot of fun, very easygoing, very straightforward to work with; he was concerned with detail, the minutiae, whereas Alex was very much concerned about where he was in the big picture. Alex was more abrasive in the studio — it was always more of a threat to him; the process was more difficult for him. And Neil, we never saw Neil. He came in and drummed and went back to his little room — and smoked wads of weed.

"There definitely seemed to be a rift between Geddy and Neil at that point," notes Kevin. "You know, I don't know that I ever saw Geddy and Alex talking to Neil. He would do his thing on his own, and they would work through a lot of stuff on their own; they were like two different facets of the same thing. Neil had his own room where he'd be writing. He'd come and do his bits, and he wouldn't be in the control room when we were recording, and I don't know why. Maybe Geddy wanted people around him that were committed to the same vision he had; I really don't know. I mean, we went to his house, we went to baseball games, we looked at his baseball collection. Geddy was definitely the friendliest of all; he was the one who enjoyed the recording more than the others. There's a wonderful version of 'Stick It Out' where he puts on his mother's voice. He does this crusty old Jewish lady's voice, and he redid the lyrics and we did a version like that, which I have to find somewhere — it was hysterical. 'Geddy, Geddy, come here, come here.' Really funny.

"We had lots of fun. We were staying up in Morin Heights and I remember we'd go out, Alex and I, and we would get pretty trashed. And then I'd go into the studio the next day, and Peter Collins would say to me, 'Oh, Caveman, it's about the drinkey-poos.' I was like, okay, I got your point. 'Caveman, it's about the drinkey-poos.'"

But again, all told, it was a battle, with Kevin saying there were "lots of fights." Ultimately, past the battle of wills, the band did things their way all through, and then to put an exclamation point on it, they did a cleaning-up process in the mix that helped make sure that in the end Kevin didn't get the sounds he wanted.

Recalls Geddy with respect to the drums: "From Neil's point of view, the whole analog approach, the whole kind of John Bonham–ish approach that Caveman took to recording his drums, Neil had feared there wasn't enough nuance, there wasn't enough subtlety in the sound. That's one of the reasons we never did that combination of people again: the heavy-handedness. He felt he was a bit heavy-handed. I didn't feel that way, although I'm kind of a sceptic — I had to be shown that going backwards was going forwards. Whereas Alex grasped it much more easily. I remember some of the songs we wanted to do a string section, and there was some frustration in finding a room because we gave ourselves the limitation of wanting to work in Toronto, and the studio situation in Toronto is kind of limited.

"Making a record is a strange dynamic, emotionally. Yeah, making any record, if there was change, had its difficulties for sure. You know, Alex not being able to use his gear and just recording the sound direct is hard, but every engineer we've ever worked with wants him to do that, maybe with the exception of Nick. I have no problem telling you if I was pissed off. It's just I don't remember being so. I mean, I didn't hedge when we discussed Peter Henderson and those frustrations, so why would I hedge on the Caveman?"

"I think they thought I was overstepping my role from the get-go," muses Shirley. "But I think that secretly Peter Collins enjoyed that they were being pushed, and I think Geddy enjoyed that they were being pushed, and he was going to work through it because he knew Peter would pull me back when he needed to. But Peter let me go. Peter sat in the room while Alex and I were having a hard-core fight about the sound — and Peter didn't do anything. He sat there with his stogie in his mouth and his legs hanging off the chair and he just let us go at it, until such time as it was appropriate for him to step in.

"And then he was like, 'All right, lads, let's take a break for lunch; has anyone got the money?' And off we'd go and have lunch at some fancy, awesome restaurant. But yeah, I think they thought I was overstepping. Like I said, Alex took me to the hotel bar to get drunk, and he wanted to read me the riot act. He was like, by the way, in case you didn't notice, I'm the royalty artist and you're the hired gun, so if I say something, it's going to go that way. I'm like, 'What if I feel differently? Then I'm going to say what's on my mind.' And so we kind of worked that out. I think one of the benefits of not knowing the heritage of the band and not being that familiar with the music is that it's hard to come at them with the sort of godly worship status they so obviously deserve. I didn't really have that sense of awe around them;

I wasn't awestruck by them, and so it was easy for me to do that. It wasn't really arrogance . . . Yeah, it may have been a little bit."

Kevin's dynamic with the band was different from the one between them and Mr. Big. Explains Kevin: "Peter and the band were very cordial, a very respectful relationship. I didn't necessarily always understand the nature of the producer that Peter was because I had never seen that before. He's very much one of letting the creative forces happen around him and adjudicating them. He's not like the elephant in the room, the great musician no one sees — he just looks at the overview. He sees when things are not working, or when they don't feel right. Neil would play a part; he'd run through the whole song, and then Neil would say, 'How was that?' Peter would go, 'Let's do another one — I think you've got a better pocket somewhere.' And then Neil would go, 'Okay, here we go again,' and he'd play the whole track again. And I was like, 'Uh, that's it?! You're going to say "pocket" every time someone plays the drums? It's like what about fix that fill or change that kick drum beat. But *pocket*? What is this, *Oliver Twist*?'

"For a start, I think the term *producer* gets used loosely. Wherever he is now, I think Terry at the beginning was more of a guiding hand. Whereas by the time they got ten years down the track, the guys were looking for inspiration. Producers are making and breaking records ten years later; the nature of the business had changed. There are people that are constructing songs, and radio is taking them to different levels, and they're selling millions and millions of units. So they go, well, maybe we need to look around a little more. Terry's great, he's friendly, we get on well with him, we trust what he does, we go into the studio. Perhaps they never feel pushed or challenged. Perhaps they never felt like they were stretched musically, performance-wise or creatively. And so it may very well be that they were looking for a kick in the ass that a new guy was going to come in and do. I mean, if Peter said when he first met them that he hated all the records that had gone before, maybe they wanted to hear that. It's like, great, guess what, we feel kind of the same way right now, 'cause we've lived with them forever — show us where you can take us. Show us if you have direction, show us if you have a vision, show us if you have a plan for us — that's where I see that.

"But they obviously had that trust, that he was going to bring out all these elements that he brought out. I wasn't there in the preproduction process either — they did this up in a studio in Toronto, where I went to see them for the first time — so I don't know how much of an input he had in preproduction. All I saw was the studio environment. Alex and Geddy had prerecorded their parts and done demos with vocals, with a click track, and then Neil would come in and play on that click track, and that would be the basis for the beginning of the song. They would build up the song with these instruments and a click track, and then put Neil on and then rebuild the instruments. And there were some times when Alex couldn't match a solo that was on the demos, where he had cut something and just didn't feel like he could get it again. So we actually lifted those parts from the demos, from the room in Toronto, and used them in the final album.

"I think a lot of bands are open to change," muses Kevin. "You'll probably find that most of them want to change. There are a few of them that stick to these formulas they have. But I think Rush was like anyone else. Rush is consistently selling one million albums, one million albums, one million albums. They almost sell the same number of albums to the unit each time — the fan base is that solid. So anything they change, they know they have a fan base, and they're always looking for something else in their fan base. Maybe we can cross over, maybe we can get like these guys, maybe we can get the bikers, maybe we can get the swoony teen girls, whatever. It doesn't surprise me at all that they were doing this. I don't think they've ever had boundaries for themselves. Maybe *Power Windows* and some of the Rupert Hine stuff was a serious, conscientious effort to try to garner some radio play and try to expand their market beyond what it consistently was — a big fan base.

"Also I think early Rush was such an experiment for them, and so much fun, just three kids having a blast, being progressive and just throwing whatever you could, time changes, this change, that change. Occasional nods to Zeppelin, occasional nods to this, that and the next thing. But I think that in the five years when it became more of a job, they started looking at selling records and, you know, not really getting out there and having quite as much fun. There's more than Molson on the rider at that point. I think we give them too much credit, when you think they are structuring their career. I think they just play — they play, they grow up, they have kids and their impetus is different. It's like, you know, tonight instead of an eight ball, we're going to have a beer, and somehow your writing changes when you do that. Or we're going to go and have dinner with my parents, whatever; things change as you get older, and it's not necessarily a bad thing, but I think that comes out in your writing."

Geddy is the first to put a positive spin on the change, as well as take the mystery out of it. "I don't know, it was just that we came out of a way of recording and the kind of gear we were using, the attitude we had, and we all wanted to make this kind of record. And you realize, well, he wants you to use this amp and really distort your bass and, you know, change. It's one thing to talk about change and it's another thing to change. I guess that's what it boils down to. For me, pulling out the Fender and the old amps, and for Alex, doing what he had to do to change, was a little prickly. You've got to kind of prove it to yourselves.

You could say, 'Okay, I'll try it. Show me it's worth changing all this stuff for.'

"And so then you do. You lay down a couple tracks and then holy fuck, sounds great! And your frustrations and your fears disappear. It's funny what you learn. Working with a lot of different engineers is informative, because every time you have a new engineer, you feel like you have to re-explain your sound to them, re-educate them, so they don't wreck your sound, change your sound. But at the end of the day, your sound comes from your fingers. The way you play says more about what you sound like, and that's one thing we all learned through that. Regardless of working with all these different people over six or seven records, it still sounded like us. At the end of the day, your sound is kind of indelible. It can't easily be destroyed. Kevin Shirley . . . finding an engineer was an interesting search. I can't remember how we ended up with the Caveman, but he certainly fits the bill. He was quite a character."

As Kevin alluded to, the band had a novel, even ingenious, way of working, using their eight-track demos as a guide to extricate Neil's parts, only doable because they were played to a click. These eight-track recordings were transferred to twenty-four-track, as it turns out, not entirely necessary, except for the fact that some of the performances were kept and used. Neil worked his way through eleven songs in three days, and then he was gone, which is pretty normal for drummers once they are recorded. Once finished, the band had difficulty sequencing the album, with Alex taking the reins with a magnetic board so the band could ponder the song order, which ultimately was predicated on the punchier tracks up front and a letdown at the end.

For the cover art applied to *Counterparts*, Hugh Syme went austere and '90s — in fact, Syme would be one of the important album cover guys that helped define the '90s aesthetic, along with Dave McKean, who did the same but at the heavier metal end of things. Syme offers a simple image in black, regal blue and faux-gold. The name of the band is rendered completely in lower case, and the album title is not included in the cover art. Lightheartedly sexual (after all, this is a rock 'n' roll band), there's a diagram of a bolt going into a nut. The roadmap-like foldout CD booklet reinforced this theme of items that are counterparts of each other. In effect, the *real* album cover consists of all these many clever Syme images collated and considered as a whole.

Wrote Neil in the tourbook: "The Concise Oxford defines 'counterpart' both as 'duplicate' and as 'opposite,' in the sense of 'forming a natural complement to another.' That's what I thought was so interesting about the word: considered in this way, contraries are reflections of each other, opposite numbers, and not necessarily contradictions, enemies, The Other. Polarities are not to be resisted but reconciled. Reaching for the alien shore. Dualities like gender or race are not opposite but true counterparts, the same and yet different and not to be seen as some existential competition — we could do without that. Better yet: we could get along without that."

Later, Peart brings it closer to home, stating, "Counterparts. Words and music. Guitar, bass, drums. Writing, rehearsing, and recording. Flying and driving and working and laughing. Alex's flashes of dazzling spontaneity, twisted humor and emotional fire, Geddy's melodic instinct, wry wit and meticulous passion, my own obsessive drive and rhythmic bombast. True synergy, I guess: the whole greater than the parts — which are, after all, just humble old *us*."

After all the teething pains, the noses bent out of shape, the expense and the time spent, *Counterparts* opens in authoritative fashion, Neil grooving like he hadn't for years, allowing himself out of his cozy matchbox so that he and his fans could breathe again. This blessing is bestowed upon "Animate": Peart's drums sounded expensive but less precious, throaty like one of his hot cars rather than fingers tapping on the jewelry case, idly shopping for watches. Arrives Geddy and all those thoughtful guitars from Alex, creating a bassy mélange that is warm and plush. An arcane and mesmerizing melody then transports the listener into the dense forest of what is arguably Rush's finest track past *Signals* until the end.

"I love ['Animate,'] offers Geddy unequivocally. "I think it's one of the great songs we've done. There's something about the bestiality of that song, the insistence of it." Bestiality might be going too far, but then again, Rush had been raising bunnies lately. But insistence, sure — not only have the band rediscovered panoramic and proper production, but they exploit it fully, filling up the sound picture with performances that are regal, bold and driving. Heck, even the lyrics read like a mysterious invocation of dark forces, reinforced by Neil's rock 'n' roll chant at the start, an unexpected count-in, casual and absolutely welcome.

While Neil applied concepts around male/female duality from both Carl Jung and Camille Paglia to his idea of an interesting love song, Geddy got busy using that Ampeg amp "on the verge of death" that Kevin had forced upon him. There's also a cool shift where Neil breaks out of his groove and creates a tribal rhythm inspired by African music. The break continues with a regular beat, Alex texturizing in the background, Geddy's bass gnarly. Escaping with a muscular fill from Neil, the band is back into another sublime verse, interesting synths bubbling in the background. Fully a creative success, and really, no breakaway from recent Rush ideals, just recorded with enough bass.

As Neil expresses in the tourbook, "['Animate'] is not about *two* individuals, but about one man addressing his *anima* — his feminine side, as defined by Carl Jung. Within that duality, what 'a man must learn to gently dominate' is *himself,* his own 'submissive trait,' while also learning to 'gently dominate' the *animus* — the male thing — and the other hormone-driven 'A-words' like aggression and ambition. We dominate by not submitting, whether to brute instinct, violent rage or ruthless greed. For the rest of it (meaning the rest of the album's songs), we can all dominate or submit as the occasion warrants, try to reconcile the duplicates and opposites, and dream of racing through life at the speed of love (one hundred and eighty-six thousand miles per second, if you believe in love at first sight). Everyone wants the ideal of 'forming a natural complement to another.' A counterpart. Friendship, love and partners in life and work are the rewards for bridging that gap between 'duplicate' and 'opposite.'"

The album's lead single would be an even heavier track, leaving no time to catch one's breath. "Stick It Out" crashes into view with an elephantine heavy metal riff played simultaneously by Alex and Geddy, no Neil in sight until a hi-hat pattern meekly presents itself. Geddy's not so fast with the praise on this one. "In retrospect, I love the riff — it's a great riff song. I love playing it, and it's a very bass-heavy song, which always makes me happy. Lyrically it's kind of a so-so song for us. I don't know, I think the best thing about that song is the vibe and the fact that it's stripped back down to a trio, back to doing riff rock. I think that was the important thing about that song. 'Animate' is more what we were after, this combination of bringing different rhythmic attitudes back into it while trying to add a bit more funk at the same time, but be big-bottomed and aggressive."

Neil agrees, saying, "We got a much deeper, rawer, rougher-edged sound, because this is early '90s now and guitar bands are back — you know we had company. Guns N' Roses, Soundgarden, Pearl Jam . . . all these bands came along and also did us the honor, with Soundgarden and Pearl Jam saying they'd been influenced by us — it's like affirmation. Because the '80s had been pretty much a 'wilderland.' Yeah, that's a good new word, a wilderness for a guitar rock band. I remember thinking at the time, where is the next generation of drummers coming from? When everyone is just using drum machines. I didn't know anyone who was taking drum lessons — any young kids or anything — and I remember having that specific thought. Well, they came, and the '90s were that time. We were affirmed by that and bolstered by that and influenced by that in turn. And *Counterparts* was a perfect answer for that."

Indeed, underscoring this idea that Rush at this point couldn't be steered or expected to change much — not by Tad, Mudhoney, Melvins or Kevin Shirley — "Stick It Out" is as grungy as the band would ever get. It is big and doomy, and it makes a statement. Even if it is off and alone at the extreme end of the spectrum, it's still one of eleven songs on the album, 9 percent of *Counterparts*.

Still, Neil found a way to make the drum track interesting on this song that hits right between the eyes, asking rhetorically of *Modern Drummer*'s William F. Miller, "How could I approach that song properly and yet give it a touch of elegance that I would want a riff rock song to have? I don't want it to be the same type of thing you'd hear on rock radio. So I started bringing in Latin and fusion influences. There's a verse where I went for a Weather Report–type effect. I used some tricky turn-arounds in the ride cymbal pattern, where it goes from downbeat to upbeat accents — anything I could think of to make it my own. That song verges on parody for us, so we had to walk a careful line. We responded to the power of the riff, yet still found some ways to twist it to make it something more."

"Stick It Out" had a grungy, gloomy video made for it too, which caught the attention of Beavis & Butt-Head, the only time Rush got called out by the dense MTV cartoon kids, with the sofa-bound critics wondering if the guy tied to the chair is Lenny Kravitz or "our lord, Jesus Christ" (might as well be Chris Cornell). The song debuted at #1 on the Billboard subchart Album Rock Tracks, representing the record somewhat deceptively given its uncommon heft. At the lyrical end, Neil is almost as dismissive as Geddy, saying the song is just a bit of fun, a bit of wordplay, with the counterpart in this instance being the double meaning of *stick it out*, specifically arrogance versus perseverance.

"Cut to the Chase" sends the message that Rush are serious about playing with more heft, with more distortion pedal, low frequency and drum ambience. Yet this one's architecture is more like the last few records, with a willingness to be quiet for the verses and Alex picking. But things start to heat up pre-chorus and then it's wall to wall power chords. "That was a solo I did on my own, on my little ADAT," Alex told Jon Chappell. "That was a spontaneous solo. I had quite a different solo for that song originally, and I thought, 'Well, now that I have a picture of what the album and the solos are like, I don't have anything very fast. Maybe I'll do a solo here that's fast.' That was really the drive behind doing that kind of solo in that song. It was as simple as that. Just to be in contrast to the other things."

Strength to strength, "Nobody's Hero" opens with plaintive acoustic guitar, followed by warm chording, while Geddy sings a dedication to the real heroes of the world, most of them unsung (until now), often because their heroism was infinitely intense to the point of immeasurable, or perhaps unfathomable across the limiting medium of a TV screen.

As Neil explained to Toronto radio legend Steve Warden for the syndicated radio album premiere, "I'd been thinking a lot about the nature of heroism and what was good and what was bad about it, and the idea of a role model, and people I'd known in my own life who were important to me as influences but weren't important to the rest of the world. So that concept of a role model but not a hero, if you like. 'Nobody's Hero' was one of the earliest ones, because that was a theme of my thinking over the last two years, and many conversations with friends around the country and so on; you get talking about the nature of heroism. So that was one that just was a growing crystal, I guess, over a year and a half or two years, and then the song was bursting with input by then."

"For a lot of young people," continued Neil, "if their heroes are in sports, or in the entertainment world, they tend to be sold and bought as perfect. Hollywood, I think, probably invented the idea of demigods and the deity of an actress or the deity of an actor. And then sports took it over too, and the sports deities, until they get old or sick or whatever, they are superhuman. And that seems like all very well and doesn't really hurt anybody — and maybe it inspires young people — but I kind of think it's discouraging too. Because when you're growing up, you're painfully aware of your flaws and your limitations, and I think perhaps you can feel too distant from any ideal of perfection.

"A role model is to me the opposite of a hero, in a sense, or a counterpart if you like, in the sense of the definition of *counterpart* is both duplicate and opposite. It's one of the reasons why I was intrigued by the word so much. So a role model is good, because there's no aspect of deity or superhuman perfection about it. It's just, 'That's the direction I want to go, and here's a person doing it the way I'd like to do it.' I thought that was a lot more healthy.

"And also the nature of heroism — something I've touched on before in songs like 'Limelight,' and even more recently in 'Superconductor,' was the nature of fame and how it affects the people in it. I've been involved, of course, in that world for a long time, and watching other people affected by the nature of fame and the nature of that kind of deification. And it really isn't healthy for them either, so I started thinking, 'Well maybe this idea of modern twentieth-century Western world heroism really isn't so good.'

"And like I say, one idea is never really enough," continued Peart. "I had the other concept of people that had been significant enough in my own life to merit almost the idea of heroism, to me. They had changed my life and prevented me maybe, in the case of the first person in 'Nobody's Hero' for instance, about the first gay person I ever knew, who was such a great role model and almost occupies a heroic space in my life, because he prevented me from ever being homophobic or for thinking there was something sick or unnatural about it, because I just knew him and worked with him when I lived in London and went to his parties, and it was all just very casual. And I guess I was young enough not to be already prejudiced, so he occupied an important part of my life. And then as the song dictates, we fell apart geographically — drifted apart, rather — and then when I found out that he had died of AIDS it was like this hole had been left, and yet at the same time, this glowing example had been set by him. So it's certainly not like his life was in vain, but his heroism was in a very small arena."

Peter Collins brought in arranger Michael Kamen, who added an extra dose of drama onto what was already a very emotional song, full of these stories of heroism. Admirably, Geddy had a lot of input here as well. "The orchestration on 'Nobody's Hero,' I thought, turned out really well," says Collins. "I particularly loved that track. I guess 'Nobody's Hero' was quite an unusual song. I hadn't heard anything quite like that before from them. Incredibly poignant lyric. We had Michael Kamen do the string arrangement for that, which is not very loud in the track, but I particularly like that. I love Neil's playing on it, and I love the way the whole arrangement worked, fabulous. And I liked generally the incorporation of more acoustic guitars, which was what I was hoping to do. And I love the punchy sound we got on that, particularly the mix, which definitely brought a different dimension. When I walked into the first mix, from where we had been listening to it, you know, the tracking and the overdubs, it changed quite dramatically, I thought, and in a good way."

Neil has also said that the way Rush had conducted their career thus far, if they aren't necessarily people who should be worshiped, they had at least served as a good example of a band with commendable ideals. On a more serious note, Peart wrote about doctors and pilots and then, in respectful and veiled terms, memorialized Kristen French, one of the victims of serial rapist and murderer Paul Bernardo, his crimes a horrible Ontario story at the time. Neil says he knows her family; French was the step-sister of his close friend Brad French. Peart's point here is that regular people are not heroes in the typical hollow sense; they are often forced to be quietly heroic. Here, faced with "a nightmare of brutality," the small victory, the unseen act of heroism, is some measure of "faith in the goodness of humanity."

"Between Sun & Moon" is yet another heavy (enough) rocker with additional welcome Peart percussive lubrications propelling a third collaboration between Neil and Max Webster/Kim Mitchell lyricist Pye Dubois, who famously wrote the skeleton of "Tom Sawyer," after which Neil performed the deep tissue massage. It's the last of Pye's suite of "moon songs," as he calls them. For Max Webster, he had penned "Coming Off the Moon," "In Context of the Moon," "Beyond the Moon" and "Moon Voices," although not really, because it's an instrumental.

"I really like his style of writing," explained Peart to Steve Warden about working with Dubois. "It's inscrutable to me, sometimes, as I think it is to other people too, but at the same time it has a certain power in his images and writing. And also, there was some strange symbiosis that seemed to affect the songs; when Pye was involved in 'Tom Sawyer' and in 'Force 10,' it made them somehow a little different musically, you know, his percolation through me. I would get his ideas and then I would add mine to them and structure it as a Rush song, and then pass it along to the other guys. Even through that chain of events, somehow there was some outside influence that was good, so we've always kind of kept the open door to Pye's ideas. Any time he had anything to submit, he would send it along to me, usually scrawled in an exercise book. And in this case that was one where we all responded to some of the images in his presentation. So again I went to work on it, shaped it up into the kind of structure that we like to work with, and then added some of my own images and angles on it. And so it went."

Any time Alex has spoken about the song, he chuckles that his sort of casual, slashing chording on it is inspired by Keith Richards, an early influence, and says the bridge evokes Pete Townshend, another influence. Alex was always impressed by how Townshend could attack the strings on an acoustic and make it sound powerful. At the drum end, Neil employs some of the counterpoint ride cymbal stuff he does on "Animate" and "Stick It Out," and just generally, he responds to the song's spirit with some really joyful fills, participating Keith Moon–like in the Who-ish break as well.

"Alien Shore" shows that the musical themes on *Counterparts* (guitars, fulsome sound) are as strong as its lyrical themes around dualism. In fact, there's probably more of a deliberate musical focus (along with a sharp turn musically) here than on any record since *Power Windows*. Everything before that record felt more like an evolution, and then so did *Hold Your Fire*, *Presto* and *Roll the Bones*. Still, the music at the verse is built of textures, so not everything has changed — it's the chorus that would have made this a candidate for opening track on a previous record. On the literary end, this song contributes to the living, breathing and expanding "counterpart" theme, one that has a life of its own. This seems at least an equal to the tidy focus on the theme of chance in *Roll the Bones* — and before that record, Neil didn't really attempt this kind of summarizing in earnest.

Peart told *Canadian Musician*'s Peter Hamilton that "with 'Alien Shore' I was thinking about these discussions among friends that I've had where, when we talk about gender differences or about racial differences, we can talk about them dispassionately because we were normal, right-thinking, generous, well-traveled people who counted all these different people among our friends and equals. I realize that these subjects are too dangerous in many cases to discuss because they are so fraught with prejudice and misunderstanding. I wanted to take that one and put it into a personal context of a conversation that, 'You and I are different but we don't have a problem with that.' Unfortunately, a lot of the people, if not most of the people around us, do."

There have been a few lighter moments up until now, but "The Speed of Love" is perceptively less aggressive than what came before. Neil's drumming is itchy, Alex is playing post-punk and Geddy is singing in the middle, all three performing more like they did on *Roll the Bones*. As Neil explained to *Modern Drummer*, "'The Speed of Love' is a kind of mid-tempo, more sensitive rock song. That song probably took me the longest to find just the right elements I wanted to have in a drum part. What made it a challenge is that I wanted the feel and the transitions between sections to be just right. I played that song over and over, refining it until I was satisfied. I don't think a listener will hear all the work that went into that track. When we go in to record, I spare no self-flagellation of playing the songs over and over again until I've got them. And it's the same thing before a tour: I spend weeks just rehearsing on my own before we start as a band. But I know it's time well spent because that work gives me the confidence to step off into the unknown with some foundation.

"When I went into the studio to record my parts for *Counterparts*, I was prepared," continues Peart. "That's why I could record all of my track in first and second takes. We put together and learned the material, we worked with Peter Collins refining the material, and then I practiced for another week to get totally comfortable with the songs and the changes to those songs. I recorded all of the drum tracks on this record in one day and two afternoons — that's all it took because I was prepared. My whole approach to life is accident by design. Everything I do has to be that well-organized, or I'm not comfortable with it. But at the same time, within that frame of organization, I'm really comfortable with contingencies, because I'm prepared. It's an interesting thing because a lot of people say it's better to be spontaneous, to breeze through and let whatever happens happen. What I find with those people is that they're not prepared to take advantage of the opportunities when they occur."

"Double Agent" sets the scene for the Rush of *Vapor Trails* with this idea of textures rather than tinkering, creating a wall of sound, everybody rocking out. With the spoken word, the devilish chord patterns, the noise pollution come solo time and the "trash" cymbal, this one evokes images of red, blue and yellow–period King Crimson, although Rush weave into this "wilderness of mirrors" some conventional modern Rush songsmithing as well.

"We were losing our minds," chuckles Geddy, telling Steve Warden about the song. "'Double Agent' was a complete exercise in self-indulgence, and really, it was one of the last things we wrote on the record. We'd written all these songs that were heavily structured, and were crafted and meticulously worked on: this note and that note. And this is a song we just wanted to kind of get our yah-yahs out and have a bit of a rave. And really, it's one of the goofiest songs I think we've ever written, but I'm quite happy with the result. In its own way, I think it's an interesting little piece of lunacy."

Speaking with Dan Neer of MediaAmerica Radio, Neil explains: "I had been reading Carl Jung last year, and I got interested in the idea of the unconscious, and I started to watch how my own worked. And I noticed that sometimes if I had a difficult decision to make, I'd be weighing up the pros and cons, and my conscious mind would be doing a lot of thinking and worrying, and then suddenly one morning I would wake up and I would know what to do. And a friend of mine was working on a book about the secret war between the CIA and the FBI and asked me to be his reader, as it were, as he went along. So in reading that, I read a whole bunch of books on the background of the CIA and the KGB, and got totally into the world of espionage. So I thought of using the imagery of espionage, and the whole romance of cloak and dagger, and the third man, to illustrate the idea of the unconscious. So espionage and Carl Jung kind of got mixed up together in my head and with nightmares and dream states and so on and it became a perfect musical vehicle. As we've found over the years, in so many different contexts, dreams are a great vehicle to carry musical and vocal ideas along too."

"I don't really play any notes in that song!" Alex told *Guitar for the Practicing Musician.* "I play a couple of chords and that's what the solo is made up of. That song in some ways reminds me of our older material, kinda like *Hemispheres* era. It's a quirky song for us. It doesn't really have a flow to it. Songwriting has become a much more important thing to me than being just a guitar player. When you think in context of the whole record or the whole song, it's not just some kind of statement you want to make as being an individual instrumentalist in the song. It's really what you do with the other players and what you do for the song that is the most important thing."

"Leave That Thing Alone" brings us one of Geddy's most memorable bass lines in ages, one that is essentially the vocal line of the song, until Alex takes over and performs that role over some tribal drumming from Neil. Then it's full-on prog, replete with church organ sounds and sublime Yes-like melodies. The tight and disciplined funk of the opening is a distant memory . . . until it returns, this time Neil getting to stretch out. At the fade, Geddy proposes in the pocket some new possibilities. Really, this is the bookend piece to "Where's My Thing?," which features similar chicken-scratch funk tone from Alex, as well as a transition to standard late '80s and early '90s melodic Rush lest we forget where we are. Both also contain middles that are pure prog noodling, although "Where's My Thing?" might even go fusion.

While affirming that the record contained "a lot of dark experiments," Neil calls "Leave That Thing Alone" "our best ever instrumental, so I don't think you can knock that." Speaking with William Miller from *Modern Drummer*, Peart opines that "the nature of the songs on this album brought out a lot of my R&B background, and I don't think that's an area I'm known for. But all the first bands I played in were blue-eyed soul bands. I played a lot of James Brown and Wilson Pickett tunes, because in the Toronto area that's what was popular at the time. All of us grew up playing 'In the Midnight Hour.' R&B is a part of my roots, and as a band I think we all played it and enjoyed it. But as we developed, we drifted off into the other styles of the '60s, and when the British progressive bands came along we went in that direction.

"'Leave That Thing Alone' is built around R&B bass/drum interplay," continues Peart. "But to make it original I had to change up parts. In the second verse I go into a Nigerian beat, like something you'd hear on a King Sunny Adé record. Later in the song I go into a quasi-jazz pattern, and all these things are introduced for our own entertainment as well as to make the piece more interesting.

"When I hear Geddy and Alex's demos, the influences are sometimes very clear to me. And I think we're secure enough to directly use those influences. If Geddy and Alex bring in a tune that has a section that sounds like the Who's *Live at Leeds*, I'm definitely going to put on my Keith Moon hat and go with it. If there's a song with a '90s grunge rock section, we're secure enough to go in that direction. All of these things are amusing to us, but they're also available to us to try and create something fresh from their inspiration."

"Geddy had this little keyboard thing for the choruses, and I had this clean verse thing kicking around from the last tour," recalled Alex, speaking with *Guitar School*'s Matt Resnicoff. "As the song developed, we thought, this is cool; it's not a big stage for showing off like so many of our instrumentals. It's a song that goes through many moods and creates very nice colors. The solo was from my original ADAT version, just a solo I threw on, but it fit. It has an almost Celtic flavour. That's the thing I love about instrumentals — we throw them down, then we give them to Neil and he figures out drum parts."

Adds Geddy on the concept of instrumentals: "They are indulgences, but they are also, in some ways, our most natural state. They're the easiest things to write and the most joyful things to play. It's our reward. It's like, 'If you get through all these eight songs, there's a little instrumental waiting for you at the end.' So it's a way of answering the incredible amount of restraint and 'taste' you have to have when you craft a four-and-a-half-minute song; when you get to the instrumental, you can throw all that out and really enjoy yourself."

"Cold Fire" is another enormous success on this underrated and sometimes forgotten record from Rush. Each of the guys has his own particular uneasy relationship with this one. It reinforces the album's theme: the verse is the typical "heavy REM" Rush of this period (but better because of the production), and the explosive chorus validates the softness of the verse through a combined sense of contrast.

"'Cold Fire,' to me, is one of my most satisfying songs, musically and lyrically," muses Neil, "although it's stuck at the second to last track there. Obviously, nobody else shared my high opinion of it, but it's one I really love. And again, you love a song for small things. I had been inspired, I think, by a Paul Simon song. I wanted to couch song lyrics in conversation — he said, she said, and all that. He has a song, maybe on *Rhythm of the Saints*, where it's in conversation. She said blah blah blah and I said blah blah blah. And I thought, yeah, what a cool idea; I'd like to try something like that.

"And 'Cold Fire' achieved that," continues Peart. "I thought about it for a couple of years, and with this song, I finally got it. I like the nature of it; it's a very grown-up relationship song. And relationship songs are never easy to do, convincingly anyway, as opposed to love songs. Relationship songs are by definition much more clinical, but this was one, I thought, that managed to be a grown-up one, with the mystified guy and the smart girl. I like the subtext of that — the guy is kind of dumb and she's really smart and cynical." Yet another pronounced use of the counterpart idea: smart and dumb, and the ultimate counterpoint, male and female.

Reflects Neil on his wordsmithing, "Again, as with the music,

I can look back at the experiments and things that didn't quite work the way I wanted them to. But it all fed and grew, and very often I can see where I tried to get at something lyrically. And that Paul Simon song, where he built a conversation into the song, I said, 'Oh, that's a cool device.' On 'Cold Fire' I got to use that device."

"That song went through many permutations," Geddy told Steve Warden. "Peter Collins's presence really pulled that song together. He came in and he pointed out certain strengths in the previous versions of the songs that we had, and he really helped us reorganize that song. It wasn't until he got there, I think, that we finally locked in on a feel for those verses that enabled Alex to play those great kind of steel guitar–like lines that he's playing, and enabled me to open up harmonically.

"I was having trouble with the verses," continues Ged. "It's a tough song, when you're dealing with this issue of male/female relationships, which is such a foreign subject for us to deal with. You want to make sure it doesn't sound trite or hackneyed . . . who needs another song about relationships? It took us a while to get the right mood, and I was really happy with the mood we ended up with in the verses. Oddly enough, as much as it was a nightmare, that song for me, when I hear the record now, I think the verses in that song are one of the strongest parts of the album."

Agrees Al, "I think there's a great balance between the romantic picture on the one side, and how the music is sympathetic to those lyrics, and then the other point of view, which is much colder, more based in reality. And the contrast between the lyrics and the music, and how they support each other, I think really worked out successfully on that song, which, from what Ged said, was a very difficult song for us to work on. Yeah, that's actually one of the songs we had a bit of a problem getting into lyrically and working on it from a musical point of view. That's right! We rewrote that song quite a bit."

Counterparts closes with "Everyday Glory," through which Neil does his authorly duty, providing a ray of hope after the fire grows cold. But first the embers extinguish completely, in the house, across the whole city. Then just as the album ends, he tells us to give our heads a shake and take control. Stylistically, from a musical point of view, the song fulfills the vague mandate in terms of the sequence, taking us out on a comfortable, predictable note — that is, if the listener had entered a state of acceptance of the singer/songwriter vibe proposed by the preceding two Rupert Hine–produced records. But "Everyday Glory" sounds like real music, ironically in this case because it's the result of an analog mix, which Geddy says lessens the harshness of the midrange. Still, obstinate and specific about his tastes, Lee is wary about the idea and its effect, cautioning that it's best to be selective about such things — really, all told, Geddy is a digital man.

Indeed, the final stage of putting a record to bed is the mix, and Geddy was going to make sure his tastes in terms of production would be maintained through to the end. These were Neil's tastes too, which is probably why Rush didn't break up. Quite fascinating, really, but for all the woody resonance of the idea of both bass and drums, Geddy and Neil were aligned in their minority love of midrange and treble and snap.

"They were insecure about Kevin's potential to be as detailed as they would want come mix time, and also his aversion to reverb," reflects Peter Collins. "They definitely wanted to have reverb on vocals and on guitars. They didn't want to be shut off from the possibility, and they knew how against it he was at that time. So I think that led to them wanting a Jim Barton–style mixer. Michael Letho came from sort of the same school as

Jimbo. They might have had enough of Kevin by the time the mix came. It seemed a fairly unanimous decision by the band. If anybody out of the band had wanted him to be in on the mix it would have been Alex."

But Kevin is pretty sure the plan all along was to have someone else mix.

"I think there was a game plan beforehand. I came in late, after they decided where they were recording, when they were recording, who is producing, and who is mixing, and I was that last cog in there. 'Who's going to record it?' 'Well, we want someone who's edgy, and maybe someone who likes to work with the tactile instruments and get organic and tough sounds, and not too processed and hi-fi and whatever.'

"And I remember it was about June 6, 1992, and I went to see Peter and he had a big cigar, and he sat back and went, 'I love it when a plan comes together.' He was thrilled with the outcome of the record, and he was thrilled with the way that it played according to his scheme of getting these natural, raw sounds, and pushing the band out of their comfort zone. Because I can be an abrasive person, and I think they found that and he let that happen. But the real instrument vibe of my recordings, the organic sound, was something they wanted to bring back. And get away from that '80s thing.

"They were pretty clear from the get-go, even before I started, that they wanted to have someone else mix it because they didn't want it to be as raw as I would have made it. Before I was even signed on they had a mixer signed on, somebody who would put the sheen on things, put the polish on things. It was a big plan, a grand scheme. And I was mortified that somebody else was going to be mixing it. I mean, I was emotionally attached to all these instruments, and then this guy came in to make it sound nice. And I was, 'Why are you doing this?' I was unhappy about that because I'm more than an engineer, just by nature of my character — I'm more than an engineer in any project.

"Peter would sit back and he'd watch things unfold. He'd go, 'This is going somewhere, I'm going to let it go, I'm going to let it work through the animosity.' It's like, 'What can I lose? The band's not going to break up. The worst that can happen is we'll fire the engineer. The best that can happen is the band is going to get pushed to somewhere else.' So he would let it go, and there'd be situations in the studio where we'd be up and at 'em, and he'd sit back in the corner of the console and he'd let it work out. I definitely think he saw me as the bigger picture guy. All I knew was that no matter what I touched, I wanted to make it sound like the heaviest rock record ever. It didn't matter if it was Olivia Newton-John or who it was, heavier is just where my sympathies lie — I like the heavy stuff.

"So when the mix process came about, I was a little dejected because I knew it was going to detract from the rawness we had in some of those recordings, the gorgeous rawness, the beautiful, beautiful, dark, gorgeous colors. And, you know, my fears were founded. It came out sounding like a cross between Sabbath and *Presto*. And I would have much preferred it sounded more like Sabbath than like *Roll the Bones*. That's where I was on that."

But this didn't mean the mix went smoothly. Alex remarked about Geddy, "He didn't seem happy when we were in the mix period. There was something that was bothering him, and I can't recall what it was now. He was very tense and seemed very stressed through that mix. We had some issues with the studio we were working in, and everything seemed to bug him at the time. I remember him coming in most days and being a little tense and antsy about it. Now that could be, at the end of a long project, everyone is tired, everyone wants it to be over and done. I thought he felt it was okay, but I know he had some issues in mastering also, about the bottom end. He quite often has issues about the bottom end — maybe it's the bass player background."

"One of the things about being in a band is that you get to say goodbye a lot," reflects Kevin, about *Counterparts* coming to an end. "So it's not that hard for them. But when we got to the end of the project, when you're three months into it, when you've been traveling around and living with each other every day, I think they were very keen to see the end of it and to see the next phase happen. But it was very friendly at the end. I certainly don't think they were sad to see me go, but maybe they'd been pushed quite enough at that point. And, you know, the record was what it was. I was thrilled to have been part of it, and still thrilled to have been part of it, thrilled to have made friends with those guys. We don't see each other often, but when we do, you know, I'm very fond of them. And I'm more in communication with Neil than any of the others, and he was never around, so . . ."

"I didn't like the making of it that much, but I like a lot of the results" is Neil's summation of *Counterparts*. "Again, not everything lives up to its potential, but 'Animate' I still like; 'Nobody's Hero' was good. 'Alien Shore,' I like the lyrics to that particularly, and 'Speed of Love' likewise."

"I think *Counterparts* was an essential learning experience," figures Geddy, looking back, though at this point, he might be forgetting the pain. "And it's a great-sounding record. It's a return to that kind of rock three-piece attitude. I was very happy to do that. It put us back in touch with some of the ways we used to record, and we used equipment we hadn't used in years and got away so much from the digital sound of things. Kevin Shirley is a big bear of a producer, whom I would consider completely unsophisticated in terms of the kind of rock he wants to make. He doesn't want you to have a super-sophisticated sound. He likes to have that big, ballsy rock sound. That was great. I mean, it was a really good change for us. *Roll the Bones* had a small sound and *Counterparts* was a complete reaction to that. We went from small sound to enormous sound. And even within that there were battles. There's always that battle between engineers and Alex about recording him, his pure sound. And with the Caveman, everything was old school, and you know what? — he was right. I fell in love with my Fender, doing that record. And I haven't really looked back."

Any struggles between Geddy and Kevin seem to have been forgotten — really, it seems like Geddy was the most open-minded of the three of them, faced with the same requests from Shirley to be allowed to meddle. "There were technical hassles, but I don't remember any personal frustrations," says Geddy. "God, I don't know, it's a day-to-day thing. You go in the studio, and you have a tough day in the studio, and then you have to do an interview, and then the frustration comes out in the interview. So, no permanent damage was suffered."

But Peter thinks the boss might have been amenable to what Kevin was saying — in fact, maybe Lee didn't think the band went far enough. "Geddy may have questioned their position in rock music given what was going on," says Collins. "And how relevant what we had just done was, given the dramatic change in the rock music climate at that time. There might have been a sense of, did we accomplish what we set out to do? Or was it more of a sop to the current movement? Geddy's constantly analyzing every aspect of everything. And we were certainly trying to fit in more with what existed. We had never done that before. I hadn't even considered that, but that's probably the case.

"As always, when you finish a record, there's a certain amount of burnout factor. You've been living with the songs for such a long time, and when you finish a record, you're releasing your baby to the outside world, and it's somewhat nerve-racking, how it's going to be accepted. And *Counterparts* was a very different sounding record to the ones they had done with Rupert. There was a little anxiety, but we were excited to get it out there and see how people perceived it. Letting go of the final mixes and no more tweaking at the mastering stage is really letting it go. So there was a little bit of anxiety, but we were confident. It was a different philosophy for that record, completely different. I always felt the blame of the fans for changing their sound so radically with *Power Windows*, so I thought I was going to redeem myself with this record.

"One of the strengths of Rush is they don't really care about how their sound is perceived," continues Collins. "They're only interested in what interests them. But they hoped the fans would go with them. Still, they're going to do intuitively what they think is best for them. So I never felt that was a consideration. With a lot of bands, that is. You know, our fans won't like it so we can't do that. But that doesn't seem to be their criteria."

"It had a lot more power to it, and it played the keyboards down a bit," sums up Alex, who describes the songs as having more hair on them. "We were all very happy with it when we finished it. With *Counterparts* it really was nice to get back to something that was a little more organic, a little more three-piece. Geddy started layering his voice a lot more, and I started layering guitars and doing things that the keyboards would have done."

The *Counterparts* tour, marking twenty years as a band for these forty-ish guys, would be quick and tidy by Rush standards, comprising essentially four months' work throughout America, from late January of '94 to early May, closing off with two Quebec dates and a hometown stand. The band was actually ready in time to hit the road quicker but was delayed because no one was champing at the bit to tour.

Indeed, the record would be well received, the album reaching gold simultaneously in the U.S. and Canada. Back-up would come from Seattle noisniks Melvins for a few shows in California, with Primus logging about a dozen dates in the Midwest. Candlebox supported for the balance, all over America. Recalled Neil of the maligned grunge-lite Seattle band, "We had them for a while, nice guys. I liked one of their songs a lot too. I don't know what happened to them." The tour closed out with a Montreal date supported by punk-popsters Doughboys, and a hometown show at Maple Leaf Gardens supported by I Mother Earth, a Toronto post-grunge band that would see considerable national success up into 1996 with their double platinum *Scenery* and *Fish* album. The U.K., mainland Europe and elsewhere would be left off the *Counterparts* dance card.

The *Counterparts* shows would open to the strains of Strauss's "Also sprach Zarathustra," which then gave way to *Roll the Bones* band and fan favorite "Dreamline." From the new album, "Stick It Out" and "Double Agent" would be intensified with bursts of pyro. Other tracks that made the grade were "Animate," "Cold Fire," "Nobody's Hero" and "Leave That Thing Alone," relegating "Cut to the Chase," "Between Sun & Moon," "Alien Shore," "The Speed of Love" and "Everyday Glory" to the set list sideline — essentially a sensible state of affairs.

"There's always excitement at the start of the tour," says Alex, "and a bit of trepidation. It's a daunting task to learn to play these songs, with the other things and the triggers and where to be at what time. After two, three, four weeks of rehearsal, it's second nature and it's not a problem at all, but very challenging and rewarding to get to that point. But all our music grows a new life when we get it on the road. We can be happy in the studio, but once we've worked on it . . . you know, this is something for us to keep in mind. It might be worth it to us to actually write a record and play it — or even take it out on the road — and then record it. Because they just develop in such a powerful way, from the benefit of playing them live — certainly *Counterparts* was like that. Getting those songs together was a task, but we were up for it; we always are. We actually did that with *Grace Under Pressure*. We played four, five songs live, at Radio City, before we actually recorded the album."

As band photographer Andrew MacNaughtan, on the road regularly, remembers, "The logo on the front cover is this nut and bolt. So they had these huge nuts and bolts built, that were like five feet high or whatever, and they were just positioned around the stage. And then as the concert opened, I had the nut and bolt that I photographed for the packaging, they took that nut and bold, and they recreated it digitally so it looked like a perfect beautiful nut and bolt. And they did like *2001: A Space Odyssey* music [sings it], and this nut and bolt began to merge together as one and started screwing onto each other. It was quite phallic, actually."

"The dynamic of the band at the time was a bit disparate," reflects Kevin, prescient, given how short the *Counterparts* tour was, and given how long it would be before Rush would record again. "Neil had his place out in the country. Alex had all sorts of other things going on. Geddy had a new family, and he had his baseball. They were definitely less communal than maybe they'd been before. I can only imagine that with money in your pocket and a desire to live something else other than the journeyman musical road life, that there was some of that to be had. And maybe making the record and pushing boundaries wasn't comfortable — maybe it all added to it. Geddy with the new child, the new baby, the new life, the new everything . . . you can have children and be on the road and you miss so much — maybe that was a big part of it. I've had babies, and I was away when they grew up. Now I'm having another baby. Maybe I'd like to see this one grow up. Maybe I want to go and make snow angels and not rush to get to the sound check."

"Golf is all about tempo and rhythm, and not trying too hard, and not getting in the way of your swing, much like playing an instrument is," says Alex of his chosen pressure release — he would soon add a solo record to his non-Rush activities. "You get out of the way and just let your instinct take over, let your hands take over and play. Everybody's got their little obsessions, particularly on the road, because it's a really important part of keeping sane and distracted. After so many years on the road, we've learned how to do it properly, and that is to stay healthy; that is the key, and it's always a bit of a battle.

"It's easy to get distracted and easy to fall into a rut and get bored, and that's what you fight mostly, the boredom. When I started playing golf in the early '90s, it was the perfect thing. And I think if you talk to a lot of other bands, they have taken that stance. It's quite common these days to get out of your hotel room, to get on a golf course for four or five hours, hit some balls, have lunch; if it's a day off, you might play a second round. It's just a wonderful escape from being in that hotel room and going through all that same stuff you always do. I love on a day off to play a couple rounds. I have dinner, I watch a movie if I can stay awake long enough, I get a good sleep and get up early the next day. I feel fit, I get outside, meet other people, and it's a wonderful, wonderful escape. So much so that I am becoming an owner of a golf club. I'm a partner with a group of guys in a very practical club that we've built. Really, out of an unhappiness with our golfing experience at other clubs. I like to say that me owning a golf club is like a heroin addict buying a farm in Afghanistan. It's like, yes, I'm set for life now; I'll just stay right here."

Geddy cautions folks who think the guys at this point didn't have a care in the world financially. Charting the course from the initial breakthrough back post–*Moving Pictures*, Lee explains: "Everything for us didn't just change. We didn't suddenly go from being poor to being wealthy, or being not successful to being fabulously successful. They were small steps and they were bumpy steps. You would have more fans on one record and then you would lose some fans, and then maybe you would lose some more fans on the next record. Our career, if you look at the graph, would be all over the place. And that's a really good thing for your life. Because you're not an overnight sensation. You've had time to adjust to every level of success that it brings you.

"In terms of success for my personal life, yeah, of course. As we made more money, I was able to pay off my house and afford certain things, and send my kids to private school and indulge my ridiculous habits and buy more stuff. Yeah, that's great, and that kind of security is what everybody wants. That was nice. In terms of how that impacted the band, it enabled us to make a bigger show, plan more extravagant effects, have more fun and try to give the audience more bang for the buck. That's the way I look at it, and I'm sure the other guys agree. We've never scrimped when it came to putting our show together. Although if you talk to our lighting director, he'll probably argue with that. 'You never gave me everything I wanted!'"

It's telling that Geddy brings the live show into it because, indeed, Rush shows got bigger and bigger as the record sales got smaller and smaller. Fortunately, a show can only get so elaborate before it becomes ridiculous, and the sales declines were only gradual across a long, long time. But still, the value that the organization gave back to the fans is the main reason Lee, Lifeson and Peart aren't as rich as your rosiest projections. Much different from Geddy's beloved Blue Jays, where all the money goes in the players' pockets.

"I've really been so fortunate," continues Ged, "that we were able to make a living, even when we were relatively not popular, you know? We were kind of a regional band at first and made enough that you could pay off a lot of your debts and get new gear. They were slow, little stages, and we were able to adjust with every stage, and as we had kids, we spent more time with the kids and made sure they were well adjusted or as well adjusted as they could be in that lifestyle. For me, personally, I always try to stress normalcy and never wanted my kids to live in the biggest house on the street. I tried to reduce their alienation due to their old man's gig. But some of that is impossible. My son grew up at a time when we were becoming most popular, and a lot of our fans were his age, so it was hard for him. He fought a lot of battles that he never made me aware of. I think that was tough for him.

"I don't know if Alex and Neil have the same attitude at home with their kids and their life, but for us it was always to stress normalcy. Get them into a good school, try to keep them regular. I wanted them to go to the best schools. I didn't want to schlep them . . . some artists take their families with them on the road. To me, that was just dead wrong. That's not making my kids normal — that's making my kids appendages to my life. I wanted them to grow up and feel that they had their own lives, their own priorities, that what they're doing is as important.

"And my wife totally agreed with that. Which was hard for her, because it meant she had to bear the brunt of it, and she had her own career too. She made a lot of sacrifices in order to keep the family normal. And in fact she probably made more sacrifices along the way, by a long shot, than I ever made. Because there's that whole thing about, well, he's the bread-winner, so cut him slack. He's got to go away for two months. Meanwhile, she's trying to juggle a career and raise the kids; we only had one at the time, so it made it easier. But it made it hard. She was a single parent a lot. But the proof is in the pudding. I've got a couple of nice kids I'm pretty proud of, so whatever we did kind of worked out, so far, for them.

"And I don't think it has anything to do with commercial success, as much as it has to do with being absorbed by a career," continues Lee. "I've often looked at producers and engineers. They have a difficult time keeping their families and lives together because they have to be there every day. You know, I can take a day off when Alex is doing guitars or Neil is working on something. I can go home and be with my family. I can provide my family with some sense that there is a paternal figure in the home, where these guys, they're there all the time. And if you examine the failure rate of marriages in the production and engineering world, and even in the road crew world, I think it's a much higher rate than musicians.

"Because we have the luxury — and maybe that's where the success comes in — that success gives you a bit of luxury to say, 'Look, take a week off, forget it. I'm gonna go home and see the family.' That's the benefit of the commercial success, to say that every three weeks, we're going home for a week. While your manager's screaming, 'But, but, but . . . how can you not be on tour for the fourth week?! Look how much money you're turning down!' It's like, well yeah, okay, we're turning that money down, but I'm investing that in my family and in my sanity. We were very fortunate that we learned that in the middle of our career, which, at this stage, seems like a long time ago.

"And that saved us — I think it really did save us. It's hard for a lot of bands to not tour, or to limit their touring. They have so much money being dangled in front of them, they have everybody in an organization depending on them going out.

And they dig it — it's the ultimate ego-stroke to be out on tour. That's why bands keep going out on tour. A lot of them, when you say to yourself, 'Why are they still on tour? Surely they don't need the money.' Well yeah, sure, they don't need the money, but they love doing it. It's in their blood. It's hard to say no. You dig playing for people. You dig writing music, playing music. Getting out on the road is such an unreal, bizarre lifestyle that it gets kind of addictive.

"Unless you're Neil," laughs Geddy. "Neil has had a difficult time with fame, much more than Alex and I. And I always tell him it's because Alex and I are stupider than he is. We're able to deal with it easier. It's hard for him. He's super, super aware of everything he's involved in. He's got such a hypersensitive reality about him. And he is a relatively shy guy. And so the more the band was on tour, as we became more successful, the more demands were put on him to be in the public eye. He's not so comfortable with that. And you say, well, what a weird thing. How can a guy be uncomfortable with the public eye when he is a rock musician playing in front of ten thousand people every night? But when he's in his drum kit, he's home. That's his turf; he's totally comfortable in there because he's doing his thing, and that's what he loves to do. But you take him out of that and put him in a party with paparazzi or whatever, and it's foreign to him. He's very uncomfortable with it. And you can't make a guy like that stuff. That's just his own innate thing.

"We tried to make it as easy for him as possible and not make so many demands for him to do that stuff, and he handles it as he can. And every once in a while something will come up that could be fun for him, and if we think it will be fun, he comes along and he enjoys it and that's great. The commercial side of things affected him the most. Success affected him the most, just in terms of his sense of himself as a private person in a public job. That's been hard for him to wrestle with. It's difficult for all of us, but we all have different skills at that. There was a period where I was kind of rebelling against public demand, and I was very uncomfortable with it. And it made me realize, just handle it, just deal with it. I'm the one who wanted to do this for a living; it's the job I wanted, and so this comes with the territory.

"We were just fried," says Geddy, on why the band opted for such a long break, upwards of eighteen months, after *Counterparts*. "A lot of albums, a lot of tours. Everybody had family issues we had to deal with. It was hard to keep going relentlessly. We figured we'd be gone down the drain by then; nobody planned for this to last this long. It's like when you're a senior citizen who didn't think he'd live to be seventy and didn't save his money, right? That kind of thing. How many bands have really been around that long? So you've got to make it up as you go along. You've got to learn as you go, and we were getting burned out. We were tired of each other's company a little bit, and we were tired of the grind of the road.

"As soon as the tour was over, 'fffttt,' we split and didn't see each other much, almost not at all. It's not like it is now, where Alex and I see each other a lot. In those days, I think the frustrations of being in each other's company more than anything, it's a test. It doesn't matter how much you like the guy you're with, seeing him every day, working with him every day, tension of the gig, tension of recording, grates on your relationship, so it's hard. And thank God we're united by this goofiness that gets you through all that. That whole laughing thing is not a small thing. I think it's saved us as a band and as friends.

"Everybody wanted to stretch out a bit," continues Ged. "Everyone was a little sick of being in a rock band, to be honest. It's a great job, but it can be all-consuming; it can just dominate your entire existence. And we're not those kinds of people. We're kind of unlikely people to be in a rock band, because we have more interests, other things we kind of could've done, or would have done, or just other things in life you want to learn about, experiences you want to share. I got sick of not being a member of a tennis club where I can play with the guys and have a regular Thursday night game. I hated that!

"So that was one of our first opportunities — we started integrating into our own communities. And then it became harder to pull us out of those and get back on the road. It's saying goodbye to a really fun life that has descended into normalized, you know, regular dinner with your kids, taking them to school, being there for the arguments, being there for the crap that is part of everyday life. At the same time, that's all the fun stuff that people take for granted. So more and more time away was self-defense, survival. It was like an innate survival alarm that was going off saying, you know, take five.

"It's also the creative thing," says Ged, perhaps hinting that the record-crafting was getting stale. "You can't be a band for forty years and just go in the studio every six months and make a record. It's not going to have the same excitement to you. For me, it's so important to let it lie, to let it get hungry again. Be hungry to work. I'm starting to get that now, where I'm thinking about working more and more every day. Every day it starts creeping into my mind. I start hearing music in my head, and that's such a healthy sign for me. It's like okay, I'm bored, I'm ready to leave my other things behind and dive into some work, and when I do, it's going to be so exciting, so fun. And when I get back together with those two guys, it's going to be great, because we'll get our hands dirty. That's part of the survival thing of being in a band for forty years. You've got to be respectful of those forty years. You've got to say, look, we're not eighteen. We can't just go in there and rock 'n' roll, 365 — can't do it. So now when it's time, we're ready to go, we're excited about it."

Charting what the guys did post-*Counterparts*, Geddy explains that "Alex was in a really different headspace from me in those days. He had quite a different lifestyle, outside of the band, than I did. And you have to allow each other that kind of grace, that respect of saying look, we spent our whole lives together, and we are really different people, so you express that in the way your personal life goes. It's so unhealthy to put constant limits on that, by the demands of your job or your working relationships.

"He was way out there and really fired up to do his own thing, to make his own musical statement," continues Ged, a motivation that resulted in the first solo album ever from the Rush camp, Alex's project modestly issued in 1996 under the band name Victor, but as much of a solo excursion as a nonsinging guitarist can make. "He was hanging out with other musicians at the time and really digging that. And that was really good for him. He had a studio in his home, and he really wanted to finally use that for his own purposes. He went totally off the deep end into Alex world.

"And me, it was kind of nesting. I returned to the whole nesting vibe, planning for another member of the family, getting a new house, preparing for that arrival. I was in a very domestic state of mind. Couldn't be more different from Alex's state of mind. And Neil was always out there, you know, traveling, doing his cycling. He's always been very good at that. The minute the tour ends, he's got rest time and then, pop, he's found some other fabulous thing to involve himself in. He was also getting much more serious about his travel writing. He was preparing for his other creative career. Alex was doing that musical thing, and I was making babies. It sounds so nice in retrospect."

Geddy says that although this was the extreme manifestation of post-tour dispersal, the sentiment had been much the same after every tour through the '70s and '80s. However, "There was one point in particular, in '89, when we came off the *Hold Your Fire* tour, and we had done a major tour of North America and it was grueling. We were really tired from that. We'd gone to Europe for a while, plus we recorded an album and then we came home, and I don't think we even had a week off, and we were in the studio, to mix that album [Geddy is referring to *A Show of Hands*, the live record]. We were so burned out, and it showed physically and emotionally.

"We were sitting in the back of the studio at McClear Place, and we all just felt like packing it in. Particularly Neil. Nobody was putting up an argument. So we kind of left it as, let's just go away before we say something we regret. Let's just go away and have some rest. Take a long break. Not our usual six weeks and then back out on tour. Let's take months off. I don't remember how long the break was; I think it was about six months. It was the longest break we'd taken at that point."

Underscoring this potential point of rupture, Alex recalls the exact same incident when asked when he thought the band as a functioning unit was ever in the most danger, barring future tragic events, that is. He says, "In my recollection, it would've been when we were putting *Show of Hands* together. I just remember sitting in the studio, sitting in a seat at the back, and all of us were just gray and tired. So exhausted and so fed up. That was the time when I thought we would break up. I thought that was it for everybody. No more. We're just going to go home."

Continues Geddy, "After that, we were all rejuvenated and fired up, and we came back wanting to take a couple of steps back and look at what was important to gain a sense of what the band was about. We took those steps back to something we had as a three-piece, and started writing in that vein. But that was probably the most critical point in the band's life, other than what had happened with Neil later."

Asked also about the *Hold Your Fire* tour, Alex says, "Yeah, well, there were days where you just wanted to cry. You just feel frustrated and worn out and just overwhelmed by everything. We were out on long runs. We played a lot of multiple shows, consecutive shows, very unlike what we do today. We'd do four or five gigs in a row, take a day off, do all the traveling. The sets are getting longer, and Rush music is not the easiest stuff to play. Not that I really know how to play anything else, but it's challenging and draining, especially over the course of a long tour."

And, says Alex, exhaustion hit its zenith "in the early '90s. Prior to that, you would always end up in each other's rooms. 'Come down; hey, what are ya doing?' Sit around, have a beer, watch the hockey game, just hang out, go for dinner — there was always this interaction in each other's rooms. And maybe that's the connection to the early days when we shared rooms, when we were a small unit. We always had this very familiar thing about being together all the time."

But come *Roll the Bones* and *Counterparts*, "there was a lot less of visiting each other. Now we never visit each other in each other's rooms. And I remember on the last tour thinking how weird it is, but we don't do that. Ged will be next door and I'll email him something and he'll email back, or maybe we'll call each other, but I never go over and visit. It was the first time we were sort of separated, where we didn't spend every day off together, and everybody sort of did their own thing. It didn't affect the work at the show or anything like that, but we seemed to crave our own independent time a little more, and we were just tired of the whole thing, really.

"It took that turn in our private lives too. We live together on the road for months and months and months, so everybody wants to have their own privacy at home. But now, I see Ged a lot. We play tennis together and we go out for dinner and have lunch, so I don't know if you're really that separated. Of course, Neil, it's a longer distance. We don't see him as much. But it's always the same when we get back together, as if we've never been apart.

"I think there's a telepathy there that you don't see," chuckles Alex, "because I never feel away or distant or disconnected from Ged. But I know we sit in our little areas, and he's checking his baseball scores and I'm doing whatever I'm doing, and we don't really have that much interaction. But we're always connected. It's not even something I'm aware of. We're just so set and so comfortable in our relationships. You know, your closest and dearest friends and mates, you can sit for hours and not say a word, and feel completely at ease and connected."

But back then, they had to make some changes, says Alex. "We decided to take some time off; I think it was about a year. Geddy and his wife were expecting, and he said, 'I'm not doing this again. I'm not going to miss my child growing up. I want to be home, and I want to be home for a year.' And that was fun for everybody — we all wanted the time off. I stayed busy by doing Victor. I kept really busy for that whole period of time, and I think we needed it. At the time, I was tired but I was always up to going back to work. Geddy was expecting and I think he felt the most stressed out of all of us. And Neil is always up for a break."

CHAPTER 3

TEST FOR ECHO

"Geddy, could you be more interesting?"

▌▌ ▌like the fact that Neil is never static," says Neil's dad,
Glen Peart. "He's never satisfied with what he's doing.
He always wants to move on. He got quite involved in
that Buddy Rich thing, big band jazz. And as much drums as
Neil has played, and he's acknowledged around the world, he
wanted to do that Buddy Rich album. He got together with
another drummer in L.A., and he was saying that he wanted
to take this drumming up, particularly jazz drumming, another
step. And Peter Erskine of course worked with him, and Peter
heard him play and he said half-jokingly, 'You are going to take
lessons, aren't you, Neil?' And Neil said, 'Okay, I will,' and he
took lessons before he did that. And of course I love the Buddy
Rich song 'Love for Sale.' It's again closer to my kind of music,
and that whole album the way it's put together, I just love that.
But he's just kept moving. He's not satisfied to stay where he is.
He always has a new challenge, regardless of what it is, in some

direction or other. And I think that's something we talk about a lot whenever we're talking together. It's usually something that either one of us got interested in and that's certainly what I am proud of with Neil, the fact that there's always a new challenge there. But you never know what worlds collide."

Now that Rush had decided to take a break and enter a period of reflection, they were more free to explore other avenues. Mr. Peart talks about Neil's side project during that time: producing and stage-managing a drum showcase album called *Burning for Buddy: A Tribute to the Music of Buddy Rich*, issued October 1994. Neil plays one track on the album, "Cotton Tail." There are also seventeen other selections played by what is possibly the greatest array of drum legends ever assembled — testimony to the respect and goodwill Neil had garnered in the industry. A second volume done exactly the same way would emerge three years later, with a five-hour DVD seeing release in 2006.

Peart was also seriously getting into motorcycling at that point, and one of his epic journeys (to Yellowknife) would inspire the cover art for the next Rush album (but more on that later).

"I got into bicycling in the early '80s, on tour," begins Neil, on how he started this huge hobby. "I was looking for some way to break out of the tightly controlled little bubble that you feel like you're in. So in Salt Lake City, actually, I bought a bicycle and started riding in different cities, and got more serious about it, got a helmet and gloves, started riding between shows. Sometimes I could ride a hundred miles on a day off. Sometimes I would set up with the bus driver to drop me off a hundred miles from town, or on a show day, I can do forty miles or so.

"I was going all around the towns of America, and exploring the downtowns on the show day, a lot of times going to art museums and all that. And I did several bicycle tours in China, Africa, Europe, through the Rockies, the Alps, the Pyrenees, on my bicycle. And I was in Mali one time in West Africa, struggling down the road on a bicycle, and I saw these two turbaned guys on BMWs in perfect formation — vroom! — on the GS like I ride now, and it just kind of lit a light. And I always liked to speed, I liked cars, and I said when I grow up, I'll have a motorcycle, and always intended that. And somehow I knew I needed to grow up a little bit.

"When I was in my forties, I always wanted a BMW, because they looked to me just like a motorcycle should look. That was ingrained in me before I even got a motorcycle. The first trip I did was to Eastern Canada, Newfoundland and Labrador, on a motorcycle tour, and I was completely grabbed by that. It was like bicycle touring times a thousand. The distances you could cover and the things you could see in a day, and the places you can get to . . . you couldn't get to Labrador too easily. You couldn't get around on a bicycle; it would take too long. Whereas in a couple weeks' time, you could go to the farthest reaches of the St. Lawrence and Quebec.

"Then I did a tour of Mexico on motorcycle, and then another one in Eastern Canada, and then up to Yellowknife for the midnight sun one year. My friend Bruce and I. We'd only been riding a couple years at the time. Both of us had totally unsuitable road bikes for that, kind of sport bike–style BMWs, but we went to Yellowknife for the midnight sun, doing a thousand miles of dirt road in the rain and mud, falling down, picking each other up. I've got pictures of me covered head to toe in mud. Why do I like this? But it was amazing. And then I went to Europe and Tunisia and the Sahara one time and came back through Sardinia, and it was adventure touring on a grand scale and I loved it.

"The curiosity a lot of times of what's around the corner," answers Neil when asked why he does it. "Or sometimes there is a place you've been to before, like the Black Forest in Germany when we toured in the '70s, where it was now about getting to know the better motorcycling places. The number of years I've gone to Britain without seeing the Yorkshire Dales or the Highlands of Scotland, or the islands off the coast, or the mountains of Wales and all of that, and now I know all of that is part of my Great Britain.

"And what are we doing tomorrow? That's another thing. It just makes the day so much more interesting. Touring, when you're stuck, sometimes you've got a day off in some town you don't care about. What can you do? I have all these possibilities. Sometimes I'm juggling, 'Okay, I've got a day off tomorrow, how can I best spend this day?' If we were in the southeast for example, I want to get to the Appalachians, ride some of that country. If I'm in the west, it's almost limitless. We have two days off on the last tour, I can get to Monument Valley the first day, I can get to Taos, New Mexico, the second day and be in Albuquerque, New Mexico, for the show the next day. That's the best possible way to spend that time.

"It's easy to over-glamourize, because a lot of times, I'd rather go home. After months go by, that's what I do to make touring more interesting — and perhaps even bearable — for me. But ultimately, of course, you are still traveling month after month, and a lot of times when I unload my bike off of the trailer in the morning, after sleeping on the bus at a truck stop, I really just want to go home. But that being said, I do have the privilege of spending my time between shows the way I want to, and getting there the way I want to, route-wise. It feeds off some of my desire for natural beauty and speed and adventure — so many of my enthusiasms are catered to by motorcycle travel."

The bike also helped Neil with his surprise second job late in life, that of a bestselling travel writer, through a series of well-received books that have made the most closed-up Rush member suddenly the most open book.

"Even on a smaller scale . . . I tend to be a morning worker, with my creative writing work and all that, and sometimes in Southern California, I can go for a two-hour ride, and it would be some of the best rides in the world, in the canyons of the Santa Monica Mountains and all that. It blows all that away. There is something existential. With motorcycling, you are on the edge of your own control and of physics, and on these twisty, winding roads with gravel, you are working as far as you can see. You are totally engrossed in your activity, and your survival depends on that concentration and perception. It's engaging and demanding to that ultimate level.

"And when you come back from a ride — with the touring and the physical exertion that it takes to play the way we do — it is an antidote. The vibration of the motorcycle all day soothes — it's almost like a massage. I feel tired all over and sore all over, but it's generalized. It's therapeutic and physical and it transports you. You're in the weather and you can feel a two-degree difference in temperature. The smell of the flowers coming up this road today, through the canyons, it just fills your helmet. It's supercharged, as a friend of mine described it. The fragrance of nature like that comes off the eucalyptus trees, the sage, and they transport you in another way. The birds and animals on the roadside . . . I'll be thinking about the geology; where do these hills come from? Back up from the Pacific plate in the Sierra Nevada, they're like snow on a snow shovel.

"Those things can go through your mind and not upset that riveting concentration you have on what you are doing. There are gaps. Similar to going onstage — total engagement and concentration, but there are gaps: 'Okay, I'm going to do this for three seconds.' Because your brain is working at such a velocity that three seconds is an enormous time, in music it comes down to milliseconds; when you are talking about tempo shifts, you are dealing with a millisecond reality. On a motorcycle, the world is coming at you that way too. And I notice in desert riding it comes at you more gradually. Any dangers are far away and long seen before they come. Whereas on a winding road, you are on another pitch.

"And there is a musical metaphor there too. Because performing is much like that. The ability to think of something else comes and goes. I'll be onstage looking at the audience, and some little thing will flash through my head, a T-shirt or a face. It registers, but in milliseconds: 'Okay, think about that; this is coming up.'

"And here's another good thing compared between the two: If I'm playing and thinking about the next part of the song, I don't want to think about what I'm doing now. If I'm coming into a bridge section, I've got to set that up physically, mentally, tempo-wise, and I want that transition to go smooth there. There's all kinds of planning that has to go with that. The motorcycle is the same. If I'm not thinking about the next corner, or as far as I can see, I'm in trouble. You can't be thinking about the world under your wheels, because that world's passing by at many, many feet per second.

"There are analogies to the state of mind too. It takes an enormous concentration and mental discipline on the motorcycle. But there's a whole 'nother kind of input, a whole different mental activity, a lot of great ideas and reflection on work and possibilities because your mind is at such a high pitch. And a lot of times I would stop, and I would have a little notebook or journal with me, with notes on maps and song titles. Because if I was that serious — 'Okay, pull over, write that thing down on that map before you forget it' — it was probably important. Before I started being a good note keeper, I'd say I've got three things; okay, remember those three things, observations about the landscape or some reflection you want to get down before you forget it . . . before something else fills your mind. All of that is part of the mechanism."

Back to the world of music making. As mentioned, on January 9, 1996, Alex would issue his first — and so far, only — solo album, called *Victor*, under a loose band concept also called Victor. This hit store shelves just as the guys were deep into the next Rush record, working against snowstorms that never seemed to let up. Though he used a collection of mostly unknowns, Alex also called on his new buddy Les Claypool to provide bass on one track and asked Lisa Dal Bello to sing on another. Edwin from I Mother Earth is the most significant collaborator, doing vocals on five tracks.

"I've always wanted to do something like *Victor*," mused Alex, doing press with *our magazine* back in early '96. "I've always wanted to work on a solo-ish project. I knew the demands that recording takes with Rush; I really needed to have a good block of time, which was equal to what we take with the band. That is normally eight or nine months, from inception to final mixes. Geddy wanted to take a year off with his baby; Neil had things on his agenda for an additional six months. I looked at an eighteen-month period and said, 'Here's my opportunity to do something.' As it was, it took ten months to do all the recording and finally finish the project in September [1995]. And then I had a couple of weeks off and began on the next Rush record. It was okay, because I get bored easily and I find I need to be focused on something to make me happy.

"I suppose the cynical world is full of anger," reflected Alex on the record's . . . not quite doomy vibe, but one that is tense, claustrophobic. "But I wanted to make a record that was dark, disturbing and unsettling. Once I determined thematically what the record was about, it was easier to make that real. I didn't do it because I sensed it all around me; it was a little more direct. The heavier, harder approach my record has over stuff I've done in the past is just what I like to hear. I wanted to have a record that had that kind of impact and power. Especially coming from the guitars.

"When you work with other people, there's always compromise. Rush has been around for a very long time and what we do is what we do. I'm completely satisfied with that. I didn't make this record because I wasn't happy with the direction Rush was taking or my relationship with Geddy or Neil. But you still compromise. That's the way it works in a democracy. Hopefully at the end of it all, you'll have something everybody is happy with. When you're the boss you can do whatever you want — and in my case I did. I wanted to have a song or two that would be considered very heavy, hard and dark and some other sadder and lonelier moments. I wanted to try to do a narrative over a song that had no guitar on it. This was something that purely started from my brain and my heart and carried through with no consideration for Rush at all."

But Alex stayed away from a "shred"-type album, of which there were many examples by the mid-'90s, some of them quite successful. Instead, there's a sense of humor despite the frenzied unease and noise — black humor, if you like.

"You would expect the guitar player from Rush to do a showcase of his guitar playing abilities," says Alex. "Honestly, I can't stand those guitar-wanking records. I mean, these players are amazing and brilliant but big deal. You listen to it once and you don't feel like listening to it again. There's nothing that really grabs you emotionally. It's just a display of talent and ability. I wanted to make a record that really had some substance to it. I wanted to write songs and work with different people and direct them and compose things that other players would play."

Offering us a few examples, Alex says, "'Strip and Go Naked' was more of an exercise where Bill Bell and I decided to get as many elements as possible into the song. Start off with some twelve-string acoustic and use some electric, then some bottle-neck, so it takes it to a bluesy sort of thing from a folky Celtic thing and then into this soaring guitar line. We just wanted to create a lot of different textures and levels. It's really honest and pure, and it came very quickly. We basically wrote and recorded it in a day. I don't get the opportunity to play that way; I wouldn't discount doing an entirely instrumental record like that.

"On 'Mr. X,' I was fiddling with keyboards downstairs and then Pete Cardinal came in with this great walking bass line throughout the whole song. I just threw some guitars on and I thought, this is my chance to do a little playing on my own. 'Mr. X' is a really fun song and it picks me up. There are so many dark points on this record, I just wanted to get a little lightness here and there. That and 'Shut Up Shuttin' Up' became those two things, to dynamically pick the record up so you don't start crying by the end of it!"

Amusingly, with everything at the time being alternative this and alternative that, when asked about the state of his main gig in 1996, Alex said, "We're still a cult band after so many years. Talk about alternative, I think we've always been the alternative band. I used to think it was luck. Now I feel that opportunities came our way at a certain point and we just worked really hard. We've been lucky because we do what we do. And if you like it, great, and if you don't like it, too bad. Fortunately for us, there are a lot of people who really love our music and have grown with us and respect that in us. They accept that we're always moving forward and doing something different with every record.

"When I got into *Victor*, that became a full-time job for me," says Alex, looking back fifteen years later. "I couldn't stop thinking about it. I recorded that record in my little studio at home, so I was down there every day. I would go out and do something and I would just race home to go, 'Oh, I gotta try this,' this little thing. I was very focused. I didn't really think about the band much at all. I know we were on a break, and whatever was going to happen at the end of the break was fine. I was doing my own thing, as Geddy was doing his own thing, as Neil was doing his. And in fact, we didn't really have much contact for most of that time, until towards the end.

"I just wanted to have some fun with music," continues Lifeson. "I wanted to play with some other people, and it was nothing to do with any sort of void I felt in Rush — Rush was Rush. But it seemed to me like this was a great opportunity to apply myself to something that would require all my time and effort, and I would have to see it to the end, otherwise I would be a total and complete failure, loser. That was a lot of it. I was in a point in my life where I felt lack of confidence. I didn't know where I was going, and it seemed to me like doing a project like this, that required this amount of work and attention, was just what I needed, to prove to myself that I could do it.

"And I did. You know, I wrote, well, co-wrote some stuff, but basically wrote everything, played everything, mixed it, recorded it, worked on the artwork, you know, did everything on that record. And I was very, very proud of the fact that I managed to do it all. It doesn't matter how many records I sold. At the end of it, if there was one album that was sold, it would've been fine. I set out to accomplish personal goals, and that's what I did. But sometimes it was a bit scary. Sometimes it was daunting and tiring, but generally it felt really good, to be in control of the whole thing, to know the decisions you made were between failing and not failing. And on a musical standpoint, it gave me an opportunity to branch out and do different stuff, from heavier things than maybe Rush does, to acoustic things, to dancy sort of stuff, to electronic. I got to fiddle around with all kinds of different music; it was a lot of fun.

"I've never been a really confident person," says Alex, reiterating the therapeutic and introspective nature of *Victor*, somehow captured in the cover art. "Like everybody, you have insecurities about certain things in life, about certain abilities you have. And I just needed a little boost at that time. And I came out of that experience a lot stronger, for what followed in Rush. And I think a lot of that is evident in our relationship, and the writing relationship, Geddy and me. I think he appreciates the fact that I went through that experience, and that I feel a bit stronger and more confident about the things I do, the things I bring, and the kind of control I'm willing to take. And it makes him feel more relieved, or not worried, I guess, about not being there. Because he's very much an in-control sort of guy; he always has been."

Indeed it's kind of cool — and surprising, and inspiring — that the first solo album to come out of Rush was from Alex. Also surprising, there'd only be one more so far (if you don't count Neil's efforts), *My Favorite Headache* courtesy of Geddy, written four years after *Victor*.

"I'm a very gregarious person," continues Alex, explaining the irony around his confidence issues. "I can put myself in any situation and feel comfortable, or take some sort of control within it. And I've always been that way, class clown. But there's always been an underlying insecurity. And my guitar playing, I've always felt a little insecure about it, and I always felt that I could be better, and that there are a lot of people way better than me. It's something to this day I still feel, maybe a little less so. I worry about those situations when they come up, and when I'm actually faced with them. It's like, what was I worried about? Being in a position of jamming, for example, or playing up onstage with another band or another act.

"I started doing these things at the Orbit Room, the club that I'm a partner at, and I played with a house band there. This was twelve years ago, and for those first four or five years, I was playing fairly regularly, probably twice a month on the weekends, and that was a great experience, because this was music I knew when I was younger but never played. Kind of the soul, R&B, funk music of the '60s. That's what was going on at the Orbit Room at the time.

"And the guys in the Dexters were all fantastic musicians. So it's really easy to get up and just kind of work your way around what they are laying down. I remember the first time I did it, I played to ninety people in the club, and it's not a big club, and I was so nervous and scared. And I never get nervous at a Rush show, whether it's the first one or the last one — it's so normal. And at home, for me to be on that stage, on this little eight-inch platform at the back of the club, surrounded by all these people sitting there drinking beer, I mean, I was really, really nervous about it. But it was great; we had a riot and it was fun, and I realized the stupid time I was wasting on feeling nervous about something like this, when it's just a fun, glorious thing to be able to do, and to have that ability. For me personally, that was a turning point. I'm a lot more comfortable about that now, but we all have our insecurities."

Victor and *My Favorite Headache* confirmed an amusing thing: both Geddy and Alex play what they like as a part of Rush. Both records sound similar to one another; both sound like the Rush of *Presto* through *Test for Echo*. Alex's is a little crazier and darker and Geddy's is a more singer/songwriter and alternative, but, almost disappointingly, they sound like Rush.

Meanwhile Neil, true to his personality, was working behind the scenes on his music, learning from jazz drum instruction legend Freddie Gruber, who completely turned around the way Neil approached his kit. "Neil's whole approach to the drums was going to be different, and quite significantly," notes producer Peter Collins, brought back for a reprisal of his role on *Counterparts*. "And I didn't quite know it until we got into pre-production. His whole body language had changed when he was playing drums; it was a much more circular movement from the way he used to play. And he was trying to incorporate different feels because his feel had always been kind of crisp and on top. And so he was experimenting with putting the backbeat a bit behind. And I think he achieved that, the ability to switch between both feels.

"That I could see almost instantly," continues Collins on Peart's new style. "His previous body language was almost tight, consistent with the drum sound and his drum feel, very much right on the beat and sometimes ahead of it. Often he would push ahead of the beat, rather than behind it, and by this time he had really mastered the ability to go both ways, which is very interesting. When he was going into the back on the beat, groove-orientated things, I could see the circular motion in his body, which was very cool. For certain songs, I think it was very effective, his choice of fills and everything. But he was rethinking the drums; it was interesting for me, and I wanted to explore further. I was very happy to push it as much as we could in that direction."

"The '90s was a great period of growth for us," says Neil. "I stopped in the mid-'90s when Geddy and his wife were having a child. We had about a year hiatus, and so I started taking lessons and completely reinvented my drumming before the *Test for*

Echo album. I really like that one. As a fan, this would probably be my favorite of the '90s albums. Yet there are some special circumstances. I started working with my drum teacher, Freddie Gruber, just before this, and I did the Buddy Rich tribute and was working with all these different great drummers and met Freddie through Steve Smith.

"So I started studying with Freddie. I started practicing every day with all these different exercises he had given me for the physical motion on the drums and so on. I spent more than a year, eighteen months I think, practicing drums every day. By the time we came to *Test for Echo*, I was playing a completely different style. That's one of the things I did willingly with Freddie. I thought, okay, after twenty-five years at that time, thirty years maybe, let's try something new. I surrendered and went back to traditional grip, turned the sticks around and played them properly, and learned all his techniques of physical motion.

"I came into this not only at a really high technical peak, but as a reinvented musical creature too. And the telling point was, when I first started playing along with the demos, Geddy and Alex were saying, 'It doesn't sound that much different to me.' And the producer, Peter Collins said, 'It still sounds like you.' But when I recorded the drum parts, and they were playing to them, they noticed the clock was different. They had to adjust their playing. Again, that subtle thing I talked about before, about nailing feels and tempos and so on; I had subtly changed my clock, my driving metronome, in the gyroscope of all my drum playing. That forced them to change theirs. So that's an example of how far-reaching the subtleties — all the subtleties — were. So that was a really important record for me.

"I made the instructional video after that, *A Work in Progress*," continues Neil, "and talked about the concept of creating a masterpiece in the true sense, the way it used to be, in the days of the apprentices. If you wanted to be accepted as a master in the guild, you had to create a piece of work; whether you're a stonemason or a guilder or carver or whatever, that was your masterpiece. You'd put it before the masters to be accepted among them, and to end your apprenticeship, as it were. I was talking about it in those terms, trying always to achieve something that was worthy of your ideal judge; if you were setting up a master in your guild to approve or not of your work, then your work was necessarily, within the craft, an attempt to achieve that mastery."

"I think I was ready to work," says Geddy on getting back to the studio. "But I don't think we were as completely glued together as we had been on certain records. Alex was still very much in that 'being his own man' kind of thing. We rented this place to write the record. Alex had done this big project, *Victor*. He worked his ass off; he'd gone out on a limb and he was kind of exhausted from it. And he got it out of his system. But I was really happy to go back to work. Because of this whole domestic headspace, I was itching to be productive."

Setting the scene further, Geddy explains that "Alex's solo experience was very turbulent, but I was coming out of a calm, low-key world. He was coming out of this high-pressure, high-powered 'I'm the boss of this record' world. It was tough, very difficult, because he engineered it, did everything on that record. It was a great weight off his shoulders when he came back for *Test for Echo*. He felt happy to be collaborative again, happy to not bear the brunt of all the responsibility.

"I know that from making my own solo record. It's nice to have a partner, you know? I had a partner for my solo record, but still, your name is going on it and there's a lot of pressure on you to do something really great. Not that there isn't in Rush, but you share that. I've talked to friends who are writers and friends who are painters, and it's one thing they always envy about my situation — my two partners, that I have two partners in this collaborative effort, this creative world. Because it's hard, and you have those moments of great self-doubt. But when you have two partners, they pick you up, they charge you back up. So you get through those tough moments, because you have each other to reinforce your confidence and say, 'No, that's great, man!' or 'No, that's crappy!' So you know what you're dealing with.

"But guys who work on their own, it's very isolating; it's difficult to make the right decision all the time. I think that's what he was going through. That's why his memories are so positive and mine were so . . . I was coming from a very laid-back position. I was happy to be working again, not changing diapers."

Geddy said Alex got something out of his system, but he seems to be missing part of the equation. Alex has expressed his perennial lack of confidence, and how some of that contributed to his decision to do the solo project, so surely *Victor* must have been a huge confidence booster as well. On that, Geddy says, "I never viewed him as lacking confidence. But, you know, maybe I've misconstrued his silence for that. I thought he was cool with everything.

"And certainly there were some big personalities in the room through that period. You've got Peter Collins, who is very decisive; in fact, that's how he got the name Mr. Big, because he would light up that cigar and he would make a decision. And I like that. And I'm very opinionated, Neil is opinionated, and we had Andy Richards in the room from time to time, who is like a tour de force. And so maybe he was a bit intimidated by all that. Maybe he felt it was moving in a direction without him. It's possible.

"Honestly, I've never thought of him as lacking confidence. Yeah, maybe he calls it that, but maybe it's more giving people the benefit of the doubt. You know, he's not one to start a creative

A *Roll the Bones* tour stop, June 3, 1992, at the Irvine Meadows Amphitheater in Irvine, California. The guys played the same venue the next night as well. Supporting was Mr. Big.

Roll the Bones–era backstage passes, ticket stubs and a hat!

May 3, 1992, at the Ahoy Sportpaleis in Rotterdam, The Netherlands. This was the last show on the European leg of the *Roll the Bones* tour. Supporting was Primus.

Neil on bike in Detroit,
June 26, 1992.

Alex at the Kumbaya Festival,
September 4, 1994.

LEFT: "Nobody's Hero" promo
CD single.

BELOW: "Stick It Out" promo
CD single.

Counterparts show at the San Diego Sports Arena in San Diego, California, February 7, 1994.

Test for Echo-related goodies: a hat, an ad, a postcard, an album flat, a promo single and a backstage pass.

Test for Echo show at the San Diego Sports Arena,
November 23, 1996.

Outdoor show at Hospitality Point in San Diego, May 7, 1997.

Promo CD single from Geddy's solo album, *My Favorite Headache*.

GEDDY LEE
HOME ON THE STRANGE

(Geddy Lee and Ben Mink) 2000 Buge Songs administered by Core Music Publishing (SOCAN) and Zavion Enterprises, Inc. (SOCAN) administered for the United States by Mo Mo Enterprises and outside the United States by Rondor Music. All Rights Reserved. Used by Permission.

1. Album Version 3:45
2. Interview Footage :42

Produced by Geddy Lee, Ben Mink and David Leonard
Mixed and engineered by David Leonard

www.myfavoriteheadache.com

LICENSED FOR PROMOTION ONLY — SALE IS PROHIBITED

ATLANTIC

ANTHEM
RECORDS INC.

300520

ATLANTIC RECORDING CORPORATION, 1290 Avenue of the Americas, New York, NY 10104. An AOL Time Warner Inc. Company © ℗ 2000 Atlantic Recording Corporation and Anthem Entertainment. All Rights Reserved. Printed in U.S.A. WARNING: Unauthorized reproduction of this recording is prohibited by Federal law and subject to criminal prosecution. www.atlantic-records.com

Promo sampler from the *Different Stages* live album.

June 28, 2002, at the Meadows Music Centre in Hartford, Connecticut. This is the band's first show back in five years, following the two tragic deaths in Neil's family.

idea. And you do get that feeling in the studio, that when there are a bunch of ideas going on that you may not agree with, you don't want to be a dissenting voice. It's tougher to stand up and say, 'Look, I know you're all gung-ho about this idea, but it sucks.' It's hard to do that because there's this kind of groupthink that takes over and pushes a project in a particular direction.

"So maybe that's what he's talking about: he didn't feel like he could stem the tide of everybody with these ideas that are coming along. And certainly, it would make sense when you think about him eventually going to do a solo album. But I never saw it as that dramatic, but maybe it was an interior thing with him. I mean, we all have our moments of insecurity, especially in the studio. If you go into a take and it doesn't come out how you want, the first person you blame is yourself. So you work harder, you push yourself. It's a tender time because the tape doesn't lie. So if you suck and they play it back for you, there's you sucking, for everyone in the room to hear. 'Thank you very much, ladies and gentlemen; I sucked today!' Unless you're an ass, you have to be a little insecure. All the best people are, I think. Because it keeps you trying to improve; it keeps you trying to get it."

And on the whole process of not being sure of what you're playing, what you sound like, Geddy figures, "That's why you need producers and that's why you need bandmates. That's the creative process. It's an insecure time because you are baring your soul. You know, you're getting ideas out of the air. There's nothing worse than saying, 'Hey, what about this?' and the whole room's looking at you like you're on another planet. And then you feel, okay, maybe not so much, you know. But you have to do it anyway; you have to speak your mind. Maybe that's something I learned earlier than he did — right or wrong, airing the idea out. We always encouraged that with whoever else was in the room. You're sitting in the room, or you're the engineer or the producer, you're part of production. If you've got an idea, even if it doesn't get used, hey man, speak up. This is a creative environment."

Creative process under way, the guys convened again at Chalet Studio in Claremont in October of 1995. At this site (which is quite inland), given the elevation, Neil says he could see Lake Ontario. Peart scribbled at one end of the house, and Alex and Geddy made noises at the other end, offering Neil bits and pieces earlier in the process than usual. Recalls Peter, "We went to wherever it was we rehearsed it, this farm somewhere in Ontario, and everyone was really happy to be there and the vibe was great. Neil was in his room writing lyrics furiously, and Alex and Geddy were still working on arrangements. I came in and there was a great atmosphere; I didn't sense any tension at all.

"I did get a sense that they wanted to be more in Canada so we didn't travel as much. The basics for *Test for Echo* we did in Woodstock, New York. But it was a fairly short time and then we went to Canada. They definitely wanted to spend more time at home with families, rather than be off in England or France or Montserrat. Geddy having a child — that's when Kyla was born — I assume had a lot to do with it. And getting to a point where they really wanted to spend some time enjoying the lives they had established from the wealth they had made. You get to a point where you just want to enjoy it, and go on vacation, go to the cabin and fish and cycle and do all those things for a lot longer than you used to."

Indeed Alex said as much at the time. "Over the years we've gone everywhere to record, avoiding working here. This time around we wanted to be here as much as possible. We all like to be at home. After twenty-one years of touring and being away all the time, it's nice to be home as much as possible. We just had this year and a half off; everybody had the chance to do other things and you got a taste of normal life. I think we'd like to continue that as much as possible."

Woodstock was home to the storied rural studio Bearsville, memorialized by the record label of the same name, both entities owned by Bob Dylan manager Albert Grossman (Grossman died in 1986, and at this point, it was run by his wife, Sally). It was chosen because the idea was to get more of a room sound for Neil's drums, and Bearsville had a cavernous drum room — this is the first time Neil's drums would be recorded in the U.S. (and really, this was the main function of the Bearsville sessions). The location, considered a bucolic retreat away from Manhattan (a little over two hours away by car), hosted myriad marquee acts but is most associated with the likes of Bearsville roster acts like Foghat and Todd Rundgren. After this, it was over to Reaction Studios in Toronto for more sessions, followed by the mix at McClear, also in Toronto.

"Certainly our writing process was the same," recalls Alex. "We wrote in the same place, in fact. We changed the schedule up a little bit, so that had an influence on how we worked. We would take weekends off, whereas in the past we didn't. Geddy was going home from the studio. It's a residential studio just outside of Toronto. He would go home just about every night of the week and come back in the morning. So that changed the whole dynamic of being there together all the time. It was positive. The *Counterparts* thing and the post-*Counterparts* thing — that was just that. And we got over it with some time and Ged having time with his daughter and his family; it fixed a lot of things. We all went through personal stuff in that period. And it was good to get back together and share our experiences of that year and a half and move forward together. I remember distinctly, when we were working at McClear on the mix, there was a really positive vibe in the studio. Everyone was feeling really good."

In early '96, when it was all still very much a work in progress, Alex explained, "In December we were in preproduction, going through all the material, the arrangements, tightening things up. And we finally got into official rehearsals. It's hard for me to make a connection to anything else. I think it's a big step forward from the last record. We touched on a couple of things with *Counterparts*. It has a real sense of power to it, but at the same time a great feel and sense of melody. And that comes mostly from Ged; that's his forte. Whereas I'm more on the heavier side."

On the process side of things, Alex said that "Ged and I will work on stuff during the day, and in the evening I will work with Neil, engineering all his drum stuff as he works out his parts for the songs. Ged has spent a lot of time working on his vocal melodies at this early stage too. The level of complexity with which he's worked out his vocal parts now really shines. I think he's become aware of that added preparation and the value of it. We're deeper inside the whole aspect of preparedness. When I listen to live tapes of the last record from the last tour, the stuff live blows away the record. I think you have to be aware that playing the stuff as a band is really important before recording. We just never had the time to do it in the past."

Somewhat contrary to the modern-day recollection, back then Alex said the guys would "work for a few weeks then we'd take a week off," pointing out a two-week break in March. "But the time frame doesn't really matter. There's no deadline and we're going to work at a nice easy pace. But we are very meticulous in our preparation. Neil and I are Virgos. We're always too anal about how we prepare ourselves. Everything is very orderly. We've reached a point in our career that we can take our time for just purely financial reasons. At the same time, you impose certain demands and restrictions upon yourself."

Back in the beginning of '96, however, things didn't look quite as rosy as they did with the passage of time. Back then, Alex divulged that "it's been a rocky marriage over the years. Especially over the last five or six years, touring has been very difficult. We all love the two hours of playing immensely. It's the other twenty-two hours in the day of waiting for those two hours. That's a lot harder to handle. We understand that that's part of it. When you're young, it's the best thing in your life. And I certainly was like that for the first ten or twelve years. When you reach a certain age, you look back on your life and recognize you had an opportunity that most people just dream about. I was nineteen when I started touring. But you miss certain qualities in your life that touring can't provide. You miss being with your loved ones and family. You miss your friends. The existence on the road is tough. You're with, in our case, fifty people and you feel lonely for most of the time you're out there. You wonder, 'Do I really need this? I've accomplished a lot. What more am I going to get out of doing this?'

"But at the same time, we recognize that it's an important part of being in Rush and you have to balance those things. I'd miss playing live. Same goes for the other guys. Neil is probably the least interested in touring. He really sets a rigorous lifestyle on the road. He rides his bike a lot and that's his release. On a day off, he's up at five in the morning, has breakfast and rides for a hundred miles. He comes back late at night, has a big dinner, then collapses. That's how he's filled his day, rather than sitting and surfing the TV or hanging out in a bar, which is a very destructive lifestyle. It's all a question of balance and discipline."

Even after reuniting for the album in '96, with the guys all in different places, there was serious talk about the band's future. Alex says, "I don't know. I wasn't sure during our first week that I wanted to continue. I was still buoyant by what I'd just accomplished with my record, and I didn't know if I wanted to get back into the same old thing that Rush represented. Ged and I spent that first week just talking about where we wanted to go as human beings in our lives. We had a varied discussion about so many things. We kind of left it as, 'Let's see how the first couple of weeks go, and if my heart is not in it, I have to say I can't.'

"Then we started playing and all this great stuff started coming out. We'd written four or five songs in two weeks, where normally we'd only write two. Everything just kind of poured out and we were so excited. This for me has been the best writing session I can remember in a long time. There's no ego, no weirdness. We've risen above so many of those feelings and we're writing in a much more mature fashion, and those results really show. There's a sense of passion and feel again that I haven't seen in a while in our records. At this point, all the pieces fit together very well. I think it might even be a little harder and heavier."

The guys might have been more confident in the writing of the album, but anxiety crept in when they were faced with having to find a new production team. "They were anxious to have someone else record the record," says Peter Collins on the switch from Kevin Shirley to Clif Norrell in the engineer chair. Clif had done Rush tunes in his own cover act and was a big fan; he would be the first American engineer the band ever had. Would it be "a little harder and heavier," as Alex threatened? Time would tell. "I worked with Clif and had suggested Clif and I can't remember how they agreed," Peter continues. "I guess they flew him in and liked him and liked the sound he got. Also the Caveman, at that particular point when I worked with him, his life was extremely fragmented on a personal level. He had a nanny and the child was coming with him and I don't think they wanted to go through all that again. To be honest with you, if it was down to me, I would've hired him in an instant. And I did hire him for Bon Jovi a little bit after that and got a great result. But I think just sort of the attendant chaos that went along with him . . ."

It's not that the band wanted to reverse the jets on the heaviness they got out of Kevin. "No, I didn't get that sense at all, actually," continues Peter. "They wanted to take it even further; hence I brought in Andy Wallace to do the mix, who had a reputation for that very punchy, very dry sound. And Alex, having made his solo record, where he got to do things absolutely his way — he worked with his son on that, and it was very good for him — he had a certain level of confidence about what he was going to do that he didn't have on the previous record, particularly with the advent of the Caveman coming in and changing his guitar sound completely.

"This time he was more confident in the way he wanted to go sonically with his guitars. And in the preproduction stage, Alex and Geddy were more together, definitely more in sync, and Alex was more proactive in the overall arrangements. I welcomed it. I didn't really know about the process Alex had gone through making his record, but he was talking about it quite a lot and wanted to discuss it. And so they'd be sitting around the computer that the demos had been recorded on, and instead of just Ged handling it, they were both inside it doing it jointly. In the past, that was more Geddy's thing. I still have that vision. I can still see them in the room kind of staring, working, sitting. Geddy had a bass in his hand and Alex had his guitar, and they were working very closely."

As for other changes, Peter says, "That was the first time I didn't bring in an extra keyboard player, and I definitely got resistance to that. Apart from that though, we just all got so much more comfortable with each other. Alex had done his solo album.

I went to Alex's restaurant in Toronto, and he would play jazz and stuff. So that was highly unusual. I mean, he was comfortable and it was a groovy scene there, and he was very comfortable going and playing and jamming with people. I'd never seen Alex in that context. I think that opened him up to different types of music, and again helped him with his confidence and with his attitude on *Test for Echo*.

"They all had developed musical entities and were more confident about what they wanted to do. When I worked with them back on *Power Windows* they were pretty much completely open, pretty much ready to do something different at that point. But *Test for Echo*, they were on a course — let's take this organic thing a little bit further. And they were excited about the idea of Andy Wallace coming in. We used more acoustic guitars, and Geddy had quite a lot to say about that and how we should texture them, and which guitars we should use. Also, of course, by that time, they'd got to know me very well, and they knew my taste. On *Power Windows*, they had no idea. They just wanted to find out. But by the time we got to *Test for Echo*, they could almost second-guess what I was going to say. Which happens when you've got a smart band. So there was probably less for me to play with on *Test for Echo*, as a producer."

Interesting comment from Peter, since that's essentially why Terry Brown was not brought back after producing every Rush record up to and including *Signals*: at any sort of decision point, the guys could guess what he was going to say, and they weren't happy with that. And indeed, no one would say there was any sort of exclamation point put on *Test for Echo*, the way there was on *Power Windows* or *Counterparts*. Rather, what the band would end up with is something between *Counterparts* and *Presto* or *Roll the Bones*. In other words, middling. If Kevin Shirley's efforts would be somewhat thwarted, anything Rush or Peter imagined they'd get out of Andy Wallace would be nonexistent, and Clif didn't bring heaviness.

This seems to jibe with Peter's memories of Norrell. "Clif was a first-class engineer who had been working with Andy Wallace; they had done a lot of records together and were a good team. And Clif was more amenable to finding out what was required sonically, whereas Caveman had a fixed idea of what he felt the sound should be, and he was going to do it the way he thought it should be. Clif had a different approach, which I think the band liked for that particular record.

"I always had something to say, whether it was right or wrong," says Peter, who avows that the band appreciated his decisiveness — famously, this was their biggest complaint with Peter Henderson, producer of *Grace Under Pressure*. "I had an opinion. And my sense of accomplishing things in a timely fashion in the studio appealed to them. I had a sense of order and, at the same time, a sense of fun. We had great times making those records, and I think they enjoyed having Mr. Big around for who knows what. I have certain little catchphrases that I live by, things like, 'If you don't love it, it shouldn't be there.' 'If it's not obviously great, it's wrong.' 'When in doubt, leave it out.' And so we could cut to the chase pretty quickly if there were any discussions, 'Is this working? Should we swirl it around in our mouth? Is it great, or isn't it?' If it wasn't, it was gone. I was very black and white — I think that's my production style. If it's not great, it shouldn't be there. We're here to make a masterpiece. And I think that's always been at the forefront with whatever I do, but particularly with Rush. Greatness was very important to them."

Peter also considers himself old school, meaning, "We don't touch the desk. I was trained at Decca Studios in London, where the engineering side was unionized and the production side was not unionized. And because we weren't in the union as 'producer' producers, we weren't allowed to touch the desks. There were tape operators — I was not allowed to touch the tape machines or the desk, as a trainee producer. I would sneak in after hours and fiddle around and learned how to do it, but that was not my interest. I saw the old-school producers coming in with great engineers, or using the house engineers, and I understood the distinction. And I understood that it must be terribly distracting, if you are fiddling around with equipment, to really focus on the performances and on the arrangements. It's all too much. In the early '80s, the engineer/producer was not as prevalent as it is now; it was more producer and separate engineer. Terry Brown was an engineer/producer.

"I have ADD," continues Collins, "and I can only concentrate on one thing at a time. So for me to sit back and really listen to the music, if anything sonically is bothering me, I'll just say to somebody, 'I don't like the way that kick drum sounds; can you do something about it?' And they say, 'Well, what's wrong with it?' 'It's too pointy,' or whatever — very general terms and not technical terms. I would rather talk in general terms to somebody who's very skilled at manipulating sound. I wouldn't say, 'I'm not sure about that five chord.' I would say, 'I think that chord there needs to be darker.' There's a lot of producers who are very hands-on and say, 'Well, I need you to play a walking bass line,' and they would pick up the bass and show them what they were thinking. Which is a style I do admire, but as I said, [Rush] enjoy the challenge of somebody throwing stuff out there, even if it's a bit abstract, and then interpreting. Part of my production style is not to compromise the style of the artists I'm working with, so whatever gets achieved stylistically is their choice, not mine; it's what comes out of them, not what comes out of the producer. I can stimulate them to come up with something, but it's their sound and their art going onto the tape."

For *Test for Echo*'s cover art, Hugh cooked up an amusing homage to Canada and to the relentless snow that plagued the album's writing and recording sessions. Frosty like *Fly by Night* and *Grace Under Pressure*, this one presents a scene from the far north, where an inuksuk, an Inuit rock sculpture used as a marker, sits on the edge of a vast waterway. Squint while examining it and scale is revealed, for it's being climbed by tiny ecotourists, a scene that evokes memories of Blue Öyster Cult's similarly blue and humorous *Cultosaurus Erectus* cover art, where a jet flies past the head of a monster, revealing its mass. Flip to the back, and there are three satellite dishes, which recalls the Very Large Array, another BÖC touchstone, as well as Rush's own "Distant Early Warning." Inside the book, nearly all the value-added imagery references winter in Canada or Canada's north. Though the typestyle hasn't aged well, nor has the fractal image on the CD itself, we'll reserve commentary on how "Virtuality" has aged for later in the chapter (spoiler alert: it squeaks through surprisingly unscathed).

Test for Echo begins with its title track, the guitar instantly recognizable as Alex and his rainy electric picking. We also get an example of the softness and fidelity we're going to be getting out of Neil's Very Large Cymbal Array. Max Webster lyricist Pye Dubois is back again, providing some raw materials, having had a credit on the last album as well — Pye's original idea led to the title "Test the Echo" as well.

Interesting choice as an opener, "Test for Echo," come verse time, is one of Rush's bluesiest songs. There are lots of hard-fit, arguably incongruous parts marbled around this brave musical section, blessed with some great Alex licks from his primordial days as a shiftless teen. At six minutes the song feels a little long, as if the guys are doubling down on trying to sell its clunky transitions. This effect is heightened by the modulation to the last verse, which sounds desperate. Not to harp, but it sounds like there were a lot of opportunities for the band to chuck things that were "not interesting, not great" and to write an absolute classic built around the mournful verse construct.

"You might get a different answer from Neil," explains Geddy, on the titular concept, "but for me, it's a call and response. You know, 'Is anybody out there?' And not only in the sense of outer space. It's like that phrase Will Ferrell used in that movie, 'Am I taking crazy pills?!' You know, am I the only one who sees the insanity in this? It's a little bit about that, and it's a little bit about, 'Is anybody listening?' For me, that's what the song says. It's like a view of things that are happening in our culture through the eyes of the instant media that we get, and the things we see that are not right. And yet it's still going on, still exploited. It's about a lot of things, but to me, it's an out of control media culture thing."

As Neil explained to storied Toronto journalist John Sakamoto, the concept explored on the title track cleverly ties in with the cover art. "I was up in Yellowknife last June on a motorcycle trip across the country, and [there was an] inuksuk above the town, overlooking it, and I was quite taken with it. I bought a postcard almost exactly the image you see on the cover, although this one's been carefully made to incorporate the other elements. I just came back with this postcard and I thought of 'test for echo.' I thought, that's exactly what these men mean when you're out in the wilderness. I had a friend who was hiking out in Baffin Island and he told me when you've been hiking for a few days and you come across one of these things, it's such an affirmation that there's life out there. Again the same thing: it's an echo; the word *inuksuk* means 'in the likeness of a man,' and that's the feeling a traveler in the Arctic would get, that it was a sign of life. The same with the satellite dishes. I was kind of referring to the search for extraterrestrial intelligence and the test for echo going out that way."

"Is there anybody out there?" wrote Peart in the album's tourbook, adding to the explanation. "That's what the title is all about. Everybody needs an 'echo,' some affirmation, to know they're not alone. Sometimes that can be life's most precious discovery — somebody out there who feels the way you do. You ask yourself, 'Am I crazy?,' 'Am I weird?' and you need some affirmation: the echo. While the answer to those questions may still be 'Yes!' it's good to know that you're not the only one. You are not alone. And we're not either. During the making of this record, my partners Geddy and Alex posted some goofy 'inspirational slogans' on the walls of the studio. Like this one: 'Individually, we are a ass; but together, we are a genius.' Like most inspirational slogans, it's hyperbolic (and goofy), but expresses a humble truth. Another previous discovery to make in life: we do our best work together. And have the most fun too (that's the 'genius' part)."

Alex, who plays a Les Paul Custom on the song, quite likes "Test for Echo," calling it "quirky" and "pure Rush." "There is something very energetic about that record from a rhythmic point of view," he adds. "There were quite a few songs in it that had that frenetic energy, things where we tried to be quite heavy and hard, and that was an offshoot from *Victor*."

"Driven" opens with a sinister, circular all-metal riff by Alex, but then the band temper it with a jazzy beat and some octave work from Geddy on bass. There's also a stark bit of acoustic come the pre-chorus, and then a chorus that's a strange melding of pop-punk and a kind of Spanish vibe — the acoustic feels vaguely Spanish guitar as well. There's also a completely unrelated heavy, doomy break, which is underscored by modulation and then textured with some aggressive, counter-rhythmic noise making from Alex. Neil counters the heft of the central premise as well with his ride cymbal off-beats, something that was becoming a signature of his in the '90s. Alex framed what Neil was doing here as behind the beat, reflective of his training with Freddie Gruber. Lifeson says he and Geddy had to adjust what they had in mind after Neil added his parts, but the general feel was taken from the title "Driven."

There's also modulation of earlier themes, a double-speed run at the chorus and then finally at the end, the full muscle car version of the original super-heavy premise, with Geddy and Neil rocking as hard as Alex, who also adds a layer of rip-snortin' guitar noise.

Comments Geddy, "Alex didn't have that frustration he had on the previous records of making that guitar statement. There were certain songs, like 'Driven,' for example, where I was experimenting and writing all these bizarre parts for it and putting it together, and I think the first time during the writing or arranging of the song, Alex actually left the room for a while and said, 'You know, I'm just going to chill.' He came back and I'd kind of put this crazy song together and he got involved in it. There was a confidence, a relaxed attitude he had. I think he was happy to share the responsibility. That whole *Victor* experience was so good for him. He had so much control there, but he was happy to share the control again, you know what I mean? I remember the writing session was amiable; we had a lot of fun. I'm not sure it's the best work, but there are some good songs on there."

"Just from a bass player's point of view," Geddy told Paul Myers, "I wrote that song with three tracks of bass. I brought it to Alex and said, 'Here's the song; I did three tracks of bass but I just did it to fill in for the guitar.' And he said, 'Let's keep it with the three basses.' So I said, 'I love you.' It was really nice to have the blessings of my bandmates to put three tracks of bass on it. I mean, who lets a guy do that in this day and age?" Geddy characterized his part as the root, a harmony, and then more of a bass frequency — the effect is something that sounds like bass chords.

"On 'Driven,' I think, Geddy's bass line arrives, and I kept pushing him. That is how I see my role," continues Collins. "I could push Geddy to come up with stuff that he wouldn't normally come up with. We would have a space for a bass part: 'Geddy, could you be more interesting?' I would challenge them. I wouldn't say, 'What you need to play should be B-flat in the third beat of the fifth bar' or whatever. I would say, 'Do something extraordinary,' and he would do it. The same with all the other guys. They love to be challenged, they love to be pushed, and if I saw an opportunity for it, I would dive in."

Next up is "Half the World," which represents the mean, median and average of the record, since it straddles between electric and acoustic guitars — a dreamy hemisphere of electricity — and blends alternative rock with alternative pop. It's probably the record's most conventionally constructed song, with not too many sections or surprises and Neil only keeping the beat!

As Geddy told Paul Myers, defining the word *straddling*, "'Half the World' is one of our finest moments as songwriters as far as writing a concise song without being wimpy or syrupy. It's got a little bit of everything — nice melody, and yet it's still aggressive. It's hard for us to write that kind of song, really. You'd have to go back to 'Closer to the Heart' to find an example of that."

"I guess in one way that song does relate to what 'Hemispheres' is about," says Geddy, addressing the "counterpart" duality of the lyric, "although 'Hemispheres' was more overtly introspective. 'Half the World' is more of a camera eye visual of the world. It relates in the same fashion. I love this song, I love the melodies of it, I loved writing it. To me, this is one of the types of songs I really like working with. Rush is always torn between its more complex, aggressive side and its softer side. Even though this song is not soft, it's melodic, so I put it in that other category. To me, this is one example where I think we were able to marry slightly edgier sound with that nice, melodic thing, so I was really pleased with this song."

You can hear in that answer why we got — and what we got with — *My Favorite Headache*.

"I think we found a comfort zone and pulled back a little bit," reflects Alex, locating that same sentiment. "I don't think we pushed it over the top like we could have. And I don't know why that happened. I don't know if it was possible or if it was Peter, or just the condition of recording and the way we were feeling. But something did happen that we didn't quite take it over the top on that record."

The studio was a world of wonders, resulting in a Middle Eastern instrument applied to one of the song's middle verses. "Yes, he had a barely workable Mellotron too, which I had to fiddle with a lot actually," recalls Lifeson. "It was in terrible shape. That was such a cool studio. That guy who ran that place bought all this old gear, a very wealthy guy. Over the kitchen, I don't know, he must've had two hundred guitars. Acoustics dating back to the '20s and every model of electric guitar you can imagine. I used a bouzouki that he had there, oh, and some old organ amp . . . not a Farfisa, but a little amp that was designed for an electric organ. It had some really cool sounds and a really cool character to it. I think we actually blew it up. It was old and cheap but it was very cool. I mean, he had violins there and all kinds of instruments, a sitar.

"I just wanted to try it," said Alex, speaking with *Allstar*. "So I just futzed around to get a feel for it, and it changed the whole personality of the song. I remember Ged when he first heard it was like, 'Whoa, I don't know about that.' It was so unusual for a Rush song to have that kind of texture, but it grew on him really quickly. I think it's probably his favorite part of the album."

"This was the first time we've had any time left after we've finished an album," agreed Geddy, in the same chat, "so I was still sitting down in the studio cutting it up and editing it and playing around. But then I would change it 'til my dying day — I'm always looking for that perfect arrangement. And how do you know when you've got the perfect arrangement for a Rush song? It's such a weird arrangement anyway. You can't judge it by conventional standards. It's why having a release date is a really important thing, because it gets it out of my hands."

Artists never finish a project — they just abandon it.

"Though when we do finish an album, I'm really high on it to a certain degree. But I'm also really pissed off at it because it didn't go exactly where I heard it go in my head sometimes. That's partially due to the democratic process, and partially due to the fact that it takes six months to make a bloody album, so by the time you've finished it you've already gone somewhere else."

Speaking with John Sakamoto, Neil said, "In the case of 'Half the World,' there was a line I ran into somewhere that said, 'Half the world hates what the other half is doing,' and I just thought it was beautiful, that one line. In many cases, there is one little quote or one line that the whole thing is built from, and they probably reflect a period of sensitivity to what's going on around me. So the thread that you're chasing there may exist, but I certainly wasn't conscious of it."

As for the acoustic guitar so richly layered into this one, "That was just my taste," shrugs Peter Collins. "I started moving into the singer/songwriter world of production, and I just wanted to hear them, for this particular record. I thought it would be a good character change for the record. I wasn't going to insert acoustic guitar where it wasn't appropriate, but I thought where there was an opportunity, let's do it — just a natural-sounding acoustic; I wanted to get back to it."

Very much so, "The Color of Right" is another one of these alternative electric pop songs that is neither here nor there, but I'm pretty sure Kevin Shirley wouldn't approve. Verses with no beat, with Neil sitting it out — it's happened a lot since *Power Windows* and it happens here. As a compromise — lots of compromising on *Test for Echo* — it's only half the verse, half the world. There's no acoustic guitar, only electric, although Alex chimes a bit, picks a bit — can a song be politely loud? A keyboard wash is a bit distant. Neil's lyric is inscrutable, or rather, the stuff of hemispheres, relationships versus science, or the metaphysical versus the physical.

"Time and Motion" is one of the great *Test for Echo* songs, full up with integrity, more "Double Agent" and King Crimson than "1979" and Collective Soul or Garbage. It's not far off Soundgarden, though it's more mathematical. It's definitely one for us nerds. It's a song that originated a few years before the sessions and was rejected and reworked. Born of the lyric first, it finally emerged here as a favorite of Geddy's, even if it sounds more like something off of *Victor*. Opening themes are returned to at the end, but the last verse finds Peart doubling up on the beat, like in "Driven."

As Neil told John Sakamoto, "A friend of mine once wrote me a letter saying that he'd realized life wasn't about how much you could get out of a day, but how much you can pack *into* it. And I thought that was really cool and I used that of course in the song 'Time and Motion': 'Like boxcars in a train / Fill them up with precious cargo.'"

"Time and Motion" houses what is perhaps Alex's coolest guitar solo since the *Grace Under Pressure* album's many. Carnal, slashing, noisy like Alex should be, but just perfect in its short space. Peter Collins figures, "Alex, to me he's Alex 'Nugget' Lifeson — you would get from him a little gold nugget of fantastic stuff, which sometimes you had to mine out of the gold field. Geddy was also great at doing brilliant stuff — you had to just look and it was there. Alex would just be free to play, and then Alex and I would go gold mining for those nuggets. I thought that was a very workable process, and I didn't sense any resistance from Alex. But Alex would come in and listen to what we compiled, and if he didn't like something, then we would have another option. But he needs to explode and just be Big Al.

"Ged would get involved, but I don't remember Neil getting involved in the guitar solos," continues Collins. "Neil and I and Alex would be involved in the vocal comps of Geddy, and I don't know if Rupert was the same, but I had Geddy leave the room when he comped, and he would come around and have a listen, and if he didn't like it, we would go back in. But I don't remember Neil being there on the guitar parts, to be honest with you.

"Sometimes Alex will do very abstract stuff, some of which works and some of which doesn't. The fact that he is mentally free to just have a stream of consciousness in terms of his guitar playing is a beautiful thing — I loved it. It was time consuming but very well worth it. Geddy could hear things that I didn't think were going to work at all, but by the time they were assembled, it made perfect sense. Geddy had a good vision of how to assemble those nuggets."

This modern-day analysis from Peter lines up well with the way Alex himself saw it back in 1996. Speaking on his tendency to just play and see what works, he says, "That's something I recognized in myself, but the other guys recognized that in me as well. I think they feel it's my job, when we're writing, to be aware of that. And they expect it from me. I could come up with a riff or something spontaneous and then Ged could take it someplace else. And that's the reason Rush works so well. Those connections this time around seem much more fluid and cleaner than they have in the past. The music sometimes tends to sound a little chunky. There's much more flow to the material this time around.

"During the *Signals* era I felt frustrated, but it was my fault," continues Lifeson, sort of charting a brief history of how he arrived at his place in the mix circa *Test for Echo*. "I should've stood up for what I felt. In all fairness, we were trying different things, experimenting more with keyboards, which were relatively new. That whole technology was new and how you applied it was new. I certainly didn't want to feel closed-minded about it. In retrospect, *Signals* was one of my least favorite records for a lot of reasons, and not just because the guitars were weak.

"The period with *Power Windows* and *Hold Your Fire* was elaborate. I changed my guitar sound around that time, going for a thinner, spikier sound. Part of that was because I couldn't fit into the same range the keyboards were in. We made the mistake of doing the keyboards before doing the guitars, only because of convenience. We were doing beds in England, and I was left with this very dense material that I had to fit the guitar into. And I thought I was one of the key people here. I was used to going into the studio with thirty percent prepared and doing everything on the day, and that was part of the fun of recording. That kind of density to the music didn't allow that approach anymore, so I had to prepare myself much better.

"The last few records we've done, I'm much more prepared when I go in. I have all my parts worked out. I have a very clear map of where things are going to go and if they're going to work. We can experiment a little bit on the day, but I have a much clearer picture of the material. Now they feel that the guitar parts are already done. That's because I've come out of my project with more confidence and a better idea of how I want to assemble everything before actually recording. It's certainly a great pat on the back that the guitar parts are as strong as they are."

With "Totem" we are back to the happy, hummable but somewhat electric vibe of "Driven," "Half the World" and "The Color of Right," only now there's more acoustic guitars and another evocation of a Celtic vibe. Agrees Alex, speaking with *Canadian Musician*, "The choruses in 'Totem' are really interesting. I created a soundscape by using harmonics with a kind of Celtic melody over it that's quite distant. In the song, in terms of dynamics, it's a really beautiful shift. Listening to it in cans, there's this line, 'angels and demons inside my head,' that was very visual to me — it's almost angelic. You can sort of see this imagery swirling around. I wanted quite a different character to the way I approached the guitars this time. I really wanted to combine acoustics with heavy electrics. I wanted the rhythmic aspect of the guitars to stand out a bit more. I used it quite a bit as kind of a flavor for the whole record. I think there are only about three or four songs that we used keyboards in; the rest is just guitars."

"Alex rediscovered just how heavy the acoustic can be," adds Lee. "A well-strummed acoustic can be really heavy; it doesn't always have to be a pretty little sound. Some of my favorite Who records have these huge acoustics. Pete Townshend has always been the quintessential rock songwriter, the Paul Simon of rock. And we were going for more of a drier, up-front sound, a bit of a throwback to earlier albums. Guitars did the job well. We threw out the paddiness and used keyboards more for counterpoint melodies, and not to just fill up space. There's keyboards on 'Limbo' and on 'Test for Echo' but they're very subtle. I think in one sense we eliminated the textural stuff because we found it was soaking up the guitar space."

Alex now figures, "With *Test for Echo* we were getting back to the core three-piece, even less keyboards now, but we were also attempting some interesting arrangements for songs — and

'Totem' is a good example. That really stood out as a very cool, very rhythmic kind of song. A lot of the record is very quick, rhythmic kind of parts. And you know, when we finished it, it left a couple of holes in me. There were a couple of weak areas . . . in retrospect when I think about it now, Peter had commented on a couple of things, and he was right."

"I've always been curious about all religions," Neil told John Sakamoto, "and the 'Totem' idea came from the Freud book *Totem and Taboo*, which I ran across at the Chalet Studio where we were working, just in the bookshelf in the living room. I had been kind of rediscovering Freud by way of Jung and getting to understand the really deep stuff he was dealing with as opposed to some of the pop psychology that we were fed growing up. And I thought *Totem and Taboo* was such a beautiful title because it's what we fear and what we worship, totem being what we worship and taboo being what we fear. What a beautiful, embracing metaphor.

"At one time, the song 'Resist' was called 'Taboo' because I wanted to have the two little set pieces of what we fear," continues Peart. "And in 'Totem' I was just trying to appropriate all religions because that's what I found looking around at different religions and different systems, is that they all have something good. So I thought why not have them all? The 'Buddha smile' is a nice thing, and I'd like to have twelve apostles — it's all great. It was really just kind of tongue-in-cheek, with all the good things of different religions. And the elements of the angels and demons came from a writer who once drew a great parallel between the good Goofy and the bad Goofy, just like in the Disney cartoons. There was a good Goofy on his shoulder telling him to do good things and a bad Goofy telling him to do bad things. I like that as far as angels and demons go, which I think all of us definitely do have."

"Dog Years" finds the band turning up the heat, creating a wall of sound but drenched in melody as per Geddy's fence-straddling mandate. In effect, through the unique coterie of production and arrangement choices made, Rush is again creating a space for themselves no one else could — or would — dare crowd. All the tones are soft, yet technically we're hearing a power trio playing energetically. It's a conundrum.

At the lyric end, Neil makes no apologies for his most ridiculed tone poem, well beyond dining on honeydew or drinking the milk of paradise en route to a last-place tie with "Tai Shan." Truth is, there are a ton of amusing but pointed observations amidst the bad puns. And if you don't get that, try having a sense of humor.

As Neil told Jill Robinson, thinking about his seven-year-old Husky, Nick, "I try to weave it in on several levels, so certainly the listener is welcome to take it just as a piece of throwaway foolishness. That's in there. Even the story of its writing is kind of amusing, because it was right when we got together for the first time, the three of us, after quite a long break apart. We did a little celebrating the first night, and the following day I was a bit the worse for wear and a little dull-witted, and I thought, 'Gee, I don't think I'm going to get much done today, but I'm a professional; I'd better try.' So I sat down all muzzy-headed like that and started trying to stitch words together — that's what I was there for, after all.

"'Dog Years' is what came out of that kind of mentality, and born of observations over the years too, of looking at my dog thinking, 'What's going through his brain?' And I would think, 'Just a low-level zzz — static.' 'Food.' 'Walk.' The basic elemental things. When I look at my dog, that's how I see his brainwaves moving. Other elements in there of dog behavior, and I've had this discussion with other dog owners too: 'What do you think your dog is really thinking about?' I say, 'I don't think he's think-ing about too much.'"

Asked by John Sakamoto about the line "We get it backwards / And our seven years go by like one," Peart explains, "That came from a columnist in the *New York Times*. She was riffing on about things and she said she's getting tired of living in dog years, where every seven years seem to go by like one. And I thought it was a beautiful little image."

Neil adds that upon pondering the lyric for the first time in his hungover muddle, "I wasn't sure at the end of it if it was stupid or smart, but I liked it and it definitely made me smile, so I passed it along to the other guys and they had the same response. That was just an example of sitting down not in the right frame of mind for creative work but forcing myself to go through the motions and something different came out of it."

"The humor aspect was great," chuckles Peter. "The one about the dog, 'Dog Years.' You know, usually the humor is reserved for the instrumentals and the liner notes, but there were a couple of real tongue-in-cheek songs."

There are all sorts of eyewinks in this one, including a roll call of clichés, various puns, and a quick tribute to *Signals*, with the line "One sniff at the hydrant." Best, however, is "In the dog days, people look to Sirius."

"Virtuality" doesn't get the respect it deserves given Neil was writing a song about the internet when the internet was barely getting started. Such is Rush, always the early adopters. Sometimes they win with that formula (*Signals*) and sometimes they get burned by it (*Hold Your Fire*). Quite admirably, Neil penned a song back then that doesn't even read as dated now, despite so many minefields he could have stepped on. There's no fax tones, no mention of AOL or MySpace, just a thoughtful message that rings even more true today. He even gets in a nod to English punker Elton Motello, whose single "Jet Boy, Jet Girl" was a minor sensation around Toronto in 1979 because the album *Victim of Time* got wide distribution as an Attic Records release.

When Jill Robinson asked if Neil spent much time surfing the net (I'm surprised that language was used in 1996), he says, "No, ironically, or perhaps not ironically, having got the message of the song itself. But I certainly do dabble in anything new that comes along, and I spent a bit of time getting netted and explored around just to see what it could do. Just couldn't resist poking a little fun at its pretensions."

The song warns people not to replace reality with this new-fangled technology.

"That's where my quarrels lay," continues Peart, "because I think it is going to be the most excellent video game in the world when things like that are available. When I think about traveling to places, and thinking how would you translate Palermo, Sicily, or Abidjan, Ivory Coast, to virtual reality, the first thing they'd do would be to take away the smells, the garbage, and de-funkify it all, make it all Disneyfied. That might make an ultimate video game, but it cannot possibly even approximate my experiences of those places. No virtual reality can take you to the top of Kilimanjaro or to Tiananmen Square, or to the heart of the Sahara. None of these places is accessible any other way but by suffering for it.

"For me to pretend there's an easy way to any more than approximate it, it can't be any more than a book or a movie or a TV documentary, except magnified of course. Maybe you can add smells and sounds, and maybe you can add the feeling of the wind, and so on. That would be great, I have no problem with that, I love things like that. It'll be a great sensual experience. My only quarrel comes with people who tend to pretend that it is as good as reality, and nothing's that good.

"I see their wonderfulness with no problem at all," qualifies Neil. "I see why they're really cool and lots of fun. It's just that differentiation between reality and virtual reality, as I said before, it can't be as good. And sometimes it can't be as bad. I've had some really nasty experiences in parts of the world that might have been Disneyfied a little for my enjoyability, but the fact is that's how they are. That's part of the experience: part of the suffering getting to these places is what you have to endure.

"I mentioned Palermo, Sicily, because I was there recently. The people were so great; the place itself just had a charm. When I was coming back into the town after being out in Sicily for the day I was thinking, 'Wow, this place is dirty and smelly and funky, but I love it!' It just won me over despite any flaws, and that would be a case of where reality is rife with reality, where all the dark sides of things are very present, to be endured or just wrapped into your package of things. All of these sides of Palermo, for instance, just made it more charming to me. That's just the way it was."

Reflecting on the line "I can smell her perfume, I can taste her lips, I can feel the voltage from her fingertips," Neil says, "That's a perfect one to dwell on, because it points out a lot of the irony of what I was trying to get across. What happens in an email relationship or something is that imagination, of course, is called upon to make it come alive. Imagination is a wonderful thing, but it's also slightly dangerous because it invites illusions. I love the image that verse opens up with, seeing a woman's face through the window in the rain; that's a really romantic image. I've had that experience, seeing a woman driving by in a car, or if I'm driving by and see a woman in the window, it's a beautiful thing. The same experience if I'm riding my bicycle down the road and a car goes by. Sometimes I'll smell a woman's perfume. Imagination, though, is a little bit of sense input, but the rest of it, if you put anything more into it, it's just imagination. All I was pointing out there is, here's a romantic little image that is imagined, so let's not pretend that it's real. You cannot feel the voltage from her fingertips, but you can imagine it. That's all I was trying to say."

At the other end of the spectrum, "Resist" is a rare, lush ballad for Rush, the band pulling out all the stops and avoiding anything trite. Instead, "Resist" is in the passionate spirit of "The Pass" or "Bravado," maybe better because it doesn't try to be a rock song. Says Neil, speaking with John Sakamoto, "I took the Oscar Wilde quote ('I can learn to resist anything but temptation') and added that I can learn to resist. In other words, the exercise of will is the weapon against futility or helplessness. Maybe I can't resist temptation, but I can learn to get along with what I don't know, and I thought that was a really important distinction."

Alex was really pleased with this one, calling it one of his favorite Rush songs. At the beginning, he plays a hammer dulcimer. On the *Vapor Trails* tour, Geddy and Alex surprised everybody by deciding to do the song acoustically after Neil's drum solo, a performance that proved popular with the fans — indeed, this is a beautiful Rush song and quite novel in construction for the band.

Next is a near-instrumental called "Limbo," or Rush "Limbo," pun intended. The sound effects at the beginning are from "Monster Mash," as is the fairly buried line "Whatever happened to my Transylvania twist?" The song was assembled as a hodgepodge of parts the guys had lying around, and it really doesn't go anywhere. It certainly is not a follow-up to "Where's My Thing?" and "Leave That Thing Alone" — it's too casual and ragged.

Test for Echo closes with "Carve Away the Stone," another one of the record's difficult but vaguely spiritual constructs, melodic but on the serious and heavy side. A sluggishness is maintained through a jagged, jammy quality, not least of which is Neil's replacement of snare with toms, his many switch-ups of the beat and his spirited end of bar fills. Alex is gloriously noisy as well, turning the song into some sort of psychedelic excursion. The exhaustive quality to the musical track makes sense, given that Neil is essentially retelling the story of Sisyphus rolling a stone up a mountain, though with a twist — the song encourages active participation in lessening one's burdens, telling Sisyphus to "chip away the stone." This theme of creating your own luck through preparation is a sort of reprise of one of the main lessons of *Roll the Bones*.

Once *Test for Echo* was committed to tape, all fifty minutes of it, it was time to mix. "Yes, and I'm not sure that I'd locked Andy Wallace into the mixing at that point," says Peter. "But that was really important for me to take this punchy organic sound another stage further. Andy Wallace was instrumental, in my mind, in getting to that point. And also working out the arrangements, trying to keep them as . . . I won't say as simple as possible because that's against their whole credo, but I wanted to bring in more acoustic guitar. And so I would look for opportunities in the arrangement to do that.

"With Rush, within what they do, to make it as heavy as possible was always the objective," Collins adds, which sounds somewhat incredulous — not sure how adding acoustic guitar helps us get there, and not sure, frankly, that Andy Wallace did anything to heavy up the sound of the record. Two things were happening though: (1) the guys were pretty fed up with listening to these songs that, as Alex puts it, they had lived with for six or seven months, and they wanted that objective ear, and (2) indeed the concern, communicated to Wallace, was to have the record not sound too layered and therefore dense. Though *Test for Echo* sounds pretty much as dense as any other Rush record, the last time we heard the band sound really electric and separated and power trio–like was on parts of *Moving Pictures*, on all of side one except for "Tom Sawyer."

Recalls Alex, of the mix, which took place in April of '96, "I think that's the first time Ged didn't feel like he had to be in the control room all the time, and he wasn't. And I think it was good for him. I think it gave him a lot of relief. For him it's always been difficult in the studio because he's always so intense about the mix and where it's going, and he finally let go on that record. And I think he's much more relaxed and better for it."

It's hard to find much good or bad to say about *Test for Echo*'s mix. One could call it bright and lively, even electric and sizzly, but there's something about what each of the guys chooses to play at any given point that ensures the record doesn't achieve heaviness, despite what was or wasn't done at the mixing stage. There's the pop melody, to be sure, but there are all these verse sections with barely a beat, or a sparse beat . . . heck, even undecided beats, where different things are tried throughout the songs. At times, it's almost as if they're demos from which they'd then start making decisions. There are also lots of stops and starts and switch-ups in mood, which add to this vibe of indecision. Modulation can sound like the result of searching for something. And then as a microcosm, back around to the mix, even *that* sounds noncommittal.

That said, there are some beautiful passages, some heavy passages and some great tones, especially with the acoustic guitars and Neil's cymbals. And you have to commend the band for making a very different record from *Counterparts* or indeed any record before or after. And as always with Rush, the story on *why* it's different is long and complicated.

"There was still a lot going on in the band creatively and expressively in the songs we were writing," offers Neil, summing up. "I like the lyrics. I've said before that for me the first Rush album is really *Moving Pictures*. When I start to like my lyrics is probably around that time. And then from *Test for Echo* on, there's a greater maturity and much more control of the techniques and the craft of putting words together in interesting ways, as well as effective ways of not hitting people over the head but still making sure there was a hammer in there. That's good too."

"I think part of it was being productive," answers Geddy, asked why he felt the need to come back after his domestic time away. "It was hard for Alex coming back to that because he had so much control making *Victor*, and so *Test for Echo* was a tough record. It was a tough record to write and a slightly unfocused record. And that's maybe reflected in the diversity of where our heads were at the time. I don't want to say we were going through the motions, but it's as close as we came to going through the motions. There were some great moments, and there was some really inspired playing on that record, but it's somehow or another unsatisfying in totality. Not one of my fondest periods, creatively, for Rush.

"There was a bit of evidence of that burnout still. We probably needed another year before we came back. I mean, *Test for Echo* is kind of an adventurous project, and the whole idea of it was pretty exciting, but I never got the feeling that we really nailed that. It's one of those projects that was great on paper, but I haven't listened to it in a long time. That's a personal feeling. My feelings about the record are mine, you know? I think it's a decent record, but I don't think it's one of our best. And why that is, I don't know. Maybe I had been too immersed in diaper changing.

"But we liked the record when we finished it," continues Ged. "We were happy with it at the time, and touring it was fun, so there was no doom and gloom about the band. When you look back and you talk about Alex's progression as a guitar player and the things we kind of forced him to change, it makes sense to go through to his solo record and get that whole total control. It made a lot of sense for him to be doing that record. After that it's like the bubble had burst for him and he was quite happy. Through the making of *Test for Echo*, he was in quite a good frame of mind, and on that tour he was in a good frame of mind.

"*Counterparts* was a satisfying record to make, in the end, in terms of what it did for our sound. *Test for Echo* was, I guess, a bit of status quo. It didn't seem like we broke down any great barriers with that record. I don't think we advanced the cause of Rush to a tremendous degree. But at the same time, things personally were good. I had a little baby at home, I was pretty happy, we just moved into a new house. Alex was feeling confident as a musician — he'd been working with a lot of other players. Neil was in a good space too."

"You finish the record and you move on to the next record," reflects Peter Collins, never to produce another Rush record. "And you stay in touch, the odd phone call, the odd email. So no, after mastering, I kind of went back home and they were doing their thing. I really didn't get much sense other than it was a very positive atmosphere when we finished the record and everybody seemed very happy. I went off to London to do a few projects, and that was it."

The *Test for Echo* tour saw the band spend October '96 until the end of the year covering a large chunk of America, with the Yule season spent in Ontario and Quebec (December 18 saw the band play a Molson-sponsored club gig in Toronto as part of the beer brand's Blind Date promotion). May '97 saw a similar jaunt, again through all parts of the U.S., winding up in Central Canada to close things out in late June and early July. The *Test for Echo* dates were billed as "An Evening with Rush," meaning no back-up act, Rush playing for a superhuman two and a half to three hours every night, traveling by private jet for the first time ever, a well-deserved perk given the nightly workout.

"That was the first tour we did that way," says Geddy, "where there was no opening act and we had two sets. We could actually indulge ourselves a little bit and try to invent some sort of dramatic or teasing beginning to the second set. We used 'Test for Echo' to open that second set, I believe. The big kind of production for that tour was the film we made for that song. We had fun using some kind of multimedia thing, exploiting the concept of that song into a fine combo of video and sound. Good tour. We had a lot of fun, a better vibe than we had had previous tours. I have really good, strong memories from that tour.

"Having to play long shows is good, and we played really well. That was the greatest decision we ever made. You know, we have so many albums, so much music. I was always so frustrated. You put your body and your life through all this torture and all this traveling around. And the yin and yang of what touring is, you get up onstage, you play for a little bit and it's over. It's like a cheat. You don't feel like you really got your money's worth. 'An Evening with' is getting your money's worth, and the crowd is getting their money's worth. You can play so much more stuff and you can get into a real groove.

"And especially having two sets. Both sets sometimes have very different feels to them. That twenty-minute break in the middle, if you've had a rough first half and you've had the twenty-minute break to get your head together, you can go and have a great second half. They're like two different shows in a way and I really love it. It's like extended touring for us because we get onstage earlier, so there's a lot less waiting around backstage and a lot less wear and tear because of that, a lot less boredom. It's hard on Neil, because of how hard he works, and it's harder on my voice, but in the end, it's well worth it.

"Our fans love it because we can go back into past albums," continues Ged, on the benefits. "We can dig up nuggets from the past or change arrangements of some songs or really stretch out. That was the first time we were able to play a bunch of songs and do '2112' as well. That helped us come to terms with who we were and who we are, and I think in a very positive, balanced way. It's good for the fans; it's good for us. We love to play. And it was nice to get on earlier; that was a big motivator for me.

"Our manager didn't like it," chuckles Ged, of Ray Danniels, who, if you think about it, is cursed with that sort of "bad cop" role with the band, if he's doing his job right. "He might tell you now that he liked it. Just like my mom, he doesn't remember those things. No, no manager likes it because if you have an opening act that can sell a few tickets, you know, it's just insurance that you're going to have a full house. But I think we convinced him that we would be so much happier and he could get more dates out of us. And in the end, that's better for him, so he kind of went along with it. And it's true — it *is* better for us; it makes us happier.

"But Neil has always struggled with being on the road, and that tour was no different. He couldn't wait for it to be over. But that didn't influence how he played night to night. He certainly was always happy to come off the road at the end of the tour. But I recall it was a very positive tour — we played well and we sounded good, with more focus on the band and getting through our whole repertoire of music."

Peart had found his own novel method of making the road spectacular, having recently become a long-distance motorcycle madman. "When the next concert tour came up, the wheels started turning," explains Neil. "How can I combine this sort of adventure touring with concert touring? And I thought, okay, if I had a bus with a trailer and a friend with me to look after the bikes and navigation, and plan the days off . . . My friend Bruce came out for the *Test for Echo* tour, and we did forty thousand miles on that tour, just in America, riding every day, five hundred miles on a day off, three hundred miles on show day, just dying from lack of sleep.

"I was thinking about traveling by motorcycle. But the logistics of doing that . . . in the past, the three of us had always traveled together on the tour bus and now the other guys wanted to fly. I really don't like flying so that was an easy agreement. 'Okay for now you guys fly and I'll travel by motorcycle.'

"But how to do that? As I say, I got a bus with a trailer so after a show I could sleep on the bus in a truck stop or somewhere like that, and then unload the motorcycle from the trailer in the morning and tell the bus driver, 'Okay, I want to be on this little road.' Of course, I don't just want to ride the interstates and freeways. I want the back roads, the smallest towns, the smallest roads, the most remote destinations, all of that.

"So eventually it evolved, the logistics to make that possible and to get enough sleep in between, getting up early and riding all day and playing a show. And when your day peaks at eleven o'clock at night, you're not going to go to sleep right away. I seldom get to sleep until two o'clock in the morning, but I like to get up at eight and get a day's riding in, so sleep has to be caught up somewhere. And especially a few tours ago we didn't have as many days off as we do now, so I would be in the dressing room before the show, and if I had twenty minutes free I would set my alarm clock for twenty minutes and sleep for twenty minutes, wake up, warm up, go onstage. My bus driver, he can sleep anytime. He just crawls in his bunk and sleeps for eight hours. In the middle of the day, in the middle of the night, it doesn't matter, because it's what he has to do.

"But it's such a source of adventure to me," continues Peart. "Every day is an adventure. I just have this hunger to see what that road on the map looks like in real life. For the last four tours and well over a hundred thousand miles now, I've been going from show to show, here and in Europe, by motorcycle. It just fills the day in such a healthy way. I'm filled with stimulation and input all day; I'm out there dealing with the real world. My life's on the line and it's as existential as you can get, motorcycling. If it's raining or cold or windy, I'm the first to know about it.

"But the smell of the flowers, and in the last couple of days riding through Saskatchewan and Alberta, the smell of the manure, the smell of fresh hay and the horses in the fields . . . it's pretty much May now, so it's late spring/early summer and the bright color of Canadian summer that is particular to this time of the year . . . The lilacs were in bloom a little bit south in North Dakota and Minnesota, and one of my favorite smells in the world is lilac.

"It's such a fulfilling way to pass the time and so free too — I leave after the show on the bus, and I'm on my own. I have my bus driver and my riding partner and we go to some truck stop, and then I go stay at some little town in a cheap motel that night. As long as I show up for work the next day, no one cares and no one knows where I am that night. That's one of the nicest feelings. At the beginning of the R30 tour — I wrote about it in *Roadshow* — the first day off we were down in Tennessee and just took off riding all day and that night settled in a Best Western hotel in Sweetwater, Tennessee. And my thought was nobody even knows where I am.

"It's liberating, especially when there is a crushing kind of insularity about touring. You're traveling around with a group of fifty people who are together all the time, every day. And the bickering and the inevitable office politics are of course a part of this life like any other. It's a traveling company going around. They used to call it a touring company in the theater sense and it's very true. And the expectations of people who would like to invade my life, you know, become my new best friend and all that, I'm so free of all that.

"But on the other hand, I don't have to isolate myself. It doesn't have to be like Roger Waters wrote about in *The Wall*, that sense of alienation. I'm out with people every day, but I'm one of them; I'm not, 'Hey, you're that famous guy.' I'm in gas stations and motels and restaurants. I talk to people every day, as people, and that's wonderful. As much as I'm shy and reserved, that doesn't apply to strangers. I'm perfectly happy to pass the time of day with somebody at a gas station.

"Anonymity is great, especially if you fancy yourself a writer," muses Neil. "I like to observe, I like to listen and eavesdrop or be part of casual conversations. My little stories for the website. Like we were in Illinois last summer, some country gas station, a little crossroads town. This old lady is filling up her Buick and here's two hulking guys going to fill up their motorcycles, big leather suits, and it's intimidating as it could be. And this old, white-haired woman looks over and says, 'I'll pay for yours if you pay for mine.' And it was just the most charming moment. I hold onto collections of those, pretty much daily, when I have some nice little encounter with someone, just as a person, and I love that.

"And it just feels artificial to me, these encounters whenever anyone does recognize me. Robert Redford described it once: 'They just go all goofy, you know?' And then I just get embarrassed. Who needs to feel that way? No one does. The other guys are obviously comfortable with it and they do the meet-and-greets every night. They're much more comfortable with that whole thing than I am, and fine, you know, they can do it and I can hide behind drums or I can hide behind my helmet and stay away from uncomfortable situations."

The prime motivation for Neil's motorcycle trips, rather

than the bicycle, was the ability to pack those grinding days on tour with experiences, and hopefully some of them would be extraordinary.

"I remember one time," says Neil, by way of example, "we had a break in the tour, and we were in Durango, Colorado, and we had to ride to Cincinnati for the next show. We stayed there with our wives for a few days, and we had three days to do the ride. And we're looking at a map, and I was looking at Mount Rushmore and thinking, 'Bruce, do you think we can get from Durango to Mount Rushmore and then to Cincinnati?' 'Yeah, I think we can do it.' We had to because we wanted to go to Mount Rushmore. When I have a day off, I want to do the most excellent thing possible. I used to sleep twenty minutes between soundcheck and dinner, and then twenty minutes between dinner and warm-up before the show — sleep anytime I could get it. Because we were up early every day and riding vast distances, but seeing so much.

"And it's another thing I said about concerts: you don't know if this is the only time you'll ever do this, so you don't want to miss anything. You want to hit every state, see every attraction from Grand Canyon to Mount Rushmore to the Hoover Dam. Nothing was beyond reach the first time.

"I learned better how to do it, of course, and every tour since, I've traveled that way. Always with a riding partner with another bike. So nothing has ever happened, but if it does, I can still take his bike and get to the show. That's the only big responsibility. You've got a lot of people waiting for you to show up for work. You can't mess around. I have to watch the distances on the show day and make sure they are doable, that kind of thing. But the freedom to feed my curiosity too, and the natural world of North America and Europe, while we are touring, is just phenomenal, to be able to do that."

And as everybody's been telling us, Neil's always had some real animosity for the road. "Yes, well, I can't imagine touring without having my motorcycle, honestly. *Test for Echo* was in '96, and the number of tours we've done since then, and the number of independent travels I've done on motorcycles since then . . . I must admit, when I get the itinerary, I look at the days off. The day off in between, great, I can ride. Because touring, again, I'm not jaded about it. I love preparing for a tour, I love the rehearsing and getting to that performance state. And when we first start flocking together in rehearsal, it's magic. I wouldn't have it any other way; I love all that.

"But for me having done a good show, it's 'Okay, done that,'" laughs Neil. "It's the repetition that gets to me. And of course, we traveled around the U.S. so many times, and in my bicycle travels over twenty years, twenty-five years ago, and then motorcycling for the last twelve, thirteen years, I've seen a lot of those roads. And usually, it's an unfamiliar road that is most attractive. So when we are on the east coast for example, you've got a day off between Pittsburgh and Boston, that can be challenging to find different ways. And I'm thinking about the route I would take. I would go through Appalachia Park, northwest corner of Massachusetts. That's how I think of the itinerary. I see the map. I described the road once as a book of dreams. And it's true for me; I'm thinking, 'Oh, where can I get to today?'"

Back at the office, besides the swallowing up of the support act space, Rush also used an increasingly sophisticated array of live camera footage, complex video, lasers and strobes. The shows opened once again with the "Also sprach Zarathustra" intro music, followed by "Dreamline." Tracks from the new album that made the first of the band's two sets were "Driven," "Half the World," "Limbo" and "Virtuality." An intermission followed, featuring B-movie trailers and the ubiquitous drive-in classic

"Let's All Go to the Lobby and Have Ourselves a Snack." The *Test for Echo* tracks in the second set were the title track, "Time and Motion" and "Resist," although the latter two only on occasion. "The Big Money" would be replaced by "Limelight" for the second half of the tour, and the impromptu "Wipeout!" was replaced with "Stick It Out." "Subdivisions" would be dropped for the second leg, with "Red Sector A" getting moved from the first to the second set.

"*Test for Echo* was a hard but satisfying tour," remembers Neil. "I thought we really played well on the tour, and I remember I documented this tour in journals and planned to write a book about it, so I have a lot of documentation on it. I remember writing notes in my journal about listening to the shows and how well Geddy was singing and how well we were playing. Very satisfying in that respect, but at the same time grueling physically. There were a lot of shows and I had the elbow problem going on toward the end, so I was in pain. But we did play really well."

Neil elaborates on his injury. "The whole end of the *Test for Echo* tour, I was wearing an elbow brace because I was getting tendinitis. But I was so glad I could play all right. You know, it hurt, but it would be much worse if I couldn't play right — that would be crushing. And I've never, fortunately, faced anything that was physically debilitating, feeling like I can't do the job. That would be an awful thing to face, much worse than a limitation of hardware or an injury. That injury hurt like hell but I could still play, right? That's all that mattered. I made that journal note at the time."

Fortunately, the elbow healed to Peart's satisfaction. "Oh, yeah! I had to really abuse the thing for months, night after night. How many times in the course of a show do I hit something as hard as I can with my right hand? You know, thousands, tens of thousands of times. So yeah, there was residual pain and recovery and all that. But I was glad to be able to do the job, to my satisfaction at least, no matter how stupid I looked with a big elbow brace and how much it hurt. That's not the point; I'm not there to feel good. I'm not there to have fun, you know?"

On the evolution of his famed drum solo up to this point, Neil explained that "every tour it gets restructured and largely recomposed, at least as a framework. I remember, at the beginning of *Vapor Trails*, I went back and listened to the solo I was doing on *Test for Echo*. And I thought, well, I'm really not finished with that framework. As far as I'm concerned, that's okay; I can go forward with that, and it still represents a vehicle of expression and exploration for me. And then I thought no, no, I can't do that. So I did take it all apart, and the parts that I kept, I reconfigured or reorchestrated or whatever.

"To me, it's a performance piece in that each tour has a different structure, but there's always a structure for the tour that gets built on. And I feel it's developed as I develop certain ideas and experiment with others, in the course of it. Because it, unlike a song, has a fixed structure of turning points and transitions and movements, but the content is not structured. It's not at all remembered. I know when I switch to a mode — okay, this is the snare drum/bass drum part; okay, go into that. But that's whatever comes out. That's a way of being structured and loose at the same time.

"And I've done that in the studio the last couple of records. For example, on 'Resist' on *Test for Echo*, I worked and rehearsed and rehearsed and rehearsed that song, and I worked out every possible kind of fill that might work. But I didn't allow myself to orchestrate them so that when I played them in the studio, I didn't know. I knew what would work, but I didn't know how it was going to come out. That's an example of how the drum solo is. I've worked out the structure of it and the arrangements and the transitions — that remains constant — but the content of the movements is strictly whatever comes out of me that night."

A career highlight for the band would take place on February 26, 1997, when Alex, Geddy and Neil were presented with their country's highest honor, the Order of Canada, both for (quietly) raising over a million dollars for charities over the years and (loudly) being Rush. The guys had long been rock heroes championing their roots, but now they were to be recognized as established and exemplary Canadians in a much wider realm, outside of mere entertainment, now part of the national fabric of the country that made a more than workable place for Geddy's and Alex's parents as immigrants.

A similarly patriotic milestone would be met in May of 2012, when the band was ushered into Rideau Hall to receive the Governor General's Performing Arts Award for Lifetime Artistic Achievement. This was followed the next year by their own Canadian postage stamp, featuring the Starman of *2112*.

"I don't think that after *Test for Echo* the intention was to take a very long break," says Alex, inevitably alluding to the tragedies that were to present themselves upon Neil and necessarily the band. "We enjoyed making *Test*; it was a very fun record to make, good vibe in the studio. The tour was great; doing 'An Evening with' was really a lot of fun for us. It gave us a chance to play stuff like '2112' in its entirety ['Natural Science' was brought back as well]. The tour went really, really well. We were healthy through the whole thing, and we got to the end of it fine. I think we were planning on taking a relatively short break and then back in for the next record. No one could know that what happened would happen."

What happened was that on August 10, 1997, Neil's only child at the time, daughter Selena Taylor, was killed in a car accident. Unthinkably, Neil's inconsolable wife, Jackie, succumbed to cancer less than a year later. Subsequently, Neil has expressed the unfathomably sad sentiment that, in fact, Jackie had died of a broken heart.

"That tour, it was mellow, it was good," reflects Geddy. "That's why that whole thing came out of . . . it was such a lightning strike. Just threw everything apart. I mean, there's no good time for that to happen, but we were in a good space. Maybe that helped, in a way, because there was no bitterness, there was no animosity, there was no backbiting between us. So when that terrible moment occurred, you can just think of him, and be there for him as his friend. You know, there was no frustration with, oh, what can we do? What do we do for him? And can we ease his pain in some way?"

Agrees Alex, "We were coming off a tour that was very positive, off of a record we felt good about. We were all in good health and in a good mental state. I think we came off tour with a little reserve energy. We were feeling really positive about whatever we were going to do next. So that made the whole thing that followed that much more devastating."

Alex remembers getting a message to call the office, and that it was urgent. "I think Geddy was away at his cottage, so he was sort of out of the loop. I called a very close friend of mine who had gone through the same thing years previously and asked him for some advice. And he was instrumental in helping me deal with it, and to find the right things to say and the right things to do. Because it's a terrible, terrible extreme to go through. So I visited them that night. I didn't go in. I slipped a note under the door, just so they knew I was there and I was there for them, and they reached out to me the following morning. And from that point on, I was there every day for two weeks. And we all took on our own responsibilities within that house of pain. It was awful; it was very, very hard.

"The funny thing is, it's as if the band didn't even exist, at that moment. The whole thing for everyone was to get Neil and Jackie strong again, and able to survive. It was really all about survival. And they couldn't do anything, as you can imagine, at that time. So there's a group of us that came there, and we mounted a headquarters and we just dealt with everything and did our best to make their lives as quiet as possible."

Geddy heard the news from Ray. "I was at my cottage. I remember my wife was out at the store. And the call came in, and when you're told news like that, you can't process it until you talk about it, until you say it out loud. So she walked in and I told her what had happened, and the two of us were sharing this; we both went white. We were at a loss; we didn't know what to do. And I think that's a common experience when there is a sudden loss. You don't know what to do with yourself. There's something atavistic about it. When you lose a kid, or you lose one of your flock or whatever, you're looking for something to do, you're looking for the right response, to find the missing person.

"So I called Alex and said, 'What's going on? I'm up at the cottage; where are you?' 'I'm in the city; I'm going to go over. They're coming back.' They were in Quebec but coming back to the city. And he said, 'Well, I don't know if they want any visitors, but I'm going over.' And I said, 'Okay, let me know,' and I think at first he just dropped a note at their door saying, 'I'm around; you can call me back.'

"That first few weeks were just heartbreaking. Shocking. So we couldn't stay up at the cottage. We were just bothered, and we didn't know whether to go be with him. And in the end, I just looked at Nancy and said I just had to go to him. There's no right answer at a time like that. So of course we just went to them, and the next few months were very painful. It was hard. It was hard knowing what to do for him, what to be for him and Jackie, and how to comfort them.

"The next few weeks they had people to their house every day, and it was just very sad, a shocking thing. And so they finally had enough. I think the people coming over were making them more miserable in a way. The pain was so evident. I mean, it was just so hard on them. We could distract him and Jackie, and try to make them tell stories about Selena, but in the end, they decided to leave. It was their course of action — it's too painful to look at all the things she used to touch, and all the things that were part of her, so they went to England and lived in England for a couple of months to try to get over the trauma. It took a long time. It just got kind of worse and worse. It got better and worse at the same time."

Howard Ungerleider, basically hired by the band the same time Neil was and crucial to the road show since day one, recalls the day he heard the news. "I was at home in Toronto at the time and it was a shock. It made me cry when I heard about it. We all knew Neil and his family very well, and we went right over to Neil's house and hung out there for days, bringing food, doing whatever. You feel helpless. There's nothing you can do. Deep down inside we all felt so . . . like we felt his pain, and you can't even describe what he was feeling. I know what we were feeling, which was horrible, you know, just to see them suffer through it.

"And I remember going over to Neil's house, and they had the French and the Mahaffy families there [both had daughters sexually assaulted and killed by Paul Bernardo] helping them as well. Because they'd gone through that ridiculous tragedy, and just to be surrounded by all of this, as a support for Neil, it's all you could've done. But it was horrible. It was one of those things where it makes you do a lot of reflecting and thinking about life. I remember Neil during that time, saying, 'I thought that life was great and people suck, for a long period of time, but then now I realize that it's people who are great and it's life that sucks,' which hit home, you know. I still get sad just even talking about it.

"I can't speak for Geddy and Alex, but I know how it affected me and my wife. But it affected them even more. It was just horrible. Nobody should experience that in their lifetime, but unfortunately, it does happen, and when that happens, you are forced to deal with it. It brings up a lot of psychological pains and conjures up a lot of demons as well as thought processes — you start drawing parallels to your life. Do you look at yourself as being fortunate it hasn't happened to you? You would have to say yes, you do. But I wouldn't wish it on anyone, much less someone I worked with for so many years. I'm just really glad to see that although this has happened, that he's come to another level in his life, and that he has pulled through it. But at what cost though?"

"I know how close he was with his daughter, so everyone was devastated by it," recalls Ray. "And it was devastating to see how hurt he was, and particularly how hurt his wife was, and he was trying to prop both of them up through this loss. And of course, the loss is magnified if you only have one child. It was everything. Whatever he wanted me to do . . . eventually, when things quieted down, the house was sold; I took on that responsibility for him. But mostly what he needed was his space, and he needed to be away. I saw him in Los Angeles a couple of times. I think, actually, one of the first times I saw him, I took him to an L.A. Kings game and tried to make sure nobody bothered him or recognized him. We went out and we talked, and he would come to Toronto and he and I would get together. Because of course his parents were here, and there were some responsibilities here, and it was tough. I can still feel it today. It's very tough. Very tough."

"It's just your spirit, something, just leaves," says Alex. "And you're so overwhelmed by the depth of the grief and the pain that you see, particularly in your friends, the pain that you feel, and it changes you for sure; it changes you forever. You look at things differently. I care in many different ways than I did then. I've always been a caring person, and by nature I like to help people and I like to make people happy, but that took it to another level. It gave me a sense of purpose. I've had a lot of sick friends lately and I deal with it so much better now. Maturing is part of it, yes, but based on what your experiences are . . . boy, something like that, you really learn a lot from it.

"I think the office made some kind of group press release at the time, but we didn't get involved in any of the sites or talk to anybody directly," explains Alex, when asked if they thought at the time that maybe this would be the end of the line for Rush. "What happened happened and that was a personal thing. We love the support from our fans, and it was beautiful to see their reaction to what had happened, and their support. But if new music was never going to happen, if that was the end of it, so be it; that's the way life goes. You can't do anything about that. We do this for ourselves. We don't do this for our fans, per se, or we don't do it for the money. Before anything else, we do it for ourselves. I think that's the great thing about our relationship with our fans; they expect us to do that."

"When they lived in England, I used to go over once in a while," continues Geddy. "You know, people would come in and see them, fly in, and we would all make contact with each other, 'Who's going this week?' and 'Are they okay?' We kept tabs on him. We just always wanted to make sure there was somebody with them. They had good friends with them; Liam [Birt], our tour manager and one of our closest friends, was with them a lot. It was very surreal. I don't know how to describe it in any way. It was terribly dark. It forced all of us into a very dark place."

And then Jackie was diagnosed with cancer, succumbing to

the disease eleven months after Selena's death. "It just became even more surreal," continues Geddy, "and it was all part of that same thing, that same continuum. They came back and we would see them, and she was surprisingly okay about being sick, because she was so grief-stricken about the loss of Selena, and I guess this is what she prayed for. Poor guy . . . after she passed away, he was lost, and you know, he describes it in his book."

And so began Neil's odyssey by way of motorcycle, which he indeed recounts in his legendary *Ghost Rider* book. Geddy would receive postcards from the open road, with Neil using one of his many nicknames. "And you'd make an effort; we would send a letter to be waiting for him somewhere. He went through what he had to go through," with Geddy intimating that the game would be played Neil's way, at arm's length, but that the contact would let him know the lines of communications were open if he wanted to talk further.

"I mean, he wrote such a great book about it as well," seconds Ray. "It was painful. It's painful to have someone you are close with for all those years go through that. It's still painful for me to know he had to live through that. You're never the same. How could you be? He and I would talk. And like I say, I had reason to go to Los Angeles once in a while, so I would see him. And whenever he came to Toronto, I would see him. We had lunches, dinners, a hockey game or two, whatever, there was contact. And of course, I was in touch with him because I was the one trying to sell the house at that point, and whatever other responsibilities came around. The one thing we didn't do is knock on his door about any business opportunities."

CHAPTER 4

DIFFERENT STAGES

*"The one thing about too much solitude is that you
don't tend to make yourself laugh much."*

"**B**asically we're talking about a journey that stretched
fifty-five thousand miles," begins Neil, on the grieving
process by way of motorcycle he embarked upon after
the deaths of the rest of his immediate family, "starting in Quebec,
and going up to the Arctic, to Inuvik, and through Alaska, around
Alaska, down to Mexico, across all of Mexico, from top across the
Mexican mainland down to Belize, and generally stopping by
night at motels along the way. I learned by then you can travel on
the fly. I carried camping gear with me, which is a great little bit
of trail craft, because you don't have to worry then. If the motel
I want to stay at is full, I can camp on their lawn. I didn't have
to; remarkably, everywhere I went I could always find a place.
I camped a couple times by choice, went down in the Arizona
desert, when it was pleasurable to do so.

"But for the most part, in North America, certainly, you can
just ramble around: 'Ah, okay, I'm getting tired now, I'd like to

have a drink, I think I'll stop, the town is twenty miles away, I'll try there.' It's the same thing I do on tour with the band now too. It's a way of being out in the world, engaging with the world. I'm on two-lane roads on that whole *Ghost Rider* journey, and to this day I go through small towns, the back roads, try to go to the independent motels, the independent diners, the mom-and-pop places, to keep all that heritage — traveler's heritage — alive. Finding how improvisational that can be is a way to travel too.

"Those are character-building lessons," continues Neil. "It's interesting to note, in that same process, I looked at it in my drumming too. Becoming more improvisational, and being unafraid to drop the itinerary. Even the early days of us touring, we would plan our days off, where we would stay that night and book it, thinking you had to. Because that's the kind of traveling I learned. And then I learned you didn't have to. No, you can improvise. If you feel like going that way or stopping earlier or later, you can. So that kind of freedom, I had that. I packed up camping gear if I needed to or wanted to, and a spare can of gas on the back, just learning the art of travel as I went. And the little interludes with people at the roadside would be so reaffirming and would definitely lighten my day.

"The one thing about too much solitude is that you don't tend to make yourself laugh much. And it's great when people like Mr. Air Mail gives you a little laugh for free. And sometimes when I'm traveling, real human beings will make me laugh more than anything else, and that would be a little gift. Like the gas station in Oregon; the town was called Irrigon, Oregon, because it was irrigated, so Irrigon, Oregon — that was funny. I pulled into the gas station, and one of those signs that usually says 'Mechanic on Duty, Officially Certified,' well, this guy had 'Maniac on Duty, Officially Certified.' And I thought that was hilarious. 'Do many people notice this?' 'No, no, not many. I just put that up for a laugh.' Yes, thank you! A free laugh there. Those are the moments that add up to something else, especially when you are trying to apply yourself back to life and appreciation of human beings, as opposed to resentment for their mere existence.

"It was a long and very desperate trip, but lessons were learned as always, and unforgettable experiences were collected along the way, and also, so many thresholds got passed. And when I said my road back was landscapes and highways, through those landscapes and the wildlife around them, that's been the path since then too. More and more nature. All the stories I write and even all those books, they're really about nature. They may be about my travels, and they seem to be about motorcycling and exploring, but it's the natural world that I am at pains to describe. Thinking about how to put in words how I might describe this to someone else who is not there.

"That became my entire drive in writing. I didn't want to write fiction anymore. I didn't want to make up stories. I wanted to capture what I saw in my travels and what I felt, and how other people described them if I could, and any dialogue I wanted to exchange. Remember that moment, remember how that conversation went and how to get that across to the reader. So the instincts that were refined down, distilled until I only had those three things left, that became the path for the next fourteen years after that. All of my writing — and even my creative thinking — grew from landscapes, highways and wildlife."

Anonymity was important for Peart, as always, but more than ever at this time. "Yeah, it is, of course, but with a helmet on you're anonymous anyway. In that whole fifty-five thousand miles, I don't know if I was ever recognized once, in a little town at a gas station or a motel or diner. Because I'm just a guy sitting there with a hat on reading a book. If you don't look to make yourself conspicuous, a lot of times you won't. And if I'm not in a town where we're playing, where people don't expect me to be, a lot of times I can slip around and be a guy. And that's all I want from traveling too — I just want to be a guy. I love your little town, I love your little diner, I love staying at this motel, I love the road we were on today, and that's life enough for me. I don't need somebody suddenly getting overexcited on me."

Seeing life in action, all forms of it, became part of Peart's healing process. "When I got up in Northern Canada and I was riding along, 'Oh, there's a bear swimming across the river over there; oh, there's a herd of elk over by the side of the road,' and that revitalized my spirit. It was those things that finalized me, the landscape around me as I moved west and north, into Northern Canada, Yukon and Alaska, and then down through Western Canada and the western U.S., the majestic landscapes. I haven't drawn these kinds of deep metaphors before, but you have to. It's your tiny existence in a different context.

"And like I said, a map to me is a book of dreams. Since I was a little kid on a bicycle: 'I wonder what's over that hill.' Down that trail in the woods. Nothing more attractive than a path that goes into the woods. And that stays with me now into the wintertime too: snowshoeing, cross-country skiing — the same fascination. I'll look at the map, 'Oh, I wonder what's over there?' Or I'm on my snowshoes and go down a cross-country trail. I have old familiar favorites that I like, but there's nothing more stimulating or exciting than a new one where you haven't been. Roads are like that, landscapes are like that, and when they are combined with the magic of life too — that holy trinity — I knew it was important. But now when I think about the resonance of what that means, the permanent world, the movement through it and the magic of eagles and elk and black bear, all these things around you remind you that life goes on, in a very primeval and evocative way. For a nature-loving kid, mind you

— so this is probably a little idiosyncratic. It's the kind of person I am — these things stimulate me."

But there was always, albeit way back in the recesses, Geddy and Alex, if not Rush. Communication was minimal, and when generated, it was by carrier pigeon and smoke signal.

"Well, this is a period in the mid-'90s, when portable modes of communication were rare," explains Neil. "I think I had a brick-sized cell phone for emergency use, but it wasn't the kind that worked in half the places I went, especially the north and the west. So I got in the habit — from my grandfather, who died at ninety-three, around the year 2000, 1999, and he was quite solitary later in his life — anywhere I went, on my bicycle trips in Africa or in Europe, I would send a postcard. And joking ones. I remember on the *Ghost Rider* trip, I was down in a beautiful little town called Loreto in Baja, California, and stopped there for a couple days. It was so nice, with a fifty-dollar-a-night hotel room and a hammock in front of it, the Sea of Cortez in front of me, sitting there reading in a hammock. And I wrote to my grandfather and said, 'Come down here, it's really cheap, you can lie in a hammock and read all day.'

"So I started sending them to Geddy and Alex on my travels too. And actually, the *Ghost Rider* title came from one of those. Alex and I had a special written language called Moronese, and it started on our grocery list one year, when we would all be together and working on stuff, and we would write down our grocery list in pure phonetics, you know, and try to outdo each other. And we would say what is the obvious way that this word could be spelled? Bread is b-r-e-d, strawberries, hmm, so we would get really creative.

"I sent Alex a postcard from the town where he was born, Fernie, British Columbia. I picked up a postcard and I turned it over and it was the phenomenon of a mountain, with the clouds collected at the top and drifted away from it, and the locals call that *ghost rider*. And I went boom, that's me — I'm riding with all these ghosts, and I feel like a ghost, and I'm alienated from the whole world: I'm the ghost rider. So I wrote to Alex, 'Eyeemthugostrydur' — 'I am the ghost rider.' Bing! Yes, I am. So that's a perfect example.

"And I remember I was hiking in Glacier National Park in Montana, and I think as anyone from there knows, there's a lot of grizzly country there and you're not supposed to hike alone. But I was alone, and the one thing they say, make human sounds. So I'm walking along singing every classic standard song that I know, every Sinatra song, Tony Bennett song, all that stuff. And when I stopped to eat, even, I kept tapping my leg to scare the grizzlies away. And I could see where they were tracking, I could smell them in the air; it was a misty, close, rainy sort of a day. And I carried a big rock with me. I always say wherever there's mountain lions around, I'll never go down without a fight. So I always carry a pointy rock in my hand. And I wrote a postcard to Geddy from there, and I said, 'I went hiking with a big rock, so if a grizzly attacks I can fight it off.' Yeah, right. So those are two examples. Yeah, those were my two modes of communication with people in traveling. Postcards and phone calls, but only occasional payphones back then. I had occasion recently when I had to find one, and it's strange how just over a decade, things can change so much."

And Neil was aware that his network of friends was worried about him. "Yeah, absolutely. *I* was worried about me. Why wouldn't you be? In the state I was in, of course they were worried about me."

Back at the office on College Street — not a particularly nice part of Toronto, but who likes to move? — staffers looked at each other and then looked for work to do. It's always been like that there. Rush is a business, and a business needs a product. And the office doesn't handle death well, in the immortal words of Pegi Cecconi. In fact Ray, in that cursed role of nagging dad with the purse strings, of administrator, of reality check, of "that lawyer is a horrible person, but I'm glad he's my lawyer and not the other guy's" — all of these roles — actually started worrying that Neil would spend all his money and wind up broke. Peart always had expensive tastes, and now he was just burning and not earning. Seemed like a good time for another live album, an obvious time, a desperate time, the only option really, a no-brainer. In effect, Rush had broken up. Nobody was saying this formally or articulating to what extent it was a given, but no matter what the reality was, that doesn't mean the brand doesn't live on, and a good manager protects and maintains and tries to elevate the brand when possible. And if this was indeed the end of Rush, no one out there in the world needed to know that. A live record could mean — if we were all willing to play along — that Rush lives.

On November 10, 1998, despite Neil's self-imposed exile, and despite voiced thoughts that the band couldn't be pressed to produce, the Rush ball was kept rolling with *Different Stages*, a mammoth three-CD live set. Besides a conventional collection, the album includes a disc comprising a Hammersmith Odeon show recorded for (but aborted as) a radio broadcast, at the back end of the *A Farewell to Kings* tour. The other two discs include three tracks from the *Counterparts* tour, a handful of other isolated and fortunate incidents, but mainly selections from the band's Chicago *Test for Echo* stand on June 23, 1997. Geddy at the time found this quite amusing, given that over a hundred shows were recorded for aural perusal. The *Test for Echo* album is represented with only three tracks, with the complexion of the album looking like a hits pack, with welcome smatterings from the '90s albums and '89's *Presto* included.

"We had been recording material for two tours," explained Geddy to the author back in '98. "We are gathering quite an overwhelming library of material actually, and, coupled with the discovery of the tapes from 1978, it was just obvious that we needed to put a package together. And in my mind, seeing that we were coming up on twenty-five years as a band, I thought it was an opportune moment to put together a retrospective, in essence, from a live point of view. And because a lot of the responsibility for this project gravitated into my corner, I just kind of decided what the concept was going to be."

Says Ged of the 1978 U.K. barnstormer, "The quality that we found on that particular show is remarkable for a twenty-year-old analog tape recording. This one was an effort to go into the realm of the idealistic. We recorded so many shows that I could choose performances I felt were as good or better than the recorded studio versions, or where there was a level of live excitement, or where there was something genuinely new that was brought to the version, as opposed to just the best possible available to me. 'Animate,' for example, evolved into something different live. So it was a more ambitious mission or goal. We accomplished a very satisfying result. In terms of tinkering, there's really none on this album. The whole purpose of this album was to record so many shows that we wouldn't have to do any."

Most definitely, hearing "2112" in its entirety is a *Different Stages* high point. "We changed a bit of the emphasis and changed the tuning of the song a little bit to give it a heavier feel," notes Geddy on the conceptual classic from 1976. "But other than that it's a fairly accurate reinterpretation of it, twenty-two years later. I was really pleased with the way that came out. It was a lot more fun to play live than I ever thought it would be."

The band takes it as a point of honor to reproduce the songs close to the way we know and love them. "For most of our songs, really, we do stick to the arrangements," affirms Neil. "The arrangements are so carefully wrought that we're quite happy to try to nail that on the night, you know? And other ones are a little looser by design. There's also a consistency of live performance that is really important to us. I always remember seeing the Grateful Dead around the early '90s. I had liked Mickey Hart's book, *Drumming at the Edge of Magic*, and I had written him a letter of appreciation, and we corresponded a little. And we were in Atlanta one night with back-to-back nights off, so I went to see Grateful Dead. And Mickey said right away, 'Well, it's not going to be very good tonight, because we just had a good show last night, and they come in fours.' And that was the kind of inconsistency that their approach to performance demanded, and their audience would forgive. So, fine. We really like more consistency, so every night is going to be good. And if we happen to be sparked up, there's always room for that to show. We notice a difference and our audience notices the difference when it's a special night."

On a more micro level, Peart sticks to the original studio structures of most of his drum fills as well. "I do, with pleasure, yeah. Again, I worked really hard on all that stuff, and it's a reflection of me and my character, how I like to see things built and the way I like to play, so why wouldn't I? It just seems obvious. There are always little details I hear in the final record and I go, I wish I knew that accent or that vocal push was going to be there. Things get built and developed along the way. There are little things like that I've added afterwards, that I wished I had done on the record. But they are small details." And in the end, there are all those air drummers to satisfy . . . "Well, they can do what they want. No, no, that's strictly about me. The drum parts are made to suit me, and consequently, they're played to suit me."

Yet ultimately, surely, there's a philosophical dissatisfaction, or deficiency, with the concept of getting out there and playing live, versus the permanence of a record that you can hold in your hand — one passes into the ether, the other becomes history.

"Well, yes, that's the distinction," affirms Neil. "Between temporary and permanent. In some ways, touring is an important evolutionary part of your progress. I used to definitely feel at the end of the tour that I was playing better and that the band was playing better than we had been at the outset. And as you're learning and growing and refining technique and all those different aspects of being a musician, there's no greater testing ground or proving ground than by performance, where you're proving yourself every single night.

"And again, playing the same songs but trying to correct flaws, or improve bits of it, get inflections, pick up what the other guys are playing, and incorporating that, listening to live tapes after the show, hearing where you might have nailed the tempo down better, or where you are playing something somebody might respond to. So many things like that go on in the course of touring, especially in the early years where things were accelerated and there's so much to learn, so you learned faster.

"Then it reaches a certain point, I find, where it's just re-creation," continues Peart. "I love rehearsing for the tour and the whole buildup for it and the band becoming tight musically and working and all of that, right through the rehearsals and everything. Then once you've played a really good show, that sets the benchmark that you struggle to live up to night after night. And then of course, if you do play a really great show, I've had this experience of coming offstage all exuberant, and then a cloud of disappointment sets in, like, 'It's gone; it's over.' So increasingly, that becomes less satisfying.

"I think to painstakingly craft a piece of work, whether it's writing or music or drumming, particularly, it's done and it's there and you can enjoy it later. It has a sense of not only endurance but accomplishment, like you've made something. A show doesn't feel like you've made something. That's the difference. You performed something and it can be satisfying or not, depending on how well you performed it. But in essence, hey, you haven't actually made anything."

As for what Neil gets out of going to a concert himself, "I would say it's more of a theatrical experience, really, for me. I don't find that live performance has ever really changed my experience of music. Everything I get out of music, I can get from the album. I love to go see a band perform, of course, but that's the essence; it's performance, it's the theater, the same way I like to watch a good play or opera. It's that kind of experience, I think, more than the intimate experience of music that you can have with speakers or headphones or in the car."

Back to Rush's own stages, Geddy addresses the topic of his understated, some say meekly delivered, stage patter. "I'm not a big talker onstage. Over the years I've loosened up a lot; I feel much more comfortable. When I was young, I was just nervous. But as I've gotten older it's much less of a big deal to me. When I talk I feel totally at ease. But I don't remember, unless somebody threw a shoe or something at me, getting pissed off and yelling at the audience. There's the occasional time where you're in a general admission situation and people are shoving too much and you have to talk about calming everybody down."

"Geddy was the one who always spoke, and he spoke very little," notes Alex, who over the years took to spontaneously cracking a regular parade of jokes, quips and impressions on any given night. "You know, other than just introducing the songs, that was it. He was never the kind of host to the evening that some people are. It was all about getting down to business, playing. And I guess that's the way it always was with us. We never worked out moves. You just reacted to the music whatever way you did and everybody was very independent."

The resplendent triple gate packaging of *Different Stages* contains a nice collage of Rush memorabilia. "It's stuff from all of us really," says Geddy, "and some fans I think. Our photographer, Andrew MacNaughtan, put the collage together. I keep stuff; I can't say I display much of it, but yes, I'm a bit of a packrat. When I see things I think are cool, I throw them in a box and put it in the basement somewhere."

Finally, *Different Stages* adds yet another bonus, a computer program, Geddy explains, that allows the purchaser to indulge in musical sculpture. "Someone at Atlantic phoned me and said they had got in contact with this Japanese artist who had developed this interesting program called Cluster Works, and there was something about the program that they were anxious to use on a rock album. And something reminded him of the kinds of things we do with our lights and our live situation, with our lasers and so forth.

"He thought there was a nice fit between our music and the ethereal quality of these visuals. He flew down and showed it to me. I've never been a big believer in the enhanced CD thing, because in the past you always kind of get lyric sheets and things like that, so they make you feel like you're getting a bonus when you're getting things you normally would get anyway. I never really thought it was much of a bargain for the fans. But this struck me as being something different, and I imagine there are a lot of fans who want to play with that. So for those who want to play with it, it's there."

With the future of Rush still up in the air, on November 14, 2000, two years after the *Different Stages* live opus, Geddy offered for the fans' consideration his very first solo record. *My*

Favorite Headache would be his only solo album to date, just like *Victor* is the only solo excursion we've seen from Alex thus far.

"This record for me is very rewarding on two levels," explained Ged to me at the time — I was doing the press rounds. "One, I'm very proud of it musically and two, I'm very pleased to be able to have worked with Ben Mink, who has been my friend for a long time. The whole reason this project came into being was my desire for the two of us to work together. And for us to work together and still remain friends at the end of it was a big accomplishment. I'm really happy about that. But musically the album is quite richly layered in terms of melody compared to where I normally operate. And it's a slightly different attitude toward groove in rock. It's a little rounder, groove-oriented music than what we end up doing in Rush. Lyrically, I guess after I got over the original shyness about it, it turned out to be a very rewarding personal experience, in terms of getting to know myself. It felt good to clarify my thoughts about certain things on paper. And the fact that can translate into a musical world also made me feel more complete.

"Well, I think about a lot of stuff," laughs Lee, asked what he learned about himself while writing lyrics. "And although my thoughts may be abstract, I think they're also in common with the way other people think. There are a couple of common threads throughout. 'Slipping' is about fallibility and vulnerability in spite of all the best intentions in the world. 'Working at Perfekt' is about creative angst and how difficult it is to achieve what you hear in your head, whether it be musically or visually. It's about getting your art the way you want it to be. It's like the old Woody Allen saying: It's really hard to get things right in life, so you try to get it right in art. 'The Present Tense' is about existential angst, for lack of a better description. You know, those moments where life feels overwhelmingly big, and yet we have no choice but to work through it. The title track, 'My Favorite Headache,' is about the recurrence and insistence of intelligence despite our best desires to hide from it. It recurs. So there are some of the themes."

Phrasing wasn't really an issue, says Ged. After all, this was a one-stop shop — no Neil. "Well, only for a while. That's the kind of thing I've been doing for thirty years. That's the easy part; it's just a matter of playing around with it until it works. That's craft; that's not so hard. It's getting something to sing about that feels worthwhile that's the tough part.

"I just take my book with me," explains Geddy, on his lyric-writing modus operandi, "and I keep it by my bed at night. A lot of times, before I go to bed, the residue of the day accumulates. And when it's really quiet I start jotting things down. They're almost never complete. It's just things I'm thinking about. And I'll look at them the next day and hate most of it, but usually there's something, a seed in there, a germ in there, that's worth working on. And I found that I don't know if I would be able to write lyrics to a deadline, because there's a real long gestation period for me in these songs. I've got to allow myself a lot of time to be dissatisfied with it before I hit on something that works. And usually it doesn't occur until there's a piece of music that makes it come to life." On whether he's brave with his lyrics, or raw and honest, "Not particularly,' answers Ged. "But give me some time and I'll hurt some feelings."

As for putting the music together, that was a case of Geddy and Ben, both with guitars, "just sitting there," laughs Mink, who shares music credits with Lee on all tracks. "Yeah, just jamming and then cutting and then jamming and refining. We used to liken it to making a garment, which it is. You know, you just keep shaping it, refining."

The production credit on the album goes to Geddy, Ben and David Leonard, who was mostly involved with the mix. Studios were used in Vancouver and Seattle (Soundgarden's Matt Cameron is the primary drummer), plus a couple in Toronto as well as Triumph's compound, Metalworks, in Mississauga, Ontario. Explains Mink on wearing the producer's hat: "Sometimes Geddy would say, 'What do you think? Do you think I should go to double-time in the bass?' or 'Do you think I should try the lower range?' But Geddy has phenomenal memory too. I've watched him pretty much improv a great bass track and then say, 'How about if I double it in the chorus?' And he'd listen to it once or twice, and his parts are not easy. It's not your ma-and-pa bass part — and then he would double it. Note for note.

"And this guy cannot read music. You know, I once used him on a . . . he was kind enough to lend his bass part to a Marie-Lynn Hammond record from a folk artist — I used to play with a string band. And I asked him to play, and I said, 'Yeah, you know when you go to the B-flat?' And he goes 'What?' And I go, 'It's the B-flat.' And he goes, 'I don't know B-flat.' 'Okay, your lowest fat string, the sixth fret, that's a B-flat.' I go, 'When you go there, don't hit it so hard.' And he really does not know. These guys are like geniuses. They've created their own musical way of communicating through complicated riffs. It's all by ear, very detailed, very complicated, and they put together incredible music based on their own sort of hieroglyphics and, you know, long-learned approach. It's fascinating to watch them work. I've been to some of their rehearsals, and it's so interesting to watch them jam and riff and to see what their years of intuition results in, because it's just incredible.

"But it was pretty natural," continues Mink, on assembling the record. "The project came about and he was here in Vancouver once, and we were in my studio, and he just picked up an acoustic bass, you know, a guitar-style bass, and I had a regular guitar. We started playing, and I realized it's almost the same way I play with Nancy Wilson. The way we hit the strings, the way we play, is very, very similar. Like-minded players will recognize this quickly in each other and realize that this is really, really natural. And we tried that a few other times and it was just like old hat. We didn't even think about it. It just worked."

Commenting on Geddy as a guitarist, Ben says, "He's good — he plays it like a bass. He pulls up on the string like a bass player would . . . he can't use a pick, really, very well. But he plays it backwards, so that he pulls at the strings like a classical guitarist would. I mean, he can strum basic chords, but bass is his thing, really. And his ability to make up parts . . . he has a complicated and beautiful way of constructing melody. He can come up with numerous melodies for a part. You know, over and over again he can come up with beautiful melodies, and very quickly. Then he hones in on what it needs. He's able to separate his instrument from the other functions. A lot of people can't do that. They'll write a melody that sounds exactly like a bass part. But he's able to put down the bass part, think of the melody, think of a keyboard. He has a really well-rounded sense of parts."

My Favorite Headache includes a large cast of characters, but, as Geddy says, "Working, it was mostly Ben and me. This project is really the result of hours and hours of being in the writing room with Ben. And the biggest difference is just the casualness of the approach. With Rush, we have a good time, we laugh, but there's this quiet . . . what's the best word to describe it? This quiet structure around us. And that structure is the band and the workings of the band. And although we're really good at not paying a whole lot of attention to it, it's still there.

"And working with Ben was completely separate from that. It was casual, it was about the music, and there was no point of reference, like you have in a band. Even when you are writing for writing's sake, or music for music's sake, it's still me, Alex and

Neil and the personalities of our instruments that are imposed on the work. And when you are outside of that and it's just a couple of guys sitting around trying to write some music they find compelling, you're out of the box. And as subtle as the box may be, you're out of it. That made a big difference to me."

A lesson Geddy learned through the making of the record has to do with regrets concerning the mix. "I don't think I will ever put myself in a situation where I have a deadline to mix a record. Because I find that the mixing process is the most delicate part. You can really wreck a song in the mix. And I'm a firm believer in allowing yourself opportunities to mix and remix. Because you have absolutely nothing to lose by remixing. Of course you drive yourself crazy, but that's beside the point. In terms of quality, the songs I remixed on this project, without question, were improved. So that's something I've learned for the future.

"I don't see why not," ventures Geddy, on whether he'd do another solo record. "It was very enjoyable and very gratifying. As long as it's reasonably well accepted, I think I would continue to experiment with that. There were a couple of players I had in the back of my mind to include, but the appropriate moment never arrived for them. So I'll just store that away for next time. And it depends on what the material is. It depends where I go writing-wise. There are a few things I would like to try in the future. I would like to try some experiments with purely acoustic instruments. I think it would be fun to put a couple of songs together just using acoustic-stringed instruments, guitars, lutes, mandolins, stand-up bass, those kinds of things. It's something I'm curious about. Plus I've got lots of stuff left over and we'll see what happens with that. Some stuff recorded but unfinished. And there were a couple of songs that are recorded that, at the end of the day, I didn't feel were successful from a writing point of view. So I just put them on the backburner to review some other time."

And then the door opened just a crack, and a continuation of the Rush story was shining through from the other side.

Says Ged, "I needed to write and I needed to be productive, and that's when I did my solo record and everybody found a way to keep themselves sane. We stayed in contact, and one day Neil felt like working again.

"I don't think I played my guitar for something like six months," remembers Alex, taking us back to the early days when Selena had died and it was just Neil and Jackie. "You know, I like taking a break when I'm off the road, but it was nothing like that. There was just no love in it, and there was no love in a lot of things. It was so painful. Every day we were living what they were living through, and trying to be supportive. They were traveling a lot. I remember writing faxes almost constantly through that period, to Neil, back and forth, just sending him stuff to keep his spirits up, jokey, funny things, whenever I could. And then it was hard again ten months later when his wife died, and there was that void he fell into. I started working with some other bands, doing some production stuff, a couple of TV projects, and Geddy did his solo record. And it looked like the band was done. I mean, we were kind of planning to move on when Neil stabilized and said that maybe he would consider coming back to work."

"I think I was the one who didn't think this was over," says Ray. "And I don't think it was wishful thinking. I had contact with him and spent time with him. All three of them, you have incredible people with huge loyalties and huge ethics. In most bands, they would've started looking for a new drummer after three years, or after two and a half years. I was convinced they were going to wait as long as it took, and I think had he waited two years longer — they still would've waited for him. They care about each other deeply, and they are incredibly respectful of each other. What would that have done to him, if they'd gone forward without him? Not a chance. If anything, there were discussions only about how important it was to have the three of them there. It would have been that no matter who would've had problems or reasons they couldn't be there: they would wait. They would have waited for Alex and they would've waited for Geddy. It's the Three Musketeers."

Danniels remembers being part of the communication. "Yes, I think it was probably more through me, at the time, that I said to them I felt he was coming back, that he'd given me indications he was thinking about it. He had met a wonderful girl, who he subsequently married, and she didn't know anything about the band. She wasn't a Rush fan; she didn't know anything about it. I knew she was curious and she wanted to see him play one day, and that would be a positive influence for him. How can you marry a guy who everyone tells you is the best drummer in the world, and you've never seen him play? Would you marry the best painter in the world and never see him paint? Or the best sculptor or the best anything? Other than maybe an aging athlete, and you couldn't do it anymore, wouldn't there be some curiosity there? So I think she was a good influence on him as well."

And then there's the whole extended Rush family, waiting, wondering, with Howard Ungerleider in the handful of employees at the top. "It's one of those things where you can't prepare for something like that. There's nothing you can do. Everybody has to do what they do best, and it's unfortunate at the time that it happens, but it did happen, but you move on in life. You have to. So everybody's future was in question. I started my business in 1994, here, and it's been running since then, so I had something to go back to. But still, what can you say? Nothing. It's just a waiting game. And it's unbelievable that Neil came back out of that. I don't know personally if I would be able to come back the way he did. It's just amazing — he's got amazing drive."

"You know what? When I stopped riding, I was ready," explains Peart. "A year and a half. I came back to Quebec for a little bit in the winter and a little bit in the summer. But basically, I traveled nonstop, and certainly was released for a year and a half. Traveling all that time."

As Ray alluded to, Neil met photographer Carrie Nuttall. They married and eventually had a daughter, Olivia Louise Peart, in 2009, before settling in Santa Monica, California. "It was when I came to rest and moved out there. I had a suitcase, a ghetto blaster and a bicycle. Those are my possessions. I moved to southern California in the year 2000, because again I was rootless. In a good way. I used to write a lot of letters, and I said I'm freer than any man ought to be or wants to be. Nothing to hold onto and nothing to be attached to. So for me setting up a new life in a new home in California, with just those possessions, music, travel, bicycle, and a little suitcase of clothes and stuff, that was as basic as life could be, but it was a wonderful place to start from."

Neil says Carrie helped him gain a sense of stability, and that's when he started thinking about going back to work. "We hadn't actually ever been apart that long," says Neil, of Geddy and Alex. "When I was getting back to Toronto I was always getting together with them. Alex and a bunch of the guys came up to stay with me in the summertime that year. And I went to visit Alex in Santa Fe; he used to have a place in Santa Fe, New Mexico. And the two of us and another friend met up there. And so no, we were never apart, really; we were in contact or in touch all the time. We saw each other frequently enough."

"How time has affected a band like us I can't really say because it's not just time," reflects Alex. "It's not just the longevity; it's the impact of what happens in that time. Really, all of us questioned whether or not we'd make another record, if we would ever work again. When this all happened, the band was the very last thing on our minds. I mean, it just didn't seem appropriate to even think about it. Music's about celebration, and there was no feeling of celebration at that time. It was circle the wagons and help as much as you can. That was the foremost thing. I didn't play the guitar. Neil didn't play his drums, obviously, for four years. A lot of things changed; it took a while to get out of that."

"It was all him — he contacted us," says Geddy. "It was all kind of formal in a weird way, because he was starting a new life in California, and I think he contacted Ray. I think he was nervous. He was nervous and shy about it. I think part of him wanted to come back but he was afraid, and he had been through so much, and Ray was such a good pal to him through that whole thing. He's kind of the safe third party. So he called up Ray and said, 'Why don't you get the guys together; we'll have dinner.' So he came into town, we chatted, and he's like, 'Well, if we did work, what would it look like? How could we set up?'

"He wasn't sure," continues Geddy. "Is there a way we can do it so he wasn't freaked out and felt trapped? So what we did was, we said, 'Look, we'll just do it however you need it to be done.' And that's when we came up with the idea of booking a studio for a year. Let's find a small studio, set your drums up in one room, set up an area where you can write, and Alex and I will set up in another part of the studio where we can jam. And then you can rehearse every day without disturbing us, and get your confidence back, go to work. And he loves rehearsing. I mean, you've never met a musician who loves rehearsing like this guy. I hate rehearsing. After a while, I need an audience or something to keep me juiced. But he can rehearse 'til the cows come home. It was very difficult, but it worked out — *Vapor Trails* was a very painful, impossible record to make."

CHAPTER 5

VAPOR TRAILS

*"It was really up to him to prove to himself that he
could start his life over again."*

"Neil had to do what he needed to do, just find some sort
of peace," begins Alex, recapping the events of renewal
that led to the return of Rush — new record, new tour,
new Neil.

"He had embarked on a long journey, a long and very painful
journey on his motorcycle, basically just going and going and
going, and never really knowing where he was going. But it's
what he needed to do. That whole process took a few years, and
Geddy and I didn't really do anything until that last year. I started
doing a little work with some other bands, I did some work with
3 Doors Down and did some film stuff, and Geddy recorded his
solo record. We were becoming a little more active musically.

"And we had a meeting, he came up to Toronto and we talked.
We talked about how we would go through this process. He
wasn't sure if he could do it, but he was willing to try. You know,
he hadn't played his drums for almost four years, so it was a very

difficult time. He was a little apprehensive, and he was afraid, I think. He wasn't sure how he felt about it, but it was a new start in his life. He was starting to find a little bit of happiness for the first time in many years. He had to go through that."

Speaking to me back in 2002 when all of this was still too fresh, Lifeson explained, "My friends said to me, you know, at the time you think you'll never smile again in your life. You feel you'll never have a happy time or happy moment ever again. And all the therapists will tell you: you don't believe this right now, but you will find happiness again. You will learn to live your lives again, as much as they don't want to at the time. I think that's what happened with Neil. But he was a little nervous. He hadn't played in a long time, and he didn't know if his heart could go into the music as it once did. Because he just didn't look at music that way anymore. He had lost too much. From the very beginning, from that meeting, it was a very fragile, tentative thing.

"So we went into the studio with just us in there," continues Lifeson. "Four block bookings for months and months and months. We were in there from January of 2001 until, well, basically Christmas at that studio, and then we went into another studio to mix and spent a few months there — the project took thirteen or fourteen months altogether. It was a very delicate time and everything happened very slowly. Neil practiced a lot and played a lot while we were writing in another room.

"You know, we were a little bit out of shape, Geddy and I. There was a lot of stuff we were writing that in review was lousy, really not very interesting at all. The first three or four weeks was like that. We were just struggling along and it didn't really feel like we were going to make it work. We took a week off and came back in, and we were so much clearer about what the direction's going to be. We started filtering stuff and started playing more, but one of the things that happened was we got attached to our demos. There was a spontaneity, and probably sixty percent of that record is from the demos. What you are hearing was the first time that idea was ever played. It's not like it was written and we learned it and we went in and recorded it — we just recorded it. Not all of it was like that, but a majority of the record was. Consequently, I think that record suffers a little bit in production. It's probably one of our weaker sounding records. I've got friends who would argue that they absolutely love the fact that it's raw and it's got that element to it. But we're usually very meticulous about how we record.

"We would only take four to six months to make a record, six being the outside. To spend fourteen months on a record is a long, long time. But Geddy, after spending a year on his solo record, really believed we shouldn't have any deadlines. We've always been very anal about the way we work; you know, six weeks for writing, one week for drums, five days for bass, two weeks guitar, two weeks vocals, mix. It's always been like that. We've been doing that for decades, and with his solo record Geddy said, 'I played so much with my songs and I could really see how they developed and how important it was to the growth of the material.' He said with *Vapor Trails*, we had to do the same thing, not worry about deadlines, take as long as it takes to work that way. I was antsy for the first couple of months; I had that four-month to six-month thing in my head, and it was three months before we even had anything written. By that point I realized he was right — forget deadlines; this record is going to take as long as it takes.

"There was a whole different mentality as we went into this project versus *Test for Echo*," continues Alex, asked at the time to address the album's nervy production tones. "We were coming out of a dark period for the last five years. We make decisions about production very early on. We decided we were going to produce the record ourselves as much as we could. And despite not really having a direction when we started, it came after a while, and once it did, it had an energy of its own. This project was more intense, even though the schedule was much more relaxed.

"*Test* was very much like the records in the past where we worked it up in a working environment, did preproduction, rehearsed it, basically learned it, then went into the studio and recorded the whole record. Whereas this record was just an evolving, growing, living thing throughout the whole process. As Geddy's said, a lot of the performances on the record were those initial jam performances. You know, they've been played once.

"It was cathartic for Neil," continues Alex. "When we started in January of 2001, he drove back from his place in Quebec, along the same route where his daughter had the accident. As he approached Toronto, it was a gray January late afternoon/early evening kind of day. The city's gray; it was rainy and slushy and the weight of everything just became too much. That was difficult for him — just that one thing — and that was before we even started working. He had to work very hard to build up his strength, and we gave him lots of time and space and support, but it was really up to him to prove to himself that he could start his life over again; that's really what it was all about.

"By the end of the record, I won't say he was the same guy he was six years ago, but he was a lot stronger, he was a lot happier, he was more determined. He's a very determined, very strong person, but all of that strength and determination was shattered.

"He's in the process of rebuilding and starting his new life," Lifeson explained at the time. "If he doesn't want to talk to anybody I can understand completely because it's going to be very awkward. He's very private anyway, always has been. We talked about it before, when we finished the record, and he said to us, 'It's hard enough for me to even think about what happened, let

alone talk to strangers about it, so please can I just not do that?'
Of course, don't even worry about it, don't even think about it."

"That's the great thing about being dear friends," related
Peart, recalling those times. "The sense of humor never went
among the three of us. And that's Alex's great gift. Other people
I know who've gone through the most horrible tragedies . . . that
devil humor is never far away. The bad jokes began immediately
and sustained us in a way — and remarkably. I had such whole-
hearted support from them. There was never any estrangement.
I never thought anything but that they were my best friends and
wanted the best for me. And that sense of support — as little as
anything meant to me at that time — mattered as much as anything, and there was no weirdness about it.

"That was all part of the healing, of course, being able to
work again. I loved coming up to Toronto and staying there, and
working with the guys every day, and socializing, at least every
week or so, despite them being with their homes and families
and everything. We would get together and have dinner — there
was the whole social side of it too that was stabilizing for me.
All that was important. And those two guys from the beginning,
honestly, they were the most stable thing I had, my family and
loved ones, and those who dared to stay around me in that time.
It was so hard that *I* would've walked."

On the mechanics of making what was to become *Vapor Trails*,
Neil figures, "We have this built-in quality control system that
if we don't like it, we stop working on it. I saw Geddy comment
on that recently — that we have no catalogue that's unreleased.
Because if we go through all the trouble of finishing something,
we're putting it out! And if we didn't go through all that trouble,
we threw it away. Or we steal — we'll take the best parts and
move on from there. A lot of the songs were rewritten many
times, some of them from the ground up, basically. 'Earthshine,'

the lyrics stayed the same, but every note of the music was completely replaced, and there were others like that too. So no, it was constant review. And again, that sense of commonality and mutual energy, that's where it shines, in places like that. 'I don't think we're quite done with that.' 'No, me either.' Those are the kinds of things we do agree on."

Dependable Paul Northfield from the Le Studio days makes a return appearance to the Rush camp, this time as co-producer of the album.

"I met with them in Toronto," begins Paul. "They were in the process of writing, and they were at Reaction Studios, which was home away from home for them. Well, it was close to home and a very comfortable writing environment. They had done preproduction for records there before. At that point, I think they'd been there for three or four months writing and getting back in touch with each other because they'd been apart at that point for probably five years. There was obviously a lot of ground to cover. It was no longer just a simple question of firing up with the same kind of sensibilities they had in the past. They found new ways to write songs, writing by themselves, or even in Geddy's and Alex's case, they had written albums entirely alone and found things they had enjoyed as part of that process, and they were not ready to give up the possibility of doing those things in the process of making the next record. So there was also this, aside from the reunification of them and Neil getting back into playing.

"I happened to drop in and visit them at that time," continues Northfield, "and they started peppering me with questions about whether I thought the studio there would be an okay place to record, because it was very comfortable for them. It was a perfectly nice studio, but it was a rather small place to record drums. They were used to recording in some of the greatest drum rooms in the world, and that was an important part of the process. On a lot of other records, the drums were recorded in a relatively short period of time. On this one, they expected to be ready to record drums throughout the making of the record, because it was done in a completely different way.

"So my first meeting with them was really just dropping in to say hi, and then subsequently I was asked to come in and talk with them about possibly making the record. Doing it at Reaction was discussed. They wanted to stay there because they could all just go home at night. They wanted to spend time with their families. Or Alex and Geddy did, and Neil was with Carrie and was comfortable, and quite fragile. It was a very, very difficult time."

As pertains the mood of the band at that time, the working dynamic, Paul says, "When I got involved, they'd already been together for five or six months. Writing. It was comfortable; they had a routine of arriving at the studio, ordering lunch and spending the day working together. Neil had a room at the back where he was writing lyrics and working on his book at the same time. When Geddy and Alex had finished working on their ideas on their computers, which they had become accustomed to doing when they were doing their solo records — great writing tool — Neil would come in and record, with Alex at the helm. This is in the preproduction days, because Alex was really enjoying the recording process at this point and so he was engineering the demos.

"When I got involved, essentially the desire was to continue to do the same kind of thing, and they wanted to know, was it going to be possible? Was the studio going to be able to deliver a drum sound that was appropriate, bearing in mind it was a relatively dead and smaller studio, or did we need to move away, something they really didn't want to do? I suggested that we essentially rebuild the interior of the studio: strip it of all of its deadening aspects and make the studio very, very live. So we did that, because I felt fairly confident that the studio size was good enough; it was just that it was a very dead studio. In lieu of moving away, we'd build a studio to our specifications, without trying to go too crazy.

"It worked really well, and we got the results we were looking for. That meant we were able to continue to work on it with the same spirit. The important thing with that record was the writing was essentially done with Geddy and Alex jamming on ideas they had, either individually or collectively, playing around with the computer, taking snippets of riffs, editing them and turning them into songs, and then having Neil play over them and experiment.

"At the same time, he was really having to get up to speed. Because I remember coming into the first sessions, when I first went to talk to them, and watching Neil play. Having stood in front of him as a drummer playing at his peak, I was aware of how intense and forceful he is as a player, and at that time he was not playing at that level at all. Even though his parts were interesting, just the force in his playing was not there. And I kind of knew there was going to be a way to go. The bottom line is you don't play at that level and then stop and then pick up a set of sticks and be back where you were immediately. As Neil himself said, it takes time to build up the calluses.

"There was quite a process of him coming to grips with what he needed to do, what he wanted to do. And I think having done it on the computer . . . I mean, I've heard criticism here and there of why didn't we record that record without a computer. And just back with two-inch tape or something like that. The thing is, that record wouldn't have been made without a computer, because that process allowed the band to experiment and put together ideas, and then gradually introduce Neil into the picture as he was getting back in touch with his performance and his playing. If the songs had all been written and then they just walked into the studio on the first day that I walked into the studio and tried to play together, I don't think the results would have been what they wanted — it may not even have come to fruition at the time. There was a big distance between where they needed to be and where they were at, at that moment.

"For me, the making of that record was to try to take all the inspiration . . . because some of the parts on the demos were inspired, there's no question. And I'm a firm believer in making use of things that are inspiring, and not just do it again 'because.' When you've done something that is spontaneous and great, use it. That was part of the philosophy of that record: to try to capture the emotion and inspiration of early performances, rather than just breaking them all down and redoing them again.

"Some of the parts on that record, Alex and Geddy would probably say they couldn't even play them the same way because they don't quite remember what they were doing. They were just ideas they had found among all of the recording they had done and taken them and made them into songs, sometimes by repeating a section. Or there was something quirky about the sound that made it really interesting. And so the idea of using those things was fundamental. I like to think of it as a record that was made out of all of the bits and pieces of inspiration and emotion and power that they came across in the process of writing. And then allowing Neil to have as much time as possible to sort of experiment and get on top of his game, to be able to play what he wanted to play on it."

Paul describes the next step: "After the song structures were all agreed upon, between the band and me, Neil would start to work on one or two songs at a time. I would do that just with him. Once we'd reached a point where he and I were both confident he had done performances that were worth consideration, then we would get Alex and Geddy to come down — with wine, invariably — so we could play it to them to see what they thought. And usually, there would be like three sort of great performances we'd want them to listen to so they could help pick and choose, in case there were different ways to approach different sections.

"Which was part of the process of being able to do this with a computer. In the past this was impossible because you would have one version, take it or leave it. In this case Neil was able to show different ways of approaching a song, and they'd just choose together afterwards what seemed to be the best. One thing that characterized the making of that record was that at every stage, until we reached mixing, I worked with them individually. They were all there at the studio, usually, and on the first part of the day, I would work with Geddy. Once all the songs were settled on, the structures and stuff, on a computer, usually in the evening, I would work with Neil. And then once we had gotten drum tracks we would get together. And then sometimes I would work in the evening with Alex.

"There was almost no time where the three band members and I all sat and worked together. It was not because of any tension; it was to do with the fact that they all needed some space and they all wanted to experiment with their own ideas. Then we would periodically get together and listen to the results and see how everybody felt about things. But I don't remember ever recording Alex with Neil and Geddy in the room, and I don't remember recording Geddy with Alex in the room — and all the drum recording I did just with Neil.

"So it's a very different record," reflects Paul. "And I think the reason they wanted me to be involved was because I'd known them for so long and I'd worked with them in a number of different circumstances — and that I was a close friend of Neil's. Those things added up to helping be the glue to hold it together. Neil had been through something very few people would survive, and now he was trying to get back on his game as being one of the greatest drummers in the world and be able to do something that was groundbreaking, from that point of view. That was equal or better than anything he'd done before — that was the goal. That's why you make records. You don't make records just because it's time to make records. Especially in their case. They do it because they want it to be interesting and something that challenges them, and that they love and that the fans would love too."

Northfield brought a lot more to the table as well. Asked specifically why they might have wanted Paul, he figures, "They knew that if they chose a producer who was strictly a producer, where they had an engineer as well, that meant there were another two bodies in the room, in an environment that was very personal. This was family getting back together to make a record, and I think they saw me as part of the family already. They felt secure with me, and they knew I would speak my mind honestly. They felt I had something interesting to offer from a production standpoint because I'd been constantly working ever since we'd worked together previously, and I was working with people they found interesting.

"I guess that's why they chose me, but also they knew they wouldn't have to do the dance of dealing with someone new who had to get to know them. I had a reference point as to the way they played their best, the way they played together, the way Neil played. Probably the biggest concern they had, that they expressed, was that because I was a friend of Neil's, would I be ready to criticize him directly, if I didn't think what he was doing was right? That was the only significant concern they had. 'If you don't agree with something, are you going to be able to say so to Neil?' And I said, 'Yes, of course, that's part of the job.'"

Paul makes an interesting comment about the lyrics on the record. "Notwithstanding it being a complicated process in the sense that they were all working individually, there wasn't too much conflict. The only small thing would've been — and it was completely understandable, really — that Neil was writing lyrically what was very much an expression of his life, what he'd gone through. And I know Geddy appreciated that and understood it, but at the same time he wanted to make sure the record was something he could sing, that was meaningful to him, and not something that was really specific to Neil.

"This was in a simple, creative, artistic sense, which Neil understood too. Geddy was uncomfortable with singing something that was very personal to Neil and would prefer to have something that was more universal. So there were a couple of times where we had discussions about that. But for the most part, the recording process went relatively smoothly, albeit long, because they had already spent nearly six months writing, and then I spent another five months with them recording."

Northfield says there was also a sticking point between Geddy and Alex around musical preferences, stemming from what they had each experienced on their solo records.

"Yes, probably the main contradiction on *Vapor Trails* was that Geddy was very into melody and harmony at that time, from a writing and compositional point of view. Alex was very into aggressive Nine Inch Nails/Marilyn Manson kind of metal. And so there was Geddy maybe erring on the side of being a bit too . . . not sweet, but melodic, and Alex maybe pushing to be a bit aggressive outside of the Rush world. That was difficult, and yet at the same time they had been together for so long and they were so respectful of each other that they were trying to make that work. There were moments of great inspiration, but it was a difficult record. It didn't seem difficult immediately, but by the time we got to the end of it, it was like wow, this has become a monster that we are trying to tame now.

"But yes, Geddy's dominant vision was melody," reiterates Paul. "And he was experimenting more with vocal harmonies as well, and allowing them in a way he wouldn't have done in the past. I made a big point of emphasizing to him that I thought it was a good idea for him to go back to singing high at that time. Because over the years, he'd gradually sung lower and lower and lower. And from a point of view of trying to capture the three-piece attitude band, singing high was actually a benefit, because you could cut through. As soon as you start going lower and lower and lower, it becomes much more difficult; there's more of a conflict to getting a vocal to be heard in a lower register.

"Some of the iconic Rush, obviously, he's way up there. And there were times like in *Hemispheres* where they wrote the whole record without realizing it was really on the edge of his range, and he had a nightmare singing *Hemispheres*. I wasn't part of that record, but when they came to *Permanent Waves*, it was like, we're not gonna have that happen again. Gradually over the years, he kind of went down and down. And then when they decided they were looking to go back to some more raw energy, it was important to think about going back up high, not maybe into the stratosphere, but pushing it.

"He'd since worked with Ben Mink on his solo record, who is also a very strong musician, arranger and multi-instrumentalist who shares a lot of Geddy's humor. They both have a sense of the absurd but also a similar seriousness about their music. And so when I came to work with him, he'd often have done a lot of his vocal stuff by himself. Working out the parts and working out the harmonies. And so when I was with him, we were working on computer. He said, 'I got used to doing a lot of this by myself.' It's kind of like . . . not a crutch, but it's a nice place to be, where you sit and you're playing with the computer and listening — it keeps you occupied. There's great value in that sometimes.

"As a bit of context, when I'm producing records, I still like to engineer things. And the main reason is, when you're busy and occupied, you don't feel like there's a big pressure to say something if you have nothing to say. Because you're involved, you're part of the process of making the record.

"And that's a difficult thing for a producer to do sometimes, to stay out of it. If things are going really well, you don't need to have an opinion. You can just let things go. And so for me, when I'm producing, I like to keep my hands busy. When things seem important to say, you say something, as opposed to sitting around going, well, I haven't said anything for the last fifteen minutes; I better have an opinion.

"Anyway, I think Geddy was feeling that he liked that, when he was working by himself — he was busy. So he said, 'Do you mind if I do this, and you just sit there at the back and tell me if it's good?' Which was the exact opposite of my comfort zone. But it was like, 'Yeah, okay, all right.' This is a challenge, but I was up for it. So basically I had to verbally tell him what I thought. And in true Geddy fashion, like when he would do bass, he'd do maybe three takes of bass and then we'd get three we felt were good takes. He'd say, 'I'll play you a take and you tell me which one you like and which bits of which one.' And he would keep playing me pieces and I had to choose. And he would either agree or disagree.

"But the amusing thing was that I wasn't aware at the time that he was testing me by sometimes playing the same piece twice to see if I had a different opinion about it. Which is the complete reverse of the tradition of being in the studio where the producers and engineers tended to force musicians — with Rush, particularly around *Moving Pictures* — to play things again and again and again, to get the perfection. And punching in again and again, to the point of absurd, sometimes.

"And it was almost like revenge," chuckles Paul. "Because suddenly Geddy was able to play the same performance back and see if I had the same opinion all the time. And I'm somewhat proud that I think I actually managed to survive that test. He said to me after a couple of days of doing that, 'You're pretty good; I've been testing you.' He's very sharp and he's watching out for bullshit, if you like, in the technical or musical department or whatever. He's got his eye out for people trying to pull the wool over his eyes.

"My take on Geddy was that when everything is going very smoothly, and everybody appears to be doing the job he expects they're going to do, he's a very relaxed and humorous guy. But at any moment, if he gets the sense that somebody's not on, not doing the job or not paying attention, he very quickly changes and becomes quite intense. It's a shocking change. You go from joking around and then suddenly, 'Oh, okay.' There's a sudden real seriousness that comes into his interaction with people. Fundamentally, he likes to joke around, but if at any point he doesn't feel like things are being done properly, he's the first person to turn up the heat. And fortunately, most of the time I worked with him and those guys, I was a pretty diligent guy. But there were occasionally times when you'd get a little loose about what you're doing, and suddenly it's like, you know."

Emerging out of the darkness on May 14, 2002, *Vapor Trails* would prove to be a very different kind of Rush album — rough, frazzled, fuzzy, noisy, claustrophobic, laden and leaden with meaning. The full arsenal is used directly at the opening salvo. First there's Neil with a novel rhythm, just like on *Counterparts*. Next Alex does his best Dick Dale — quickly two tracks of it — while Geddy enters gloriously bassy of tone, perfectly meshing with Neil's booming bass drums. Ergo "One Little Victory" starts twice but with the same theme, more focused and purposeful than so many Rush songs that start twice or three times, often without logic to the stitching. A couple of waves of the surf theme soon give way to a considerably heavy riff that hits that place between British blues boom and doom, last heard on "What You're Doing" and "Working Man," something that will return again in a few hot spots on *Clockwork Angels*.

An apt opener and a sensible enough lead single (there's a conceptual and sonic uniformity across the album that means all the songs are candidates — and none at the same time), "One Little Victory" begins the record on a hopeful note, before moody introspection sets in. This whole record is a latticework of little victories, one supporting the next, carrying forward into touring again and yet more records. The choice of this song for the pole position also makes sense given it's a bit of a showcase for Neil. Even if he cites a certain amount of "anger and confusion" in the part, he really cooks up something interesting, using double bass drum as an extra treat. The plan was for Neil to insert this part at the back end, but Geddy cajoled Neil into opening the record, solo-style. Also, as Paul alluded to, Geddy unpacks his high register, singing the first verse middling and then jumping an octave for the second push.

Geddy continues unpacking for the long haul come "Ceiling Unlimited," where he plays bass chords as well as some bass harmonies. Up-tempo rock like the opener, in this one Alex is characteristically textural, with Neil bashing away and Geddy not plonky but simply emitting tone. Bass players usually really dislike when their articulation is missing, and indeed there was so much regret about the mix of the album that it came in for a rare remix, with *Vapor Trails Remixed* issued on September 27, 2013, complete with new cover art, mixed by modern prog maven David Bottrill.

Add the title of this one to Neil's suite of weather titles, even if the song itself is not about weather. It means, essentially, very thin cloud cover, a term Neil picked up while on the tour bus with the TV tuned to the weather channel. Peart's lyric for the song is jam-packed with concepts for pondering, much of it societal, balanced (in the booklet, literally) against inscrutable lines that could apply to his remarkable circumstances.

Alex continues to explore where he fits across the layers of Rush's now re-densified sound, picking individual notes as he often does, plus hitting chords.

"It gave me the opportunity to explore areas of the guitar I could use for textures, the sorts of things the keyboards used to do in the past," says Lifeson. "And I love that; it's fun to make that instrument sound unlike how it's supposed to sound. And that's what we did with *Vapor Trails*. It's always the most recent record that sits best with you, but even trying to be as objective as I can, it's probably my favorite record that we've done."

Still, as Alex explains, the record emerges as downright inscrutable, with respect to its relationship with the guitar. "The direction I really wanted to go in for this record was a very anti–rock guitar direction. Geddy plays a lot more chordal stuff, and that comes from his solo record. He wrote a lot of those songs on bass. You play chords to sing along to, and he naturally gravitated toward that style. And when he would do things like that, it took me somewhere else. I could play single-note lines, play more of a bass part when he was playing more of a rhythm guitar part. So we were changing roles and that interested me; I really like trying to go in through the back door if I can."

At the lyric end, Neil gorgeously and with discipline describes his motorcycle-mounted healing process, creating a soundtrack song to his celebrated book, in progress at the time. Reflects Alex, "Everything had so much weight to it, every note and every idea, and of course the writing lyrically was very therapeutic for Neil. It was an opportunity for him to get a lot of stuff out of his system. And in many ways he's very honest, as he was in *Ghost Rider*, the book he wrote about his feelings and the things that were happening around him. He's a very private guy, and he spoke very openly about those very private issues he has, which he usually holds very close."

Ghost Rider serves as a microcosm of a wider album that feels like it needed to be written, art that was screaming to come out despite the difficulty of its birthing. If in the past, records might have been made just because Rush are responsible adults and they need to make stuff, the whole of *Vapor Trails* feels like a work of art, one that is conceptually purposeful even from a musical point of view. In other words, it marks a shift in direction, one too fragile and arcane ever to be repeated. It's an odd song though, but one that works, thanks to an urgency from Alex on hard-rain guitar, with Geddy passionate and pushing air, Neil bashing along with open hi-hat, hitting lots of cymbals, leaning into spirited fills. And yet there's a strong melody. You might almost think it's some kind of post-punk ballad from 1983.

"'Peaceable Kingdom' is one of my favorites because I think it's a great example of all these different elements, of shifts in tempo and shifts in rhythm and of melody," notes Alex. "For me what was important was to get the guitar to sound dissonant at times, and very rich harmonically, with a lot of noise going on in the background of whatever the melody was, counterpoint as much as possible to what Geddy was playing and sometimes to what Neil was playing, not only in terms of rhythm, but also in terms of texture and melody.

"Almost all of 'Peaceable Kingdom' is from that one jam we did, then we made the song up from that, added a couple little embellishments, the drums of course. But basically guitar and bass are from that one time — that's the one time it was played. I really love that idea."

When asked to clarify whether this means that much of the record comes from live interaction between Geddy and himself, Alex says, "Well, I wouldn't say almost all of them, but at least half, in terms of performance. Generally, Geddy and I would jam for three days. And then we would spend a couple of days compiling, weeding out the crappy stuff from what we thought was good, and then from there, we would start assembling songs. The deal was, if we could better the performance, great, if we can't, fine. And songs like 'Peaceable Kingdom' had a certain feel and energy to them. You know, you get into the studio and start playing, and you start thinking about it too much — everything is like that — and it becomes a little safe. When you're not thinking and just playing, it's coming from a different place; you don't care and it just goes. And it's a beautiful reflection of where you're at that very moment. That's what I love about it."

Again, there's a through line from things tried on previous songs, Geddy singing moderately high (albeit, back in the mix, smeared by open hi-hat and his own bass chords), along with some really heavy caveman rock, only achievable when the bass is this low of frequency, and Neil pounds away freely like he would on *Clockwork Angels*.

The artful and understated tarot card theme Hugh used for the CD booklet (contrasted against his gratuitous image-barfing on *Test for Echo* and *Counterparts*) reveals the "Tower" card as we arrive at "Peaceable Kingdom." Indeed, this one has Neil addressing the then-recent September 11 terrorist attacks. Hard hitting, action packed and opaque, there's even a plot of real estate on which to underscore the album's tarot card theme.

"The Stars Look Down" keeps up the side in terms of the band creating a helluva din. There are backward guitar parts, acoustic massaged in, obscure bass chords, but the river running through it is fat bass, Alex with lots of electricity and Neil bashing away hitting lots of cymbals. "This started with Alex and me just riffing together in a funky way," Geddy explained to *Bass Player*'s Karl Coryat. "When we hit the chorus, everything changes; I go into a finger-picking bass chord pattern, with three or four chords that circle around. He joins me at the end of the song, doing the same thing on nylon-string acoustic, which makes for an interesting orchestration."

The title of the song comes from an A.J. Cronin novel from 1935 (and the attendant 1939 film), but it's really just a jumping-off point. Again, Neil is cryptic with the point he's making across the verses, but the chorus is pretty clear, Peart looking at an unresponsive cosmos and asking, "Was it something I said?" and "What are you trying to do?"

"How It Is" is a curious one, a left turn. Structurally, we're back to *Roll the Bones* and *Presto*, or *My Favorite Headache*, given the song's load of melody emphasized by soft strumming from Alex. Yet the verse is somewhat new wave, recalling the band's ardent explorations of '80s bands finding new and somewhat antithetical ways to combine guitar, bass and drums. As Geddy told Coryat, "This song fell together easily; the melody just popped out of my mouth and worked well with the lyric. But every time we tried to 'produce' it, we lost something, so we decided it was best to go back and work with the original jams that inspired the melody. Alex added some mandola in the beginning and middle, but overall this tune was a 'jam to disc.' I just tried to find the busiest, angriest bass riff for the verses — a bit over the top — to contrast the chorus' sweet, melodic nature."

This song contains one of many nods to literary sources for Neil, who itemizes a few of these in the *Vapor Trails* tourbook. "Lyrically, no overall concept emerged, but I can trace some interesting sources for particular lines, like Thomas Wolfe in 'How It Is' ('foot upon the stair, shoulder to the wheel') and 'Ceiling Unlimited' (Wolfe's title *Of Time and the River* and looking at a map of the Mississippi Delta suggested the 'winding like an ancient river' lines). 'Ceiling Unlimited' also offers a playful take on Oscar Wilde's reversal of the Victorian lament, 'drink is the curse of the working class,' while Joseph Conrad's *Victory* gave the 'secret touch on the heart' line. 'There is never love without pain' echoed from my own experience and the novel *Sister of My Heart*, by Chitra Banerjee Divakaruni, and W.H. Auden and Edward Abbey (*Black Sun*) influenced certain lines in 'Vapor Trail.'"

Continuing with his method of essentially creating the official statement on albums as they got toured, Neil explained that "an article in the magazine *Utne Reader* called 'What Do Dreams Want?' contributed to my ideas in 'Nocturne,' as well as the enigmatic mantra, 'The way out is the way in' for 'Secret Touch.' And I was also struck by a psychologist's approach to analysis and dream interpretation, 'without memory or desire.' The nineteenth-century Quaker folk artist Edward Hicks painted no less than sixty versions of the same biblical scene, 'Peaceable Kingdom,' while a series of works by Canadian painter Paterson Ewen helped to inspire 'Earthshine.'"

The record's (almost) title track moves musically like a combination of "One Little Victory" and "Test for Echo," one part surprisingly leading to the next, tribal drumming coming out of nowhere, sophisticated melody and counter-melody tickling the senses. Incidentally, one might wonder, why not the Canadian and British spelling of "vapour"? It was Neil's decision to go with the shorter U.S. spelling, where both Geddy and Alex would have readily gone with *vapour*. The same issue emerged with Geddy's solo album, where the decision was made to go with "Favourite" for copies sold in Canada and the U.K. and "Favorite" for copies sold in the States.

Peart's "Vapor Trail" lyric feels sharply autobiographical. Heartbreaking is the line "All the stars fade away from the night / The oceans drain away." It's a tribute to W.H. Auden's poem "Funeral Blues," read by Neil's brother Danny at Selena's service.

"That was definitely Paul Northfield," says Alex, on the subject of the record's big drum sound, almost dominant on "Vapor Trail." "Paul came into the project about six months after we began. We had a couple of songs we still weren't too sure about in terms of arrangement, and Paul really had an objective ear. He helped out a lot in fine-tuning some areas of the songs we were a little unsure of, having lived with them for so long. We went to Reaction Studio, which is not known for its live room, as a drum room. It's actually quite a dead room. It's a jazzy room, very dry. Paul came in and just built it up to his specs — drywall everywhere. Every open space he could find was re-drywalled. He really brought a lot of life to the room, and I think he did a great job on the kit. The kit sounds to me very immediate. It sounds like you're there in the room, which is not an easy thing to do."

Alex addresses the topic of Neil's intense yet eerily spare lyrics. "Obviously, having gone through what Neil went through, and what we all went through, it was definitely going to impact where this record was going to go. To me the record is very optimistic. It's all about recovery and about hope, about a future, rebirth and moving forward. There are some dark moments, some sad moments, but generally, it's really about those things I just mentioned. And the course the lyrics it takes to get that message across covers a lot of ground, from a very personal experience to a more universal representation of it. Geddy and Neil worked very, very closely on getting that idea across. Neil has always been, I think, a writer who has written from an observer's point of view.

He doesn't dictate one way or another, but he lets his feelings out and they are taken in a universal manner. With this record, it was a very personal experience, and they worked closely together so the idea that Neil was trying to get across could be presented by someone else, in this case by Geddy — he has to sing the lyrics with conviction. So they worked very closely and it was very professionally done. There was no question of a personal thing in it. It was more about what the best way was to get this across."

In this author's opinion, the most artistic, magical, emotional moment on any Rush record past *Signals* occurs at 3:44 of "Vapor Trail." At the tail end of an impressive and fresh sort of '80s new wave passage — Waterboys meets Big Country meets Midnight Oil — there's a massive drum-propelled crescendo. Once the tension lifts, the band collapse into a sad and almost Sabbatharian groove, over which Geddy repeats the "in a vapor trail" refrain. Quickly it's normalized by Alex adding REM-like picked electrics, but for a brief moment, at the outset, from 3:44 until about 3:53, it's just epic sobbing notes from Alex atop Neil swinging for the fences. Not even sure there's a bass track in there, and if there is, it's just supporting these awful "Working Man" chords that emerge from Alex, considerably blackening what is already a bleak combination of music and words.

It's hard to believe that "Secret Touch" was picked to be the album's second single. Peaking at #25 on the U.S. Mainstream Rock chart, this one's a bit more challenging for the listener. There's bass chords to open, there's a dissonant wall of sound for the verse, and there's shocking bursts of almost Voivod-like heaviness.

But no real guitar solo. "I don't solo nearly as much as I used to," explains Alex, speaking with me at the time. "I think I used to have a solo on just about every song on every record we've made, but I've gotten out of that for some reason. I love soloing and I think relatively and objectively I'm a good soloist when it comes to composition of solos. But for some reason on this record, it just wasn't in my heart. There are a few, but I just didn't find it as important. I thought it would be great if those quote-unquote solo sections were more a band solo section where we just get into an instrumental thing and we're all grooving and playing off each other; that was far more satisfying."

Indeed, "Secret Touch" has one of those, where each of the players stays respectful to the root but can step off briefly or offer a variant. Here a crazy sound collage gives way to a sinister metal riff from Alex and distorted bass from Geddy on what can only be called a casual or spontaneous break, before the band brings back one of the song's already established melodic themes.

"This was a great platform for exploration for me," continues Alex. "The guitars are loud on this record, for sure. Everything is. The bass is loud, the drums are loud, the guitar is loud. We managed to capture that, and that's really what our goal was from the beginning. I tried to create guitar parts that were simple yet sounded more complicated or complex than they really were. I really got into this idea of guitar dissonance and playing across keys and using keys that are usually against the wall and creating tension that way. Geddy's playing a lot of bass chords lately, and on this record, they become a little more dominant with all this other guitar noise in the background. It created a sense of depth and greater dimension by doing that."

"This is a bit of an extravaganza," explained Geddy, again to Karl Coryat. "We built the song around these repeating bass chords that I thought sounded like French horns. The tune has a hypnotic feel, and because we weren't happy just enjoying that feel, we had to smack it up with some power. When we get to the middle section and all hell breaks loose, there are these stuttering bass punctuations. I double tracked them, but on one of the tracks, I went in and digitally truncated the notes to make them sound really abrupt and punchy. There's another point where I'm playing straight 16th notes, and when we were jamming originally, we could hear the sound of my fingers slapping against the string, but when we played it back it didn't have the same 'smack.' So we put up a mic and recorded the sound of my fingers while we were laying down the parts, and we used it subtly in the mix. I don't know how much of it survived under all the guitars, but it's there."

"Earthshine" is another tense rocker, Geddy singing high, Alex most clearly stomping a distortion pedal in comparison to elsewhere on the record. Geddy's bass has more of that old-school Rush articulation to it here, old school meaning back to *Moving Pictures* and earlier and not so much the hyperarticulation of the late '80s/early '90s. The dark heaviness lets up for one of the band's slightly Celtic choruses, *Celtic* also somewhat of an apt descriptive for Alex's seagull-scream of an ersatz guitar solo late in the track and then the returning high atmospherics even later, which almost sound like Mellotron.

"'Earthshine,' which was the first song we wrote, was completely rewritten," notes Alex. "Even the lyrics were changed around. Musically it was a completely different song from what it was, and it was a complete song in the beginning. We had all the parts, the lyrics; we worked it out, it was there. But there was something about it that just didn't knock us out."

In a sense, this was a revelation to the band: that with no deadline — and really no predictable outcome or future — they had the luxury of discarding ideas generated over the first long writing period, five or six months. In Geddy's view, the original music didn't live up to Neil's majestic lyric. Not really a weather phenomenon but in the wheelhouse of Neil's nature musings then, "earthshine" is an effect that occurs about once a month, where the night side of the moon is illuminated by "earthlight," which is, in reality, sunlight bouncing off the earth.

"Sweet Miracle" is a comparatively conventional song on the record, melodic hard rock, somewhat singer/songwriter-ish. It's one that came very early, with Geddy particularly touched by Neil's almost spiritual lyrics. Geddy sings it in his comfortable lower range, although he adds some higher background harmonies. Once more, Neil is just hammering away at his cymbal array, making casual and bar-room rocking a song that is sort of ballad-esque.

Geddy says that "Nocturne" came from tail-end writing sessions that resulted in five or six songs coming rapidly, arising from jams between him and Alex that he thought were some of the best they ever had. To characterize it, it's quite raw and wildly bass guitar–centric — the verse is built of two or even three very distinct bass tracks, no guitar, with Neil essentially playing hi-hat. But as the drama unfolds, there's some intrusive and vicious guitaring from Alex, and then a break that is almost punk rock. Supporting Neil's lyric — a fearful exploration of the dream state, essentially — the musical backtrack is both murky and agitated. Interestingly, the threat of the narrative isn't so much of nightmares, but of dreams being too powerful, a night-mining threat to waking sanity.

"Freeze" gets a subtitle indicating it is Part IV of the "Fear" trilogy, Rush smashing the rules of trilogy-making in the process. Of the four songs, it's the most about fear, literally being frozen by fright, nominally in some sort of early morning confrontation downtown. To recap: Part I of the trilogy is *Grace Under Pressure*'s "The Enemy Within;" Part II is "The Weapon" from one record previous, *Signals*; and Part III is "Witch Hunt," from the record previous to *Signals*, namely *Moving Pictures*.

At the musical end, this is Rush at their most experimental.

What we get is pretty much Primus without the sailor smoking a corncob pipe, although a modern-day King Crimson is also evoked. All told, it's a gem hidden way at the back of an album that is almost seventy minutes long. Do bass chords make for good music? Debatable — in all cases across this record the songs might have been stronger without them. But "Freeze" is a full-on noise-prog workout, all the white-knuckle circumstances of the album coming to bear, almost as if the guys are executing a final flameout ignited by fumes.

As Geddy told *Bass Player* magazine, "We were dying to work in some screwed-up time signature because we hadn't done that in a while, so we came up with a jam that was in seven. But then I got the idea to digitally form the jam around the song's lyrics. The more I played with it on the computer, the weirder the time got. I decided the bass and guitar should be repetitive and hypnotic, but I threw out any rules for the time signature; I shaped the time of each verse section to the number of beats I needed to fit in the vocal properly. That's why it's hard to count that song. There aren't any rules as to when a beat is dropped or added. The middle section is a bass-and-guitar jam, which we left virtually as is."

Last track on *Vapor Trails* is "Out of the Cradle" and back come the bass chords, although Geddy says some of the intention was to use bass to create what a traditional piano part would sound like. Neil holds down a song breaking to get free, through the device of replacing expected snare whacks with tom-tom, and then a typical non-beat for a bit. But of course, as often is the case, this is to set up following verses and choruses where the beat is back. The music is on the happy side for the album, and so is the lyric, with Neil celebrating the miracle that is life, endlessly rocking (until the end) from the cradle forward. Peart was inspired by a Walt Whitman poem called "Out of the

Cradle Endlessly Rocking," which is much longer and covers a lot more ground. However long gone are the days when Neil would essentially summarize Coleridge — this is much more of an abstraction that takes the initial idea and explodes it. In interviews, Peart has likened riding a motorcycle to being rocked and soothed, and so it's a fitting summary of events. Of course there are ties between the concept and actual music, ties that Whitman also regularly made.

Alex ends "Out of the Cradle" with a squall of guitar noise, but that isn't the end of *Vapor Trails*. As alluded to, the album would get a full remix, the guys spurred on by favorable reviews of remixes of two tracks, "One Little Victory" and "Earthshine," executed by Richard Chycki for the *Retrospective III* compilation.

"Right up to the point where we got to mixing, everything was going well," explains Paul Northfield. "The difficulties — the big difficulties — with *Vapor Trails*, came in the mixing. We mixed it at Metalworks. I started the mixing, and before Christmas we'd gone into their big studio, which is a very, very large control room, with a new console in it, and initially everything was very smooth. Before Christmas, I'd mixed about two-thirds of the record, and everybody was really happy. It was like, 'Wow, this is the easiest mixing session we had ever done.'

"And after Christmas I came back and I got a call from Geddy, 'Oh, we need to talk.' He said, 'We've been listening to stuff, outside the studio here; the mixes sound very compressed — it doesn't sound right.' He wanted to play me a bunch of records he liked, and we played them in the control room, and it was like, well, it sounds a lot different outside. The differences between the records he played in the control room and what we were doing were not as noticeable, and so we started to sort of question the control room itself, or the room we were mixing in, which was frustrating, to say the least.

"So then we decided — or I decided — to move into one of the other rooms in Metalworks, which I did have good experience in mixing in, and we started from scratch again. Essentially it was going pretty well, but it was difficult. Alex was interested in a more intense and aggressive approach to mixing than maybe . . . I wouldn't say it was between Geddy and Alex, because it wasn't like that. Even me, I wasn't necessarily comfortable with being quite as aggressive, from a guitar point of view, as Alex was looking for. But I guess that was his frustration to some degree. So mixing became difficult, and the decision was made that they would get somebody else in to do mixing, someone who hadn't been involved. That was a decision taken, and I can't disagree with them. I mean, that's just what happened.

"And so Dave Leonard was brought in to mix it, somebody Geddy had worked with. I thought he brought some interesting musicality to some of the mixing, but ironically at the end of it all, the very criticisms we had at my mixing in the beginning, which was too compressed, ended up the problem with the album overall. Whether it was mixing or predominantly the mastering, it was a problem. At that point, I was not involved in the record. I was busy making another record at the time, with Porcupine Tree. So in the final month of the mixing and the mastering of the record, I was mostly at home in England and subsequently working on another project.

"It had been such a long journey making that record, that by the time it was all done, I think everybody was so worn out with it, they weren't ready to sort of sit and be critical again. Consequently, the overly aggressive mastering, in retrospect, is plain for all to see. I think everybody would agree with that at this point. By the time it became clear that was going on, I think it was too late. All the guys in the band were pretty much exhausted with the whole process.

"And at the same time, there was a lot of enthusiasm for the record," continues Paul. "For every person who was concerned about the sonic quality, there was a whole bunch of other people who were very excited about the energy of the record, the fact that it was a powerful record. Musically and songwriting-wise, there's some really excellent stuff on there. But I'm glad it got remixed. It really does benefit from somebody from the outside going through what is there. Because there are some great performances and some great musicality on that record. It was a time and place — a very difficult time emotionally — making that record, and that comes through."

As Neil explained in the *Vapor Trails* tourbook, "In the self-contained universe of our work, everything had been going very smoothly, and it was only when we moved into the final mixing stage that we got bogged down. It seemed that all of us, Paul included, had become too deeply immersed in the material, and we could no longer step back and hear the songs whole. After a few unsatisfying attempts, we called in a specialist, David Leonard, and he was able to sift through the parts and make them bright and new again, to find the hidden dynamics and textures and bring out the subtleties of the music and the performances. And so it was that we suddenly found we had been working on this project for over a year.

"While putting so much time and care into every detail of the content and performance of the songs," continued Peart, "we hadn't paid any attention to their length, and now we began to worry if all thirteen songs would even fit on a CD, which can only hold seventy-four minutes. There was some talk of saving a couple of songs for a compilation or something, but Rush has never left any 'previously unreleased tracks' for anybody to capitalize on, and we weren't about to start now. All of these songs had taken a lot of time and effort, and we simply couldn't imagine leaving any of them behind. Fortunately, they added up to just under sixty-seven minutes, so we were spared any painful choices.

"The last big challenge we faced, as always, was the running order of the songs, and we fiddled with that right up until the last minute. However, we never doubted which song would open the album, for 'One Little Victory' made such an uncompromising announcement, 'They're ba-a-a-ack!' Knowing our music is nothing if not idiosyncratic, and doesn't really cater to popular 'taste,' we also envisioned advertising slogans along the lines of, 'If you hated them before, you'll really hate them now!' or 'And now more of everything you always hated about Rush!'"

Alex's complaints with the *Vapor Trails* mix were that certain guitar nuances, especially the acoustic playing, got lost, but also that there was distortion, crackling sounds, and compression. The most salient changes in the remix are that Neil's bass drum and snare drum get more attack and whack, also something applied to Geddy's bass playing. It adds to the tightness and energy and vitality of the songs. Most thankfully and impressively, none of the power was lost — the new version simply sounds more stadium-rocking and expensive, less muddy, but Bottrill didn't turn off the bass and make *Vapor Trails* into *Presto*.

"It's one of my favorite records that we've ever done," summarizes Geddy. "There's something about that record that is really raw and really passionate. And in some ways, even though it's nothing like it, it has a kind of focus that reminds me of *2112*, in a way, just in its kind of balls to the wall attitude, the playing. It's a real album of playing out. Alex and I wrote a long time. The first stuff we wrote was not very good, and we threw a lot of stuff away. We almost needed to write a practice album before we got to the real one. It had been so long, so many years, since we'd written together. But we had to get a lot of stuff out of our system, shake off the rust.

"But when we finally started getting to the good stuff, a lot of it was just jamming, playing, that we recorded. We just left the machines running and recorded it and shaped the songs out of that spontaneous performance. We learned a really important lesson from that. You have to respect a performance, especially one that is improvised. And I think a lot of the spirit of that record comes from the fact that some of those are the original jams. A lot of those songs, or the final guitar parts and bass parts, were just things we had jammed together. There's a real honesty about it."

Adds Alex, "I think *Vapor Trails* really requires four or five listens before you get a sense of what it's about and where it's going. It requires a commitment from the listener to get into it. There's a lot of meat on dem bones. For us, that's what music is all about. In our music, we like to challenge the listener and make it so that every time you put it on, you hear something else or you get a different emotional reaction to a song you didn't have before."

Hype was sky-high for Rush's first tour in more than five years. Ticket sales were brisk, giving the band a glimpse of what can happen when you make yourself scarce, something they had only toyed with in the past, be that with touring, records or indeed even interviews. One must also remember that making oneself scarce can blow up in one's face — you can be forgotten — and that emphatically didn't happen here. Remarkably, the *Vapor Trails* tour proved that Rush could be an arena-level headline act for an uncommon twenty, twenty-five years, indeed for every tour since 1980, and really, with only moderate scarcity practiced, more like a gentle and relaxed elasticizing of its record/tour cycle beginning in the early '90s.

On the subject of playing big shows versus the grinding gigs of the club days, Alex offered at the time the following observation.

"You know, we played a small gig in Germany on the last tour. It was a 1,200-seater, a little kind of club thing. And people always ask that: Do you miss the old club days? Being right there with the audience? And no, I don't. We've been doing arenas for so long that that's where we're quite comfortable. To us, that *is* an intimate setting. There's a greater sense of power, I think, in an arena. The lighting can be more dramatic; the smoke onstage can add a sense of mystery to what's going on."

Ultimately, Alex and the band saw a flurry of activity in all corners with the arrival of *Vapor Trails*. Rust had to be shaken off, a new show needed designing, and of course, many, many interviews had to be conducted to tell the world that Canada's prog icons were back. "It's a little overwhelming," remarked Alex. "We've always done a lot of press before a release but the work-load this time around is three or four times what it's ever been before. I think it's because we've been away for five years. Times have changed. The internet has become so much more import-ant, so there's a lot of website interviews that we do now. I think we've made a really good record and people are either surprised by it or very interested in it. It's just upped the amount of work."

"That stands for all of us now as a difficult time," explains Neil, with some distance. "There were sonic battles on the melodic side of the band, and Alex and Geddy had both made a solo album in that interim. So they came back as little dicta-tors. I don't think they would mind my saying that, and knowing they had done it all themselves, written music, been in control of everything, produced it, the art direction and everything, made it the way they wanted it. So they were coming from that place.

"I was coming from such a lost place. I love the image of the ghost rider, and of vapor trails, and it was a way for me to process all that horrible experience, and what I might've learned from it. So that was very difficult too, for all of us to find a balance, the commonality that I described, that we needed. The common energy, even if we don't agree on things. So if you can find a central point, okay, that's what will satisfy us all. And it's not a compromise; I choose the word carefully.

"That was a difficult time coming together. Uneasy, for me to start writing lyrics; you know, what was I going to write about? Being angry and confused. That does come out. But I was very much interested, years later, in hearing that in my drumming. I can hear what I built from with that, and I knew where I was coming from at that time. But it was such a reflection of who I was then. Afterwards, I hadn't listened to *Vapor Trails* in six or seven years. We'd grown from there and made *Snakes & Arrows*, which comes from such a different place in our lives. And ultimately good."

"But *Vapor Trails*, like *Hemispheres*, had to be made," continues Peart. "'What cannot be altered must be endured' is one of my sayings. That was the case — we had to go through *Vapor Trails* to get to *Snakes & Arrows*. That's the price to pay. And we had to go through *Hemispheres* to bust out of that. And just to backtrack a little — because it's such a beautiful circle — at the time of making that, we already decided that we would never make another *Hemispheres* again. It took so much out of us and we realized, okay, we're done with that. We knew we were moving on, stylistically and song lengths and approaches and dropping the big thematic thing. And the interesting thing is that it was organic, in the moment. Okay, done!

"And *Vapor Trails* too was a struggle to get right and had some of the very same obstacles as *Hemispheres* did. Nothing seemed to click easily, and it took a much longer time than any of the others because we recorded it as we went, and made demos, and made the record all in the same country, which was all good. Now I can see what was successful and what wasn't successful, and what the flaws are, and why my anger and confusion is sometimes good and sometimes not good in my drumming — I can see that clearly. But it doesn't take away from that record being so important and on the whole such a positive step."

As mentioned, concurrent with the making of *Vapor Trails*, Neil was toiling away on *Ghost Rider*. In his book, Neil truly opens up about himself. Though Neil is famously at odds with the interview process, through his writing, he bounds from last to first in openness. Starting as a famed recluse, his book shoots him past rock stars who chum with fans regularly and take every interview that comes their way; he amusingly winds up the guy who is the open book, literally.

"Well, there's the double irony of it all, I guess," chuckles Peart. "Despite being so private and introverted, yes, I love to tell about my life — but I decide what that's going to be. And you know, website stories are a perfect example. It's been kind of my creative writing outlet for the last year or so. Every break on the tour, I'll put together an essay with photographs describing my experiences and little stories like the lady with her Buick and little incidents that I like, and observations I've made about nature or weather or whatever — all of that's in there. But it's not private, you know? There are no pictures of me with my friends, or my wife, or of my house or anything like that. It's about my working life. There is a very clear distinction to me, what's public and what's private. And yeah, my books are about my life, and all four of my books are autobiographical travel books, which ought to be as un-private as can be but it's still not. As a writer-to-reader thing, same as any of my favorite writers. I've never been tempted or even desired to be part of their lives. I must admit the cult of celebrity never affected me even as a kid. Like, I never wanted to force myself into Keith Moon's life, you know? I could play his songs on my desk at school, and that's all I needed."

Once the *Vapor Trails* tour started rolling — to many a fan's disbelief — Rush-starved crowds were treated to fully five tracks from the new record, namely "Earthshine," "One Little Victory" and "Secret Touch," as well as "Ceiling Unlimited" and "Ghost Rider" on alternate nights.

"Geddy and I sat down and listened to a lot of material," explained Alex at the time, about coming up with a satisfying raft of songs. "We decided we wanted to shake up the set list: freshen it up, drop a lot of those songs that maybe a segment of our audience had gotten used to expecting, and mix it up a bit, play songs we've never played before or in a long time. That required us to go through all the albums and listen to everything. We listened to *Caress of Steel*, *Hemispheres* and, man, we hadn't listened to those records in a long, long time.

"And generally our feeling was they held up pretty good," continues Lifeson. "Our recollection of them was much different from what we discovered. *2112* has held up well; it was such a great period. There's a lot of anger in that record, and I think it stands up as an idea as well as a musical piece. *Hemispheres* was a transitional record for us, the last of those big concept things we did. There was always a question of whether it was a really great work of ours or maybe not such a great work of ours, but I think it stood up musically. There are some songs we can't get around like 'Tom Sawyer' or 'Spirit of Radio;' they're great songs to play anyway, so that's okay. But some songs you do get quite tired of playing over and over. It would be nice to challenge ourselves a little more, particularly with the older stuff that was challenging to play even back then."

Further on the process of going back and listening to the old records, Alex says, "My recollection of it was that things were a lot smaller and more amateurish. When we listened to all of those old ones, *Fly by Night*, *Caress of Steel*, *Kings* particularly,

Hemispheres, they stood up pretty well. There was great energy, power and spirit in the playing. When you listen to something that you did twenty-five years ago, and you haven't heard in twenty years, it can be an eye-opening experience. We felt a lot better about our catalogue at that point. We realized that some of these songs really improve with maturity. We'll approach and attack them a little differently than we did in our early twenties when we wrote these things. We'll definitely play them with a different sense of feel and rhythm."

The first show back was in Hartford, Connecticut, on June 28, 2002, this after closing out the *Test for Echo* tour in Ottawa, July 4, 1997, almost five years previous to the day.

"Hartford, Connecticut. Wow, that was amazing," reflects Ray, who says that after the show Neil was so happy. "He came over and he hugged me, and he was like, 'It was good, it was good.' Some self-confidence was back. That's why we were in Hartford, in a secondary market and not somewhere big. But that's the Rush style. Rush could've capitalized on it and used it as a big deal somewhere, but that's not the way Rush works."

"He's a bit of a stage fright guy anyway," remembers Geddy, who took it upon himself to keep Neil engaged and amused during the set. "It's part of my job description. But it was very hard for him. It was hard for all of us to keep our cool because it was so emotional. And I don't think we expected it to be so emotional once we hit the stage. I guess he did, but I didn't. I figure, back to work, and Alex too. There was a moment when we gathered around Neil's drums, first song. You know, you make that eye contact. We have little devices of contact that we always do to each other, and that makes you smile. And by three or four songs later we were fine."

"You can ease yourself into the songwriting and recording part of it, and if it doesn't work, come again," figures Neil. "A show doesn't work that way. There's a whole other resonance on it, and a whole 'nother vulnerability to it as well. Trying to do your best onstage, and failing. Always. Nobody is always at their best. So there's a constant undercurrent of self-examination and insecurity there; you are literally vulnerable, and also internally so. And so coming back to that night, there were several moments when we looked at each other, and if a face could speak, we spoke volumes to each other. The emotionality of it, and having come through fire back to that essential being . . . but backstage we were just so anxious and intense and focused. It was a remarkable state of mind, not nervousness exactly, but it's tense, all right? I was super focused on one thing: 'I've got to do that show now.'

"I must admit, I did," says Neil, asked if he felt the pressure of all eyes upon him that night. "Again in that whole time, I was vulnerable. And I don't like people to know that much about my life. It was unavoidable of course at that time so I had to deal with it. But there is an internal place I'm at when I'm playing, and the outside is a luxury. When I'm concentrating, I'm in such an internal world of milliseconds and shades and expression and all of that, and exertion. You know, working at an intense physical ability as well as mental. So when I do have the opportunity to come out and observe others, it's a luxury. But that's what that night was like."

Recalls Alex, "It was interesting, because being the first gig, there were a lot of friends and guests there. It was just a beehive of activity in the dressing room, and we like to have a very quiet dressing room, a peaceful place. And of course, they really wanted to be a part of it. We went out into the gig, and I remember looking out at the audience and there were people crying, you know, in those first few rows, because they were just so happy we came out of this dark period and that we were still there. I think it gave them something to latch onto, that in our darkest times, there's a light somewhere. And I remember a couple of points for the three of us where Geddy and I were right there with our feet on Neil's riser and just totally connected, and it was an amazing feeling. A lot of lumps in our throats that night."

"It was hard because everyone felt the sadness Neil experienced," explains Howard, part of the senior team tasked with making an experience like this run smoothly. "That's where it was hard as far as what we do. We had to get back up on the horse and go, but that's second nature for us, for the band, for everyone. I mean, it's time to go. I look at this as a really cool kind of camping trip. Especially when I was younger, when I ramped up a tour, it was like getting excited because you got together with a bunch of your friends and you are going to go camping. You are going to have a good time, and this is what it's like for us. You get on the buses and go to all these cities and it's like a big camping trip. So the camaraderie and the drive and incentive of what you want to accomplish keeps you going. You just get right back up there and do it. It's easy for everyone to do this. The hard part was to deal with the emotional side of what just happened, and be sensitive to it.

"After five years, you don't know," reflects Ungerleider, on the real possibility that what was happening in Hartford would ever happen again. "Who knew? But a painter never stops painting; a musician never stops playing. I worked for a guy named Brian Auger, amazing Hammond B3 player, and he was one of the guys who taught Keith Emerson how to play keyboards. This guy has to be in his seventies and he still plays; you just never stop. Once you're great at something, you are not going to stop unless you're physically made to stop. Even Oscar Peterson had arthritis in his later years before he passed away, but if you're a musician, you're going to go. If you are creative, you're going to go. And these guys seem to be a wealth of creativity, especially when it comes to writing music. You have the best drummer in the world playing drums. I mean, it's pretty cool.

"But it was still unbelievable," continues Howard, on when he heard Neil was coming back. "You had no idea what was going to happen. And we didn't expect it to ever happen, because Rush is Rush. There are three guys in Rush. You need the three guys to have Rush. But yeah, he did come back, and not only did he come back, he came back with a vengeance, which was unbelievable. I got a call from Geddy, saying, 'Hey, we're going back on tour.' And Alex said the same thing: 'We're going to go back, record a record,' and I was just so happy when I heard that. I wasn't happy for myself; I was happy for them. But it was one of the best news bulletins we had. Just the process of Neil coming through that, it was outrageous. And that's why you have to respect what he wants. You have to give him his privacy and his quiet or his downtime, whatever he wants to do — give him his space because he deserves it.

"To see the power and the musicianship back again, yeah, just great," continues Howard, on Hartford. "It was an outdoor shed show, at the Meadows, and it was a very good feeling. The first shows back on any tour are kind of edgy because you haven't done it in such a long time. You're memorizing all these cues, and they have to remember all their lyrics and everything else. There's a parallel to it. It's sort of like a marriage with lighting, choreography and musicianship. But it was really, really, really good and from that point on, it just rolled forward.

"I mean, their legacy is having three of the best musicians to ever exist," says Howard. "There will be people who would disagree, but I recognize the talent because I'm here watching it every day. I challenge people who are out there to try to take on what these guys do onstage every night, and do it as well as they do it. Rush is a band that people will definitely remember for generations, and the fact that already they have three generations of fans, that's pretty impressive."

Part of that fan base over the years included an increasing number of famous folk. "Oh for sure, there are loads of celebrities who are Rush fans," agrees Ungerleider. "It's surprising, but there are a lot of ballplayers. Randy Johnson was up onstage in a chicken suit, basting the chickens. There are a lot of pro golfers who come out. Jack Black comes out. We'll see other bands come out — there's constantly other bands. You know, the younger bands idolize Rush. The guys from Tool came out. My company that I own does production design, and we do a lot of other tours. We do lasers for Tool; so we're friends with them. Maynard owns a winery, and he brought some of his wine to Las Vegas and gave it to the band — very cool guy. I heard Will Ferrell was at our show. People you don't expect would pop up. It seems more people are coming out of the woodwork now."

With Howard's help and other specialists, one of them Geddy Lee, who by this point had become a keen visualist not without technical acumen, Rush created a grand cinematic experience for the *Vapor Trails* tour, offering a symphony of images (the main ones revolving around a dragon motif) to operate in sync with major and unmercifully regular pyro effects ("sweltering hot this tour, I can tell you," laughs Alex), not to mention a bank of white clothes dryers, the day's wash spinning around throughout the show.

"George Steiner on our crew went out and got them," says Alex. "He sourced them down and kind of fixed them up a little bit, took the heating elements out of them so they were working but not heating. And he installed aircraft landing lights in them so that when you opened them up, they glowed. You had to put Canadian quarters in to keep them going. Every night we tried to have guests up onstage, to pump quarters into the machines to keep them running." On the subject of other domestic chores, Alex lets on that the kitchen was also very well equipped. "We brought our own chef out on tour. Our food was always fresh, organic. And we could tailor the menus to whatever we wanted individually. So it was great having him out."

Geddy offers a bit of color to the story of Rush's celebrated live film work, the *Vapor Trails* jaunt the most extensive yet. "I have a group of animators I work with. Norm Stangl at Spin Productions here in Toronto has been my point man for over twenty years, in terms of making weird animation and rear-screen stuff. And every year we try to do something different or try to invent some interesting effect or gag, and we've had a lot of fun designing different things. We usually use different stylistic animators every time out just so we get a different visual look. It's really one of the most fun parts of my gig, and it's something I always look forward to in preparing for a tour, sitting down with new creative people and having one of these great meetings where we just throw around all kinds of whacked-out ideas.

"And this time I wanted to do something very fresh and very spontaneous," continues Ged. "We were put in touch with this guy named Greg Hermanovic over at Derivative who has invented this touch software that is really very cool, which has allowed us to have an actual live VJ, kind of, on the road with us. And what we would do is design live concepts for about fifteen different songs, and he would design elements that he would blend live every night. Some of them would be purely abstract, some of them would be representational, and it really opened up a whole new area.

"As a result, no two shows were the same because Jim Ellis, who was our operator, had the ability to improvise on a nightly basis. And sometimes the combination would just be magic. But you could go to two shows and they really wouldn't be the same, although the elements would be the same. Depending on how he was feeling it, and how the band was feeling that night, the show around us would vary. And of course, the longer the tour went on, he would start throwing new ideas in, so the show kept growing visually. It was really fantastic, and I thought it worked terrifically, better than I ever expected. It was a wonderful addition to the show."

Geddy adds flesh to the tale of the dragon, prevalent in the film, and then talks about the packaging of the tour's subsequent live memento *Rush in Rio*. "In the original *Vapor Trails* design, Hugh Syme had one version of the cover where on the back, very small in the corner, was this tiny dragon, who was the cause of this great vapor trail. And when we were doing the preproduction for the tour, I was looking for animation ideas to use live. I wondered what it would be like to exploit that little dragon a bit more, turn him into a character, which people at Spin Productions developed into a full-blown character that we used during 'One Little Victory' live. It was a cool, humorous way to use this dragon. So again, the dragon was picked by Hugh to become the representative of the show in Rio, and of course, he's got him dressed up like Carmen Miranda."

"The live experience and the studio experience have always been two different things for me," says Alex, looking back on the tour that was. "The kind of energy that is required in the studio is quite different from the live show. Looking back, the live part of the whole experience has come full circle, the *Vapor Trails* tour in particular. We played the best we've played; we were really tight. The level of satisfaction on a night-to-night basis was the highest I think it's ever been. Very few shows are tens but we had, I think, a lot of nines. And the energy level seemed to touch on an earlier time. I guess it might be because

Vapor Trails was more of a three-piece kind of record, and we had come full circle in that respect.

"We also brought some stuff back like 'By-Tor' and 'Working Man,'" continues Lifeson. "They were truncated versions of the originals, but they were pretty true to their original form. I would say we've always prided ourselves on being close to the record but with that added element of it being live, with the energy you create onstage. It was always a disappointment to me to go see my favorite bands and not hear the original versions of the songs. That always seemed like a bit of a cop-out. So from an early point, we always wanted to reproduce what we did in the studio fairly faithfully. We might have eliminated some of the keyboard stuff here and there, or eliminated some of the vocal harmonies that Geddy does. I try to help out as much as I can in that department, and we do have some samples. But he really loves to layer his vocals and he does a terrific job at that. But those are some of the things that are expendable live. I don't think they get missed given the energy of the live show.

"Certainly 'Resist' was different on that tour," says Alex, "going from an electric version to an acoustic one. We always wanted to do something acoustic but we weren't quite sure. We always resisted the urge. We didn't want to do an unplugged thing, which always seemed so trendy. But we thought it would be a nice break in terms of the three-hour show. Plus it would give Neil, depending on its placement, an opportunity to catch his breath after his drum solo. And to do it with quite a dynamic shift. So we worked on sort of a folk version of that, and I thought we pulled it off well. Geddy and I both had a lot of fun just breaking down for those few minutes."

Offering comment on the notable set list switch-ups put in place for the *Vapor Trails* tour, Alex reiterates of "Working Man" that "it was a real treat to bring that back. We weren't sure about it; it's such a simple, kind of straight rock song, but it ended up being a great opportunity to jam and to really play your heart out, for all of us. The same thing with 'By-Tor.' Some of those '90s songs, they come and go. They'll come into the set for a couple of tours and then they'll go and something else will come in. 'The Pass,' for all of us, is one of our favorite songs to play, if not our favorite song to play. And 'Bravado,' the same thing; we hadn't played 'Bravado' in a while, and bringing it back was a real treat because it's got such a nice mood."

"All the new material, generally, requires the most concentration," adds Geddy. "Because as a bassist and a singer, those songs aren't as firmly entrenched in my memory banks, so it usually requires a huge amount of concentration for me to remember to keep my bass lines grooving with the drums, to make sure I trigger all the samples with my feet at the right time and to sing in key. Even near the end of the seventy-date tour, it's still a challenge. Songs like 'One Little Victory,' 'Earthshine' and 'Secret Touch' are by far the toughest part of the show for me."

Concerning the new record's extensive use of bass chords, Geddy figures, "That is not so much of an issue, in and of itself. The issue is playing them, singing and triggering all at the same time. Some of those songs have very complex backing vocal effects, loops that are put on synthesizer that I have to trigger at the right time, otherwise they sound fucked up. So I'm basically triggering some vocal effects while I'm singing, while I'm playing bass. It's a bit complicated up there at times. And if you can't hear it all, you're in big trouble. In terms of older songs, I think the highest one to sing is '2112,' parts of it. That's probably the toughest vocal song. 'Red Sector A' is one of those songs I love to play because it gives me a break from the bass, and I can just go over to the keyboard and get into a whole different realm. Plus I think it's a great textural change for us live. And it's one of those songs that is just a perennial. But of the new ones, I think 'Secret Touch' is my favorite song on the record and I love playing it live. It's got a great intensity about it."

"We were doing 'Bravado' and 'The Pass' and both of those are impossible for me to play without feeling the emotion of them," says Neil, offering his perspective on certain high-water marks of the set list. "That's a nice thing. A lot of times it can be just a performance, where it's 'Okay, here's the song I have to play and all these elements of subtlety go into playing it well, so here's what I'm going to do.' Whereas other times I do get swept up into the song itself and hearing the lyrics and watching the response of people through that. That's another special thing about live performance, on the emotional side. Apart from the excitement and the cheering and the adrenaline reaction, when you see an emotional reaction to songs like that, and see people swept up in it — and feeling it yourself — that's kind of an underappreciated and unglamorous part of what live performance can be."

"Neil will practice for anywhere from twenty minutes to half an hour immediately before the show," offers Alex, on the subject of gearing up for show day. "He has one of those little five-piece practice kits that's just pads. But he pounds the crap out of them and that's his way of warming up. It's basically like him doing a drum solo for twenty minutes. He really plays hard on the thing. I like to do the same and warm up for a minimum of half an hour before the show. Depending on my mood, sometimes it's an hour. Geddy, not so much. I don't think I saw him practice once on the tour before the show. Although toward the end of the tour he had some tendinitis in his hand, so I do remember, actually, him spending a little time just warming up his right hand."

Other than that, "you'd be very surprised. Backstage before a Rush show — and when I say backstage, I mean the dressing room — is much like a library. It's very quiet. Neil is usually sitting in a corner reading. There is no psych-up. We get dressed, we chat a little bit about whatever, and somebody comes and gets us and we go on. There's no group hug or prayer or anything like that. We just do our thing."

"I'm not very hard to please," adds Neil, when asked about food requirements, riders and such. "I like some salty peanuts and some ginger ale and a tuna sandwich on the bus. But there's one thing; we always like to go to the show in the afternoon, for example, and do soundcheck and stay there. We always felt a certain uneasiness about leaving. There's some kind of, almost superstition, where we think we won't get back in time for the show. So that's a pattern we established early on, and we always stuck to. I don't think any of us has ever left the venue after we go there in the afternoon, whereas most people do. We were always more comfortable going to work and staying there, basically.

"Just being able to have dinner and have a rehearsal room . . . those are the kinds of things for me. Being able to have dinner when we want it, between soundcheck and the show, and having a room to warm up in. And then I leave right off the stage, so the rest of it doesn't affect me. There's a certain pattern to the day though, and you feel it winding up inside you through the course of the day. It's a show day, which is unlike any other thing. You go to the venue and do soundcheck . . . when we did the big Toronto show last summer, I didn't have a warm-up kit backstage, and it upset my whole rhythm of things, so to speak. That's the kind of thing that becomes a really important part of the day, just to go in for half an hour and warm up on my little practice kit. That's not superstitious obviously, but it's important."

Finally, I asked Alex if there was any time on the tour where the band experienced a real musical breakdown, due to miscommunication or what have you. "Not really. We wear in-ear monitors, so we're very aware of what's going on and where everybody's at in terms of train crashes, which is what we call them. But I can't really think of anything on the last tour. Although it does happen. I'd say it happens twice, maybe three times, over the course of the tour, where suddenly somebody does something and everybody is lost, and it sounds like very outside jazz, and then it just immediately goes back to the song."

Before we move on, we must mention that, while not part of any tour per se, as alluded to by Neil already, Rush ended up playing to their biggest crowd ever, eight months after the end of the *Vapor Trails* campaign. The occasion was the Toronto Rocks concert on July 30, 2003, billed as an economic booster for a city reeling from a bad tourism season due to the outbreak of an infectious virus called SARS and reduced travel in general due to 9/11.

Headlined by the Rolling Stones but with AC/DC receiving most of the effusive press, the day-long festival found 400,000 people tramping off to a retired military base amidst perfect summer conditions. Rush played third to last — a thirty-five-minute set — and were the hands-down hometown heroes, although the Guess Who (on just before Rush) were appreciated as well. Earlier in the day, the Tea Party played their well-known cover of "Paint It Black," and amusingly Rush returned fire, with an impromptu and brief jazzy version of the poisonous Stones classic, segueing into their last song of the day — Rush's set proper consisted of "Tom Sawyer," "Limelight," "Dreamline," "YYZ," "Freewill," "Closer to the Heart" and "The Spirit of Radio," in that order. The band looked impressive in black, and yes, the clothes dryers survived SARStock.

As Neil is wont to say, as the years went on, his life "got bigger." Such was the same with everybody in the band. On tour, any number of activities would fill out the days of the guys. Upon being asked if Geddy had become a pretty serious book collector, Alex replies that "I think to a degree he is; I don't know. He's a collector, period. He collects wine, he collects baseball memorabilia, books. He's the kind of guy who gets very interested in something and likes to really learn as much as he can about it."

"I have lots of interests," adds Geddy, on this same subject of leading big lives. "I play tennis, I travel a lot with my family and on my own. We go to France once a year to Burgundy to do wine tastings and things, so I'm a busy guy. I got pretty big into cycling this last summer, so I did a lot of cycling and long-distance riding. I make sure I plan at least one or two bike trips every year somewhere in the world. I'm a huge wine collector; it's a great passion to me. Literature, of course. Films; I love cinema. It's always been a big interest of mine."

"I'm fifty, and it's hard to lose weight!" Alex told me at the time. "Really, really hard. I've been really good about eating. I don't eat any bread, potatoes, no real empty carbs. I used to *think* about losing weight, and I'd lose it — not anymore. I do yoga practice for an hour and a half once a week and I try to do a couple other days, but generally it's just that once a week. I work out at a gym twice a week. I do at least two tennis clinics; one is two hours, one is an hour. I try to play on one other day. You know, I'm doing a lot! And it's not budging.

"But I feel better, I feel stronger, and it's important to get into shape for the tour. You really feel it out there, not so much in the first month or two months, but after it's a real curve. You just get tired; you don't have the same level of energy. It's difficult to travel and your hours are screwed up. You get into that two or three o'clock in the morning slot where you're going to bed. And I can't sleep in anymore. On the road, really, the first half of the tour, I'm up six thirty, seven. I like getting up early, especially in the summer. Again, I try to do my yoga daily on the road and I love playing golf. Then halfway through the tour, that catches up to you, and by the end of the last tour, I was sleeping until eleven. You're out of gas.

"Neil is the same way as Geddy," continues Alex, comparing his two bandmates and what they do to stay sane. "If Neil's into something he will exhaust it before he moves onto something else. When he got into motorcycles, for example, he *really* got into motorcycles. Now he does a motorcycle tour when we're touring. He rides thirty thousand miles on a tour, and he writes his journals, based on his experience on the bike. He did the same thing with cycling — he got so into cycling. Writing for him, writing these travel journals, has become a really big thing. He published for the first time on the last tour, but he's been writing these things for years now. He'd do a short, limited run of maybe 150 books for his friends. So he's been learning how to do that and building up the confidence to have finally released a major work. With his last book, *Ghost Rider*, I mean, the material he had to work with was so powerful. But I think he really learned how to put it into print by doing all those other things. He's always been super, super focused, quite disciplined.

"The last two tours — *Test for Echo* and *Vapor Trails* — he had the motorcycle," clarifies Alex, on Peart's extensive itinerary. "Prior to that, I think he cycled at least two tours, if not three, and he did other bike trips. For him, it's the perfect thing. He's not into sports. He doesn't play any sports at all. He's very uncoordinated, which is great for a drummer, but not for a tennis player. But he's quite clumsy otherwise. But cycling for him, because he's a solitary kind of guy . . . Maybe less so now, but in the past he really enjoyed his private time. He would get on his bike and ride out fifty or sixty miles and ride back, nobody but him. He could focus on his — whatever you would call it — cadence, the tempo of his bike riding.

"A little bit the same as motorcycling," continues Alex. "He could shut out the rest of the world and focus on staying on the road, you know, looking out for other cars. This is his kind of escape and how he dealt with being on the road. You try to deal with being on the road in positive and constructive ways. Because it's so easy to slip into bad habits. And we're lucky. We've managed to stay away from those pitfalls. But to say that we didn't come close on occasion would be inaccurate."

CHAPTER 6

RUSH IN RIO

"You gave us goose puppies!"

Victory-lapping it up around North America for only five months, Rush would cap off the *Vapor Trails* tour on an extraordinary note — playing Brazil for the first time ever. Three triumphant shows, the net effect captured on a live CD and DVD package called *Rush in Rio*, released to great acclaim on October 21, 2003. It won the Juno for best DVD in April of 2004. Serving as a sense-overwhelming exclamation point to the short summer and fall tour, the Brazil stand represents the global phenomenon that Rush had quietly become. And this without cultivating that status — despite being world travelers individually in their personal lives, Geddy, Alex and Neil never got out much together as a band.

Rush in Rio captures the mania of the band's three-night stand in Brazil, consisting of shows on November 20 at Olympic Stadium in Porto Alegre, November 22 at Estádio Morumbi in São Paulo and November 23 at Maracanã Stadium in Rio de Janeiro.

Until that point, Rush had only toured Japan once, did the hula in Hawaii twice, toured Europe with limited atlas-cracking imagination and hit Mexico for one show on the *Vapor Trails* tour. That was it for globe-strobing. Also bear in mind that South America loves hard rock, heavy metal and progressive rock, being quite the hotbed of the two natural convergences of the three: power metal and progressive metal. Tucking Rush under the equator and under those flame-thrown conditions would prove explosive.

Geddy offers a glimpse into the machinations that took place to make something like this happen in the first place. "Usually we get this yearly request to go play the Rock in Rio festival in January. And every time they held one, and they've invited us, we've been either in the studio recording — and you can't just stop that and do a one-off gig — or we've been not on the road at the time or not working; it's just been bad timing all these years. And the promoter was just determined to get us there this year, so he kept negotiating with us and pleading with us to come down, saying, 'You have no idea your popularity down here,' which of course was true. We had respectable record sales but we didn't realize how much of the record sales can't be accounted for because there's such a huge counterfeit record market down there; you have no way of knowing what you really sell."

Surely then, there must have been certain guarantees. "Oh yeah, they promised us they'd pay us a certain amount of money per gig, and they'll pay for our expenses and they'll send us the cash up front. Our manager, being exceedingly xenophobic and paranoid, wanted to make sure all these things were in place before he sent us down there. That wasn't in question. And I don't think we had much doubt about that, quite honestly. Because our agent down there is the same as our agent in Europe and the rest of the world, and he's very experienced. There's no way he's going to connect us with somebody there where we're not going to get paid; that wasn't really in doubt. What was in doubt was whether we were as popular as he said we were, or whether they could provide the technical assistance we needed to put on the kind of show that we do. But I had talked to some friends of mine who had played down there in other bands, plus other managers and stuff. People have been doing gigs down there for quite a while, so really, I don't think there was much to fear."

"We'd had offers for years to go to South America and never really added it up, or it never felt right or whatever," confirms Ray, back at the office. "Neil is an adventurer, and he would rather go on an adventure off on his own than carry this thing called Rush with him. It's tough enough just to get these guys to Europe on a regular or semi-regular basis. So when it came around this time, I'd made them aware of it, and Alex and Geddy had said they really want to go and they were ready to go. I had a promoter who had been trying for at least a decade, more like fifteen years, to get them. So I kept putting demands, requests, roadblocks, whatever, of what it would take to get them. And we had this very aggressive promoter who just kept saying yes, yes, yes, and we ended up going. And much to our surprise, it was as big as he thought it was going to be.

"But understand, there had been big shows in Brazil," continues Danniels. "They'd had this Rock in Rio series for years. I had gotten feedback, over the last five or ten years or whatever, that we were becoming the biggest band that had never been there. And that in itself was an attraction. U2 had been there, plus Rolling Stones, Chili Peppers, Iron Maiden — bands that were perceived as bigger than Rush had been there, as part of Rock in Rio or on their own. So there was this legacy about Rush, that we hadn't been there.

"And when we got there, I understood. First of all, you're coming to a country of a hundred and eighty million people. It's a lot of people, a big country, and São Paulo was a place of over twenty million people, seventeen million in the city itself, over twenty in the area; in Rio, probably six million in the area. These are big cities. And radio stations there sound like radio stations in secondary markets in North America — they play everything. Granted, because we were coming there, we were getting extra airplay, but I'd been in São Paulo for a couple days and I was hearing Rush between the Chili Peppers, Rolling Stones, the Yardbirds, Eric Clapton, Tool and whatever else is going on today. They just play rock music. They play Bob Marley on the same station. So I got it. Once I was there, I got it. It's a show, it's an event, we had some fans, but then it becomes bigger than that. And they promote — the promoters do a very good job. It's massive television advertising; it's newspaper, radio, you name it."

But outside Ray's purview, boots on the ground, "All hell broke loose every day there," says Geddy with a shake of the head. "You know, you never know what you're dealing with when you go to a country like that. When they ask, you tell them what you need technically and they say, 'Oh yes, we understand.' That doesn't mean you're going to have it. That just means they understand what you want. This was the fine line of semantics that we discovered.

"So every day there was a new surprise, in terms of the technical aspect of getting the show up, let alone twenty cameras and a recording truck. And the recording truck, by normal contemporary standards, was quite basic. And I think the same is true with a lot of the photographic equipment they were using. But they had some good cameramen and they had a great director and really good crew and a lot of experience in the periphery.

"But again, you just never know what's going to happen. We hadn't counted on it being such a circuitous route from São

Paulo to Rio. It took the truck about eight hours to get there. And because the shows are so much later . . . I mean, we didn't go on in South America until ten thirty, and we play a three-hour show, so do the math. And of course for the show in São Paulo the previous night, it was raining throughout, so the gear was all wet. So it was a case of loading trucks in the middle of the night, in the rain, and then driving eight hours. By the time they got the first piece of equipment on the stage, it was about two in the afternoon. We usually arrive at six in the morning and the show is ready to go by six in the evening. They were up against it, definitely."

Howard recalls all too well the logistical nightmares of the trip, but this was balanced by the excitement of the fans. "The Brazilian audience is passionate and they actually love the band," explains Ungerleider. "We never realized how much they loved the band until we went down there for the first time. I mean, I remember sitting next to Geddy and we looked at each other and Geddy went, 'Who would have thought? Look at this.' There were people who'd come up to us in the hotel and they'd be in tears crying. As Brazilians say it, 'You gave us goose puppies!' It's goosebumps but they called them goose puppies; I thought that was pretty funny. And we were staying at a hotel where the sushi chef carved the man in the star out of a radish and put it up there, not because the band was there but because he loved the band. There was all this passion.

"On the other hand, Brazil doesn't have buildings that are really conducive to playing in, other than the soccer buildings. You see where the people come in, the openings, they're tiny. You can't get your equipment in. The trucks can never get into the facilities, so you wind up pushing all your equipment a quarter of a mile from where the trucks can make it to, across plywood, over grass, over a moat that people usually urinate in during soccer events . . . think about what the smell would be.

"So you're loading equipment in past all this stuff, and then it's raining and everything's turning into mud. Then when we get to the stage, we have to zigzag around an area that goes back and forth for sixteen feet. All the equipment has to go across the lawn, over the moat, down here and up. It took a long time. And people were just filthy. There was a point in time with that Rio show when we didn't think it would go down. Everything was late getting there, and your stagehands are trying to understand you but there's definitely communication errors happening. But that show went off and it was magic. This magical thing happened, and it just became this brilliant, amazing rapport between the audience and the band.

"But yes, it was raining for the first part of it, raining all day, and that's where all the mud came from and it was really hard. I remember hauling cables through mud, and things were filthy and everybody was stressed out. No one really slept the night before because we had to go from São Paulo to Rio on a bus, and not a tour bus but a regular street bus that was uncomfortable and bumping around. None of us slept. We were up for forty hours, and then we had to do all this. But we pulled the show off and they shot it. I remember the first five songs, where I normally use ten spotlights, I only had two, because the generators had gone down right when this show started — no one knew but us. Still, everyone loves that video to this day. They're like, 'Wow, that's the best!' And the crowd was amazing, just incredible."

Long-time crew member Tony Geranios corroborates Howard's harrowing tale, admitting, "I got a little unhinged. I actually walked off one of the trucks I was loading. A little immature of me. But these guys didn't speak any English, and we were supposed to have somebody in the truck. I load the band gear every night. I don't physically load it anymore — I point. We have the union people that do that. And I'm trying to tell these guys — I'm supposed to have an interpreter there — 'This has to go on like this, man on each corner, lift it together.' And I'm in there now lifting as well, and getting this thing up. And two of the guys on the other end just walk away when I'm lifting it and it falls on me. Didn't get me, but knocked my glasses off.

"And I got pissed off, and I go, 'Fuck you, guys. I'm out of here.' Road manager got really pissed off at me. But as Howard was saying, we had to ride these trucks from the semi, because the semi couldn't get into the arena because the entrances were lower than these trucks could get through. Everything is loaded from the semi into an open-back truck, and then driven to the stage and unloaded from there. And that day it rained. It took us eight hours to unload all our trucks and we didn't have that many trucks. Eight hours to get to the stage."

But again, the end result made it all worth it. "Totally blown away," laughs Tony. "Had no idea. Had no clue whatsoever. It was very impressive. We were welled up with pride, you know?"

Still, Tony understands why this type of thing wasn't a regular occurrence. "Sure, I mean, for us just to do that Brazil stuff, we had to rent a 747 for about two weeks. And half the time it didn't fly — it just sat at the airport. You have to have different truckers. We had to transfer the gear when we went into Mexico, for example. Just the amount of production cost. Why we haven't gone to Australia, why we haven't gone to Russia, why we haven't gone to a lot of countries, it's the fact that this band won't just pack up their instruments and go into a festival type of situation and use whatever rental gear is there. For them, every show they do, they want it to be the show they're presenting, no matter where it is. There's a benchmark.

"Plus you can't really change the show a lot because of the way the synthesizers and the samples are set up. For a long time, we didn't have much flexibility of being able to change things around or shorten things because one song goes into the next one. I make the switchover. The samples from the last song are still playing as I do the switchover to the next because all of them are online at the same time. The only thing that differentiates what you're hearing is the output. I have eight discrete outputs per thirty-two inputs. There's thirty-two inputs going into eight outputs at the front of the house. So it's a matter of making the switch. Anyway, point is, when you switch over to the next song, that other machine is still playing."

"Awesome audience — it's a World Series audience," recalls Ray, on finally getting to see the shows themselves happen. "It's a big deal, a big event. Traditionally, in South America, they don't put the shows on top of each other. Usually they want to make sure there are three weeks to six weeks between shows like this. So the show takes on a life of its own. That said, a big part of the audience was hard-core Rush fans who had waited a long time, and some of them were twenty-five and some of them were forty-five. It was a pretty broad section of people."

Adds Neil, "We had no indication of record sales or conventional measures of success like that. That led us to believe we had a small loyal following there. That's what we went expecting."

Instead Rush played to their biggest crowds ever (excepting Toronto Rocks in 2004), and so onstage, Peart's main concern was "the mental congruence of things. We were trying to film sometime during that tour and it never happened and it never happened. And then it was suddenly, okay, we're going to film the last show. Okay. And the story's been told before: the weather, the trucks getting there late and so on, there was no soundcheck and nothing was tested until literally the minute before we hit the stage. And we're just going, 'Okay, we've got nothing to lose here. It can only be terrible.'

"But it was just magically elevating. And you can't say, 'Okay, it's the last show, I'm going to be better.' That's kind of a self-defeating prophecy there. Because you can't will yourself to do that. It has to happen and that's what we did. We just came out there and played against all these odds we couldn't blame ourselves for, so we weren't feeling that way. It was like, 'Okay, we're going to do this better than anyone has a right to expect under these conditions.' It was a magical night.

"And then going back to the hotel, the three of us, and all our wives were there, so it has that feeling that almost never happens at the end of a tour. There's actually time to reflect and glow in it collectively. The Snakes & Arrows Live tour, I remember, Indianapolis, we flew home, separated. It was all great, but Brazil, after the show we were with all our families. 'Yeah, we did it.' That was one of the rare occasions that we could actually bask in the glow of having accomplished something. Not only that great show, but that tour and everything that brought us there. That was one of those beautiful moments for the three of us and loved ones to share. If anything, the first show on that tour was the 'we're back' sort of thing, and by that time we were into the progress of the tour, surviving night by night, and then playing in Brazil for the first time ever, and in these giant soccer stadiums. All of that was so unfamiliar that survival alone was perfectly acceptable."

Again, a huge part of making mere "survival" acceptable was having to contend with the weather. We've heard about preparing the show in the rain, but now the band had to execute onstage.

"We had rain on the first two nights," says Alex. "In Porto Alegre, which was the first gig in the south, it was raining hard. By the time we went on it had stopped, but everything was wet. The stage was wet, our carpet was wet, some of the gear was wet. There was a problem with the console; it got wet. We managed to get it all going and working; it was a real miracle. The next gig in São Paulo, we do a three-hour show and we split it with a little intermission between the two sets. Towards the end of the first set, it started to rain. And during the second set, it rained. And I don't mean it rained on the audience and we watched them get wet — it rained everywhere. And the wind was blowing towards the stage. So really, all of us, including Neil, were soaked, water just pouring off us.

"The advent of radios makes things a little less dangerous up there," explains Alex, when asked if electrocution concerns might have stopped the show. "So you're not really worried about making a connection from one point of electricity to another, for example from the guitar amplifiers to the mic PA, so we just carried through. But toward the end of the set, my pedalboard started to short out. Some of Neil's electronic kit started to short out, but we made it through that set.

"The following day, which was the following gig, in Rio, it was a long drive," continues Lifeson. "They just started setting up when we would normally be doing our soundcheck. So no soundcheck, no line check, no video line check. There were problems with the power; requirements had not been met. There were problems with the staging. Everything that could go wrong did go wrong. The audio truck for the recording of the DVD . . . boy, it was a relic from another era. But we managed to go on at ten thirty and the show went off without a hitch. The camera setup for the DVD all worked. It was amazing that we got away with it. All the equipment problems we had the night before had miraculously sorted themselves out, thanks to our terrific crew.

"But yeah, we never expected that kind of response. We had no idea we had that sort of popularity in Brazil or anywhere in

South America. We heard stuff, but to be there and experience the energy of those crowds down there was remarkable. Plus we'd made this record that was not easy to make, and we had done this relatively long tour, considering we'd come from where we had come. So finishing like this, it was a crazy show."

Geddy chuckles about one incident during the filming of the event. "Alex was having a problem with a cameraman in the first set and he started freaking out at him, lost some concentration and had a gaffe in one of the songs, during one of the solos. After the set, we had to kind of cool him off and remind him that you've got to forget about that; you can't let those things bother you during a show you're filming. Because there's just no sense looking pissed off on tape."

"There's a little more of that Latin influence," laughs Alex. "Things that we kind of consider important here — work, efficiency, those sorts of things — exist to a lesser degree there. Their priorities are more family, friends, having a good time, having a good meal, enjoying each other's company, much like it is going to Italy or Spain or something like that. We could learn a lesson from that."

"He got the message, but it was very hard," continues Ged. "There was so much going against us that day. We were going on cold; everyone was going on cold. And to add to the confusion, there were all these extra lights that the camera people had put onstage without discussing with us. So there were these wires running across the front of the stage that were inhibiting our ability to go to the front and ham it up with the crowd. And that was really disconcerting for me, because I'm used to just roaming around and having some fun. And when I'd venture to the edges of the stage, I suddenly had to look at my feet to make sure I didn't trip over these stupid cables. The way you want to record a show should be ideal, and the last thing you should be thinking about is all this crap, so this was pretty fucked up in terms of our ability to stay calm, cool and collected."

Because of the rain, adds Neil, "Some of my stuff wasn't working and I was playing around it all that night, which is . . . if you consider the mental mechanics of playing the drums anyway, and then to be playing in two places, as it were, mentally, of 'What about when I get to that song? That's not going to work. What should I use instead for the electronic sound and how can I cover up *that*?' And imagining my whole drum solo. At some other part of the set, I'm playing some other song but thinking ahead, 'Okay, my drum solo; that's not going to work, so I'll do this and this and this.' It's restructuring in my head as I'm going. I've often said about drums — or probably any instrument — if you're not at least eight bars ahead of yourself, you're in trouble. If you have to think about what you're doing right now, you're probably in trouble. And it's that kind of distraction — when something goes wrong, that jars you. Suddenly you're just thinking about where you are and keeping up with it. That upsets a performance and makes you less satisfied with it.

"So in the general flow of things, I'm way ahead to the next transition, for instance, setting up mentally and physically for moving into that flow and keeping its mood and nailing the tempo — all the tiny little things of technique. So that's all flowing through your head in the course of the show. If something's gone wrong, it affects everything, and then you're completely and mentally just solving equations. I compare playing drums for Rush to running a marathon and solving equations at the same time. When you're solving equations in real time and in future time also, it's not pleasant, you know? You can do it and survive it and 'Whew, we made it,' but it's not fun! That's the only way to say it — it's not fun."

And the trip was all business, says Alex, no fun. "In Brazil, no, because it was always a whirlwind. We got down there and there were a couple days off, but we were traveling around a lot. There was a lot of press to do. We always do a meet-and-greet before the show, sign a bunch of stuff, take pictures with fans. There was a very robust schedule for us in terms of the promoter and record company keeping us busy. And then we had dinners every night; they wanted to take us to all kinds of different restaurants and things like that. So we were kept pretty busy the whole time down there. But on the course of the *Vapor Trails* tour, yeah, I play a lot of golf; Geddy goes out and plays with me maybe half the time. We also play a lot of tennis. Ged likes to go to art galleries and movies. You know, just try to do normal stuff and keep busy.

"Going onstage, for all of us, our heads are in performance mode," continues Alex, addressing what Neil discussed, namely onstage concentration. "When you're playing, it's down to business. For us, there's not a lot of room where you cannot be concentrating; you're really inside of what's going on. It's very busy onstage, and I find that if you get into the zone, then you're fine. You can sort of sit on top of it. But there are distractions, technical problems, in which case it's very difficult to keep up the concentration.

"But in terms of the audience and those other external thoughts, you leave them for other times. Instead, you're thinking about where you're maybe speeding up in a certain song or things to look out for from the last gig. We tape every show, so we're constantly updating what's happening with the show. I guess our approach is professional and performance-oriented before we go on. And then other times you go on and think, 'Wow, I can't believe people are paying me to do this.' It's just such a joy and it's so much fun. Particularly, the *Vapor Trails* tour was great. We had an amazing time. I thought I played really, really well and the response was terrific. It was nice to do a summer tour. We had never done a summer tour before. We had come off five very difficult years where we weren't even sure we were going to tour again, which made it that much more special. I don't think we took a single moment for granted."

"All of our wives came down," adds Geddy. "Pegi [Cecconi, important figure at Anthem and all-round Rush enabler] as well. We forced Ray to come on the whole tour, just to prove to him that it's okay to be in another country. We had a lot of fun and it was really a terrific time. The people in South America treated us very, very well."

On the subject of meeting the fans, Geddy confirms that Rush held meet-and-greets every night of the *Vapor Trails* tour; Brazil was in some ways just the end point of that tour. "We posed for photos and signed autographs; there are contest winners. It's a very short fifteen minutes, but we get all kinds, as you can imagine. We've got people who've named their children Alex, Geddy and Neil. Most of them are very hard-core fans who are just thrilled to have the opportunity to talk with you for a couple minutes. So it's kind of a sweet moment and I don't mind doing it."

Extending that experience to all of the years, Geddy says, "I think we've signed everything from picture discs to baby pictures to women's breasts. You just never know what's going to be put in front of you to sign." Alex adds a comment on gifts the band's been given. "Some people have done some very big paintings, some small ones. You get some things that are almost like school projects that have diagrams and drawings, basing something on a song. Japanese fans would send paper fans, boxes of incense. I remember getting an engraved glass goblet from a fan in Manchester, England. Um . . . I haven't seen anything lately. People are getting too cheap." Another memorable gift was a set of dolls (this was in the early '90s, before Bobbleheads — a Rush set exists), which both the boys and the crew found a little eerie because of how closely they resembled the guys.

Pretty much the fondest or most lasting memory from the Brazilian campaign was the manner in which the fans participated in the show.

"So enthusiastic and knowledgeable of every song and every note," explains Neil. "They set the precedent for all other audiences to come. Here's the highest tribute I can pay to the Brazilian audiences. They sang along with instrumentals, and instrumental passages, and even a counter-melody to parts. I'm thinking, maybe the end of 'Natural Science,' there's a counter-melody that they'd developed and sang on the video, that everybody else started doing from then on. And 'YYZ,' instrumental, they sang every note of that. Since that time, other audiences in North America and Europe saw that DVD, and they learned the Brazilian way to respond.

"Sometimes a big crowd gets unruly and it can be frightening. You see things going on, maybe a fight breaks out, a ripple of things going on. We used to play a lot of no reserve seats, festival seating as they called it in the olden days, and you'd see people getting pulled out by their legs; all this chaos, which is really hard on a soul to watch. But with the Brazilian audience there was no sense of that. There was a smile, warm enthusiasm, great engagement, singing every note. That's probably the ultimate — everyone wants to be the best rock crowd in the world, but there's a rock crowd that changed all audiences after. I don't think you can say more about them than that."

"'YYZ,' that was one of the audience highlights of the show," seconds Geddy. "As soon as we started playing that song, that whole crowd started bobbing up and down in time with it. And at one point they're waving their arms doing a 'We are not worthy' thing in sync. And what was amazing about the

Brazilian crowds, when we played some of our instrumental stuff, they would be singing parts, like a lyric part for it on top of an instrumental. I don't know whether they were soccer chants or what. It was amazing to me that they were singing well and adding new parts to our instrumental stuff. I was amazed at how young people were, as well. There were so many young people and many really good-looking young women too, which was a pleasure to look at. That's always a nice surprise at a Rush show.

"But yes, they wrote their own parts; they're very creative. And then other audiences did that. I love that. It happened in the U.S. and it happened in Europe, and it's all from their example. The Brazilians wrote the part for 'YYZ' that other fans were later singing when we played the song. I think 'Natural Science,' they wrote a part too, that people joined in on. I think it showed Neil that it's fun to play new places. It doesn't have to be a nightmare. He needed to know that, and I think he had fun. He may not admit to it, but I think he had fun."

"That's hard to do," chuckles Ray, remembering the sudden appearance of vocals on "YYZ." "I still can't do that. The next step after that is learning how to dance to that song, I imagine."

"It's surprising how in tune they are with everything; all forms of music," adds Alex. "They don't speak a lot of English down there, yet the audience was singing the whole night. And they very easily sung along with songs from *Vapor Trails* as they did from *2112* or *Moving Pictures*. I went down thinking that Brazil would be . . . not backwards, but yes, lacking, but it was really the opposite. It's a very advanced culture. They've been around longer than we have. And I think in a lot of ways they are the pride of South America; certainly a city like São Paulo is, which is technologically advanced and is the center of commerce and technology for Brazil."

Rush would play to twenty-five thousand people in Porto Alegre, forty thousand in Rio and an astounding sixty thousand in São Paulo, making that show the biggest crowd Rush had ever played to as a headliner, next biggest outside of the Brazil dates being far less, namely twenty-thousand, at the Gorge in Washington state during the *Test for Echo* trek.

Although the band played three shows, as Geddy explains, they wound up shooting only one. "It was a roll the dice kind of thing. It was actually the last show of the tour and not really our first choice. Originally, we were scheduled to shoot a show in the U.S., on the east coast, but at the last minute there were problems with the venue and it suddenly got canceled. And we said, 'Well, what are we going to do?' Because we had planned to do it as more of a high-definition photography experiment using really state-of-the-art gear.

"And then we changed to a completely different kind of video and it was suggested, 'Why don't we shoot one of the shows in South America?' Because those shows will have more color and kind of a concept to it. Rather than just being the band performing in a technical environment, it will be this interesting slice of life. So we had to throw everybody into panic mode, such as the production house. And actually my brother, who is in the film business and has done a lot of work with us and various companies, took over as executive, kind of a production overseer, coordinating all the various departments. And they set up the production in Brazil, which was quite interesting, a combination of our own people and cameras and using what we could find there. There were over twenty cameras involved in the shoot."

As alluded to, the aftermath was imbued with a sense of summarized victory. Relates Alex, "After that gig we went back to the hotel. We get together from time to time on the road, all of us together, especially when the girls are in town. We go out for dinner and try to do something, but because Neil travels separately, it's not always easy to coordinate those things. So at the end of that tour, all the wives came down for that trip. We were staying at the Sheraton in Rio, and we were all sitting at the table together and there were tons of people there. It was a big celebration. The crew guys were coming in after they'd finished, and it was a chance to say goodbye and hug and all that stuff. But the six of us were at this table, and we just felt so connected and so in love with each other. It was a really remarkable way to finish off a very exciting ride."

"To me Rio represented a willingness to accept new experiences," reflects Geddy, "and to expand our view of the world as far as Rush touring goes. To arrive there and to have this wonderful new experience in this new culture . . . I remember Neil sheepishly saying after one of the gigs, we were driving back to the hotel and he said, 'Hey, that made me feel really international!' or something to that effect. And I think that was a good sign. It made us realize we had gotten really narrow in where we were playing and what we were doing. So that's when I knew in my mind that we had to keep pushing."

The highlights of the resulting *Rush in Rio* CD and DVD are many. The video is packed with behind-the-scenes stuff, including hotel footage and Neil's warm-up regimen, the involved and meticulous show setup, plus travel shots. Musically, the package is distinguished by the inclusion of *Vapor Trails* material (most of it more frantic and quick of tempo than the originals), including "Earthshine," "One Little Victory," "Ghost Rider" and "Secret Touch." Disc three of the CD is retro heaven (and funny as hell, once Alex takes over the mic), ending off with "The Board Bootlegs," namely a slamming, highly electric version of "Between Sun & Moon," recorded in Phoenix, and an intimate, new wavy "Vital Signs," captured in Quebec City. Obscurely, "Driven" and

"Resist" are included, the latter, as discussed, in gorgeous acoustic form. "Leave That Thing Alone" percolates madly, leading into Peart's solo extravaganza, now known as "O Baterista." The crowd sounds like waves crashing ashore — that is, when they aren't singing every syllable and then some, which is seldom.

Alex offers a few comments on the construction of the DVD, framing it as "a lot of work. When we came off the road, Geddy and I sort of decided that if there were any video decisions to be made, he would look after that. Any audio decisions that needed to be made, I would look after that. We started mixing it and I thought I'd be in every other day for a couple of hours. I was in the studio every day from noon until four in the morning for eight weeks. So it was a lot of work. The original intention was just to do the 5.1, and then Atlantic decided they wanted to release the CD, so there was that added, and it was the whole show again, in a stereo version. The work just piled up and piled up. So I worked really hard that summer, a summer where I just expected to kick back. The previous two years had been very busy and very hectic for us, so it was nice to just have that fall off."

On June 29, 2004, Rush surprised the heck out of everybody by issuing *Feedback*, an EP of covers, twenty-seven minutes of music consisting of eight songs. The math is frustrating because eight songs is near the lower bar needed for a record to be considered an LP, while twenty-seven minutes . . . well, at least back to the '70s, add ten more minutes and you'd have an LP. At this rate, a double raft of sixteen songs wouldn't even have made for a particularly long CD — fifty-four minutes, falling well short of the approximate seventy-four-minute limit of compact disc technology. But this presumes an LP is universally viewed as preferred. Perhaps this is just messaging that *Feedback* is not to be taken all that seriously. Furthermore, at EP length, it's easier to leave it off discussions of the "official" catalogue: the catalogue of LPs (which of course are further distinguished by being comprised of Rush originals).

"We've always ignored these anniversaries," Geddy told Michael Mehle of *Rocky Mountain News*, addressing the fact that it had now been thirty years since the *Rush* album saw release. "Your manager is the one who wants to exploit every one. I kind of felt that way this time as well. I would have preferred if the thirtieth anniversary had passed by quietly, but the other guys thought, 'You know, this is an accomplishment. Maybe we should stop and appreciate all we've gone through. Maybe it's okay to have a moment of nostalgia and reflection.' Maybe they were right about that.

"Over the last ten years, we've talked about doing a cover song as one of our encore tunes in concert," continues Ged, "so the idea wasn't completely foreign. Once we started, everyone said, 'Hey, this is fun.' Everything we tried turned out pretty darn good. The criteria was that it had to be something we could call our own, but at the same time we wanted to pay homage to the people we liked without wrecking the song. That was the number one rule: we couldn't wreck the song.

"We wanted to do a Jimi Hendrix song because he was so influential," says Geddy — rumors also exist of the band getting semi-serious about King Crimson and Jethro Tull. "But you can't touch Jimi, man. He's untouchable. We put together a rough version of 'Manic Depression,' which is just an awesome song. But you put my voice on that and it just sounds all wrong. You put this skinny little white guy from Canada on there, and it's just not the same vibe. I found the same thing with Zeppelin songs. It's so much about the people playing them. But we could have done an entire album of nothing but Who songs. We could have done an album of nothing but Yardbirds songs. We went back to fiddle with some of them, but mostly we just added a few great moments of feedback. We tried to get feedback in each and every song."

Hence the title, which also embodies the idea that Rush is offering feedback on the subject of their roots, opening dialogue beyond name-checks in interviews and substantially paying tribute.

And as Geddy explained to Brad Parmerter, there was really no risk in trying. "A very good friend of mine, one of my closest friends, suggested it to me. It was the kind of thing that came about very slowly. I thought about it for a while and I thought, 'You know what? Maybe it would be a fun idea.' And I ran it by the other guys. They both responded positively rather quickly, and we approached the whole idea in a kind of 'nothing ventured, nothing lost' way. We thought, 'Well, we'll just play around with these songs and if they turn out great, fine, and if not, then fine too, we don't have to release them. We can throw them away. Because nobody knew it was coming, there was nothing expected from us. We took a very casual approach to it.

"Vocally on *Feedback,* there are a number of different arrangements to that of the originals," notes Geddy, in the same chat with FYE.com. "You can't go in with the idea of just copying a song directly, although 'The Seeker' is really not that different. There are a few different dynamics and a few different harmonies floating around there. You need to make the songs your own in one way or another, otherwise you can't really sing them convincingly. Once we put the initial arrangement together, I played around with what suited me in terms of singing that song."

But put aside vocals and look at the guitar, bass and drums — and even the mainstream song choices themselves — and you'll see a lack of imagination, a tentativeness. The countless covers and "tribute" albums that had emerged in the business beginning in the mid-'90s to this point had collectively raised the game for such pursuits — *Feedback* falls flat on all fronts. Fans rolled their eyes reading the track list and then were not wowed by Rush's versions. Talk to the deep fans, and sure, they would have appreciated a run at Zeppelin, but *obscure* Zeppelin. Same with King Crimson — this is Rush, so nerd out. Since the guys are known Who fans, something a bit more adventurous than "The Seeker" would have been cool. And why not Kansas, Queensryche, Dream Theater, the Police or Primus — an expression of the band's much-lauded sense of humor and self-deprecation? Or at least, closer to the mandate of influences: Yes, Genesis, maybe a little taste of Taste.

"Our vision was 1966, when we were teenagers," expressed Neil, speaking with Don Zulaica. "We just decided to pick songs from our youth that we liked and make a tribute album to the people we grew up on. For instance, we did 'Summertime Blues' and kind of combined the arrangements of Blue Cheer and the Who, and did Buffalo Springfield's 'For What It's Worth,' and this other obscure '60s band called Love, a song called 'Seven and Seven Is.' All of us loved being freed from the material — in other words, not being responsible to think it up. And we did it our own way, of course, but we paid a little due respect to the times. We called the project *Feedback* because when Geddy and Alex were working on demos, they decided to have feedback and backwards guitar on every song."

"When we got into the studio, we set up a whole bunch of candles and lava lamps, and brought in some rugs," Alex told Doug Elfman from the *Las Vegas Review-Journal*. The sessions were produced by David Leonard, everybody working at Phase One in Toronto in two or three weeks traversing March and April of 2004. Leonard had worked with Geddy on his solo album. Here he gets a lively and electric sound but one that seems to fall victim to the volume wars, the compression craze that was making CDs harsh at the time. Getting into the spirit, vintage gear was used, albeit computer manipulated.

"We set up in the room, recorded off the floor together, the three of us. We toyed with the idea of including a Beatles song, or two Beatles songs — maybe 'I Feel Fine' or 'Day Tripper.' We sort of jammed out on that a little bit. There was some stuff that seemed sacred, that didn't seem right, and 'Manic Depression' was one for sure — it's such a personal song for Hendrix. And instrumentally, it sounded fine, but with Geddy's voice, it sounded too alien and weird.

"We thought it was a lot more fun and appropriate to pay tribute to some of the music we played when we were twelve and thirteen years old and learning how to play, before Rush, when we were in little basement bands," continues Alex. "Going through this stuff for *Feedback*, I realized how much of me is Jeff Beck and especially Pete Townshend. When I list the people who inspired me as a kid, I usually say Eric Clapton and especially Jimmy Page. But really, I think Townshend's probably one of the biggest influences I ever had — he really taught me something about chords and how to create a big guitar sound without turning it up really loud."

The EP opens hard with "Summertime Blues," and as Geddy explained to J.D. Considine, "The song has been done by a lot of people, but the first version we all loved was by the Blue Cheer. In fact, we played a few Blue Cheer songs back in those days. They were our heroes because they were the loudest power trio in the history of power trios. We really dug that!"

"I've never really heard Eddie Cochran's version," Lee told Michael Mehle. "My first exposure was Blue Cheer's version. It was a pivotal moment in my life, hearing this raucous three-piece band with all this feedback."

Next is the Yardbirds' "Heart Full of Soul," on which Geddy

employs some mild falsetto — the whole song is mild, originally and in this version. "We changed it up a little bit," figures Ged, speaking with Considine. "The verses are very simple, and the choruses kind of kick in with a block of harmony that I wrote. I think it's one of the best things we've ever recorded. As soon as it comes on, it sounds contemporary, but it sounds like the '60s too. It feels like there should be an Austin Powers movie running with it simultaneously."

Alex has called Buffalo Springfield's "For What It's Worth" his favorite song of all time, so there's the reason that one's on there, even if it's legitimate that we're all surprised Rush cared at all about music from the Troubadour's avocado mafia. Lifeson remembers being in the car with his dad, pre-Rush. "We were going to a shopping mall or something like that," Alex told Doug Elfman, hearing in his head that song on the radio. "It was a sunny summer afternoon. I had my little blue granny glasses on. I just connected to that whole moment. It wasn't the first time I listened to it, but I think I was just becoming so aware of moving on to a different point in my life. And it was all connected to that, in that summer, to that song."

Track four of eight on *Feedback* is "The Seeker," a bit of a deeper album choice, so . . . fair deal gone down. As Geddy told Considine, "There were so many other Who songs that we wanted to do, but there was something about 'The Seeker' that we all liked, and I think it's because in our own songs we never play that slowly! We're always so hyper, and there's something about that song and that feel that's so classic."

"Mr. Soul" by Neil Young (for Buffalo Springfield, circa 1967) is entirely incongruous but there's a darkness there that suits Rush, and Geddy is recorded down a wind tunnel, adding urgency. As a positive, the arrangement coheres with the comparatively rockier material on the EP, and the end result is a uniformly loud — even raucous — trawl through the band's teenaged roots (even if no one asked for this exercise).

"One of the weirdest songs ever written," says Geddy of Arthur Lee's "Seven and Seven Is." "Pure surrealism. Alex and I loved this song when we were kids, especially the chord progression. The lyric is probably the goofiest thing I've sung in my life. We had some fun with it because it's lightning-fast, and Neil plays one single snare roll from the beginning of the song right to the end."

Those snare rolls continue across Yardbirds classic "Shapes of Things," yet again another song on *Feedback* played with no irony, oddity, obscurity or extrapolation. Still, we get to hear Neil solo profusely, or at least we hear him make a lot of noise. And then, of course, there's some feedback. Why didn't Rush cover the Amboy Dukes?

Feedback closes with "Crossroads," and again, one might venture the guess that the fans would rather have heard a Cream original. Geddy told J.D. Considine, "It's a very simple version of the song, quite unlike anything else on *Feedback*. We just set up and played the song live; afterward, I did just a single track of vocals. When we mixed it, we even set up the stereo field so that the guitar is off to on one side and the bass is off on the other side."

Along with punking the Rush faithful, *Feedback* also served the function of new Rush product, fulfilling the old promoter's corollary that the purpose of a tour is to support the new record. Technically, Rush was delivering a record, thereby creating a reason to tour. The campaign, like the EP, was framed around the band's thirtieth anniversary. They played May of 2004 through to the first day of October 2004, and filmed and recorded their Frankfurt, Germany, show on September 24 to release as an extravagant CD and DVD live package called *R30*.

"They're a blast to play," Geddy told Brad Parmerter, with respect to the covers. "I love playing them. I wish we could play

Fourth show of the *R30* tour, May 31, 2004, at the Post-Gazette Pavilion in Burgettsown, Pennsylvania, a suburb of Pittsburgh.

R30–related items: congratulatory poster, enamel pin, promo sampler and a couple of passes.

September 15, 2007, at the Centre Bell in Montreal, Quebec.

October 17, 2007, at the Ahoy Sportpaleis in Rotterdam, The Netherlands. This show as well as the previous night in the same venue were recorded for the *Snakes & Arrows Live* album and DVD.

BELOW: October 19, 2007, at the Konig-Pilsener Arena in Oberhausen, Germany.

June 13, 2007, at the Hi-Fi Buys Amphitheatre in Atlanta, Georgia. This was the first show of the *Snakes & Arrows* tour.

© PATRYK PIGEON

© PATRYK PIGEON

© PATRYK PIGEON

June 12, 2008, at the Centre Bell in Montreal, Quebec.

July 17, 2010, Air Canada Centre, Toronto, Ontario.

July 5, 2010,
Charter One
Pavillon,
Chicago,
Illinois.

June 18, 2013, First Midwest Bank Amphitheatre, Tinley Park, Illinois.

June 19, 2015, Air Canada Centre, Toronto, Ontario.

ABOVE: Postcard from Rushcon 15.

RIGHT: Promotional brochure for Kevin J. Anderson's novel version of *Clockwork Angels*; 32 pages plus cover.

RUSH HEMISPHERES FORTIETH ANNIVERSARY
CROSSWORD

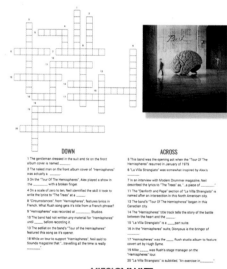

DOWN

1 The gentleman dressed in the suit and tie on the front album cover is named _____

2 The naked man on the front album cover of "Hemispheres" was actually a _____

3 On the "Tour Of The Hemispheres", Alex played a show in the _____ with a broken finger

4 On a scale of zero to ten, Neil identified the skill it took to write the lyrics to "The Trees" at a _____

8 "Circumstances", from "Hemispheres", features lyrics in French. What Rush song gets it's title from a French phrase?

9 "Hemispheres" was recorded at _____ Studios

10 The band had not written any material for "Hemispheres" until _____ before recording it

13 The setlist on the band's "Tour of the Hemispheres" featured this song as it's opener.

18 While on tour to support "Hemispheres", Neil said to Sounds magazine that "...travelling all the time is really _____

ACROSS

5 This band was the opening act when the "Tour Of The Hemispheres" resumed in January of 1979

6 "La Villa Strangiato" was somewhat inspired by Alex's _____

7 In an interview with Modern Drummer magazine, Neil described the lyrics to "The Trees" as, "...a piece of _____".

11 The "Danforth and Pape" section of "La Villa Strangiato" is named after an intersection in this North American city

12 The band's "Tour Of The Hemispheres" began in this Canadian city

14 The "Hemispheres" title track tells the story of the battle between the heart and the _____

15 "La Villa Strangiato" is a _____ part suite

16 In the "Hemispheres" suite, Dionysus is the bringer of _____

17 "Hemispheres" was the _____ Rush studio album to feature cover art by Hugh Syme.

19 Mike _____ was Rush's stage manager on the "Hemispheres" tour.

20 "La Villa Strangiato" is subtitled: "An exercise in _____".

MUSICVAULTZ

Items from the in-studio listening party for the fortieth anniversary edition of 1978's *Hemispheres*.

The last Rush
show ever.
August 1, 2015,
at The Forum
in Inglewood,
California.

Neil Peart's
high school
yearbook
missives —
on his way
to greatness.

them all, but there's a fine line in my view with what Rush fans want to hear and what we want to play. To lose four songs that people have been waiting to hear from our previous albums in favor of four cover songs is a jump enough, but to do four more would start boring them. People are digging them. I think they're kind of a breath of fresh air in the set, to be honest.'

The *R30* tour was primarily American, two shows in Canada, about three weeks in Europe. The world-beating buzz from Brazil had given way to pragmatism and practicality.

Qualified Alex, "If there was someplace we could go where we could have the kind of response we had in Brazil — which quite frankly, we had no idea we had that kind of popularity there — then it would be worth it. But at this stage in our career, to go to a country that is exotic and play for a couple thousand people is really not something we're interested in. Our show is big, it's costly; we don't like to compromise it, we don't like to do festival sorts of things. The occasional special event, yes, okay, but we like to be in control, and we like to present the band in a certain way. So it has to be the right place."

In fact, it was touch-and-go whether Rush would tour at all; the band very nearly decided on making a new studio album instead. But the tour was to go ahead, and they packed in many shows, even if the United States got most of the attention.

On November 22, 2005, *R30* emerged. It's another monster-length live album, following up rapidly on a couple previous with a couple more to come not long after. The specialness of these was being lost, especially when the line between CD and DVD became blurred. Beginning with *Different Stages*, live albums from Rush became mortar between the bricks and not events of their own the way *All the World's a Stage*, *Exit . . . Stage Left* and *A Show of Hands* were. But we shall move on, because fortunately, Rush wasn't done writing.

CHAPTER 7

SNAKES & ARROWS

"With this record, you need to remember who you are."

After the painful experience making *Vapor Trails*, but also after years of life-affirming live performances, in 2007, Rush again found themselves in circumstances a little closer to normal; they were back in the studio, working on a new album. What would become *Snakes & Arrows* emerged from cocooning while Geddy and Alex worked in their home studios and Neil worked remotely, having set up a new life for himself in California. The modern method of swapping files back and forth would be used often, with Neil showing up when needed and then going home again.

"It might've been five years between studio albums, but we were very busy at that time," relates Alex. "We put out two DVDs, we did two world tours. Typically for Geddy and me, we don't do anything until that first day of writing. We don't bring stuff in that we work on individually. We don't really do that anymore.

We used to, years ago, but it's much more exciting, more fun, if you arrive on that first day and play that first chord together."

Alex, inspired by seeing Dave Gilmour in concert, chose to write on acoustic guitar, going so far as to thank the Pink Floyd legend in liner notes for his comment that a song's mettle is proven by whether it could be played on an acoustic or not. Acoustic guitar would figure prominently within the record's mix, enigmatically whether the song was a rocker — of which there are many — or not.

"We'd become very good at layering and density and intricacy," Geddy told Philip Wilding, agreeing with that premise, "but we'd forgotten the wide-open rock feel that is a joy to play and write. Covering songs by artists like Cream and the Yardbirds [on *Feedback*] reminded me of that. And Alex wanted to write on acoustic this time because if a song is lame it sounds really lame on acoustic guitar. On electric you can fool yourself because you've got distortion, you've got power, this whole edginess and this technology that can lull you into a sense of false satisfaction.

"I think we had five songs when Nick came up," explains Lifeson, speaking on embarking on a relationship with yet another new producer, Nick Raskulinecz. "We got in touch with a few different producers, and we were talking to one in particular at the time, but a lot of these people need a lot of notice, obviously a guy like Bob Rock or Rick Rubin, who was also on our list. In fact, Nick heard about the project through Rick. And of course, Rick is booked years in advance and couldn't do the project for ten months or something. So Nick got in touch and wanted to come up and talk with us about doing the record. At the time we hadn't decided who we were going to work with, or were we going to work with anybody, or maybe we would just do it ourselves with Rich Chycki.

"And then Nick came out in May of '06, after we spent a few weeks with Neil in the studio getting caught up and getting him up to speed with the arrangements and the songs and all of that. We sat down and we talked about lots of stuff: music, song construction, songwriting, the value of the chorus, all these things, as well as the war in Iraq, family and everything. We really got to know him. And he was just so enthusiastic and he said all the right things. And he was young and his track record was fairly diverse. He had done a lot of heavy stuff as well as Foo Fighters, which is very, very strong, I think. We just thought we would take a chance on his youth and the things he was saying."

Noted Ged on Nick, in conversation with J.D. Considine from *Bass Guitar*: "He was kind of refreshing for us, because he was such a positive human being, and I really hadn't worked with a producer who had so many ideas so quickly in a long, long time. So he was a real treat. It's kind of weird, the way he appeared in our lives, because we were kind of set to work with another producer. But the negotiations were not going well, so we said let's look around some more."

Listening to Nick's work with the Foo Fighters, Geddy figured, "It was very impressive, just in the sense that someone made this that had a real love and knowledge of music. No matter what song or style, the reel was showing off good material or good sound or good production whereas a lot of reels we listened to, there aren't very good songs on them. And I'd think, why would you want to hire a guy who can't tell the difference between a good song and a bad song enough that he puts kind of a mediocre song on his reel just because it's got a mix he did?"

Also, says Lee, Raskulinecz "offered to fly up on his own dime too, which is unheard of in the music business. So he flew in, and Alex and I met him at my house. He's such a lovable guy, you can't help but like him. Anyway, we played him a couple of our songs, and he flipped — but kept it quiet that he was really a huge Rush fan. He said he was a fan of the band, but I didn't know how seriously he was *really* a fan of the band."

As the sessions played out, Geddy says of Nick and engineer Rich Chycki, "Every once in a while we would hear these two guys singing lines from songs I had forgotten I had even written. They were singing the words from 'Chemistry,' fer cryin' out loud, from the *Signals* album. I'm like, 'Chemistry'? Geez, that's obscure. That happened all the time. And in the evenings sometimes, when we were doing bed tracks, Nick would want to jam every night. So everybody's in there jamming, and of course those two always want to play Rush songs. It was really sweet, actually. Never did I think we would work with someone who was one of our fans. But we found the right one to do it. And it meant a lot to him to do this record. He put his heart into it. And I remember when he left after that first meeting, he said, 'I will not let you down.' And he didn't."

After Steven Wilson from Porcupine Tree had read an interview with Alex where Lifeson had professed to being a fan of the band (Neil and Porcupine Tree drummer Gavin Harrison would become friends as well), Wilson asked Alex if he would do a guest cameo on the band's upcoming record.

"I wanted to ask Steven if it would be okay for me to play on the entire record," Lifeson told *Classic Rock*'s Philip Wilding at the time, ultimately playing on a track called "Anesthetize." "I was in the process of writing and preproduction for *Snakes & Arrows*, but I loved the song and it gave me room to stretch out. Porcupine Tree are a great band and it was my pleasure to play a small role on *Fear of a Blank Planet*."

As Wilson told me at the time, "Alex was recording the Rush album when we were back in England recording *Fear of a Blank Planet*. So that was done by mail, effectively. But to be honest, I don't think anything would have been different had we been in the studio. Because if you think about it, if you're going to ask someone like Alex Lifeson to play on a new record, you don't want to direct him too much. Because the whole great thing about having someone like that is you already love what they do, and you love the way they approach music. I certainly love the way he approaches things. He always surprised me. So other than a little bit of direction in the sense of 'This is the section we want you to play on,' I didn't want to tell him what to play or how to play. Alex played on a couple, but so far we've only released the one on the album. In fact, Alex played such a wonderful solo — we did four or five takes — and he played so beautifully that when we got the files back, we actually extended the sections to accommodate more of his soloing."

Back in Rush world, the band found themselves ensconced at Cherry Beach Sound in Toronto for preproduction, the month of May and then later September and October, before transitioning to Allaire Studios in Shokan, New York, to close out the year. Leaving Toronto, the guys were fresh, coming off a break for summer and bringing with them eight songs. Tennessee native Raskulinecz, thirty-two at the time, had co-produced two records for the Foo Fighters — *One by One* and *In Your Honor* — but really was just getting started. Foo Fighters and Rush made his name, and Nick has gone on to amass an illustrious list of credits, including Alice in Chains, Ghost, Evanescence, Deftones, Mastodon, Korn and a second full-length studio album with Rush, the record that would be their last.

"Nick had very good engineering skills, from what we had heard," continues Alex. "We still wanted to use Rich, because my relationship with Rich has been a little more diverse. We'd been doing some independent projects together, and I think he's just a spectacular engineer. He is so, so good. He has such intuitive skills and a real solid grounding in engineering. As Nick does too. But it took the pressure off Nick so he could just concentrate on the music and where we were going, and the performance.

"Neil had some stuff he had been working on," says Alex, taking the baby steps up the *Snakes & Arrows* board. "Because he sent it along to us. And Geddy and I worked in a very casual manner with this record. We worked a few days a week for five or six hours, and we maintained the rest of our lives. We had a balance, and it was exciting to come in to work. It wasn't like a slog of working five days a week, from noon until midnight. You force yourself to try to be creative, and it doesn't work that way.

"This is all here," clarifies Alex, meaning Toronto. "In fact, we worked at Geddy's place. I only live five minutes from him. He has a cozy little writing room. Not a studio per se, but a nice little writing room, and it looks out on his garden. And it was great to be working in there, really, really casual, very relaxed. We started in March of last year, and we got some stuff from Neil, got him involved, in mid-April or so, went up to his place in Quebec and spent some time together and went over the material. And he came to Toronto and we worked for a month in a local studio here, then we took the summer off and got back into it in September. In September/October, we went back to the same studio and just continued working on the demos and writing and getting familiar with all the material.

"And then we went to Allaire. Now, we only meant to go there for about twelve days, to get the drum tracks. Neil had worked in that room and was well aware of the advantage of working in that big, beautiful drum room. But a surprising thing happened: we fell in love with the place when we got there and decided to just stay and do all the recording. So we spent five weeks there."

Musing over what some of these other guys might have brought to the table, Alex figures, "Well, they're so different.

Brian Eno was a very interesting choice for us because it would have been something completely different. And that's kind of what we look for. That's the excitement of working with the new guy, especially somebody like him. We kind of know already what we want to do with the record, a direction, which is a little different from a producer who really takes control of the whole project. But Brian Eno, for example, would just take us into a whole different area and bring to light certain things we would never consider. That's always very interesting for us, to work that way. Bob Rock too is a very skilled producer. He's done a lot of great work, a lot of different work. You know, a lot of these guys are very selective about the kind of work they do, and their schedule for working, particularly if you're in the big time. And a lot of these guys take a long time to make a record. Nick didn't seem to be that type of person. Things were going to happen a lot quicker; he's much more energetic."

And fortunately it worked out. "Yes, the sessions were fantastic. We had a riot, and he was very motivating and very inspiring. One of the great things about Nick working with us, Nick saw us play when he was eleven years old. It was the first concert he had gotten to [Nick says he was twelve, and it was his second concert, on the *Moving Pictures* tour]. His mom took him. His mother was a big fan and she still is, which is really fantastic, especially for Nick, as it's kind of gone full circle. But he's a very gregarious, outgoing guy, and he knew a lot about the band. But one of the interesting things he said was, 'You guys forget who you are sometimes. And with this record, you need to remember who you are. Because you have a lot of good things about your history that you overlook or ignore.' And I think he's right. Left to our own devices, we tend to leave everything behind and move forward, almost to the point where we lose touch with where we came from. And he really wanted us to keep that in mind, what the strengths of the band have been over the years. And he brought that out. He challenged everybody to play to their best abilities, and he really got that."

Allaire Studios, up in the Catskills, was picked at Neil's suggestion; he had worked on his *Anatomy of a Drum Solo* instructional DVD there. As Alex says, the plan was to whack down rhythm tracks within the space of a couple of weeks (or at least half of Geddy's bass), but the guys enjoyed the estate so much, they decided to do guitars there as well, scotching the original plan to work in Alex's home studio on that piece of the puzzle. Vocals were recorded at Allaire as well, across the band's extended stay of four to five weeks.

Neil, for his part, liked the idea of the three guys being away from home working and playing together, like they did in the old days, either at Le Studio or more grandly, burning money, in the U.K. It was he that insisted on Allaire, with Geddy resisting, saying he was becoming a curmudgeon in his old age and preferred being able to go home after a day in the studio. Alex was typically pliable and was sold on the place by the second day.

"It's hard to tell," Alex told me back in '07, asked to compare the record to the rest of the catalogue. "For me, it sort of encompasses our whole history. When I hear it, I hear different aspects of our songwriting and different approaches to the way we recorded, how we constructed songs. But it's all in this very fresh sound package. It's the heaviest record I think we've done in a long time. And the richest sounding record, for sure. *Counterparts* was a pretty driving record. *Grace Under Pressure* had that thing to it, because it's kind of dark, sort of gray-ish, not a black record but a pretty dark gray record [laughs]. It has a bit of that heavy character to it. Yeah, I don't know if we'd ever had a really heavy record, to be honest. *Counterparts* would be the one from that period — it wouldn't be *Presto* or *Roll the Bones*."

Lifeson is right about that, and he's also aware that *Counterparts* stood apart. It's interesting that he'd comment on Rush never having a heavy record. To be sure, there are flavors of heaviness across the catalogue, from the early distorted guitars to punishing rhythm grooves to lyrical darkness, but he's right: all of that has never come together in one place. Nor does it on *Snakes & Arrows*, mostly because of two things: the acoustic guitar and the hopeful, yearning, soul-replenishing lyrics, which arrive laced into *My Favorite Headache*–style melodies.

Notes Alex, concerning the creative back-and-forth between Neil and Geddy, "Sometimes the lyrics pile up. It's not unusual that he pushes something every time around: 'Have a listen to this now' or 'Check this out.' But we gravitate to what we gravitate to. And it tends to be something more modern or current that he is writing. I have to say that Geddy and Neil working together, it's a marvel how they get it all together. It's so professional and respectful. It's gotta be tough for Neil though, to spend all this time writing a song, and Geddy might pull one line from it and say, 'This I really like. Can we build a song around this one line?'"

"Oh, man!" says I. "Yeah!" laughs Alex loudly. "And I'm sure that's the response! And Neil says, 'Yeah, I'll have a look at that, I'll see what I can do.' And Geddy comes in and then, 'This whole chorus is happening. Can we just do a shift? What if we actually move this to here?' He's really great that way. That's not with all lyrics. Like 'Far Cry' was almost verbatim. It's like, perfect! But I think it's always for the best. And then Geddy can sing them with conviction."

Asked if Neil ever suggests a vocal melody, Alex says, "No. I think he trusts us. He leaves that up to us. He might make a comment about an arrangement or a musical part he feels maybe doesn't work as well as another, but no, he kind of concentrates on lyrics and learning the drum parts."

Being a trio has always helped Rush get through these mine-fields. "Out of all the numbers it's probably the easiest," reflects Lifeson. "You know, it's a lot easier to convince the one hold-out of the merit of your ideas than if you had three against two or two against two, or any other combination. That's always the way it's worked for us. And if it's not unanimous at something, it doesn't happen."

And by the time of *Snakes & Arrows*, one of the main sticking points, namely the use of keyboards and the collapse into other dated '80s values, was in the rear-view mirror, says Alex. "Geddy knew I was always sensitive with the keyboards, so we would joke about it more than anything. But when it came down to a crunch and there were serious conversations about it, everybody was open. For me, probably the most difficult record was *Signals*. The guitar really took a background position. A song like 'Subdivisions' for example, I listen to it now and the keyboards are so incredibly loud in that particular song, and the guitar struggles. Why am I looking for a different place? I shouldn't be looking for a different place. What's going on with these keyboards? They are not even real — it's not even a real instrument, if you know what I mean. That was the way I was feeling about that at the time, because I think the guitar is the heart and soul of a three-piece rock band, or any rock band. That's where all that emotional stuff is coming from. You know, playing with Geddy and Neil, who back then were really active players, I had to be the glue, I had to kind of hold it together. There was a bit of a reversal of roles. Now I think we're playing more of a traditional kind of setup where the rhythm section is back here, and the guitars are up here."

Indeed. And across *Snakes & Arrows*, Alex offers a double charge of those barsy guitars: acoustics joyously strummed along with electrics, as Geddy and Neil more often than not rock away, all warm and analog, thanks to Nick and engineer Rich.

"He *is* bossy, but that's in his nature," chuckles Alex, putting a positive spin on Geddy's assessment of himself, that more so with every record, he acted as the leader of Rush. "That's a good thing. He wants things done the right way, what he considers to be the right way, and he works hard to achieve that. And in terms of our relationship, I'm a little on the other side. I lose interest quickly, short attention span. I'm very spontaneous, but then I move on. He's more fixed and he works through things. We balance each other really well in that respect. He knows what to use from me, judging by my character traits, and applies it to the way he molds things. So when we write together it's a wonderful way to work. I explode into my little things, and he takes those and he works them in and he adds his thing and he fits that in, and it's a great way for us to work. I'm free to do the kind of work I like to do in the fashion I like to do it, and I trust him to be there to put it all together.

"*Snakes & Arrows* was written with such gusto and excitement and confidence," continues Lifeson. "It just all came together so perfectly at the time. There were no obstacles or difficulties that weren't surmountable. Everything was fine — 'We'll get it' — and we couldn't wait 'til we got back in every day. It was like brash and bold in every respect, whereas there was a delicacy and fragility to *Vapor Trails* in every aspect of it. I mean, now what we're doing more is recording off the floor, which we haven't done in a long time since those early records, and there's a very different vibe and a different energy to the way those songs translate when you're all in a room playing together. For the last five years I've been playing a lot. I have a studio at home and I've been writing an awful lot. For me it's like going to the gym; it's all exercises. And I don't mean playing scales; it's exploring sound and what sound can do generated by a guitar. So for me it wasn't really so much challenging as it was liberating. It really gave me a chance to pursue the stuff I like to do. I like coming in the back door and creating weird things. There's a dissonance to a lot of this record that is very appealing to the ear. It sounds like three or four guitars when in fact it's only one or two."

But Alex marvels at where Geddy had arrived by this point.

"I think a lot of it comes from his early training, the players he listened to as teachers. But I think a lot also comes from the fact he is a vocalist and he wants to create a good base for his vocals. So that there's a good connection between the vocal melody and the bass melody. As a rhythm section, he and Neil have a great understanding of each other. It's uncanny to watch them when they're working parts out, because they just naturally fall into the thing. You know, the way it's meant to be for them. Even in soundcheck jams, to this day, when we start, they immediately lock in together; they are very, very natural that way. It's a combination of those two elements: basically the vocal melody is what's driving the bass melody, and then the rhythm stuff is a little escape and fun time."

In terms of the songwriting at this juncture, while Alex is exploring writing on acoustic, he says, "Ged sits down to write on his bass; he'll play a lot of chordal stuff. Because he's blocking vocal melodies and he knows this is what the guitar is going to do, so he'll play these chords. And then when we come down to actually do the arrangements, I'll obviously replace those chordal parts with guitar, and he'll develop a bass line. But a lot of times he's incorporated those chords into the actual bass parts he's playing, more so in the last few records. It's a really interesting jumping point for me because I have to come up with something that fits around the density of those bass chords, which can be all-consuming, in the sonic area. So I'll write a part that's more single-line or up in a higher register, to work around it. It's interesting when we're writing and those parts come up because they do often. Especially if he's just sitting around doing some noodling on his own. That's what he goes to as a starting point. So we were quite adept at understanding and reading each other in those ways."

Peart's themes circling faith are reflected obliquely and richly in the cover art for the album. Explains Alex, "The cover came from a game board called Leela. It's an ancient Indian game. It's the source of the game we're familiar with as snakes and ladders. It's a game of karma, and you go through the squares and move up on the arrows, whatever karmic number you land on, on the square, and your bad karma sends you back down the snake, on the back of the snake. A lot of the record deals with that duality of east/west, good/bad, love/hate, and it's really about life, this record. To me, thematically, it's a little broader than it has been for a while. We always work on some sort of theme, but with this one, it touches on a lot of different aspects of the human condition and how we live together, things we believe in, things we don't believe in."

Religious extremism was very much on Neil's mind at the time, and in effect, the lyrical canon is the work of a self-sufficient atheist grappling with the positives and negatives of religious faith. The overarching theme came from the song "Armor and Sword," where he posited that faith in a positive sense can manifest as armor, whereas all too often, it is used to justify violence, use of the sword. The visual couldn't be more intellectually rich: a crusader or medieval warrior (of either Eastern or Western tradition — armor and sword were used everywhere) "killing in the name of," as it were, while in the act, consciously or subconsciously, believing his protection is imbued with spiritual support beyond the steel.

Alex readily admits the messaging is aimed at both Islamic terrorism and the paroxysms of the religious right in America, Neil being particularly affected by the religious sloganeering he saw on billboards while zooming on his motorcycle across the U.S. "Yeah, it's both, totally. They are just as fanatical as they are in the East, at least in terms of what we read. It's my experience that you have to look at both sides of the story before you take a side, but it has a lot to do with that. It's about the goodness that religion can bring and also the negativity that it brings."

Notes Neil, "On *Snakes & Arrows*, it's very much a conversation with the world; I've described it in terms of Robert Frost's epitaph: 'I had a lover's quarrel with the world.' In a lot of the songs on *Snakes & Arrows* I used relationship devices deliberately, but they're not about one-to-one [connections] at all. They're about me and my lover's quarrel with the world, but they're couched in what seem to be romantic situations. That's a way of putting the particular across in a general way — it makes it sound personal. That of course is the key to connecting with an audience in many art forms: to make something come home to someone personally."

"We always really care about the presentation of the whole album," says Lifeson, when asked about the album's booklet providing "cover art" for every song. "I mean, we are old, so we remember what it was like to have those albums, to look at it and listen to it and read the album cover, turning it over and over — it all becomes part of the process. And that's changed over the years. I guess on iTunes you can download covers and look at them while you're listening, so it's getting back to that. But it's always been important to us to provide something tangible that you can hang onto and look at. And doing a separate jacket for each of the songs — and really, just the songs with lyrics — is a nice way to provide a platform for the lyrics, first of all, to make them readable in an easy way, but it also makes for a good visual to look at while you're getting into it. And to do the whole package with the game board and the DVD, the documentary and stuff, it's a nice way to put the whole picture together."

Regarding the title, Neil had also been inspired by the Hamlet phrase "slings and arrows." Peart did some online searching to make sure his title hadn't been used for a record before and he found Harish Johari's Leela game board, which he then showed to Geddy and Alex. They approved of the idea, and the art was given to Hugh Syme to convert into a full-blown album cover.

Snakes & Arrows, Rush's eighteenth album, emerged as a digipak CD on May 1, 2007, brightly colored and boldly recorded. Instantly, upon the opening movements on first track "Far Cry," it became plain that this was Rush's most richly analog record in terms of production tones since the '70s. Of course, fans had already gotten the song as a taste of what was to come, since "Far Cry" was issued as an advance single on March 12 of that year. The song would reach #22 on the Mainstream Rock Tracks chart, get the full production video treatment and be featured on every tour the band ever did moving forward, until the end.

"It's much bolder, richer sounding," agrees Alex on the production job, "and it's heavier, it's stronger, less personal. I don't find very much in common with *Vapor Trails*. Maybe a couple of tracks . . . 'Earthshine' I could see coming out of this record. But that was a much more personal record, a much more difficult record to make, for sure. This record was just a joy. There wasn't a single difficult time we had on this record."

This was certainly the case with "Far Cry." The song emerged from a particularly satisfying jam between Geddy and Alex. Neil had left some lyrics for the guys to consider, and Geddy was amazed how seamlessly Neil's words lined up with this jammed song fragment he and Alex had just created, particularly the chorus, which Neil had highlighted. The end result is a hammering, rhythmic celebration of power trio rock, notwithstanding the extra guitar, the acoustic. Most notably though was the warmth from all corners, and no keyboards.

"We took the keyboard experiment as far as we could," says Alex, of a transition that began in the early '90s. "But it seemed to naturally come to an end. We found that the core of the band was the three-piece, and that's where we wanted to go back to. It wasn't like we said 'no more keyboards'; it was more like let's get back to the core and fit the keyboard stuff around. We went on from there; more guitar parts were written than keyboard parts, and I found that more rewarding. It was a lot more fun to come up with parts that were pads and atmospheric. And now, of course, we're basically no keyboards."

Though friction over keyboards was out of the way, tensions over sonics and textures remained on records like *Counterparts* and *Vapor Trails*. And in between, *Test for Echo* wasn't fully satisfying either, both sonically and in terms of the songs, the writing. Now Rush had settled on a new sound, only hinted at on *Vapor Trails*, this sense of a "bashing" three-piece plus acoustic, which would carry them through to the end, *Snakes & Arrows* and *Clockwork Angels* comprising a two-project suite.

No Wal bass either. Raskulinecz had Geddy playing his Fender Jazz, along with his Taurus pedals, which he uses on every track but two. Peart played a Drum Workshop kit and Alex used a number of guitars, but mainly a Les Paul, a Stratocaster and a semi-acoustic Gibson ES-335. But it was mainly Geddy's use of the Fender Jazz and Neil's lack of electronic drums that helped the band get a timeless sound, along with procedural things like partial use of takes live off the floor, all three of the guys hammering out in the room together. Nick also egged Neil on to swing and let loose, suggesting fills, resulting in the guys' nicknaming their new producer Booujze, a moniker amusingly as hard to spell as his last name. The made-up word refers to a sound Nick used to describe a bar-ending fill he wanted Neil to do on "Far Cry," with Nick also imploring him to go nuts over the "YYZ"-like monotone chord bits, something Peart readily agreed to.

With respect to the lyric, "Far Cry" is essentially a microcosm of the album's composite or general theme, becoming the spokesman track. It's the title track in all but name. Geddy instantly fell in love with the concept of "Far Cry"; it easily passed his test of something he himself could get behind. There's negativity there, the idea that the ideals of the hippie generation failed, but also a sort of exasperated hope that one can learn to cope and "get back on." Ills are only hinted at, ills like poverty and religious extremism, and also, poetically but so quick it can be missed, perceived ills like the electronic wiring-up of a younger generation, something that was only beginning to become an issue in 2007.

Speaking with Phil Roura, Geddy framed "Far Cry" as "full of indomitable optimism. It's about the idealism we have for the world. It's about what we have been given to deal with — and that's okay." Generally across the album, said Ged, "We wanted to reflect a lot on the issues of the day, how our lives are reflected by extreme religious behavior — both near and far away. The point Neil is trying to make in his lyrics is that it's not just the world of Islam. Any extreme religious behavior is bad, whether it be Middle East or the Middle West. You walk through airports and see what everyday folks have to deal with. That's the world we face. This album is more topical. The world has changed a lot in a very short period of time. There's been a lot of conversation, a lot of books written recently about religion, of how God plays in people's lives."

"What does lyric writing do for me?" asked Neil rhetorically, just after the release of the album. "Self-expression, like drumming — it's the perfect thing. And a belief that it matters, I guess. One of my dad's maxims in life was always if a thing is worth doing, it's worth doing well. So that drove me as a drummer, certainly, and obviously if I'm going to write lyrics, then I have to make them as good as I can. Another one of my dad's maxims that got drilled into me big time in working at the farm equipment dealership, if he sent me off to do a job, clean some shelves or arrange the parts, then I'd come back and say, 'There, I've done it; is that good enough?' He said, 'If it's perfect, it's good enough.' So these are words to live by that, again, are clues to my character, that it would be spent in the pursuit of excellence.

"Drumming has been such an odyssey for me, an odyssey of influence and of refinement and understanding and work and practice and teaching and learning. All of that — a circle that never ended. And lyric writing is exactly the same, as I got more interested in it and learned more and read more widely and learned to understand metaphors and the rhythm of words. One thing I think is important is that being a drummer, the rhythm of words came so naturally. My drumming is very much phrase-built, in the way I like to orchestrate drum parts, in a conversational but architectural format. Words became that too, where I could focus on them in that rhythmic sense.

"And then there's the sensibility I guess you need to have for the power of words and images and communication, of saying what you want to get across effectively. Because normally you just can't say in as few words what the subject of the song is going to be; you gotta dress it all up. That's the perfect analogy for drumming too. I'm not just going to play the beat; I'm going to dress it all up. So much of my life is built on the idea of 'It's not going to be just what I have to do — it's going to be as much as I can do.' That's it. And like drumming, lyrics grew in that way too.

"I mentioned before about the conversational idea, composing a song as a conversation between people. On *Snakes &* *Arrows*, again, it's worldly matters expressed on a personal one-to-one basis. Those are devices, but at the bottom of that, it's still me saying this and caring enough to write about it, whether it's inspired by anger or outrage or passion for nature. I always like to get weather into songs and I like to get nature into songs, because I love them. You know, speed . . . I've written about cars, I've written about motorcycles, because I love them too. Everything I love about drumming comes out in my drumming, and everything I love about life comes out in the lyrics. Those things are genuinely there.

"So when people do respond in that way, in a genuine way, and when people have said . . . you know the quote that I use: 'the soundtrack of my life,' when people have said they've been fans of Rush for twenty years, thirty years, through their whole lifetimes and all the changes that brings, of becoming a parent and getting a responsible job and still keep coming to our shows, that's perfect. That kind of continuity of all the people that I look out at every night, who just have that simple joy of relating and are so glad to come and share that at a live show, with all the other people who obviously feel the same way, and to sing along and air drum along or just to be, to feel part of that spirit . . . that's the satisfaction.

"But much larger than that is, of course, what it's meant to their private lives. When people tell me our music or my lyrics or my books have helped them, then of course it's a wonderful feeling. I must admit . . . honestly, I can't even begin to deal with being an impact on anyone's life, a positive influence on anyone. Me? Are you kidding? But it is nice. I feel that whatever influence people attribute to my lyrics or my books, they had it already. They maybe just needed the affirmation. Because I've had that experience, where I'll read something and go, 'Yeah, that's just how I feel.' And that affirmation, that's worth a lot. But it's not the same as inspiration. So what I receive back, without getting overblown about it, is just that they relate, right? And not that I elevated their lives. I don't believe that — they elevated their lives. But if they could relate to my passion or my struggle or my anger, then it's a sense of affirmation. Like, I have a circle of friends all over the place, and we don't see each other a lot. But they're a constant affirmation to me about what I do and why. Because I know there are a few people who go through their lives the same way as I do."

Indeed "Far Cry" is as much joyous drumming as it is meaningful lyric. The imposing sense of rhythm on the song and across the album came out of the relationship with the band's bounding new producer.

As Neil explained to Jonathan Mover from *Drumhead*, "I've seen it in studios, where multi-tracks were going by that were just tape, splice, tape, splice, tape, splice, tape, splice. I would accept that reality if we had a ten-minute song and there were two or three takes to make it up; then okay, fine. But mostly, even today, I like to feel that I can perform a good take every time, and then you look for something special.

"Like when Nick Raskulinecz would send me out to go crazy. We were both looking for the seat-of-the-pants fills, and there are some on this where you can hear the rim shot as I just barely made it, and I just barely get back to 'one.' And that's so exciting; it's not replicable. So Nick's suggestion of capturing a good take gave me the satisfaction as a musician of having done the job right. There are two sides to that story. Yes, you can fix everything, but then the drummer feels, 'Well, I didn't really have very much to do with that performance.' That has got to undermine your confidence — and your satisfaction — in the work. And all of that intangible stuff is really important in the long term: how you feel about what you've done and the music you've made. So I like to have all of that and then the delight of hearing something just so over the edge and so on the edge. You know, it gives me a smile. There are certain fills on this album and certain figures I hear that I just have to smile at, like, 'I can't believe I got away with that!'"

Continues Neil, on the logistics that allowed this to happen: "We were in Allaire Studios and the way we were set up, the control room was off to this side and I couldn't see Nick. I said, 'I want to see you. Stand over there where I can see you.' On one track he came out and drummed along with me in the room. I could tell by his response, even looking through the glass, he'd be all vibed up. So there's a barometer of excitement there, and a lot of times everybody knows. Everybody's around if we're doing the basic tracking together, and everybody's there vibing off it or not. And I'll come in and it'll be like, 'You got it!'"

"Armor and Sword" continues in this spirit of groovy drums, lots of cymbals — not to mention, at the onset, a sample of whacked sheet metal! — and three-way chemistry between players. It's an odd one, arguably with ill-fitting parts, but it's highly creative. What's more, it adds to the idea that Rush is deliberately building an arcane new sound, one that will last across this record and *Clockwork Angels*. Neil attributes the opening polyrhythmic signature on the song to something Buddy Rich does on "Mercy, Mercy, Mercy." A cover of this composition, featuring Chick Corea drummer Dave Weckl, is included on Neil's *Burning for Buddy* tribute project from 1994.

Recalls Neil on "Armor and Sword," "I remember with a couple songs done, coming in one day and we just couldn't get anywhere. We were working on 'Armor and Sword,' and it wasn't getting anywhere and I was thinking, 'I can't do this anymore, I suck,' just wanting to give up and go home, and then coming back the next day, facing it again, making a little change. So your whole existence does rest on that. If you are able to imbue everything in your spirit into the job, like nothing else in the world is more important than getting those two lines of lyrics right, you will apply yourself. And finally on the third day, boom, I had a breakthrough and wrote the whole rest of that song and part of another one, 'Far Cry.' Yeah, that's one that came out of that blockage. Perseverance, in that case, is what it took. *Vapor Trails* had a lot of hardships, but they were existential and internal. Time wasn't part of it. And same with *Snakes & Arrows* — we were able to work hard and rewrite to our hearts' content with nobody holding a gun to our heads."

Explained Peart in the *Snakes & Arrows* tourbook: "While I was working on those lyrics, the battlefield imagery reminded me of a line, 'Where ignorant armies clash by night,' from a poem I half-remembered. It turned out to be Matthew Arnold's magnificent 'Dover Beach,' and I was so excited by its synchronicity with my own preoccupations in many of these songs that I had to put in one line from the poem, as a tribute, 'Confused alarms of struggle and flight.'

"I was also thinking," continues Neil, "like Richard Dawkins in *The God Delusion*, about how children are usually imprinted with a particular faith, along with their other early blessings and scars. People who actively choose their faith are vanishingly few; most simply receive it, with their mother's milk, language and customs. Thinking also of people being shaped by early abuse of one kind or another, I felt a connection with friends who had adopted rescue dogs as puppies and given them unlimited love, care and security. If those puppies had been 'damaged' by their earlier treatment, made nervous, timid or worse, they would always remain that way, no matter how smooth the rest of their life might be.

"It seemed the same for children. To express that notion, I came up with, 'The snakes and arrows a child is heir to / Are enough to leave a thousand cuts.' I thought I was only combining

Hamlet's 'slings and arrows' with the childhood game Snakes and Ladders, to make something less clichéd. And indeed, when we were discussing *Snakes & Arrows* as a possible album title, Geddy remarked, 'I like it because it sounds familiar, but isn't.'"

The third track on the record and arguably second most celebrated, "Workin' Them Angels," takes its title from something Neil overheard on his motorcycle travels. An elderly woman had been chastising her husband for driving too fast, saying he had been "workin' them angels," meaning testing fate, one of the themes of the record at large. The lyrics are very much about this idea but applied to Neil, given all the driving, flying and white-knuckle motorcycle touring he had been doing.

At the musical end, this one's yet another example of Rush demonstrating enthusiastically their new hard, progressive rock proposal, bluster set dynamically against acoustics.

Explained Peart, on taking the reins and doing his own writing, in *Modern Drummer*: "This song shifts between 3/4 and 4/4 several times. Early on in the arranging, it was my suggestion to change the choruses to 4/4, to take the 'lilt' out of the song for a minute. However, once we did that I found it surprisingly difficult to feel the transition sometimes. The point where Alex and Geddy chose to make the shift from four to three, for example, sometimes made sense structurally but could be a real head-breaker for me. Still, it forced me to come up with some creative ways to bridge that change — jump that fence — like at the end of the instrumental passage, after the one-handed snare figure with tom flams on the triplets (inspired by a fill Matt Johnson played in 'Last Goodbye,' from Jeff Buckley's enduringly brilliant *Grace*). I resorted to calling a 'time-out' by throwing in a pair of rumbling quadruplets with double bass and floor toms, rising to a snare flam to kick into the last verse. When Geddy heard me pulling off stuff like that, he would shake his head and say, 'Now that's comedy!'

"And all this time, Booujze was always encouraging both Geddy and me to 'get crazy,' until we decided we were 'the world's funniest rhythm section.' We began to think this album ought to be called *Don't Try This at Home*. Otherwise, this song is all about feel, the right looseness for the verses and a relentless drive for the choruses, then a gentler groove for the instrumental passage."

"There's no solo in 'Workin' Them Angels,'" noted Alex, speaking with Joe Bosso from *Guitar World*. "What happened was, I originally recorded a solo over this section of very Celtic-sounding mandolins. It was a cool solo, nothing wrong with it, but just before we mixed the album, I called Nick and said I didn't think the solo was necessary, that it sounded better with just the mandolins. I was prepared for a big disagreement but Nick was like, 'Dude! Absolutely. I was thinking the very same thing.' I hate to disappoint guitar fans who are waiting for solos, but sometimes you just don't need them."

The guitar solo as embedded event is back come "The Larger Bowl," but again, the overriding signature is the use of acoustic guitar. Alex calls the song "experimental" and says that it is "acoustically driven; there's a very cyclical thing about it. Lyrically it's a pantoum. I think it takes lines two and four of every four-line stanza and makes them the first and third of the next. Or the first and second of the next. I never get that quite right. It's something Neil has been working with for a long time, lyrically, how to use the device. And the music is written in a way that it's looping. It's only four chords, but they keep looping through the whole song. I think it's a really interesting approach for a song, from us."

Further on the use of acoustics, Alex told me, "Before we actually started writing, I mentioned to Geddy that I thought it would be refreshing to take an acoustic approach to writing. He thought that was a great idea. In fact, we both started out on acoustic, and it lasted for about five minutes, and then he put the acoustic down and he picked up the electric bass. We wrote like that in the old days, but he hasn't played guitar in decades. It's not really the best way. The best way is how it ended up: me being on acoustic and him being on bass. And the whole writing process on acoustic, I don't think I played electric . . . no, I didn't play electric once while writing. And of course, the album has a lot of acoustic on it, either in a primary or secondary role. I love using acoustic as support. I think it adds a richness to the heaviness, of this record in particular. And certainly guys like Townshend and David Gilmour were masters at using acoustic to make a big statement."

Asked about other acoustic inspirations, Alex says, "I went to see Tommy Emmanuel play a couple of times, and I was so blown away watching him. He did an acoustic set, just him and the guitar, and that was spectacular, really inspiring. I went to see Stephen Bennett play. We got together afterwards. I'd never met him before, and we had a couple of drinks and we jammed a little bit and played and talked about the harp guitar, and he tried to show me a few things. It was impossible. And he gave me a capo that I ended up using on a couple of things. I just found I was playing acoustic a lot more at home. Friends would drop by and you would have a glass of wine and sit in the backyard and strum away, for hours, and it's really a lot of fun. And I started fooling with different tunings. So I was in that headspace when we started working."

Also notable in the song is a track of real tambourine and sampled tambourine played by Neil. As for the solo, it's typical obtuse Alex, laden with lots of chorus, played over a track of electric and a track of acoustic.

Fate is addressed even more directly in "The Larger Bowl," where Neil muses over economic disparity — who winds up with the larger bowl, as it were. The pantoum structure adds a hypnotic quality, like a chant or a blues song, both of which use repetition to focus one's thinking on an idea. Explains Peart in the tourbook, "The title for 'The Larger Bowl' came from a bicycle trip in West Africa, as described in *The Masked Rider* when a song with that title wafted through a feverish, hallucinatory 'dysentery dream.'"

This took place in 1988 at the Happy Hotel in Cameroon, where Neil was on a bike tour with four friends. The dream had him whisked back to Toronto in an armored helicopter and then to Halifax in a truck where he did a phone interview in a clothing store, where a song called "The Larger Bowl" was playing. The title is also partly inspired by seeing women in Africa carrying bowls on their heads.

"Waking in a sweaty tangle of twisted sheets, I only remembered the title, but I knew I had to write that song. Make a dream come true, as it were. Back in the early '90s, I gave that title to some words partly inspired by the dream's location, Africa, about life's unequal 'fortunes and fates.' The front of my rhyming dictionary had an index of traditional verse patterns, and I tried writing in some of them, as an exercise, like solving a crossword puzzle. Among sonnets, villanelles, and sestinas, I particularly liked a Malay form called the pantoum and wrote several lyrics using that scheme, including 'The Larger Bowl.' However, I never even submitted them to my bandmates until this album — fifteen years later.

"It must have been the right time, because, to my delight, Alex and Geddy responded to the challenge of 'The Larger Bowl' and its unusual construction. Musically, the song seemed to benefit from stylistic influences we discovered, or recovered, during our *Feedback* project, when we recorded a number of cover tunes from our earliest influences. That spirit of youthful enthusiasm, and the spirit of the '6os, is alive in several of these songs, from the blues sections in 'The Way the Wind Blows' to the 'feedback solo' in 'Far Cry,' and the simple rhythm section backing for the melodic guitar solo in 'The Larger Bowl.'"

"Spindrift" is another of Neil's weather reports, crashing waves tossing Peart into existential crisis. The ominous music echoes the literary sentiment, just as it did back on "Jacob's Ladder."

As Peart described in *Modern Drummer*, "Beginning with the punches and rolling hi-hat, it steps through several different movements, and the parts are deceptively simple. Detail is the god here. The first verse, for example, uses only 8th note bass drum accents, while the second one introduces 16th notes, to kick it up a little. The whole song is a 'muscular' performance, and I had to concentrate hard on laying it down and on locking in with the vocals. That is sometimes an underrated part of drumming and of being an accompanist: if you're playing a song, with words and music, the singing is often considered . . . oh, let's say, 'important.' For that reason, and perhaps because I write the lyrics, I give a lot of attention to the vocals, trying to frame them effectively and unobtrusively, while punching them up rhythmically when I can.

"Years ago I saw a documentary on the making of *Who's Next*, and Roger Daltrey was talking about how much Keith Moon, for all the apparent wildness of his drumming, was actually very sensitive to the vocals. Daltrey demonstrated that quality by playing a bit of the multi-track tape of 'Behind Blue Eyes,' soloing the drums and then adding the vocals. Keith was clearly doing what I describe — framing the vocals, punching them up with accents — even though in his case it might have been his natural, instinctive musicality rather than my studied approach.

"Between vocal lines in the choruses, I was able to come up with more of those fills launching from the left floor tom (even deliberately repeating one, to Booujze's shock, but hey, sometimes repetition can be effective). It was Booujze's idea to reprise the intro after a false ending, and once again he urged me to go crazy in it, so I did. We rarely use fade-outs these days, but this one seemed inevitable, and I was pleased to find that Booujze was amused, as I have always been, by the notion of putting a 'comedic' fill right at the bottom of a fade."

The false ending to "Spindrift" was in the Rush tradition of songs like "The Spirit of Radio" and "The Big Money" — because of the band's prog predilection, this device always came with twists, extra features. Acoustic guitar in this one is heard only during the break, where Alex dips his toe into the idea of soloing but then recoils. There's also a bit of individual note picking — King Crimson–like — but this is executed on electric. The song as a whole is relentless and roiling like an agitated surf; it's a fairly heavy number very much with a *Clockwork Angels* feel, with particular kinship to that record's "Seven Cities of Gold," and for that matter, "Earthshine" from *Vapor Trails*.

Noting Raskulinecz's contribution, Alex said that "Nick came up and threw himself into the situation. A few songs we didn't touch at all. Some songs we moved a few things around, and there was one song called 'Spindrift' that we made radical changes to. We were very impressed with Nick; he wasn't afraid to tell us we had the song all wrong. Most producers are afraid to do that with name bands. Also, he allowed us to re-record anything we wanted, as many times as we wished. A lot of producers these days just want to Pro Tools parts together."

Next up is "The Main Monkey Business," the band's first instrumental since "Limbo" on *Test for Echo*. This one explores further this idea of acoustics atop bludgeoning rhythms. One is also reminded of the connections between Celtic music and Indian music, across the buzzing acoustic guitars, Neil's poly-rhythmic drumming and the exotic, ethereal keyboard washes. There's a bit of a cheat on the idea of instrumental, as Geddy sings a bit, mirroring the key parts. Even Alex's guitar soloing shares those Far Eastern melodic touches with the likes of King Crimson's Adrian Belew and Robert Fripp — incidentally, Fripp is the other famed guitar craftsman Steven Wilson collared to guest on *Fear of a Blank Planet*.

As Alex told me at the time, "I remember 'Main Monkey Business,' when we were doing that, thinking, we'll never play this live. So let's just track it up and make it a lot of fun, a really great thing to listen to. And of course, there's no way we can't do it live — so it's definitely on our list! We're going to try to do seven or eight songs from the record. But until we actually play them, we don't really know if we're going to have trouble with anything. It's always difficult in the beginning but you work around it. A lot of those little details, like tracking the acoustic for example, you can approximate that stuff live. And the energy of the live show makes up for a lot of those little details that might be missing. But I've a feeling that when we start rehears-ing and get comfortable with the songs, they're going to sound really good live."

Indeed the band would play much of the album 'til the end, and as Alex stated, the *Snakes & Arrows* songs came off as rip-roarin' rockers, benefitting from the molten electric leveling that takes place in a hockey arena, something that also greatly improved selections from *Power Windows* through *Roll the Bones*.

Explained Alex further, speaking with *Guitar World*: "We wanted to do an instrumental that had some real substance, but we were getting pretty deep into finishing the record. So one day we started jamming and the song started to emerge. At first, it was extremely complicated — it probably had about twelve different parts to it — and Nick really helped us whack it down and simplify it. The only problem is, to play the song live I might have to bring out the double-neck. Man, I dread it though; that thing weighs a ton! You feel it the next day in your neck and shoulders. Maybe I'm just getting old."

The band did do "The Main Monkey Business" live, but Alex opted for an acoustic guitar mounted on a stand along with his Les Paul slung around his neck, which he plays for the lion's share of the piece. Not that he was the focal point — "The Main Monkey Business" came off as more of a percussion showcase than anything.

The title of the track comes from something Geddy's mother once said to describe someone up to no good. "What kind of monkey business?" Geddy asked. "The *main* monkey business," which Ged found amusing. The song was a *Hemispheres*-level work of origami to assemble. All that monkeying around led to a sprawling odyssey that was originally eighteen minutes long. In the beginning, Neil challenged himself by playing the piece without snare to support the song's world music feel, but eventually added some piccolo snare at the point of Alex's solo. There's also all sorts of sampled percussion sounds, including sleigh bells.

"On *Snakes & Arrows*, the instrumental, of all things, 'The Main Monkey Business,' took longer than any song," recalls Peart, "because we had such high expectations of what we wanted to be in there and what we wanted to get out of it. We were rewriting and rewriting and rewriting, all the way through. But that wasn't arduous the way *Hemispheres* was. That's what we wanted to do — we weren't pressured by time."

"The Way the Wind Blows" ambles in as old-school 3/4 blues before retaining that frame and becoming near heavy metal, or to strike a compromise, a hard blues reminiscent of "Whipping Post." But soon, come chorus time, we're into lush, Celtic acoustic strumming, the sun-dappled melody at this point taking us back to *Test for Echo* or *My Favorite Headache.* The solo break finds both Alex and the backing track arcing back to the album's Eastern (or Moroccan, or Turkish) touchstones. Add to this the overt references to the Middle East and Middle West in Neil's lyrics, along with lines that further explore fate, and you have across the record an emboldening of concept: religion across borders and cultures and free will versus predestination. This is all set upon a musical backtrack that also compares East and West.

Noted Alex of both "The Way the Wind Blows" and "Bravest Face," speaking with Mac Randall: "The bluesier stuff on those two songs was just so fresh and so much fun to play, and it's true, I seldom play like that, so it was a great opportunity to stretch out. In both those cases, the idea and the tone came together at the same time. Some of that was due to the fantastic selection of amps at Allaire." A few precedents exist for this kind of playing by Alex, albeit they're sparing. The beginning of "Available Light" and the outro solo in "Ghost of a Chance" are nice examples.

Geddy, speaking with Philip Wilding, explains that Nick Raskulinecz was central in this song coming together. "His phrase was, 'I'd be curious to hear . . .' You knew then that you were going back into the studio. We were working on 'The Way the Wind Blows' and we were very close to nailing it. And I come into the room and Neil's playing the part and I see Nick's face, and it's almost like he's stroking his chin, you know? So he asked Neil to come in and he said to him, 'I'd be curious to hear you play . . .' and he describes what he wants, and Neil says, 'So you're asking me to completely rewrite both verses?'

"Neil had a look on his face like he was going to explode. But he wasn't — he knew Nick was right. He trusted Nick's ideas; he wasn't threatened by them. He was a little pissed off because his hands were killing him, but he says, 'I'm going back in there' and on his way back in he was like, 'Oh fuck, what am I going to pull off here?' Then he realized he had this part that might work, so he threw that in and you should have seen the room. It just lit up. I was just dancing — yes! He transformed the song totally. Nick had this big grin on his face and he brought Neil in to hear it afterwards and Neil went, 'Well, when you're right, you're right.'"

Next up is another instrumental, "Hope," with Neil lifting the title for the song from the "I still cling to hope" line that is part of "Faithless." The twelve-string acoustic number with a two-minute-long solo finds Alex delving deeply into his new love of acoustic guitar, Lifeson virtually writing a tribute to U.K. acoustic revival figures like John Renbourn, Bert Jansch and Davy Graham, not to mention the Jimmy Page of "White Summer" fame.

Alex told Mac Randall that the song is tuned to D-A-D-A-A-D, adding that he'd "been messing around with a few different alternate tunings at home, and during the writing sessions, whenever Geddy was working on vocals — and I wasn't sleeping on the couch — I'd sit in the corner and strum my acoustic. I just fell in love with the sound of that guitar and that tuning in particular, and that's where 'Hope' came from. It was nice to do something on my own for one of our records; I haven't done that in a really, really long time. What you hear on the album is the first full take, which we mixed right after we recorded it, so it's about as pure as you can get. Rich Chycki had his tape measure out and measured the mic setup right down to the inch, and it was very effective — you feel like you're sitting right in front of the guitar."

"That's the thing with Al," mused Geddy, in conversation with Philip Wilding. "He's so spontaneous that if you walk in and he's playing something, you have to run and hit record; you have to grab it. Three minutes later you'll ask him what he just played and he'll be, 'I played what?' That's the story of my entire relationship with him: 'What was that, Al?' 'What was what?' He did 'Hope' live; we let him have a go at it twice. I actually thought the first take was good enough. I was standing in the booth going, 'That's it!'"

Neil echoes Geddy's sentiments: "Alex can just pick up the guitar and not even be paying attention and Geddy will be like, 'What's that you just played?' And Alex goes, 'I don't know.' In the most beautiful sense, Alex doesn't know what he's doing."

Reiterates Geddy, "Yeah, when I'm up at the desk editing or doing my vocals you can hear him in the background either noodling away on his acoustic guitar or asleep on the couch. I've got the demos we did for this album, and you can hear him in the background on them, either playing or snoring."

A live rendition of "Hope" was included on the two-CD *Songs for Tibet: The Art of Peace* album issued in 2008. This was a different version than what was included on the band's own *Snakes & Arrows* Live album from four months previous.

"Faithless" is one of Neil's most direct expressions of atheism, and to underscore his tough words, the song is serious and seriously slow, especially for Rush.

"Using the Mellotron was cool," adds Alex. "And they just happened to have one. It's interesting, at Allaire they've got a whole room full of equipment, primarily guitars, acoustics, electrics. They must have 150 instruments there. I mean, not just crappy instruments, beautiful instruments! This is just outside of Woodstock. The owner of the studio is a major collector. He's got amps and keyboards, everything, so they had a Mellotron there, and we talked about orchestrating a couple of things, like 'Faithless' for example, and rather than putting an orchestra on, we tried the Mellotron and it added this really cool '70s strings vibe to it. It's a cumbersome, out of tune, gigantic behemoth of an instrument, but it was still really great. It suited the track really well. And we got Ben Mink to play some violin on it as well, to bring some real strings in. So it really worked nicely. Bouzouki I had on a song, mandolins."

"This is another arrangement tour-de-force, combining lots more 3/4 and 4/4 combinations," wrote Neil in *Modern Drummer*. "Early in the songwriting, Geddy had half-jokingly lamented, 'Why do all our songs have to be so fast?!' Despite the obvious association with our name (and our natures — we come by it honestly), we decided to try something a little less frantic. This song achieves a stately majesty as a result, especially in the choruses. In fact, the choruses are slowed down even more, by two beats-per-minute, the first time we've tried that device. It's hardly noticeable to a listener, or even to me while I played it, but gives the arrival more weight. A slower tempo also gave me a different framework for fill construction and placement, allowing me to explore some fresh directions in that area.

"A couple of the little hi-hat figures before the bridge vocals were particularly fun to try, and I guess those bridges stylistically kind of reference early Bill Bruford and Phil Collins. A little Nick Mason returns in the verses and choruses, though maybe there's some 'me' in there too, being passive-aggressive again. And one more great drummer to mention: I recently heard 'Purple Haze' on the radio, and was immediately reminded of the influence Mitch Mitchell has been on my drumming. I think you can clearly hear his inspiration on a few of the fills I played near the end of this song. I liked Booujze's idea for the delicate military snare roll trailing off at the end. We drummers call that an "existential metaphor' (don't we?)."

"Faithless" would serve as a rare entry into the ranks of songs not played on the tours immediately following their appearance on a record but then trotted out later. Earlier members of the club include "A Passage to Bangkok," "Entre Nous" and "Between Sun & Moon." In this case, "Faithless" would be a surprise addition to the Time Machine Tour.

"Bravest Face" is a sort of up-tempo pop ballad, one where the acoustics win out over the electrics, although come chorus time, there's quite the mighty churn. As Alex told Joe Bosso, he had gone to see Stephen Bennett live, and "Stephen gave me a half capo, which I'd never seen before, and I thought it was really cool. You can move it around but still have open strings. What an awesome little thing! I used it on 'Bravest Face.' Because this album was written on the acoustic, I was so hot going in. We talked about *Moving Pictures* and how I'd play solos cold. This record was the exact opposite: I knew exactly what I wanted. Writing a lot of the songs on the acoustic offered me a wonderful way to sketch out the album; I knew that if everything worked on the acoustic, everything would be ten times more powerful on the electric."

"This one is another drummer's feast," wrote Neil in his *Modern Drummer* track by track on the record. "Dynamics range from, well, nothing, to delicate double-stroke snare work, subtle timekeeping and vocal-framing, staccato punches, all the way out to semi-chaotic machine-gun fills (for once, those were not Booujze-inspired but fairly tightly composed). The drums follow the vocals pretty closely once again, both framing and accent- ing, and in fact, in the last chorus where Geddy sings 'There's no magical place,' Booujze suggested that lyrical change from 'magic' because the extra syllable would kick with the drums better. So sometimes it goes both ways.

"Generally, I stayed away from the splash cymbals on this record, because as much as I like them, it seems to me they are a little too 'common' lately, not to say overused (Booujze agreed). However, there's one little whim I've long wanted to find a place for: a staccato, choked splash figure like Gene and Buddy used to do. I put one in at the beginning of the second verse, and it makes me smile every time I hear it."

"Good News First" is the strongest example supporting this curious premise of Neil's — of addressing universal concepts through vignettes of people's relationships. The extra layer of meaning makes this one of the more enigmatic lyrics on the album. Set to sturdy and linear yet impassioned and angsty music, "Good News First," buried at the end, becomes arguably the record's hidden gem.

Penned Neil, on his drum part, almost distractingly tribal beneath verses that are almost balladic, "When Alex and Geddy first start putting a song together, sitting in the studio with guitar, bass and vocal mic, they use a drum machine for tempo and accompaniment. Alex does the programming, sometimes coming up with highly unusual parts that can inspire me with a non-drummer's vision — especially a great non-drummer like Alex! The 'Neanderthal' verses in this song came about that way, and naturally I used my Troglodyte cymbals and Einstein heads.

"The hi-hat chokes that alternate in the intro, and again later, are the kind of funky stuff guys like Vinnie Colaiuta seem to pull off effortlessly. For me, they're the result of much work and experimentation, and in this case, playing them with my left hand proved to be the trick (I used that again in the next song too, because it was new to me). My loose approach to playing behind the guitar solo, and the bridge out of it, channels the spirit of '60s Toronto 'blue-eyed soul,' with a bit of Keith Moon, a style known as 'Wholiganism.' Those stabbing triplet figures [also found in] 'Workin' Them Angels' return going into the last chorus, and these are all results from the Tao of Booujze: 'Just go crazy!'"

Does the "Neanderthal" drum part constitute good music making? Debatable. Does it, through drums, serve as metaphor for the helpless exasperation and emotional exhaustion in the lyric? Most definitely. Can this writer hear blue-eyed soul and Keith Moon in the drum part behind the guitar solo? Not even remotely!

"Malignant Narcissism," or "MalNar" as it has been deemed in near-Esperanto speak by the fans (and then amusingly the band themselves), became Rush's fifth nomination and fifth loss in the Best Rock Instrumental Performance category at the Grammys. Short like "Hope" but loud like "The Main Monkey Business," this one's a drum and bass guitar workout, with Alex hitting droning chords demarcated by murky atmospheric sounds. Since 1980, Lifeson's tireless exploration of texture has resulted in a trademark sound for the guitarist, along with a secondary characteristic, a sort of slashing approach to chording that comes from Pete Townshend, a trait also heard on this short piece. Like other songs on *Snakes & Arrows*, it's vaguely in a King Crimson zone, but pegged more to the Adrian Belew era(s) of that band.

It makes sense that Alex sounds disconnected from the proceedings. "Malignant Narcissism" was recorded in less than a day and as the last track slated for the album while Alex was away in Florida. His parts were added after the fact.

Geddy plays a Fender Jaco Pastorius Jazz Bass on this one, which significantly is a fretless. As Geddy told J.D. Considine, "It's one of the coolest instruments I've ever played. I picked it up, and within half an hour of owning it, I was just jamming with myself between vocal takes, playing this riff that just felt so fun to play. Our producer was listening, and he started recording the riff through my vocal mic, just acoustically. He said, 'Man, that's a song right there you just wrote.' Neil happened to be hanging around, and he had this four-piece drum kit set up. So the next day we took that bass and the amp, sat down, and threw an arrangement together."

Ged found the fretless "scary. Me playing a fretless bass is like, 'Jumpin' Jehoshaphat, I hope you don't want any other instruments added to this, because tuning's going to be really interesting.' I figured if I played fast enough, the wrong notes wouldn't have time to be heard, really. The passing notes will just pass too quickly. I think it worked out well because it's such a damned beautiful bass to play and to listen to. Now everybody associated with the session wants me to get them one. That's a good sign. Fender was kind enough to make me a fretted version of it. I'm going to play around with that as well and bring them both out on tour with me."

As for Neil's energetic, funky contribution, Peart says he was inspired by the drum styles of no less than Terry Bozzio, Steve Gadd, Buddy Rich and Tony Williams. At this late stage, Neil had already packed up his drums, resulting in him using the four-piece kit Geddy refers to. He wanted to leave a basic beat machine for Nick to use when he left, and so it was available for Neil to pound mercilessly on this two-minute showcase — one barely misses the tom-tom array, with Peart firing off combinations that, through the confusion of the fusion, remind us how John Bonham and Mitch Mitchell could be so interesting despite small kits.

There's a short and fairly indecipherable bit of spoken word at the halfway point of the track, a lift from *Team America: World Police*, which the band aired at Allaire for Nick, who had never seen the film. A female voice explains that "usually a case of malignant narcissism is brought on during childhood," referring to Kim Jong-il.

Neil closes the record with another relationship-steeped song, "We Hold On," picking up on the themes of "Good News First" and "Cold Fire" from back on *Counterparts*. Similar to both of those, the chord changes are melancholy and ominous.

An ill fit to *Snakes & Arrows*, Neil is playing trashy while Alex leaves off the acoustics. There's lots of noise everywhere, even though the song features one of Rush's characteristic drop-downs to a verse without much beat, tilting it into a ballad zone, albeit up-tempo.

But it's all according to plan, as Neil explained in *Modern Drummer*: "These verses begin very simply, the later ones punc-tuated with sharp 'tattoos' on the high toms. The first jagged one-hander is another Mark Craney dedication, while the others offer nods to several reggae drummers and Latin timbale players, plus Stewart Copeland, Nick Mason, Kevin Ellman (the first guy I ever heard using 'concert toms,' with Todd Rundgren's Utopia) and — hey — me again! It's always great to find a place for a fill that goes up the toms, too, like the last one.

"The choruses were influenced by Booujze's ideas (like the little snare 'skip'), while the double bass pedal fills that repeat (though each time different) between sections were developed in live performance — in my solo, the usual crucible for new devel-opments, but also in one of our oldest songs, 'Working Man.' During the past couple of tours, introducing a new style of fills into an old song helped keep it interesting for me. Other varia-tions of that device appear as a repeating motif in 'Far Cry' too.

I can also trace the development of that approach back through the past couple of Rush albums, in double-pedal rhythmic pat-terns I used in the songs 'Test for Echo' and 'One Little Victory.' Starting from that foundation, I opened up those patterns and moved them around the kit, finding new variations all the time.

"It is also fitting, and fun, that this final song concludes with the kind of 'rock flourish' we might use to end a song onstage. Taking note of that, and some of these other observations, I can't escape a gnawing realization: apparently playing live is good for my drumming."

Record tracked, "We mixed in Los Angeles," explains Alex, "the first time we actually made a record in the United States in all these years. We mixed in L.A. because they had this particular console we wanted to use at Ocean Way [a Neve 88R]. There are only a few of these consoles around. Nick lived in L.A. and Neil lives in L.A. So it was nice, especially for Neil, for a change, to work in his hometown. And it worked out great. It was nice to be there for a month; it was kind of fun and we made the best of it. L.A. is a really weird city. It's like a big giant subdivision. It just doesn't have a core. It just goes and goes and goes."

The venue was Ocean Way Recording, and the four-week mix was started January of 2007, conducted by Rich Chycki, assisted by Nick and Scott Moore.

"It's funny, mixing and getting the right balance in our songs is always, by far, the toughest thing about recording," Geddy explained to J.D. Considine at the time. "We go through these phases where we get paranoid that the guitars aren't present enough and loud enough, and that was the way we were with *Vapor Trails*, where it was very much, 'Let's get the guitars really raw and steamy and rockin'.' On this album, after the songs were written, the production team of Nick and Rich — Nick in particular — was driving to put the guitar into its own space, so that the rhythm section can be big and bold and beautiful, and the guitars can be present without smashing up all those other elements of the rhythm section. And what it brought to light was that interplay between Neil and I, and the fact that we can create a rhythm section that holds the melody — and holds the heart of the song, with the guitar free to play all those lovely inversions and unusual chordal parts that are Alex's forte. I thought that took a lot of maturity on Alex's part, to back away from the giant wall of massive, heavy guitar, in order to bring back some nuanced sound to his style."

The tour in support of *Snakes & Arrows* folded in on itself and expanded like a black hole, given that an entire second campaign was launched after a five-month break, now in support of *Snakes & Arrows Live*, not just any live album, but one that featured fully nine of the root album's thirteen selections. In other words, what Rush did between April and July 2008 intensively across North America was continuing to support this eighteenth studio record of which they were intensely proud.

With respect to the set list, this tour would see the biggest overhaul since the band's major shake-up back at *Signals*. In recent years, the band had admitted they would make new set lists by swapping out a handful of things but keeping the structure much the same. Opening with "Limelight" was new, as was tearing into "Digital Man" as the second selection. "Entre Nous" made its live debut, and they played nine songs off of the most recent album.

The first leg of dates took place between June and September, in North America, with the European tour commencing October 3 in Glasgow and ending October 29 in Helsinki. The October 16 and 17 concerts at the Ahoy Rotterdam in the Netherlands were recorded for use across *Snakes & Arrows Live*, the DVD version of which contains extra material from the July 22 Atlanta, Georgia, stop on the 2008 campaign.

The *Snakes & Arrows Live* album seemed to represent further proof that Rush was on some sort of victory lap, flooding the market with product. Not only was the live album twenty-seven songs long, but there was a DVD as well. Then there was a spate of compilations: *Gold* in '06, *Retrospective III: 1989–2008* and *Working Men* in '09, *Time Stand Still: The Collection* and *Icon* in 2010, and then *Icon II* in 2011. Finally, before we'd see another studio album, Rush would conduct their Time Machine Tour (the one and only time they ever played Ireland!), capped off with yet another live souvenir of said tour, *Time Machine 2011: Live in*

Cleveland, which featured all of *Moving Pictures* live. Again the package was issued on CD, Blu-ray and DVD, with the concert in Cleveland shot by Banger Films, which had of course crafted the *Beyond the Lighted Stage* documentary back in 2010. Topping it off, there were vinyl releases and box sets. All of this took the spotlight off what was arguably the reason for Rush: lack of new songs as they appeared on studio records.

However, that would be remedied soon enough, with the first quakings to be found right there on the *Time Machine 2011* live album, in the form of "BU2B" ("Brought Up to Believe") and "Caravan," two crushing new tracks of progressive noise pollution. Stacks of reconstituted and repackaged Rush stuff obtained and piled aside, space would have to be made to sit comfortably — brandy snifter in hand — and digest the epic, full-on concept album to come.

CHAPTER 8

CLOCKWORK ANGELS

"Because there's so much furious stuff happening
before that, you need a mental break."

After a full dance card in 2007 and more than an honest day's work in 2008, Rush took a full year and a half off, not playing live between July 2008 and June 2009. December of '09 rolls around and the band conduct a summit in California, Neil's turf, to talk about what to do next. Vague plans toward a concept record slowly begin to take shape, and Geddy and Alex return home to work on music.

The only wrinkle in the plan this time, aside from the concept album device, was that the band had finished and released two songs — "BU2B" and "Caravan" — well in advance of the album, and in the interim, they hit the road again, breaking up the sessions.

As Alex explained to Jeb Wright, "We spread this one out over a couple of years, and it ended up being a very nice way to work. It gave us a bit of breathing space, as we wrote in groups of songs. I think that always helps to get a little bit of variety. When you get into the studio and you record everything together, then it brings that consistency through it. I think we really achieved an interesting dynamic. We have a lot of songs that are different from each other. I think a lot of the songs are very cinematic and part of the story. The first batch we did consisted of five songs that we wrote several years ago. When I think of the songs on the album, I think of them in the little groups that we wrote them in. But overall I tried as much as possible to keep it simple. That's one of the refreshing aspects of the record. It has a lot of space in it and you can hear the drums clearly, you can hear the bass and the guitar — everything can be loud at the same time."

Comparing making records back in the '70s versus the way *Clockwork Angels* transpired, Alex muses, "Youth is a very volatile thing. When we were younger, we thought differently about our songwriting and our playing. We set a very high standard for ourselves and we always wanted to reach our goals. We put a lot of pressure on ourselves and we worked very fast. We, generally, had very little time to work on our records because we were touring so much. Everything that we ended up doing had this giant ball of energy attached to it. Today, we feel a very relaxed confidence about our music and our songwriting and also about our playing. We absolutely respect and trust each other now, more than we ever have. That's a very important aspect to working the way we work and how we put records together. You have to be able to trust each other and not hold your own ideas as the most precious. We all try to do the best work we can as a band. There is no one person more important than the whole. We've learned over forty years that this is the key to our success and our integrity."

"Originally, we planned the tour and I didn't feel right about going out without having anything new written," Geddy told Jerry Ewing, with respect to the Time Machine Tour back in 2012. "Because what we like about playing live is getting our juices going playing new music on stage. We'd discussed the idea for the album and decided we'd just get at the writing. We had a great writing session and recorded those two songs ['BU2B' and 'Caravan'] very quickly. That tour was originally supposed to be only about three months long but it was going so well and we were playing *Moving Pictures* as well, that it was wrong not to bring that tour to Europe and South America. It was a special show and we weren't prepared to let it be a small tour. So we decided to put the album on pause. Alex and I had a jam session on that tour and we wrote 'Headlong Flight' and 'Carnies.' And when we got back off the tour and we got really close to finishing the album, I rediscovered those jams and those two songs came out of them. So it's weird that this album is made up of music that's been written over a two-and-a-half-year period."

Concerning the decision to do a concept album, Geddy told Chris Neal, "It was an idea that came along through Neil that we found intriguing. We started talking about the steampunk aesthetic and how much we liked that. We thought it would be fun to do a set design around that, and that led to some musing that he'd had about the story. The idea was interesting, and when Alex and I started writing the music for it we made sure that it was a different kind of concept record — more of a rock opera, in a sense. We wanted every song to stand on its own, to have a point and something to say that could be removed from the context of the other songs and still be valid."

Neil's *Clockwork Angels* narrative was built from the ground up, from nothing, although as he relates in the *Clockwork Angels* tour-book, inspiration came from the likes of William Manchester's *A World Lit Only by Fire*, a treatise on the middle ages, along with John Barth's *The Sot-Weed Factor* and Voltaire's *Candide*. More specifically, Peart also cites in the booklet "Michael Ondaatje and Joseph Conrad for 'The Anarchist,' Robertson Davies and Herbert Gold for 'Carnies,' Daphne du Maurier for 'The Wreckers' and Cormac McCarthy and early Spanish explorers in the American Southwest for 'Seven Cities of Gold.'"

Most intriguing is the introduction of alchemy, a topic or hobby that was pretty much over by the steampunk era, replaced by all manner of hand-wringing over ghosts. Peart vowed to keep plot pretty much out of the songs, addressing the concerns of Geddy, the guy who had to sing all this, who insisted the songs be given a fighting chance of staying strong and independent on their own. As he hinted at previously, Geddy didn't want them to be dependent, from a literary standpoint, on understanding the rest of the bank of lyrics. Toward this end, Neil had his private notes on plot, he had visuals in mind, and then in the end, in the booklet, he provided a few helpful stage directions atop each of the song's lyrics.

Early 2010, Neil had written enough lyrics for Alex and Geddy to complete the two songs they would be performing on the upcoming Time Machine Tour. The band also had "The Anarchist" and "The Garden" written by the time the tour kicked off but didn't present them live. After four dates on the Time Machine Tour that found the band playing São Paulo, Rio de Janeiro, Buenos Aires and Santiago, they took a five-month break and resumed work on the record. But progress was slow, marred by difficulties getting Neil's words to line up with the jams Geddy and Alex had. Still, much of "Headlong Flight" and "Carnies" got done at this point.

Given the extension to the Time Machine Tour, the band scotched plans to return to Blackbird Studios in Nashville, where in April of 2010 the first two songs had been recorded, Nick Raskulinecz returning as producer, Richard Chycki finishing up with the mix, which took place at the Sound Kitchen, also in Tennessee. Instead they wound up at Revolution Recording in

Toronto's east end. "Toronto is home for Ged and me," Alex told Chris Neal, "so the studio was about ten minutes away. It's a brand-new place, and they were barely done by the time we were ready to come in. But the room sounded great and had a great console in it, and it was nice to be able to go home every night after work and spend the weekends with the family. We'd spent years away from family while we were recording in the past, and it's nice to be there now. We mixed in Los Angeles, which is home for Neil these days, so it was a bit of a trade-off. He came up and spent a couple of months with us in Toronto and then we reversed it."

"The only funny thing about it was that it was so spread out," said Alex, speaking with Mick Burgess. "We did little spurts here and there but once we got into the meat of it, it was really a joy to make. We had a great time and had a lot of fun making it and it was very vibrant in the studio. It was great working with Nick Raskulinecz. He's such a music lover, so enthusiastic. He's such a great presence to be around in the studio. With this record, we really wanted to play and wanted to stretch out a little bit. We wanted to have fun playing and also to strip things down a little. I think *Snakes & Arrows*, in retrospect, was a little bit dense because it was written on acoustic guitar, which played a major role in the production. We layered a lot of acoustics and electrics and we got a little cloudy at times. I really like the record, but with the hindsight of living with it for a while we realized that we overcooked it a bit. So we really wanted to strip it down and have more of a three-piece feel to it. There's no rhythm guitar during the guitar solos and such, which are things you end up doing as you like the sound of it because you like all the color. But it's not always necessary and I think the album comes across as a lot more powerful as a result."

The band at this point also switched from Atlantic in the States to feisty mid-sized metal label Roadrunner. Says Alex on the switch, "The industry is changing so much and I think Atlantic Records has changed a lot too. Atlantic used to be *the* rock label and I don't think it is anymore. Roadrunner has become that label. It's in the family; it's a cousin of Atlantic. I think the feeling was — and it was a mutual feeling — that we would get better attention in a very difficult industry at Roadrunner. I have to say it was the right decision. Being on Roadrunner is very different from being on Atlantic. We had lots of friends at Atlantic we dearly loved, but a lot of the people we got to know over the years are long gone now. Roadrunner were straight out of the gate working very, very hard, particularly in the U.K. We are very happy to work with them."

Deal in place, the sessions at Revolution ran from October to December of 2011. Meanwhile, into 2012, sci-fi writer Kevin Anderson, a buddy of Neil's, had been writing a novelization of Peart's story, issuing it on September 4 of that year — a sequel called *Clockwork Lives* would emerge three years later. Summarizing *Clockwork Angels*, Anderson wrote, "In a young man's quest to follow his dreams, he is caught between the grandiose forces of order and chaos. He travels across a lavish and colorful world of steampunk and alchemy, with lost cities, pirates, anarchists, exotic carnivals, and a rigid Watchmaker who imposes precision on every aspect of daily life."

Explained Neil in the tourbook: "My friend Kevin J. Anderson was among the pioneers of a genre of science fiction that came to be called 'steampunk' — a more romantic, idealistic reaction against the 'cyberpunk' futurists, with their scenarios of dehumanized, alienated, dystopian societies. Our own previous excursions into the future, '2112' and 'Red Barchetta,' had been set in that darker kind of imagining, for dramatic and allegorical effect. This time I was thinking of steampunk's definition as 'the future as it ought to have been' or 'the future as seen from the past' — as imagined by Jules Verne and H.G. Wells in the late nineteenth century."

The world Neil creates is "driven by steam, intricate clockworks and alchemy. That last element occurred to me because I was intrigued by Diane Ackerman's use of a few alchemical symbols as chapter heads in *An Alchemy of Mind*. They seemed elegant, mysterious and powerful. Soon I learned about an entire set of runic hieroglyphs for elements and processes, and as with the tarot cards for *Vapor Trails* and the Hindu game of Leela for *Snakes & Arrows*, I became fascinated with an ancient tradition. As the lyrical 'chapters' came together, I chose one symbol to represent each of them, for the character or mood. Those would end up arrayed on the cover clockface, as first used on the 'Caravan'/'BU2B' single in early 2010. Since then they have shifted a little, as the story has grown, but you can find brimstone at one o'clock for the faith-bashing 'BU2B,' gold at six o'clock for 'Seven Cities of Gold,' earth at eleven o'clock for 'The Garden,' and so on (the 'U' in Rush stands for amalgamation)."

Behind the clock of alchemical symbols are storm clouds in a rich red, but one could easily imagine it as the type of colored flash powder alchemists would use to impress the royals who are paying good money for golden results — and if not that, a little bit of Renaissance-era pyrotechnics. The clock is set to 9:12, which on a twenty-four-hour clock equates to 21:12. Throughout the booklet, long-time designer Hugh Syme touches down on story points here and there, while other times staying more abstract. There are various visual references to steampunk, including the airship — pertinently, across Victorian-era America, there had been the "airship mystery," namely a rash of UFO sightings. Most graphically, Syme shows us the "most famous City of Gold," Cibola, an image that conjures thoughts of another Victorian-era Fortean pastime, hollow earth theory.

Into the record, and *Clockwork Angels* opens with "Caravan," the shock of its heaviness cushioned by the fact that fans had already heard it, both an in-studio version and delivered on live stages. The song was not re-recorded for the album but it did go through a remix, with Alex remarking that when people suspect they hear different parts, it's because of what got raised in the mix and what got lowered. Instantly one hears Rush's most powerful production job in years, in fact, maybe the bassiest and heaviest ever in terms of guitars, even if Alex doesn't cut with the same no-nonsense distortion as he did in the '70s. Indeed though, Geddy has given up articulation for bass as frequency, and Neil is set a bit back, splashy, overwhelmed by bass and guitars. Alex has left behind his *Snakes & Arrows* experiment of acoustic guitar massaged in with the electrics — what he described earlier as a type of "overcooking." Another way to describe it is that it sounds like a woofer with a rip in it. The distortion pedal track is the correct one, but then there's this buzzing.

The second early track, "BU2B," is most definitely in the same bashing, crashing zone as "Caravan." Lyrically, while "Caravan" sparingly speaks of an embarked-upon journey, "BU2B" brings up questions of faith, fate, karma and the embodiment of such in the character of the Watchmaker. The hero of our story, Owen Hardy (a wide-eyed Candide of sorts), experiences a transition much like Neil's, both leaving a childhood in the country (but with shore and ships) for "Crown City." Both also, in tandem with the trip, take up as intellectual hobby the philosophy of religion.

In the preamble to "BU2B," amidst the pondering over predestination, Neil offers a fresh and amusing take on alchemy. Rather than the set idea of a bearded man toiling away in a tower working in vain to generate gold from economic nothings, Neil posits a team of alchemists as the hero inventors of the electrical grid.

Asked about "BU2B" by Jeb Wright, Alex noted that "I used my Les Pauls and my Telecasters, which is a combo that I used to use quite frequently. It really was heavily layered with guitars and that was the idea for that song." Raskulinecz said that in contrast, "Caravan" made use of a couple of Gibsons, Alex's "Les Paul Goldtop and his tobacco sunburst 335. We put those through a Marshall and a Bogner."

Unlike "Caravan," this one got some extra sauce added to the version that came out earlier. Alex explained to Joe Bosso, "I recorded a new opening that wasn't on the version of 'BU2B' we put out last year. Mixing can be terribly tedious. You want to come in when the mix is ready so that you can be very objective about it. So there's a lot of sitting around and 'Hmm, what am I going to do today?' I had Logic set up in my hotel room, and I was goofing around and doing some writing. I had a few guitars — there was one of my Gibson Axcess models and a Martin I borrowed from the Guitar Center — and I got a mic. We had talked about doing this little segue, so we stuck the mic outside my balcony and recorded some background sounds: Los Angeles in the morning, cars going by, stuff like that. With the balcony doors open, I did a little guitar pass, and then Ged did his vocal thing. We messed around with a few effects and created the piece. It was all done very spontaneously in just a few minutes."

Further, Nick called "BU2B" "a heavy-hitter. It's dark and a little out of character for Rush. It went through something of an overhaul from the version that was put out last year. We added the intro section Neil always envisioned. Alex and Geddy actually recorded that in their hotel room. Like 'Caravan,' this one was quick. We spent a day on the drums, then immediately did the bass and guitars. After that we did overdubs. We did Taurus pedals and we did a theremin too. That really cool, squiggly ascending part in the middle is Geddy playing a theremin.

They had one in the studio, just lying around in Blackbird; it's such an amazing place, the things you find there. So we took the theremin, plugged it into an amp, put some delay and a phaser on it and he did a solo. I think he might have played one back in the '70s. His performance is cool. He did it once and it worked out great."

"I hope that's in the live set forever," noted Peart of the third track, "Clockwork Angels," speaking with Philip Wilding. "Alex gave us a demo way back before we started writing and right away I pointed at that song and said, we've never done anything with that feel as a drummer, so I wanted to play it. It's so unusual for us, but it still has all the intricacies and techniques, the challenge and the performance." Indeed, Nick says that Neil played this one once and that Alex's guitar solo was lifted from the demos.

"There's a real 'shooting from the hip' feel on this record," Alex told Mik Gaffney from *Powerplay*. "You know, Geddy and Neil are always a very tight rhythm section, but there's a real looseness to their playing, as you said, a funky, groove approach to their playing. A lot of that was down to the way that Neil approached the way he recorded the drums. Normally, he would work on arrangements for weeks and then he'd practice them over and over, ingraining it, and then he'd record the parts. This was a lot more spontaneous. It was all about the moment. I think it shows in Neil's playing. He's very creative and very, very active on this record, even for such an active drummer as he is.

"Geddy really reacted to that," continues Lifeson. "Even when he and I were working on the demos, we were really grooving to the songs; it was there in essence right from the very beginning. Neil is an amazing drummer, arguably the best rock drummer in the world, and the things he can do are incredible, but I think sometimes as a musician when you work on some things too much, you lose something and it becomes more of an academic exercise. You lose the spontaneity, the gut instinct to hit the cymbal at that moment or to go for that drum fill, and that's more apparent on this record, I think. I really don't think Neil expected to enjoy things as much as he did. He's a real creature of order and pattern; he's a typical Virgo in that way. He likes to have everything in a straight line, so to do something like this was a real eye-opener for him. He was like, 'I'm just going to play whatever I'm going to play, and then I'll learn it later, rather than the other way around.' Which I think was really good for him."

"That song began with an experimental instrumental sound-scape Alex wrote using technology, resulting in some amazing textures," explained Geddy, on the record's title track, speaking with Chris Jisi from *Bass Player*. "When the lyrics came along, I saw a way to break down what Alex had into several sections and write some melodies over the top, and before long we had created this interesting rock/electronica song. The trick, both in recording and mixing, was to retain the spacey, mysterious sounds while keeping the song urgent and somewhat organic. Neil had that swingy, shuffly groove in mind when he first heard the demo, and when the song was finished we both couldn't wait to tackle that feel."

Lyrically, on "Clockwork Angels," the roles of the Watchmaker and the Clockwork Angels are left obscure, and for that matter, it's hard to tell where the Timekeepers and the Regulators fit in all this. Suffice to say that past the preamble, Neil is simple and descriptive enough in his lyrics in a visual sense that we get how this all plays out — the angels are highest upon high, beyond the glowing orbs. As well, he focuses the lyrics chiefly on the dynamic of the angels and how they elate and placate the masses who worship them in turn.

The strong sense of tribal rhythm, along with the melody and texture found throughout "Clockwork Angels," is reprised with "The Anarchist." In fact, the entire record thus far seethes with bluster and energy, arrangements similar across the first four, with exotic ear candy added regularly, and all of it sounding strangely antique, evoking images of the steampunk world, implied but not exactly described in concrete terms.

"One of my favorites, but I could say that about all the songs," explained Nick, speaking with Joe Bosso for *MusicRadar*. "To me, it's all about the riff, and this riff takes me back to the old days. That was one of the cool things about working on this record, helping Rush to know that it was okay to be like this. 'You guys can do this. You guys did it a long time ago; you can do it again. You own it!' There's a lot of interplay happening between everybody. There was a demo, but we added a keyboard and the high strings — it morphed. Vocally, it was about getting Geddy up in that high register where he belongs. His energy level is pretty cool here. I've said this for years: Alex Lifeson is the chameleon of rock guitar. He's got so much feeling. He brings me to tears when he plays; in fact, he's in tears while he's playing it! Some of his solos were from the demos, some he played in the studio a few times, and there were a few that he tracked multiple times. In every case, he had pure emotion."

"The drum pattern on that song is one that I put together and Neil connected with it," noted Lifeson, interviewed by Jeb Wright. "I think I come from a different place than Neil does and sometimes he will find what I do as an interesting approach that he would have never thought of himself. It gave him a launching point."

But Geddy had his hands full. As he told Phil Ashcroft from *Fireworks*, "As soon as I recorded the bass line for 'The Anarchist,' and then put the vocal on it, I looked at Nick and said, 'This song is going to be a motherfucker to play live!' And he goes, 'What? Really? It's not so complicated.' The thing is, it's not about what's complicated; it's about the direction they're moving in — the bass is moving in one direction and the vocals are moving in another direction. I'm going to have to play that fucker so many times that I can't think about it anymore, and that's why we've left ourselves more rehearsal time before this tour than we have for any other record, because I think we're going to need it — at least I know I will!"

True to Geddy's lyric specifications, the songs on the record remain substantially independent — the comparison he used was to the Who's *Tommy* — "The Anarchist" bears none of the plot trappings of what came before, with Neil painting a psychological picture of a bitter anarchist. Not particularly prone to anarchy through thoughtful politics, this particular individual wants to blow things up because nothing has gone right for him — anarchy is a satisfying way to bring all those more fortunate to his level. Neil's preamble brings into view the character of the peddler, who asks the loaded question, "What do you lack?" When the anarchist hears this, he answers "vengeance," evoking images of James Dean in *Rebel Without a Cause* or Holden Caulfield in *The Catcher in the Rye.*

"Carnies" underscores another gathering sentiment across the first half of *Clockwork Angels* — when the band is aggressive and heavy on this record, there's an element of early blues-boom hard rock about the riffing, circa Led Zeppelin and Free, bleeding into early King Crimson. "Carnies" oscillates between these tank-like passages, an almost Killing Joke–like sense of post-punk, and then more up-tempo, melodic playing circa Rush back on, say, *Permanent Waves* or *Grace Under Pressure.*

At the narrative end, Owen Hardy finds work with a carnival, again like Neil, who worked the amusement park back home in St. Catharines as a kid for a summer job. The difference is that Neil manned the booths before his trip to the city and Owen is doing this *in* the city, although the carnival also travels. Neil readily admits the parallels, telling Mike Doherty, "Ah, the classic dreamer, and one of the lovely distinctions that Kevin and I wove over the character with reflection to our own pasts. When I was in the band J.R. Flood in St. Catharines, where we were doing pretty well, I said to my bandmates, 'Let's go to London.' I did, on my own, but it surprises me to this day that no one wanted to go with me. I went hungry and wasn't finding fame and fortune as quickly as I'd fantasized, but there was nothing daunting to me at the time. Like Owen, I did stumble into things, and a trail of events that could not have happened otherwise in one sense led me toward the person I am today. I lived away from home for the first time; I got a real job and proved myself in a workday situation, and thus I was never afraid anymore. As crises came up later on, 'Oh, we have to compromise, and the record company wants to do this,' I'd be like, 'No, I don't have to.'"

Owen confronts the Anarchist, who is about to conduct an act of terrorism at the Midsummer Festival in Crown City. The Anarchist throws the detonator to Hardy, who is then run out of town, presumed to be the perpetrator. In the lyric, Peart unambiguously relates this odd tale to the concept of fate: Hardy wishes out of this noisy and sense-overloading job, and then his prayers are answered by the angels, but mischievously, with edge.

Underscoring the oppressive nature of the song's structure, Alex brings many weapons. As Nick told *MusicRadar*, "Geddy sang the song and after he finished, it was time to come up with the soundscapes. We have three guitar tracks — one on the left, one on the right and one in the middle — and they all have different clean amps with tremolo, panning effects and phasers, Leslie speakers and filtered little sounds. Alex doesn't really discuss what he's thinking before he does it. He'll lay his parts down, and then he'll call me into the room. I'll either say, 'That's fucking amazing!' or 'It can be better' or 'It's done, it's perfect.' Nine times out of ten I'll say, 'It's perfect.' This solo is so cool because of the carnival atmosphere, and that's all Al. He made those sounds and did all that brilliant guitar work — he had such vision and so many ideas. It was pretty inspiring seeing him follow it all through."

"I love the opening riff with the cool harmonics," Alex told Joe Bosso. "It's got a little bit of Hendrix or Robin Trower about it. The choruses are strong. The carnival-type vibe and the sounds make them quite different from the verse and bridge sections. The climbing bridge is reminiscent of something, but I don't know what it is. A lot of moments on the album are like that: I'm reminded of something, but I couldn't tell you what song it is or what era it's from. That's a great thing, though — people gravitate to that."

Other than special case "BU2B2," track six of twelve, "Halo Effect" is the shortest song on the album (at 3:14). It's also the closest thing to a ballad on the album, and it's consistent with soft Rush since *Test for Echo* as it sounds vaguely Celtic. "There are only really two shorter songs," remarks Ged. "One is 'Halo Effect,' which is quite a beautiful and unusual piece of music. It's shorter but I don't know if it's what you would term as accessible. I suppose it is to a certain degree, but to me that was just a thing the record needed to give you a break. Because there's so much furious stuff happening before that, you need a mental break just to give it some dynamics."

Accompanying a casual Neil playing open and cymbal-dominant, Geddy plucking hard on bass (uncommonly articulated for this record) and Alex strumming acoustic (also rare here) is the string section, added in California.

"It's hard because you start hearing them everywhere," remarks Geddy, on the temptation. "At first we just wanted strings on

'The Garden.' Then we thought 'Halo Effect' would really be beautiful with strings. And then you listen to other songs . . . that was Nick's thing, Nick always hears strings on everything. Then you start thinking, 'Well, there's a little bit in "The Anarchist" that would sound great with strings.' And before you know it, they've taken over the whole record if you're not careful. I think it's okay to indulge ourselves at this point, and I felt so confident in the strength and the solid bone structure of the songs that I think they can take the extra enhancements without losing the essential thing."

The first stab at strings on this came from Alex, who added electronic strings to his demo. The actual string section used on the record was in fact commandeered by David Campbell, life-long Scientologist, father of famed alt rock talent Beck Hansen and arranger on over 450 gold and platinum records. Noted Nick on the acoustic guitar work, "Alex played his Gibson Dove acoustic. We used two tracks, miking him with a U47 tube mic. I put the mic about three feet away so you can get the nice body of the guitar. It's a pretty gorgeous sound."

Lyrically, Geddy is really getting his way with this one, "Halo Effect" reading like a simple love song completely detached from plot. To be sure, it is our main character, Owen, who finds himself spurned by a potential love interest who is part of the circus troupe, but unlike "Carnies," there's no relating of the plot point to questions of fate, much less a grand religious debate. What's remarkable about the lyric is how unremarkable it is — or at least how plain-spoken; stylistically, one would never suspect Neil was behind it.

"Another epic riff," remarked Nick, on "Seven Cities of Gold." "It sets the tone for the whole song. You know, there's nothing in the world like a fucking cool Rush song, and that's what this is. There's a lot going on, so as a producer, I want to make sure that we don't lose the song. I love the way it builds up, coming out of this chaotic funk, and then you have Neil just slamming. It makes me want to drive fast. We created a lot of spacey stuff in the middle section. For his solo, Alex played live off the floor. We put him out in the room with his headphones on, and he was right in front of his amp. We wanted to get the screaming feedback coming at him. I think he nailed it in one take. I'm so privileged to have witnessed it — and many moments like it."

Asked by Chris Jisi at *Bass Player* about the wacky opening bass workout on the track, Geddy chuckles. "It's sort of a retro white funk feel mixed with crazy, Robin Trower-y guitar licks. I'm plucking and hammering, while muting with my right hand. It feels like the opening to an old softcore porn movie! Part of it is stiff and not very funky, yet I'm trying to funk it up. It was a weird moment that we just liked and kept. I love the song — it has a nice tempo that you can kind of hold back on and play in a bluesy rock vibe."

As for the inspiration for the lyric, Neil was amused by this idea that Spanish explorers traipsing around what is now the Southwestern U.S. were always on about the search for the City of Gold. In essence, our protagonist, our global wanderer and searcher, has encountered his second gleaming city, this one very different from the first. No steampunk airship could reach it, so he gets there by water and then a trek through Redrock Desert (a sly reference to the celebrated concert venue). There's a nice reference to the "alchemy mines," another concept that is Neil's alone. Is the first city powered by ore from these pits? Are the cities of gold built from lesser minerals mined here and then transformed by a separate class of alchemists? Musically, this is just a big, loud stadium rocker with a grinding hard rock groove. Again, built into the riff is the story of how the British blues boom begat heavy metal, which Alex had understood as far back as "What You're Doing" on the very first record.

"It's very cinematic," reflected Lifeson on this one, in a *Total Guitar* interview. "You can hear the danger of the big city as our traveler approaches. Then when Neil comes in and we break out the riff, you're there — you're in the city with all of its excitement and opportunity and trouble. The song has a swagger to it. It turned out exactly as I envisioned. I love the end . . . the guitar squealing and spitting as you leave the city."

"The Wreckers" feels like the band's homage to the Who — if only for the opening fifteen seconds! Neil is Keith, Geddy is John, Alex is Pete and no one plays Roger. Then we're into replenishing Rush pop songwriting, mid-tempo, lots of electric guitar, Geddy singing in a comfortable range. Strings creep in, but nothing can take center stage from the song's hooky power ballad chorus.

"It was very cool, the way that came about," Alex told Mik Gaffney. "We were on a little bit of a downtime in the studio and Ged picked up one of my guitars. I have all my guitars in the studio — it's like a family get-together. I might not use ninety percent of them, but they all like to be there. Anyway, I had an old acoustic there, in Nashville tuning, which is like the octave tuning on a twelve-string, so it has a light, airy sound to it. Ged started playing on it, grabbed some lyrics and said, 'What do you think of this?' He started playing the verse melody and I said, 'Wow, this is great!' Ged wanted to throw it down real quick in the studio so I grabbed a bass and played along, and that's how we ended up writing it, with him on guitar and me on bass. It was really interesting because Ged plays guitar by using one finger and strumming back and forth, a lot like he plays bass, and I don't do that, so he was getting a really different sound and feel to it. I play bass totally different to him. So the whole song had a different feel, which was very revealing to us."

Elaborating on this, in conversation with Jeb Wright, Alex said, "On the original demo, Geddy played guitar and I played bass. When it was recorded, Geddy played the bass but he learned my bass part. He said, 'I would never play this song like this.' I learned something from him from the way he played the upstrokes on the acoustic, as I tend to use mostly down strokes. I found that with the Nashville tuning that he used, the upstroke had a particular effect on the song and the shimmering quality. The song eventually evolved and became a different thing but it's still great when you can evolve and influence each other on your instruments just by looking in a different direction."

"Just talking about this song chokes me up," remarked Nick on "The Wreckers" in his *MusicRadar* track by track. "It's got the spirit of the '60s and '70s, a real purity to it. I tried to get the two of them to switch for the tracking — Alex on bass and Geddy on guitar — but they decided to stick to their designated instruments. The tune is so big, it's got such bounce and swing, but it took some effort. The guitar part in the verse was probably the hardest thing on the record for us to find. Alex had some difficulty playing the part Geddy had written — it was great, but it didn't feel right to him. He had to search for the right part, and it took all day with me going, 'Nope, that's not it; nope, that's not it.' Finally he stumbled onto a picking figure, and Geddy and I just stood up and went, 'That's it! That's the part.' The tune came together real fast after that. It's a very melancholy song. It's almost mournful but in a positive way. I think the song is about trust. See, the wreckers were people who would make fake lighthouses on the coasts and the shores, and they would guide merchant ships into rocky waters in order to wreck them so that they could plunder the ships."

Neil picked up the idea from a Daphne du Maurier novel called *Jamaica Inn*, which describes wreckers operating on the coast of Cornwall, in southwest Britain. Peart frames their crimes as a "shocking example of inhumanity." In his "Seven Cities of Gold" lyric, Neil has Hardy narrowly escaping death in the desert and onto his next adventure. After the wrecking, he is the only survivor. In the lyric, he ruminates that sometimes things are too good to be true, in this case, the salvation of the ghostly light. In truth, everyone wants gold: the alchemists and their patrons want it conjured from nothing, Hardy wants to see a city of it, and the wreckers want to snatch and scavenge it, scooping it up from the ocean bottom, hopefully without survivors from the ship getting in the way.

Next up is blasting rocker "Headlong Flight," which was launched as the record's second single, two months before the issue of the full record. The song limped to #84 on the Canadian charts and #23 on the Billboard Hot Mainstream Rock charts — not that much could be expected beyond that. "Headlong Flight" was arguably Rush's heaviest song since "Stick It Out," and it was both dense and chaotic to boot, while featuring some of Neil's most spirited fills to date, but centered around rapid-fire snare rather than tuned toms. Geddy says the song began life as an instrumental to be called "Take That Lampshade Off Yo Head!" but that Neil's supplied lyric fit so well, they had to turn it into the slashing late-period — last gasp? — heavy metal anthem it became. There's a vague similarity in some of the guitar figures to "Bastille Day"; in case anyone missed it, Neil draws attention by directly quoting the 1975 classic on the drums.

As Geddy told Jerry Ewing, "There are nods to our past but specifically when it suits the story. For example, 'Headlong Flight' is the story of our protagonist looking back over his life, so it seemed apropos to do that in musical terms as well. So we looked back at some things we'd done musically in the past and put a new twist on that just for a moment before jumping headlong off in another direction."

In terms of the bass part, Geddy told Chris Jisi, "I'm trying to come up with melodies that work around what's going on, to add a level of orchestration. I do that pretty much by ear as opposed to specifically following the harmony. 'Headlong' is interesting; the opening main riff is a repeating figure throughout, but in different forms and time signatures. That's how the song got going, out of this furious jam I had with Alex. I was jamming with him in the lower register, and he'd start riffing on my riff; then I would move up the neck and he would go somewhere else. When we found that line, it seemed to be such a classic, circular riff, with so much propulsion to it. I knew when Neil got to sink his teeth into it, it would really start to move."

On the lyric side of things, Geddy took the message of "Headlong Flight" to be that Owen Hardy had looked back on all the positives and negatives of his life and come to the conclusion that if he had to live it all again he wouldn't change a thing, a sentiment corroborated both by Neil's preamble and dead-easy lyric. This is a Nietzschean sort of intellectual exercise, or on a lighter note, also the conundrum conjured by the Bill Murray film *Groundhog Day*. Gold is mentioned and there are musings on the idea of fate. Also "quoted" is Friedrich Gruber, a reference to both Friedrich Nietzsche and Neil's drum instructor in the '90s, Freddie Gruber.

Raskulinecz talks about how the song came shortly after Neil enthusiastically and animatedly, in his breathless all-or-nothing manner, laid out over twenty minutes what he'd like to do from a literary standpoint with this record, which he now had come around to accept as a concept album. This took place in the space between the two legs of the Time Machine Tour, and the steampunk ethic used there helped inspire the steampunk over- and undercurrents that would wind their way through the record, always felt but, in fact, rarely described.

Next on *Clockwork Angels*, officially track ten, is a spot of both segue and reprise, a time-honored tradition with concept albums. "BU2B2" is a reinterpretation of the earlier rocker, at 1:28, arranged like John Cale in the Velvet Underground, comprised essentially of a Geddy vocal over avant-garde strings.

"There's no guitar or bass on it," Nick told Joe Bosso. "We constructed it using different elements of instruments. Alex wrote a great string part and put keyboards on it. It's kind of a segue piece. Geddy's vocal is almost bluesy on it. It's pretty special." Adds Alex, "This is a moment that's integral to the story for Neil; he really wanted to have it in."

And one can understand why: Neil throws himself into both the preamble and the brief lyric, making this quiet and fleeting piece central to the dizzying panorama. Life is bleak, meaningless, maybe even horrible, but Hardy chooses to live. We're immediately taken back to the bipolar bumper car sounds and sentiments of *Vapor Trails*. We're disoriented because we don't know what to think, but we're wiser for it. Hardy in his fiber feels what the anarchist does but chooses not to detonate.

As we near the end, steeped in *Candide*, we arrive at "Wish Them Well," where the band rocks out, sparkly and optimistic, in concert with Neil's lyric. Woodstock and the *Feedback* EP and the Who are conjured once again, Geddy, Alex and Neil finding the fountain of youth.

As Geddy told Phil Ashcroft, "'Wish Them Well' is probably the most accessible song on the record, and that's a song that almost didn't exist. I kept writing it; Alex and I would work on it, and then it kind of sucked so we threw it away and tried again, and that sucked a little less but it still sucked, so we threw it away again. Then at the eleventh hour we had this last jam session and came up with this song. It's a more immediate kind of classic rock song, and I really think it's a breath of fresh air when it appears near the end of the album. Everything has to have a purpose in the context of the total thing, but shouldn't be dependent on the other songs to be valid."

"We got a set of lyrics from Neil that we really liked and we tried to develop some musical ideas but it didn't seem to be working," said Alex, talking with Mick Burgess. "With the first version we had parts of it that we really liked but the longer we spent on it the less we liked it. We went ahead with a couple of the other songs and did the tour and then when we returned to it we decided to scrap the music. We felt the lyrics were strong and were important for the story. The music just was not happening so we developed a completely different thing and lived with that for a little while and that was still not getting us off. Finally, we went with the approach that you can hear now which was much more strident."

Asked if "Wish You Well" was single material, a valid proposition given the effusive explosions of riff and fill throughout, Alex demurred. "I'm not the guy who you should ask about what should be the single, as the first single off this record is seven and a half minutes long! [He is referring here to 'Headlong Flight,' technically second single, but first in temporal space with the release of the album proper.] That's the right way to be. A Rush single should be seven and a half minutes long. The thing about 'Wish Them Well' is that the approach we settled on was a very classic, traditional-sounding rock song. The drums are really strident and marching along and the nature of the chords and the chord progressions makes for a classic rock sound."

Adds Geddy, talking with Jerry Ewing, "I love the lyrics and I loved the sentiment behind this song, and I felt it was really important to the concept of the album. It's about how you look at people in a non-judgmental way, and I thought that was important as a part of growing up and achieving adulthood. The first two versions didn't do the lyrics justice. So I kept rewriting it with Al and that's the luxury of having two and a half years to work on material for a record. We got it third time lucky."

Wrote Neil in the tourbook: "Typically, there was one 'trouble child.' Out of all the seemingly more complicated songs, the music for 'Wish Them Well' was written and scrapped twice, and the song was almost abandoned. But Geddy liked the lyrics enough to keep trying (thank you!), and the third version pleased everyone. That song also put Booujze and me to a lot of trouble over the drum part, much more than any other song except 'Headlong Flight' — that one for its perverse complexity, rather than the exacting simplicity of 'Wish Them Well.' Booujze and I spent many hours trying out different basic patterns and juggling their arrangement. The guys always laugh when I come out of the studio grumbling, 'I hate that stupid ignorant song!' They laugh because they are the ones who made it that way. 'Wish Them Well' was equally elusive vocally — or at least lyrically. The day Geddy and Booujze recorded that vocal in Toronto, I happened to be at home in California, and all day we exchanged texts and emails over the tiniest of alterations, line by line, sometimes word by word. Ultimately it turned out very well, but I admit I still have a bit of a grudge against that song."

As he told Mike Doherty from *Maclean's*, "There's so much life experience in this story — it's not just a far-blown fantasy. 'Wish Them Well' [offers] a very mature response to the world that it took me a long time to learn. In a lot of our early stuff, my lyrical inspiration was anger, for sure. There's still a lot I'm angry about, a lot of human behavior that's appalling and despicable, but you choose what you can fight against. I always thought if

I could just put something in words perfectly enough, people would get the idea and it would change things. That's a harmless conceit. With people too, you constantly think, 'If I'm nice to people and treat them well, they'll appreciate it and behave better.' They won't, but it's still not a bad way to live."

Finally, we arrive at "The Garden," the culmination of all that came before, more strings than before, more acoustic guitar than before, more heart-wrenching melody than before, a conclusion in every sense, and perhaps unbeknownst to the band themselves, the conclusion to the band's studio canon.

We're essentially in a ballad zone, as with "Halo Effect," but we're rocked along. As well, Geddy reminds us of the strong role of the bass player in this band, telling Chris Jisi concerning the intro passage, "That's me fingerpicking, like a classical nylon guitar; the part came to me while jamming with Alex. I like to play around with fingerpicked chordal pieces, but it's rare to find a place for that in Rush because it doesn't cut through. 'The Garden' is delicate enough that I could do it. The first time around I use a pure, clean tone, and when the part returns I add some amp sound for dimension. It's the piece I'm probably the most proud of on the record. The lyric wraps the sentiment of the story of this person's life, and it has a universal sensibility everyone can relate to. We wanted the vocals and the song to be heartfelt and relaxed, without being wussy or syrupy. That's hard for a rock band that likes to pump it out — to play those gentler moments and make them feel authentic. I felt we accomplished it, though."

Explained Alex in a chat with Metal Express Radio, concerning "The Garden": "We put down keyboard, sample strings, and we really liked it but we thought rather than use sampled strings we'd bring in a real orchestra. Geddy and I were the catalysts for that. He's a real sucker for those sorts of things. David Campbell did a great job. That really tugs at your heart. There's something that's really classic about that arrangement and really heartfelt. The song works really well as a closer, the final chapter of the story. That single cello note at the end is very poignant."

As Geddy told Philip Wilding, "'The Garden' is such a different song for us; it's a side of the band I've always wanted to push more. The melodic side, the orchestration, more thoughtful and reflective, maybe. The lyrics just felt perfect. I loved the fact that it had stepped outside of this concept, dealing with these universal truths, so I wanted it to be heartfelt. It just flowed and we had a good day, as we call it; we had a good six minutes."

Concerning the song's orchestration, Geddy told Chris Neal, "We wanted to see what the music needed and felt that those songs would benefit from a different orchestration — and not synthesizer strings, which we could do easily. We wanted something with a more organic and emotive quality to it."

As for the piano part on the song, it came from Alex, who then handed it over to Jason Sniderman, of Sam the Record Man fame (a Canadian retail institution, courtesy of his dad), who played the part for the album. Raskulinecz told *MusicRadar*, "The chameleon of rock, Alex Lifeson, wrote a really gorgeous piano part and demoed it. We had one of Geddy's really good friends, Jason Sniderman, come in and play it for real on a nice, beautiful Steinway. The Alex Lifeson guitar solo you hear on the record is the original one he recorded for the demo — that's the demo guitar solo. What you're hearing is Alex by himself. He's at Geddy's house, it's late at night — I think Geddy was sleeping on the couch — and he's just playing a guitar solo. When you get something that great, it's not a demo anymore. There wasn't even a discussion to try to do it again."

Add in the six violins and two cellos marshaled by David Campbell and you have a rousing yet soft and sympathetic tour de force, a strident yet fitting close to this album star-crossed by dizzying travel and adventure.

"It's probably the most beautiful song on the album," muses Nick. "It's reflective. It's the end of the journey, and it's got the long outro. Originally, we were going to fade it out, but it has such power the way it is that we decided against it."

Lyrically, as Neil relates in the preamble, it's straight out of *Candide*. Mercilessly beaten up by life, Voltaire's character shrugs and says, "Now we must tend our garden." And essentially Owen Hardy does the same. Past the Hemingway-clear preamble, Peart's lyrics go further, proposing this and so much more as he wraps up the tale in a way that's so compact and intense we are left only with more questions, all of them related to the overarching philosophical issues of the tale, and none of them about anything as material as the narrative. We've let go of plot and are left to ponder universals rich and deep — coming fast and furious even though we are supposed to be done.

Rush closed out 2012 by embarking upon what was to be a first leg of touring in support of *Clockwork Angels*, playing about a dozen shows per month across North America, from September through to December 2. After a long break, the guys emerged with a bang, April 18, 2013, participating with gusto at their induction ceremony into the Rock and Roll Hall of Fame at the Nokia Theatre in L.A. This particular induction has gone down in lore as one of the most egregiously overdue, and it's now considered as one of the big victories of the people over the gatekeepers.

On April 23, 2013, five days after their induction party for the Rock and Roll Hall of Fame, Rush were in Austin, Texas, to resume their tour in support of *Clockwork Angels*. The set list was back up to man-sized, after playing only "Tom Sawyer" and "The Spirit of Radio" at their induction ceremony, while also participating in an all-star jam of "Crossroads" and opening with

"Overture," accompanied by Dave Grohl, Taylor Hawkins and Nick Raskulinecz.

As expected and as was their duty — it was America, in particular Middle America, that made this band — Rush finished playing every corner of the U.S., but now also played England along with frustratingly few dates in mainland Europe as well: two in Germany, one each in Finland, the Netherlands and Sweden, the latter being a rare festival date for the boys. Of note, France did not get a date, and had not seen the band play there since the *Roll the Bones* tour in 1992. More of Canada got played than usual also, with the band closing up shop August 4 in Kansas City. On July 24, the band had to relocate to Red Deer, Alberta, after the dramatic and costly flooding of Calgary due to the Red River overflowing its banks.

On November 19, 2013, Anthem and Roadrunner issued the latest in a succession of mammoth Rush live albums, this one called *Clockwork Angels Tour*, built from three shows almost exactly a year before in Phoenix, Dallas and the Canadian hard rock–loving San Antonio. The staging for the tour was gorgeous, the use of video absolutely top shelf, and the filming — the set was issued on DVD as well — captured every steampunk detail, the Rush organization building upon the steampunk premise already in place on the Time Machine Tour, inspired now by the album and its quiet undercurrent of a future imagined over a hundred years ago.

The band perform ten of twelve tracks from *Clockwork Angels*, leaving out "BU2B" and "BU2B2," joined by a nine-piece string section conducted by David Campbell — strings are also featured on additional, non–*Clockwork Angels* songs. The rest of the set is themed almost entirely as songs from the '80s and newer, and some of them quite obscure, such as "Force Ten," "Grand Designs," "The Body Electric" and "Bravado." The encore features "Tom Sawyer" and the band's jubilant eight-minute "2112" highlight reel.

CHAPTER 9

"IN THE END"

*"Three young guys who grew up together in
music and in life, going through everything
music and life can throw at you."*

As alluded to in the last chapter, Rush were finally inducted
into the Rock and Roll Hall of Fame on April 18, 2013,
by Dave Grohl and Taylor Hawkins of the Foo Fighters.
Once it was their turn to talk, Neil and Geddy were typically
respectful and Canadian with their acceptance speeches, but
Alex delivered the notorious "blah blah blah" oration, a speech
in which all he said, over and over, with various animated actions
along the way, was "blah blah blah." The end effect was that he
got to say what needed to be said — albeit in charades — while
Neil and Geddy looked on a bit uneasily about what was going
down.

Complain about it all you like — and indeed the relevance
of the Rock and Roll Hall of Fame is endlessly debated — but
in the music industry realm, this is the biggest accolade, a pretty
big deal, as Neil mused in his speech. For all its bad press along
the way, usually because of who was getting in and who wasn't,

the Hall has fought its way to undeniable traction. After all the gold and platinum records, their triumph in Rio, a star on the Hollywood Walk of Fame, the celebrated *Beyond the Lighted Stage* doc and getting named to the Order of Canada, Rush's induction into the Hall turned out to be the band's ultimate career achievement, as it is for any band.

"I may have told the story about the author Tom Robbins," reflects Neil, on the subject of validation — both from the inside and the outside. "He published a novel called *Skinny Legs and All* that got the most scathing, insulting, moronic review in the *New York Review of Books*. And as an admirer of his work, I wrote him a letter, and just said, 'Look, this does not represent your readers. As far as I'm concerned, each one of your novels has gotten better.' And he wrote a very nice letter back that said, 'If there's one thing I've learned . . .' a long time ago he stopped reading his reviews. Because he realized that if he believed the good ones, he'd have to believe the bad ones.

"And I really took that to heart. It was the right time for me to learn that lesson too. And I really have stopped reading — and continued not to read — reviews, good or bad, and try not to be touched by that. Because they are hurtful when they're bad, and they are perhaps falsely inflating if they're good. And what Tom Robbins said is true. The approbation is a kind of vindication, but I think Geddy made a comment once: our fans, they're being vindicated for their faith in us all this time. We had the music and the career and the success, you know, enough, honestly. We've always had to keep working and everything, and we certainly never have been a huge band on any level. We've had a really long, successful career and I can't complain about that. And how much does critical approbation mean? If you don't read it, it doesn't mean a thing. So the positive things like that are nice, of course, but I do agree with Geddy in that respect. It's also nice because it's a fan thing. It makes a fan feel better about their band, to appreciate them a little more. We've always appreciated ourselves.

"Honestly, I think it's generational," continues Neil, on the string of late-career accolades the band seemed to be attracting. "We've noticed for a long time, over the last twenty years or so as our fans grew up and became more mature, more active in the world, suddenly Rush fans are working for TV shows and they're working for film companies and they're working for book publishers and they are doing theater design. I hear from people who have all these interesting walks in life of their own. They've got their own lives now.

"And if they can find a way for their lives to intersect with ours . . . like if you're working for *The Colbert Report*, and you can get Rush on there, you know, you're going to. That's what a lot of it is. It's so fun because they bring such a sense of appreciation to what we do already, and again, it's a kind of vindication of themselves too, that they've arrived at a point in life where they can rub creative shoulders with us. That's happened a lot over time. A lot of people we work with, they're just enough younger than us to have been Rush fans. It's a difficult balance there. Of course, the scales have fallen from their eyes and there's no adulation involved anymore — they can just be friends. But there's a shared sense of accomplishment."

As to how the attention makes him feel, "Discomfort is the right word," chuckles Neil. "Honestly, always uncomfortable. Always embarrassed. And those are the right words. It was never a sense of, how dare they bother me? Oh, what do they want to bother me for?! Some people are more outgoing than others, and people who aren't shy don't understand shyness. That's one thing you learn in high school. Anyone who is shy is stuck-up. Back to that time in your life, people were judged that way. If you look at them as adults, they're just quiet and shy. Nobody thinks they're special when they are sixteen. Everyone's a loser. But if they were quiet and shy, that's what needs to be explained, almost, that the real emotions people are feeling are discomfort and embarrassment. That's all. I like the work that I do and I'm proud of it, and I'm glad other people like it too. But some people go way over that line, and I'm just not comfortable with that. It's not a big deal; it's just a matter of my character. I happen to be shy and reserved, not outgoing, so it just makes me that way. As I've said, 'People are different, and Alex is a great example.'"

Neil can marvel with a laugh at how Alex's approach to fame is the polar opposite of his own. Then in the middle there's Geddy, who seems to have worked out his position along the way, organically.

"Yes, well, fame doesn't bother me," ventures Lee. "There was a time when we first started getting recognized that I got a little touchy about it. I remember one time, it was the end of a tour and we were playing a gig in Germany. I was so exhausted from the tour, and my wife had come out to meet me, and we rented a car, and I was driving and just wanted to take off; we went on holiday after that. And at the far end of the parking lot was a group of fans from Italy, our Italian fan club, and they were kind of blocking the exit. And you know, I didn't want to deal with them. I was tired and I turned around and drove the other direction.

"And I cannot tell you how much sleep I lost over that. I felt like such a dick! You know, these guys have come all this way to see us, from Italy . . . and I know maybe it's not so far — everybody has a different rationalization. Maybe it was a fun trip for them. But I felt bad that I didn't stop for a second and thank them for coming all this way. I was exhausted and I had my reasons, but that whole holiday, I started thinking about fame and how you deal with it. And I said to myself, that's not how to deal with it. Because all I did was create a negative experience for them and a negative experience for me! And I can guarantee you, it was much more negative for me than it was for them. It stayed with me longer than them. They didn't really expect me to stop. You know, why would I stop? I was jetting off somewhere.

"So that was kind of an epiphany," continues Ged. "And I said to myself, I'm not living that way. I may live my life and go where I want to go, and if someone comes up to me and is nice to me, and they want an autograph, I'm going to have time for them. It's no big deal. I'm going to turn what could be a negative experience into a positive experience. It really was a turning point in my life and the way I deal with a lot of things. I just decided I would tend to the positive and not the negative.

"And Alex kind of shares that with me, where Neil is not that kind of person. He has a real struggle with fans. It's not a personal thing — it's a shyness thing. He's not able to be as relaxed around strangers as Alex or I am. And that's all it is. He's figured out his complex way to rationalize and justify it, but in the end, he's uncomfortable and he doesn't know what to say and it could be awkward for him. He doesn't like the way it makes him feel, so he avoids it. He gets embarrassed. And it's funny when he's with me, he's like, 'I need all these security guys around to protect me.' I'm like, 'It's okay — I'm your security guy; it's fine. I'll take care of it.' A fan will come up to me and I'll say to him, 'Here, sign this.' He'll give it back to me and I'll give it back to the fan. I swear, give him to me and Al for two months, just walking around together and we can fix that! But that's the way he is. He doesn't mean to hurt anybody's feelings. He's not trying to be rude; he's just not comfortable. It's just the way he's built."

"He's always been very sensitive to it," agrees Alex, on how Neil deals with accolades, "and I think unfortunately for him, he comes off as being rude sometimes, only because he is very embarrassed by the adulation. He's very uncomfortable with that celebrity, so he pushes against it. I'm pretty easygoing. I always have been. For me I can brush it off a bit easier, smile and chat a bit. I understand that these are your fans and that they love what you do. There's been a moment in their lives where your music or something you said has been so important to them that it's changed their path; you hear these sorts of things often. And I think that happens with a lot of musicians. People find something in music that is so important to their souls. And to take a couple of minutes and just chat, shake a hand or a hug or something, it's not a big deal. It's easy for me to deal with it.

"I think in our band we've been fortunate in that we haven't had this really crazy kind of fame, where you fear for your life. I mean, I live up above the city, so it's not there all the time. Geddy, more so, because he's got a very distinctive look about him. But generally people are very polite. They don't want too much from you. But we're at this stage in our lives where there is perhaps a little more respect for your elders. So that's a little easier to take. It makes it smoother; it's not a big deal. We've never had to have bodyguards or that crap, or those trappings of fame that drive people to think they're more important than they are.

"I think the more you travel, the more you realize that there is this Canadian thing. It's like Neil's thing about being embarrassed with all the adulation. It's so 'I'm Canadian.' We're not supposed to get like that. We're polite and we say thank you and even 'Sorry if you don't like me,' and I love that. When you travel, particularly in the States, you really get a sense of the difference between the two countries. It's apples and oranges from the other side of the border; you see those differences. But there is this thing about growing up in rock 'n' roll that earns you respect from your detractors, because you've managed to live through it, you managed to get there. And we managed to do it with the same team all the way through, which is unusual. Maybe that's a Canadian thing too."

To be sure, there's a Canadian-ness to the sense of grounding, but Alex also cites the guys' middle-class origins, "particularly Eastern European. Both Geddy and I agree that when you come from an Eastern European household, that it's pretty strict for the most part, or let's say old fashioned, in the way your parents want you to grow up and behave and express courtesy and believe in things that matter. But the humility is a Canadian thing, so it's natural that it's really embarrassing when you get all that attention."

"Psychotic fans, yes. All the time — constantly," says Neil, further on the subject of attention. "That's a reality of life. It's not remarkable, I have to say. To be surrounded by craziness, by organized crime, union corruption, and by corruption of all kinds throughout the music industry, record companies, radio stations . . . I mean, it's a part of these times, so consequently, it's a part of our lives."

"But it's fun," muses Geddy, reflecting back now on where the band fits in the world, at the Hall of Fame juncture. "It's always been weird, the way we're perceived. In Canada, we're very mainstream, although in different parts of the country, we're perceived differently. I think in America we're pretty much mainstream too. I mean, everywhere I go, I'm spotted. Brazil too [laughs]. But country to country it's different. Because we don't have a lot of pop hits and we're not on Top 40 radio, we can be incredibly popular in a place and still most of the people who live in that place won't know who we are. Biggest cult band in the world? Yeah, I think it's true. There's something that has kept us out of the main, main, mainstream. But it seems to be that we're filtering through. Even in a nonmainstream way, we're filtering into different areas. Because what's happening is that a lot of our fans have grown up and they have jobs in media outlets. They are radio people, TV people, they are writers, composers, and they've grown up with us. To them, we're just another band they love, so they're always happy to share the secret."

As alluded to, on June 25, 2010, Rush got their own star on the Hollywood Walk of Fame (granted, it was the 2,412th!). This follows up a star on Canada's Walk of Fame in Toronto, added in 1999. Guest speakers included Smashing Pumpkins leader, Billy Corgan, who spoke so passionately about the band in the *Beyond the Lighted Stage* documentary, along with Donna Halper, radio personality from Cleveland who helped break the band.

"I think it's really cool!" remarks Geddy, with a laugh. "You know, I'm glad some hobo is going to be sleeping on our name on Hollywood Boulevard. Listen, are those things important to me? Not really. But are they nice when they happen? Absolutely! It's nice to be recognized for something you do. It makes the family smile, and that works good for me here at home. I have to remind them why they should respect me."

"Their creativity knows no bounds," muses long-time Rush producer Peter Collins, on why they are so deserving of this late-career victory lap. "There are no boundaries for them. And they're not particularly concerned about what their audience thinks. They are there to please themselves and do what is musically satisfying to them, and hope the audience comes with them. Which, clearly they have. And unlike a lot of bands that followed, they've created a genre. In my production world, if I'm producing a young band, I would say, 'Let's make that a Rush-type moment.' They became a genre unto themselves."

"Because nobody does what they do," answers Peter, on why the fans stuck with them 'til the end, not to mention their success in pretty much shouting them into the Hall of Fame. "Neil has an extremely interesting point of view, in the way he sees the world. The musicianship is always incredibly unique. The way they approach anything is unique, to them. And I can see why young musicians would continue to be interested in what they had to say, musically and lyrically. You take a band like AC/DC, and their whole mantra is to make the same record over and over again; that's what they strive to do. Rush, on the other hand, just had a very different philosophy. They wanted to develop a new direction with each record. They wanted it to sound fresher. They would be bored with making the same record over and over again because of the kind of people they are. They are continually growing in their lives, and they wanted to grow with their music and lyrics also.

"Also the fact there is clearly a brotherhood between the three members of Rush is very attractive," continues Peter, who is always happy to talk about how much fun he had with the band across the four albums he did with them, four records from two entirely different eras of the band's development. "It's three guys who actually love each other. I'd never experienced that with all the other artists I've worked with. With bands, there's always huge rivalries and tension within the band, that at any given moment, the band could implode — that's what I was used to. I was not used to three guys who actually really cared about each other and were looking out for each other. And I think their fans sense that as well, particularly when they're onstage and having a good time. They can actually subjugate ego and everything else for the bigger cause. And they all understand that. And they just genuinely care about each other. They care that they are, physically and mentally, like three brothers."

But Collins also understands that for all their success, Rush was never a hit with the critics. "It's because they don't follow any set style. They insist on just doing their thing. They're unpredictable. I would think those are the things the press would like, generally speaking. They love Rush or they hate Rush — there's not much in between. And to real Rush fans, they haven't changed their sound that much. It's still, you know, Neil playing what he plays and Alex's style of parts and Geddy's vocals and his style of bass playing. All those elements remain true from album to album; they don't change that much. What we're talking about more so is the decoration changes. Sonically they changed a bit, but it's not radically different, I don't think. And their songwriting has obviously developed over the years, but it's still them. I think there are very few people who are in the gray area: 'Well, we kind of like Rush; they're quite good.' You don't get that."

Summing up, Peter figures, "The core element is a three-piece that plays very punchy music. It's tight, interesting and technical, and I don't think that's a negative word to use, in the context of Rush. They're extremely high-end, very skilled musicians. But yes, I think the critical mass finally caved in and realized there's got to be more to them to survive and sell out huge stadiums and be so popular — it's undeniable."

"It has to do with the material," explains Terry Brown, producer of choice before Peter, on why Rush is deserving of their elevated place at this point. "It occupies a special place in a lot of people's psyches. They grew up on Rush, and once you grow up on something, it's hard to give it up. And a lot of these folks who were going to see them have young families, so you're going to take your kids along. Also staying together, I think, is something that has made them so successful. We haven't seen a revolving door of players, which can be very detrimental. It's still the same guys playing great and entertaining thousands and thousands of people worldwide. It's become a household name."

"It's perseverance," agrees Primus bassist Les Claypool, who, as we've heard, toured extensively as support band to Rush and became friends with the guys. "Continuing to do what they do and doing it well. There's a comfort in knowing those guys were out there, the same three guys, coming around, what, every two years or something? There is a glorious comfort in that. Pink Floyd can't do that. The Police just did it for the first time in twenty years or whatever. There aren't too many bands that can come back as the original element and keep coming around. So perseverance is a big thing.

"Trends and whatnot, they come and go in waves. But there is that element of youth that wants to see musicians who are exceptional on their instruments, because they haven't seen that in a while. And now with *Guitar Hero* and things like that, where you are actually being rewarded for playing more intricate stuff, the kids are looking for those guys who really took it to the wall. And all three of those guys really took it to the wall. And they are inspiring kids to take it even further.

"They're sort of the unsung heroes," continues Les, which fits the narrative concerning the apparent ill fit of the band to the assumed critic class ideals of the Rock Hall. "In certain regions of the United States, they are very much revered, and in other regions not so much. I mean, punk rock was a direct rebellion against bands like Rush. So in a lot of the coastal metropolitan areas, it was harder to find the Rush fans. They didn't get the props in *Rolling Stone* or any of these magazines. They weren't the darlings of MTV.

"I'm sure when Stewart Copeland first came along with the Police, he was making fun of those guys. I know Stewart, and I'm sure that was the polar opposite of anything he thought was cool or exciting. They carved their own path — and some of it is not necessarily by choice either. Some of these little carrots that are waved in front of you as an artist . . . I don't think they got a lot of those carrots. So they basically stuck to what they were inclined to do. They weren't propped up by the media as this or that or the next thing, so I don't think they've ever had a time where they had to live up to that. To an extent, it's been a blessing they didn't have all these people poking at them saying, 'If you did this, you could sell X amount of records' or 'You can get on the Jay Leno show' or whatever. They sort of scooted by somewhat under the radar. That notion of being consistent and doing what you want to do, I think your fan base relates to that and respects that and they will be there for you."

Signer of the band to Mercury, back in Chicago in 1974, Cliff Burnstein — later at the pinnacle of band management with Q Prime — has an interesting perspective on the band's notable new attention in the 2010s.

"I'm not really sure, but I think it helps when you are kind of ignored in the early years. Then the people who latch onto you are more partisan because they have something special. They've got something special that other people are maybe putting down or denying, or are ignorant of. When you have a stronger negative it creates a stronger positive on the other side. Maybe that's why Rush fans are so strong in that way. Besides the music part of it — which pretty much any heavy metal or progressive fan would really like — you have people who were becoming obsessed with Neil's lyrics. Those meant a lot to a lot of people; it was kind of an extra dimension that took Rush well beyond what some of the other bands were doing at that time."

"And don't you get points for longevity in this world?" continues Cliff. "That has a lot to do with it. Plus there are a lot of people — let's say guys — who were eighteen in 1978 and were crazy Rush fans. Now they produce TV shows or they're editors of magazines, all kinds of jobs where there's power. If I'm not mistaken, at the press conference Metallica did for the Rock and

Roll Hall of Fame, when they initially officially announced the inductees, Kirk Hammett specifically said he felt that Rush had been slighted by not being in the Hall of Fame. And he's not the only one who felt that way."

Certainly not. The same year Metallica was inducted and Kirk mentioned Rush, Gene Simmons of Kiss also said that Rush deserved to be there. "Of course they do. As opposed to what? The Ramones?! You're killing me. There are bands in there that wouldn't make enough to pick up my garbage. Grandmaster Flash. What?! You've got rap acts there! And that's a perfect example. Rock and Roll Hall of Fame. It's twenty guys in the music business who decide who gets in. But if you talk to the masses, they never voted in Grandmaster Flash or Run-DMC, people who have nothing to do . . . who can't play guitar. Madonna is in the Rock and Roll Hall of Fame. Rush is not?! Give me a sharp object now. Let me kill myself. You're killing me. It just shows that the people who decide these things aren't qualified to wipe my ass for me. But the fans know. The question is: does it matter? I don't think so. Rush are too nice to say that, but let me say it my way: I'm too rich to care."

And Cliff Burnstein certainly understands why it took so long, echoing some of Gene's thoughts. "It's a different constituency. There's not that many voters in the Rock and Roll Hall of Fame, and it's certainly a different constituency than the usual Rush fan. A lot of the constituency actually are the same people who maybe in the '70s even wrote bad reviews of Led Zeppelin. They're not easily going to be converted over to saying Rush was important, when at that time they didn't consider Rush highly. I think that's really the problem — that they are tied to their past opinions."

But Cliff comes back to the curious original premise, that the sort of cultural quietness of Rush's origins imbues their story with a little extra pixie dust. Citing the lack of Top 40 hits, Burnstein ventures that "if you don't have those things, then what you have is this kind of pure, pure memory for people. They don't think you ever sold out and they're more willing to raise their hand and be behind you for a long period of time, than if it was merely somebody who they liked, then they had some hits, then they started to suck because their attempts at hits became lamer and lamer, and then it's like oh geez, I don't listen to that anymore. You just get rid of it — you banish it from your collection. But Rush never did that. So you're always proud to have it and to listen to it. And then the quality of their work, plus the fact that they made albums rapidly, you have a large catalogue of work of very high quality. All these things lend to the longevity."

Like our other speakers, Cliff also likes the steady ZZ Top–like lineup. "You have essentially the three original members — after all, Neil was there from the first date in America. When you have three people and there are no personnel changes for forty-plus years, people will identify with you, I think, more strongly as individuals. Plus that shows something, a strength of character, that they lived through some difficult times and there was no, you know, fake version of Rush during those times. People appreciate that."

Citing another admirable quality of a band of three merry men, Cliff reminds us that "the power trio format is very unforgiving. Because there are only three players, each one of the three better be really, really good or the whole enterprise is going to fall apart. As a result, with the great power trios, people know who all three of the guys are. Because each one is holding up a lot of weight, each becomes famous on their own. And of course in the '70s when Rush came out, people did actually care more about who made the music. Funnily enough, because there wasn't MTV, people actually learned who was in the band by reading about them and by reading album notes and by exchanging information with their friends. Maybe because the information was harder to come by, it was more precious. Later on, with MTV and the internet, information became very easy to come by and therefore less precious."

Cliff makes yet another curious point, essentially that Rush managed to wind up where they are today by a confluence of two things way back when, namely rock fans accepting Geddy just as the band got good.

"I think that overall, people got used to the sound of Geddy's voice," explains Burnstein, "while at the same time, like a lot of other bands, Rush figured out a musical format that was consistent with what they were doing, but slightly more palatable for the radio people. I would say their most played songs today on the radio are from albums seven, eight or nine, or something like that. That comes from experience. You become more skilled and better songwriters, and those skills were put to use at the same time that people were getting used to Geddy's voice and to his style. So you wind up with these monster classic rock hits like 'Tom Sawyer' that become part of the generational culture."

Manager since the beginning, Ray Danniels agrees with these other industry folk that somehow it was now, finally, time for Rush to get its due.

"You want me to describe Rush fans?" laughs Ray. "They are ninety-percent-plus male, but until recently they were generally late twenties until late forties. But in the last few years there has been a shift where, partly because of *Guitar Hero* and video games and whatnot, there is a younger generation who has discovered them. Suddenly it's like, 'Dad, can we go see Rush when they come?' So you have a fair number of fathers with their fifteen- and nineteen-year-old sons, which was not something we would have had for a long time. So the audience got bigger because of that. And it's not a metal audience, it's not a nerd audience, it's a pretty mainstream cross-section of people.

"But probably the biggest reason is that if you surveyed a hundred percent of the people in the arena, somewhere between eighty and ninety percent of them would say, 'This is my favorite band. This is the band that is most important to me.' Most bands don't have that. I go to see lots of music in a year. I'm a music fan, but I go to see lots of bands that are not my favorite band. Most of the fans who go to see Rush, that is their favorite band. Or worse, top two or three."

"Rush fans are so dedicated and so inside the band," agrees Alex. "The loyalty is something that's really remarkable. Some of them have been around for so, so long. And even the ones who are younger and haven't been around that long still have that same passion about it. It's really astonishing. In the early stages it was a very young male audience, almost a hundred percent male. We got a little older and after a while someone would bring a girlfriend or a wife or something who hated to be there; that was a good thing.

"But now what we're noticing, or certainly what I've noticed, is how many young kids there are, eight, nine, ten years old. Sure, there are lots of young teenagers and mid-teens, but now there are really young kids, and they sing not just the new material but all our stuff. We did a gig and there was a girl who couldn't have been more than nine years old in the front row with her mom and she sang everything. And it wasn't like she was trying to show off. She was just into it. I could see her mouthing all the lyrics and kind of doing the accents — that blows me away. I mean, I know a lot of these games like *Rock Band* and *Guitar Hero* have a lot of influence, and that these young kids are hearing us from their parents, but it's so odd to me to look out and see really young kids who are in there for the band. We still have lots of people in our age group, mid-forties to mid-fifties, and there's that broad demographic of mid-twenties to forties, but it's the younger ones who stand out."

"I think if you stay around long enough, they eventually acknowledge that you must be doing something right," figures Ray, putting it all together. "I have my own theories on it. I think there's less than a handful of bands that are influential, that are still together, that have the original members or close to the original members. If you do the checklist of what it would take to be a great rock band, great career, lasting a long time, Rush is one of the bands that get that. And I think we are finding that the younger generation of reviewers and writers, the guys in their thirties, get Rush way more than the guys twenty years ago did, who would probably be sixty now. This generation of writers in their thirties likes this band and likes them a lot and respects them. And gets them as players.

"But it takes time. Look at the resurgence that AC/DC had. Very different from Rush, very simple. Rush is complex. A lot of the same people are going to see both bands now. There's never an overabundance of really good rock bands. That's become apparent, and I think they get the benefit of that. They are acknowledged as that now."

"Really there are no rules in this business," muses tour mate, label mate and close friend of Rush since the early '70s, Kim Mitchell. "Who knows? You can't explain any of this stuff, why it happens, why a band hits and strikes a nerve with so many people. I just think the fact that they were asked by record companies to do this, asked by their managers to do that, asked by all kinds of people, 'If you only change stuff like . . .' And they didn't — it was just the three of them. This is our life, man, this is our band, this is our music, this is what we want to do, and this is how we want to go about doing it.

"Maybe some of that comes through in their music, their attitude toward life. Maybe that's the reason for the longevity. And because of that they kept searching for new stuff to do. I remember when their keyboard stuff started happening and a lot of fanatical Rush fans started going, 'Ugh [thumbs-down], keyboards!' And I'm just going, wow, this is amazing. They're reaching for new things. How beautiful is that? How could you be so closed-minded? I mean, if you don't like it, fine, but you've got to keep reaching and that's what they did."

Which takes courage and conviction, says Kim. "Yes, well, record companies want to sell records and that's all they're concerned about. So when they see something that is selling, they want more of that. 'When you guys do this, it sells.' And Rush were more like, 'Yeah, that's great, but this is where we're at right now. We got together, we've been talking about it on the tour bus, we've been jamming and Alex is writing this riff, and this is where it's going to go.' They didn't care if the floor fell out, if the plug was pulled. That wasn't a concern. Which is the best way to live your life."

Agrees Ray, "Rush are the only act I've worked with that has always measured their success internally. They don't look at the charts. If I tell them the record is #1, they say, 'That's nice.' And they always had top three records when they came out. But they always measured it internally, so there has never been friction or disappointment or any sense of failure. It's kind of like the peaks are never that high and the valleys are never that low. There's that sense of integrity throughout their career, where 'This is a record we made, we're happy with the record, we wouldn't put it out if we weren't happy' and they get behind it and they work it. And I've seen other acts I've worked with, the minute there's a dip in the sales, it's a catastrophe. Rush have seen records do five million and they've seen records do five hundred thousand, and I've always been amazed at how unaffected they are by it. Which is a big part of how you stay together for forty-plus years.

"And that's given me a license to where I go out and I chase success, and they back me up on it, but you aren't judged by it," continues Danniels. "You're not judged by commercial success. You're judged by whether they feel good artistically. And you know, they're as apt to do more shows because we're in a successful cycle as they are if I went to them and said, 'We need more shows because it's not so successful.' Either way there would be a discussion. Incredibly realistic."

All of a sudden it was 2014, and it was discovered it had been forty years since *Rush* by Rush, the band's Led Zeppelin–slaying, badder than Bad Company debut, a record so good they had to name it twice. So what better way to begin the party than with a deluxe vinyl reissue? This indeed happened, in April, commandeered by Universal label archivist and Toronto industry legend Ivar Hamilton, working with Pegi Cecconi and Meghan Symsyk at the Anthem office and a band expert from Buffalo, Ray Wawrzyniak. Ray has also been the consultant on a number of my Rush books and a full contributor to *Rush: Album by Album* from 2017. He's been an increasingly valuable asset to Hamilton over the years, generously offering materials from his archive for reproduction as well as recently beginning to contribute with liner notes.

The reissue of *Rush* included a poster, three repro promo photos, a print of an original recording reel and a Rush family tree, along with the album reproduced with the original Moon Records' red Rush logo (it was pink for the regular issue) and a blue and gray Moon Records record label on the actual remastered vinyl record.

The celebration continued in November of 2014, with *R40*, a massive six-Blu-ray/ten-DVD book-box, essentially a coffee table book of photos with the DVDs tucked in at the end, opened with liner notes by the author. The set comprised the previously released concert DVDs *Rush in Rio*, *R30*, *Snakes & Arrows Live*, *Time Machine: Live in Cleveland* and *Clockwork Angels Tour*, but also the coveted footage found during the making of *Beyond the Lighted Stage*, Rush performing eight songs at Laura Secord Secondary School in St. Catharines, Ontario, back in 1974. There's also live video from 1976 and 1997, along with footage from the band's induction into the Rock and Roll Hall of Fame.

On May 8, 2015, Rush embarked on what would be their final tour. Dubbed R40, the campaign would encompass North America only, cities of all shapes and sizes, up and down the States with five Canadian dates, closing out at the Forum in Los Angeles, Neil's hometown, August 1, 2015.

Just before the tour kicked off, Alex hinted in the press that this might be the end, or at least the last large-scale tour, because of his psoriatic arthritis and Neil's long-time and painful tendinitis. Alex said he'd had the condition for about ten years at this point and was really starting to feel it in his hands and feet, while Neil's persistent injury had essentially been tennis elbow, notoriously hard to heal.

As Neil told Ilya Stemkovsky from *Modern Drummer*, "As you can see, I often refer to what I do as athletic. It's not low impact. At this point in the tour you have no reserves. So a thing like this attacks, and it wears down your resistance in every other way too. And there's no getting better. I got tendinitis in one elbow on the '96/'97 *Test for Echo* tour, and then I didn't have it again for fifteen years — and it was the other elbow. For the rest of the tour I have to wear a brace to play, and I wear a brace at night. People say, 'Oh, you just need to rest it.' 'Okay, I'll do that. We'll just send these ten thousand people home tonight while I have a rest.'"

Neil also began to struggle with leaving his new wife and six-year-old daughter at home, after getting a second chance that many a rock star wishes for in terms of watching their kids grow up firsthand and not from the road, using whatever technology was current at the time, be it cell phone or Skype or the payphone on the corner outside the Motel 6 and, yes, even postcards and handwritten letters.

No one wanted to use the term *farewell* though, having seen the debacles around the industry with that. Later looking back, Geddy told Eddie Trunk that the guys didn't want to milk the word. In actuality, the band couldn't quite be sure that this was the end, but as the tour progressed and it looked like there would be no end to Neil's pain, it quietly became clear they'd hang it up after L.A., even if the question would linger after L.A.'s eerie waves from the stage.

There's another dynamic at hand. I'll never forget something Pegi told me once at the Anthem office, how no one is good with goodbyes there and how they don't handle death well. We've heard about how Neil would rather not glad-hand with people and talk about nothing. Imagine him having to say goodbye to thirty to fifty industry people in every city. Imagine even Geddy or Alex having to do that. Imagine how many names across all those cities the guys would be expected to remember. Not all or most of them, obviously, but there's always that threshold above which anybody, in each of their own unique situations, is expected to know a bit about who you are. The stress of looking self-centered and ungrateful is always there with these guys. Think about all those radio personalities and writers, record store owners (and if you don't think that's high up enough, how about record store *chain* owners?), local label reps, venue operators, concert promoters. If it's all over the press that this is the last time through Columbus or Dallas or Detroit, that's one heck of a long and uncomfortable goodbye.

Plus there would always be hope that bodies heal, not to

mention the idea of wanting to hang onto what is a pretty fun job. Neil always would have been happy doing less, and at this point even more so — despite what was to come, he always mused about doing other things. Geddy and Alex might have had another tour or two in them but then Alex's hands were hurting, and, let's face it, Geddy wasn't always singing so good. It's not to be discussed, I know, but in general it had been the talk of the town. David Coverdale, Ian Gillan, Rob Halford, Paul Stanley, David Lee Roth, Vince Neil, Don Dokken, Stephen Pearcy, Ozzy Osbourne . . . they had all been getting the gears from the fans for ducking, croaking, rallying and then the next night crashing, and Geddy's name was also regularly starting to be included in that conversation.

In terms of an itinerary, Europe, also spurned on *Counterparts*, *Test for Echo* and *Vapor Trails*, was left out of the routing, although, granted, the band had just done a pretty good job of delivering for those fans two years earlier on the *Clockwork Angels* campaign. Also left out were Pittsburgh and Cleveland, probably the first two cities that should come to mind when thinking of where the band planted their flag in the U.S., although St. Louis, which got a show May 14, might be included as well. The curious non-relationship with Miami continued, as did Rush's lack of connection with Eastern Canada, although Rush did set up shop for two consecutive nights at the Metro Centre in Halifax on the previous tour.

Further giving rise to the idea that this particular tour might represent something extra significant, the guys came up with the novel idea of a set list that chronologically moved from the latest album, *Clockwork Angels*, all the way back to the self-titled debut and then even beyond, into a sampling of non-LP/pre-LP selection "Garden Road." One wrinkle was the jump taken from *Roll the Bones* to *Grace Under Pressure* — nothing from *Presto, Hold*

Your Fire and *Power Windows*. Then again, this period was covered surprisingly well during the *Clockwork Angels* tour and, of course, there are a lot of hits that need to get played, especially if this is the end.

Brilliantly reinforcing the concept, the band stripped away their stage presentation as they regressed into their past, in a rough reflection of what tools they would have used at the time of each song's inaugural presentation. Numbers of amps were reduced, drum sets contracted, vintage instruments were trotted out, and the band's video display — the best in the business — reflected these historical markers and signals as well.

Also special on this tour, the band played *Signals* classic "Losing It," bringing out the guest violinist from the original recording, Ben Mink, to perform with the band in Toronto on June 19 and in Vancouver on July 17. Jonathan Dinklage, from the *Clockwork Angels* string ensemble, performs the role at three additional concerts, in Phoenix, Irvine, California, and the band's final show ever at the Forum in Los Angeles.

And yes, concerning that L.A. show: the wave. At the end of a concert, rarely does Neil clamber out from behind his set and indulge in the arm-and-arm wave to the crowd the way he did that night, further taking pictures from behind his kit before taking center stage. The whispers had grown to a medium murmur by this point about this being it, built sensibly from the accumulation of musings from management and band, and so what happened at the end of the show at the Forum took on additional resonance.

After the tour was over, in December, Neil had gone on record saying he was retiring, amusingly noting that his daughter had begun referring to him as a retired drummer. But Geddy downplayed the remark, with both he and Alex saying in the press that various things related to Rush could still happen. Even

Neil joined in and muddied the waters. But soon the picture became clearer, and very sadly, we now know why. Alex confirmed in 2016 that there would be no more "large-scale tours," with Geddy following up with "no plans" and "zero plans" and "no chance," later admitting that Neil is not only retired from Rush but retired from drumming.

In what almost seems like an act of self-fulfilling prophecy, in November of 2016, a second high-quality Rush documentary called *Rush: Time Stand Still* emerged. With heart-wrenching drama and gorgeous cinematography, the film documented the R40 tour with a pervasive sense of finality that almost made the end okay.

The flow of Rush product continued, even if the guys watched on from the sidelines. November 20, 2015, saw the release of *R40 Live*, documenting the band's last shows ever in Toronto, which of course meant the Ben Mink appearance was captured. A year later, we saw the fortieth anniversary box reissue of *2112*, followed by *A Farewell to Kings* and *Hemispheres* in 2017 and 2018, with more in the hopper planned as those birthdays come upon us.

In 2015, Anthem was acquired by Ole Media Management, with all manner of high-stakes publishing money deals getting swung in the process, millions of dollars changing hands. June 2019 saw Ole rebrand itself as Anthem Entertainment, complete with new logo. Of the three guys, Geddy has come back the most active, having put together a plush celebration of his collection and beyond in *Geddy Lee's Big Beautiful Book of Bass*, for which he has conducted a signing tour that has crossed into the realm of a speaking tour at times.

In 2019, Geddy spoke with Jane Stevenson from the *Toronto Sun* about his book and all things creative moving forward, explaining that "I try to go down at least once or twice a week to my [home] studio and get to know these instruments a bit more and put some ideas down, but I don't know what will come of them, if anything. Time will tell. They're going to keep me busy [with the book tour] until next Christmas and then I'll be free as a bird, and probably next spring I'll start looking at some serious musical ideas."

Asked whether he misses touring, Geddy says, "I don't miss leaving [my family], but I miss those three hours onstage with my buddies. That, especially in the last ten years of touring, was so much fun and so gratifying."

On L.A., Geddy explains that "Neil insisted that that was his last gig. And you know, Alex and I would look at each other and go, 'Yeah, yeah, yeah, he's just saying that.' So I think we kind of knew, we should have known, it was the last show. But I think being eternal optimists we hoped that after a break we would be back out there. That never materialized."

As for what the guys were up to, Geddy noted that "Alex is turning into this super session guy. He loves playing on other people's records without the responsibilities of having to write anything other than his solo. I know he's really digging that. I've been doing this project, but we talk, quite a lot. We see each other quite a lot. And we visit with Neil quite often. So we're all close but I don't think we would ever do a project, the three of us. It's certainly possible that Alex and I would do something down the road. I can't see the three of us ever really doing anything.

"I get hit up with a lot of ideas on how to keep Rush music out in the public eye, so we listen. But there's nothing we can announce at this point. But as I said, I'm reluctant to leave my family again. So for me to do another musical project that would involve touring etc., it would have to be something I feel really strongly about. I'm not saying I wouldn't do it. But I would have to be so charged up about it, it's worth that separation."

Geddy's remarks are indicative of his keeping respectfully

quiet about the secret that would hit the world hard on January 10, 2020 — the announcement of Neil Peart's death from glioblastoma, an aggressive brain cancer, on January 7, at the age of sixty-seven. It is the same disease that took another Canadian icon, Gordon Downie from the Tragically Hip, and now it had taken a man widely lauded as "the world's greatest drummer," after a long degenerative battle following a diagnosis three and a half years earlier. Geddy and Al and the extended Rush family had known for a long time before Peart's passing that there would be no more Rush albums or concerts. They helped wrap up Neil's affairs with trips to L.A., managing to keep his situation out of the news until that shocking winter day. Out of respect for Neil and his family, other than to say that the final months were very tough, we will leave it at that. On January 7, 2020, the rock world was thrown into shock, and accolades poured in from around the globe in the days and weeks that followed.

"I know this is a very unusual life to have led," Alex told me back in 2003, his perspective on what he and Neil and Ged had accomplished, still salient in light of the news. "And you know, I've wondered for a long time why is it that I'm blessed with this whole thing? It is a very unusual and special gift, I think, that we've all been so generously given." Remarking that if he could do it all again, he'd have four kids (he's got two sons, Justin and Adrian). He affirmed, however, that "creativity is really important to me, but it's not the forefront of my head. When I sit down and do something creative, it's a powerful thing for me; it's physically powerful. I feel, well . . . different from normal, when I go through that kind of experience.

"For example, I have a studio and my son writes electronic music, kind of trancy stuff. And last weekend, on Sunday, he wanted me to play guitar. We wanted to re-create a kind of a Middle Eastern flavor. So we used the banjo, and it sounds a lot like a guitar, depending on how we tune it. And it's a weird tuning, so your head has got to get into that mode and I just sort of got lost in it. We spent hours doing this stuff, and it felt like minutes! Everything was all over the place. The tuning was crazy, playing the banjo was not easy, but we got great stuff! It was really unusual. And at the end of the night I was shaking, just from the excitement.

"And sometimes as I get older, I'm just not in that place as much. Whereas when I was younger, I was always in that place. But it was all part of my life, and I kind of took those things for granted. You know, I've always been a very 'go with the flow' kind of person. I've never been great on making plans. When we work, I'm the one who is spontaneous. My best work is in those first few takes. Geddy's the opposite. He likes to develop an idea, experiment, try everything before he makes his final decision on what he thinks is good about what he's doing. And his may be a more intelligent approach, whereas mine is more from the gut. And I think that's why we complement each other and work so well together. I think if I didn't have that creative outlet, I would be very unhappy. But like I say, I don't really think about it. It's such a natural part of my life and who I am. And I guess that's because I've been allowed to have it that way."

As for the future, Alex says, "I love playing with people. It's really easy and great to just be a player and kind of put on a couple coats of a color on their masterpiece — that's really, really enjoyable. I'd like maybe to do some production work, but it's a huge commitment to produce a band, especially a young band. And the rewards, other than the satisfaction of helping a young band out, are negligible these days. It's tough these days, unless you have a real love for it and you don't mind giving up your family life and everything else that you are already giving up by being on the road for eight months of the year. Just like it was for us back in the day, it's all about scheduling and there's very little time."

Years later, Alex reflected that "it was always about the music; it wasn't about the lifestyle. Other than a few things here and there, we've never had that much notoriety and haven't been in a lot of magazines. It took us decades to get in *Rolling Stone*, but to be honest, I like that. I like the fact that we're sort of in the background and not that present all the time. It allows you to come home and hang out with your grandkids and go to the club and play tennis and do all those sorts of normal things that everybody does and still feel connected to the normal world. And it's always been like that with us. Partly to do with us having families early. All three of us had families early — relationships started early in our lives."

"Integrity and work ethic," answers Ray Danniels, on how this grounding in reality led to so much. "Those two things. And nothing has ever gotten in the way. All the horror stories that you hear about what breaks up rock bands, whether it's girlfriends, wives, drugs, addictions, distractions — never happened. Never happened. We lived through the awful things that happened in Neil's life, but with the exception of that, there have never been any distractions. They are really normal, nice people. Their great work ethic and their integrity run parallel to them and their personal lives.

"And it's the Three Musketeers. Whatever is good for one is good for all three of them, and it's amazing to watch that. And rare — they've managed to have the same manager their entire career. We've been through three agents in forty years. We don't chew people up and spit them out. They had the same tour manager and lighting director they've had since they were starting out on the first record. They give loyalty and they ask for loyalty, and I don't know how many other bands can say that."

Agrees Alex, "We've always done the work that we love doing, that we really believe in, but outside of that, we've had a strong family core, individually. I've got a couple of grandsons who I would give up everything for. They are the most important thing in my life now. I love guitar, I love Rush, and I love playing with those guys, but those two little guys mean everything to me. And I think it's important to have that balance in your life and know what the real important things are, have that perspective."

As Geddy has remarked in interviews, with Alex now back in Rosedale in downtown Toronto, the guys live five minutes away from each other and see each other all the time.

"Well, with Ged, he's such a dear friend, really my best friend," says Lifeson. "He's a very thoughtful, intelligent guy. He's very generous and he's . . . how do I put it? He's so intense about the things he loves, and he's a real champion of the best things in life. He's a gourmand, he's a wine collector with a knowledge that would blow your mind, he has a baseball collection, again something he's passionate about.

"Anything he's passionate about — architecture, art, anything — he's fully absorbed by it, and I really respect that a lot because I'm not like that. I'm much more flighty and have a short attention span. But he dedicates himself to the things he loves, and I really, really respect that. And he's got a great sense of humor and is a lot of fun to be with. Neil's a very private guy. I mean, he's very open with his friends, but he likes to keep his group of friends on the smaller side, I think. He's very sharp, very, very bright, and he's very well read as everybody knows. But he too has a great personality for laughter and is very open that way, and very sweet and generous."

In December of 2015, shortly after that last show in L.A., Neil took it upon himself to set the record straight about why now was the time to quit, in one of his own articles, this time for *Drumhead.*

"Not being one for celebrating personal 'occasions,'" penned Peart, "I am always content to mark milestones like birthdays quietly, privately. Not that I deny them — each September I am proud and grateful to have survived another year, and lately, at age sixty-three, to be in my seventh decade. I just don't like to make a big deal about it, or have others make a fuss. For that reason, it was a few days later when I realized where I had spent my fiftieth anniversary of playing the drums — at a concert at the Hollywood Bowl. Having played there a few times with Rush over the years, it was fitting in that way. But this time I was with my wife, Carrie, and six-year-old daughter, Olivia, to see the Psychedelic Furs and B-52s. Lately Olivia has been introducing me to new friends at school as, 'My dad — he's a retired drummer.' True to say, funny to hear."

Continued Neil, "Forty-one years with one band, three young guys who grew up together in music and in life, going through everything music and life can throw at you. All the while we were doing what we wanted, the way we wanted to do it. That's the quality I'm most proud of, really — just that we can stand as an example, in the face of what often seems like a factory of corporate entertainment. If nothing else, we showed that it is possible to make a career of music without giving away — or selling — your soul. You just have to be determined. And of course, lucky.

"Now after fifty years of devotion to hitting things with sticks, I feel proud, grateful and satisfied. The reality is that my style of drumming is largely an athletic undertaking, and it does not pain me to realize that, like all athletes, there comes a time to . . . take yourself out of the game. I would much rather set it aside than face the predicament described in our song 'Losing It.' In the song's two verses, an aging dancer and a writer face their diminishing, twilight talents with pain and despair ('Sadder still to watch it die / Than never to have known it').

"You have to know when you're at the top of your particular mountain, I guess. Maybe not the summit, but as high as you can go. I think of a Buddy Rich quote I used in a book, *Roadshow*, about our R30 tour, ten long years ago. Late in his life, Buddy Rich was asked if he considered himself the world's greatest drummer, and he gave an inspiring reply: 'Let's put it this way: I have that ambition. You don't really attain greatness. You attain a certain amount of goodness, and if you're really serious about your goodness, you'll keep trying to be great. I have never reached a point in my career where I was totally satisfied with anything I've ever done, but I keep trying.'

"I recently picked up another great quote, this one from Artie Shaw. As many readers will know, he was a celebrated big band leader and clarinetist who famously gave up playing at age forty-four. This summation of his career really resonates with me now: 'Had to be better, better, better. It always could be better. When I quit, it was because I couldn't do any better.'"

No need to prove anything more, now it was time for Geddy, Alex and Neil to apportion more time and effort to normality. Whatever the guys were planning to do moving forward, it was never going to look like *Rush in Rio*, but then again, those particular mountains, as Neil calls them, well, they've been peaked.

"We just naturally are that way anyway," figures Alex, confident that he and Geddy and Neil were never the type to spiral out of control once the limelight fades. "I see a lot of people with bodyguards and the whole celebrity bullshit, and we managed to stay out of that. Once you start surrounding yourself with people like that and people who are telling you you're important all the time, you start to believe it. That's a one-way ticket. We all cherish the fact that we're all pretty normal guys. You know, I got married when I was young, I introduced Geddy's wife to him when we were teenagers, I had a family early. Like I say, I have grandkids I adore who are the most important things to me in my life. I love the fact that I can be a grandfather and give them all my love and spend as much time as I can with them. That's where my perspective is, and this is a very fortunate thing I'm doing.

"And rare — I understand that," continues Alex. "I recognize and appreciate how special and fantastic it is. I love playing live, but it's not the most important thing in my life, and I don't think any of us feel it's the most important thing in our lives. Maybe that's what makes it all that much more normal. It's not something we thrive on, that we need to feed our egos or some kind of crazy desire we might have. We're proud of what we did, we worked hard, and we set high standards and high goals for ourselves as musicians. We always have — it's good to go to work and do a good job; it feels really, really good. But it's a lot better to go home after work."

DISCOGRAPHY

A few notes: I've provided the greatest level of detail for the studio albums, then less for live albums, then compilations, etc. As well, this is a U.S. discography, with U.S. chart placements, U.S. certifications, and when we get to singles, official U.S. singles only (save for the all-important independent debut).

There is no Side 1 and Side 2 designation because all of these records originate, essentially, after the switchover from vinyl to CD. Where possible, I've endeavored to reduce repetition (i.e., for live albums that were issued both in audio and video format). Catalogue numbers are the originals, as are the issues — I've not gotten into first and second and third appearance on CD, remastered, audiophile recordings, etc.

Summing up, the idea was to limit this to the core, relevant discography (and, yes, videography). Anything that came out only as digital (no physical issue) is also not included. Also, I've skipped chart placement for videos and DVDs. I figure the only chart measure that carries enough significance to mention is the actual Billboard 200, for albums. One other thing — and I'm sure there are a few more of these gremlins — originally and then occasionally, it's "Freewill" and other times it's "Free Will."

A: STUDIO ALBUMS

Roll the Bones
(Atlantic 82293-2, September 3, 1991)
PEAK U.S. CHART POSITION: #3
U.S. RIAA CERTIFICATION: Platinum
PRODUCED BY: Rupert Hine and Rush
>   1. Dreamline 4:38; 2. Bravado 4:35; 3. Roll the Bones 5:30; 4. Face Up 3:54; 5. Where's My Thing? (Part IV, Gangster of Boats Trilogy) 3:49; 6. The Big Wheel 5:13; 7. Heresy 5:26; 8. Ghost of a Chance 5:19; 9. Neurotica 4:40; 10. You Bet Your Life 5:00

NOTES: Issued on vinyl in some overseas territories.

Counterparts
(Atlantic 7 82528-2, October 19, 1993)
PEAK U.S. CHART POSITION: #2
U.S. RIAA CERTIFICATION: Gold
PRODUCED BY: Peter Collins and Rush
>   1. Animate 6:04; 2. Stick It Out 4:30; 3. Cut to the Chase 4:47; 4. Nobody's Hero 4:59; 5. Between Sun & Moon 4:39; 6. Alien Shore 5:46; 7. The Speed of Love 5:01; 8. Double Agent 4:51; 9. Leave That Thing Alone 4:06; 10. Cold Fire 4:29; 11. Everyday Glory 5:11

NOTES: Issued on vinyl in some overseas territories.

Test for Echo
(Atlantic 7 82925-2, September 10, 1996)
PEAK U.S. CHART POSITION: #5
U.S. RIAA CERTIFICATION: Gold
PRODUCED BY: Peter Collins and Rush
> 1. Test for Echo 5:56; 2. Driven 4:27; 3. Half the World 3:41; 4. The Color of Right 4:48; 5. Time and Motion 5:04; 6. Totem 5:00; 7. Dog Years 4:56; 8. Virtuality 5:43; 9. Resist 4:22; 10. Limbo 5:28; 11. Carve Away the Stone 4:05

NOTES: Last Rush album issued in the U.S. on cassette.

Vapor Trails
(Atlantic 83531-2, May 14, 2002)
PEAK U.S. CHART POSITION: #6
U.S. RIAA CERTIFICATION: n/a
PRODUCED BY: Rush and Paul Northfield
> 1. One Little Victory 5:08; 2. Ceiling Unlimited 5:28; 3. Ghost Rider 5:41; 4. Peaceable Kingdom 5:23; 5. The Stars Look Down 4:28; 6. How It Is 4:05; 7. Vapor Trail 4:57; 8. Secret Touch 6:34; 9. Earthshine 5:38; 10. Sweet Miracle 3:40; 11. Nocturne 4:49; 12. Freeze (Part IV of "Fear") 6:21; 13. Out of the Cradle 5:03

NOTES: Also issued in the U.S. as a double LP album (83531-1) and overseas as a cassette (83531-4).

Snakes & Arrows
(Atlantic 135484-2, May 1, 2007)
PEAK U.S. CHART POSITION: #3
U.S. RIAA CERTIFICATION: n/a
PRODUCED BY: Nick Raskulinecz and Rush
> 1. Far Cry 5:21; 2. Armor and Sword 6:36; 3. Workin' Them Angels 4:47; 4. The Larger Bowl (a Pantoum) 4:07;

5. Spindrift 5:24; 6. The Main Monkey Business 6:01; 7. The Way the Wind Blows 6:28; 8. Hope 2:03; 9. Faithless 5:31; 10. Bravest Face 5:12; 11. Good News First 4:51; 12. Malignant Narcissism 2:17; 13. We Hold On 4:13

NOTES: Also issued in a Walmart bonus edition and on vinyl as a double album (79980-1).

Clockwork Angels
(Roadrunner 1686-176562, June 12, 2012)
PEAK U.S. CHART POSITION: #2
U.S. RIAA CERTIFICATION: n/a
PRODUCED BY: Rush and Nick Raskulinecz

1. Caravan 5:40; 2. BU2B 5:10; 3. Clockwork Angels 7:31; 4. The Anarchist 6:52; 5. Carnies 4:52; 6. Halo Effect 3:14; 7. Seven Cities of Gold 6:32; 8. The Wreckers 5:01; 9. Headlong Flight 7:20; 10. BU2B2 1:28; 11. Wish Them Well 5:25; 12. The Garden 6:59

NOTES: Also issued on double LP in the U.S. (1686-17656-1) and as a *Classic Rock* magazine fan pack issue, featuring a 132-page magazine and full CD.

B: LIVE ALBUMS

Different Stages
(Atlantic 83122-2, November 10, 1998)
PEAK U.S. CHART POSITION: #35
U.S. RIAA CERTIFICATION: Gold
CD1: 1. Dreamline 2. Limelight 3. Driven 4. Bravado 5. Animate 6. Show Don't Tell 7. The Trees 8. Nobody's Hero 9. Closer to the Heart 10. 2112
CD2: 1. Test for Echo 2. The Analog Kid 3. Freewill 4. Roll the

Bones 5. Stick It Out 6. Resist 7. Leave That Thing Alone
8. The Rhythm Method 9. Natural Science 10. Force Ten
11. The Spirit of Radio 12. Tom Sawyer 13. YYZ

CD3: 1. Bastille Day 2. By-Tor & the Snow Dog 3. Xanadu
4. A Farewell to Kings 5. Something for Nothing
6. Cygnus X-1 7. Anthem 8. Working Man 9. Fly by
Night 10. In the Mood 11. Cinderella Man

Rush in Rio
(Atlantic 83672-2, October 21, 2003)
PEAK U.S. CHART POSITION: #33
U.S. RIAA CERTIFICATION: Gold

CD1: 1. Tom Sawyer 2. Distant Early Warning 3. New World
Man 4. Roll the Bones 5. Earthshine 6. YYZ 7. The Pass
8. Bravado 9. The Big Money 10. The Trees 11. Free Will
12. Closer to the Heart 13. Natural Science

CD2: 1. One Little Victory 2. Driven 3. Ghost Rider 4. Secret
Touch 5. Dreamline 6. Red Sector A 7. Leave That
Thing Alone 8. O Baterista 9. Resist 10. 2112

CD3: 1. Limelight 2. La Villa Strangiato 3. The Spirit of Radio
4. By-Tor & the Snow Dog 5. Cygnus X-1 6. Working
Man 7. Between Sun & Moon 8. Vital Signs

Snakes & Arrows Live
(Atlantic 442620-2, April 15, 2008)
PEAK U.S. CHART POSITION: #18
U.S. RIAA CERTIFICATION: n/a

CD1: 1. Limelight 2. Digital Man 3. Entre Nous 4. Mission
5. Freewill 6. The Main Monkey Business 7. The Larger
Bowl 8. Secret Touch 9. Circumstances 10. Between the
Wheels 11. Dreamline 12. Far Cry 13. Workin' Them
Angels 14. Armor and Sword

CD2:   1. Spindrift 2. The Way the Wind Blows 3. Subdivisions 4. Natural Science 5. Witch Hunt 6. Malignant Narcissism — De Slagwerker 7. Hope 8. Distant Early Warning 9. The Spirit of Radio 10. Tom Sawyer 11. One Little Victory 12. A Passage to Bangkok 13. YYZ

Grace Under Pressure 1984 Tour
(Mercury B0013252-02, August 11, 2009)
PEAK U.S. CHART POSITION: n/a
U.S. RIAA CERTIFICATION: n/a
    1. Intro 2. The Spirit of Radio 3. The Enemy Within 4. The Weapon 5. Witch Hunt 6. New World Man 7. Distant Early Warning 8. Red Sector A 9. Closer to the Heart 10. YYZ / 2112: The Temples of Syrinx / Tom Sawyer 11. Vital Signs 12. Finding My Way/In the Mood
NOTES: Reissue of audio CD that first appeared in the *Replay X 3* package.

Moving Pictures: Live 2011
(Roadrunner 016861766016, November 8, 2011)
PEAK U.S. CHART POSITION: n/a
U.S. RIAA CERTIFICATION: n/a
    1. Tom Sawyer 2. Red Barchetta 3. YYZ 4. Limelight 5. The Camera Eye 6. Witch Hunt — Part III of "Fear" 7. Vital Signs
NOTES: Released digitally and on vinyl only.

Time Machine: Live in Cleveland 2011
(Roadrunner 1686-176655, November 8, 2011)
PEAK U.S. CHART POSITION: #54
U.S. RIAA CERTIFICATION: n/a
CD1:   1. The Spirit of Radio 2. Time Stand Still 3. Presto 4. Stick

It Out 5. Workin' Them Angels 6. Leave That Thing Alone 7. Faithless 8. BU2B 9. Free Will 10. Marathon 11. Subdivisions 12. Tom Sawyer 13. Red Barchetta 14. YYZ 15. Limelight

CD2:   1. The Camera Eye 2. Witch Hunt 3. Vital Signs 4. Caravan 5. Moto Perpetuo (Featuring Love for Sale) 6. O'Malley's Break 7. Closer to the Heart 8. 2112: Overture / The Temples of Syrinx 9. Far Cry 10. La Villa Strangiato 11. Working Man

Clockwork Angels Tour
(Anthem/Zoe Vision 1686-175982, November 19, 2013)
PEAK U.S. CHART POSITION: #33
U.S. RIAA CERTIFICATION: n/a

CD1:   1. Subdivisions 2. The Big Money 3. Force Ten 4. Grand Designs 5. The Body Electric 6. Territories 7. The Analog Kid 8. Bravado 9. Where's My Thing? / Here It Is! (drum solo) 10. Far Cry

CD2:   1. Caravan 2. Clockwork Angels 3. The Anarchist 4. Carnies 5. The Wreckers 6. Headlong Flight / Drumbastica 7. Peke's Repose (guitar solo)/Halo Effect 8. Seven Cities of Gold 9. Wish Them Well 10. The Garden

CD3:   1. Dreamline 2. The Percussor (I) Binary Love Theme (II) Steambanger's Ball (drum solo) 3. Red Sector A 4. YYZ 5. The Spirit of Radio 6. Tom Sawyer 7. 2112: Overture / The Temples of Syrinx / Grand Finale 8. Limelight (soundcheck recording) 9. Middletown Dreams 10. The Pass 11. Manhattan Project

R40 Live
(Anthem/Zoe 01143-38256-02, November 20, 2015)
PEAK U.S. CHART POSITION: #24

U.S. RIAA CERTIFICATION: n/a

CD1: 1. The World Is . . . The World Is . . . 2. The Anarchist 3. Headlong Flight 4. Far Cry 5. The Main Monkey Business 6. How It Is 7. Animate 8. Roll the Bones 9. Between the Wheels 10. Losing It 11. Subdivisions

CD2: 1. Tom Sawyer 2. YYZ 3. The Spirit of Radio 4. Natural Science 5. Jacob's Ladder 6. Hemispheres: Prelude 7. Cygnus X-1 / The Story So Far (drum solo) 8. Closer to the Heart 9. Xanadu 10. 2112: Overture / The Temples of Syrinx / Presentation / Grand Finale

CD3: 1. Mel's Rockpile 2. Lakeside Park / Anthem 3. What You're Doing / Working Man 4. One Little Victory 5. Distant Early Warning 6. Red Barchetta 7. Clockwork Angels 8. The Wreckers 9. The Camera Eye 10. Losing It

C: SELECTED COMPILATIONS

Chronicles
(Mercury P2 38936, September 4, 1990)
PEAK U.S. CHART POSITION: #51
U.S. RIAA CERTIFICATION: 2 x Platinum

CD1: 1. Finding My Way 2. Working Man 3. Fly by Night 4. Anthem 5. Bastille Day 6. Lakeside Park 7. 2112: (a) Overture (b) The Temples of Syrinx 8. What You're Doing (live) 9. A Farewell to Kings 10. Closer to the Heart 11. The Trees 12. La Villa Strangiato 13. Freewill 14. The Spirit of Radio

CD2: 1. Tom Sawyer 2. Red Barchetta 3. Limelight 4. A Passage to Bangkok (live) 5. Subdivisions 6. New World Man 7. Distant Early Warning 8. Red Sector A 9. The Big Money 10. Manhattan Project 11. Force Ten

12. Time Stand Still 13. Mystic Rhythms (live) 14. Show
Don't Tell

Retrospective I: 1974–1980
(Mercury 314 534 909-2, May 6, 1997)
PEAK U.S. CHART POSITION: n/a
U.S. RIAA CERTIFICATION: n/a

> 1. The Spirit of Radio 2. The Trees 3. Something for
> Nothing 4. Freewill 5. Xanadu 6. Bastille Day 7. By-Tor
> & the Snow Dog 8. Anthem 9. Closer to the Heart
> 10. 2112: Overture 11. The Temples of Syrinx 12. La Villa
> Strangiato 13. Fly by Night 14. Finding My Way

Retrospective II: 1980–1987
(Mercury 314 534 910-2, June 3, 1997)
PEAK U.S. CHART POSITION: n/a
U.S. RIAA CERTIFICATION: n/a

> 1. The Big Money 2. Red Barchetta 3. Subdivisions
> 4. Time Stand Still 5. Mystic Rhythms 6. The Analog
> Kid 7. Distant Early Warning 8. Marathon 9. The Body
> Electric 10. Mission 11. Limelight 12. Red Sector A
> 13. New World Man 14. Tom Sawyer 15. Force Ten

The Spirit of Radio: Greatest Hits 1974–1987
(Mercury 440 063 335-2, February 11, 2003)
PEAK U.S. CHART POSITION: #167
U.S. RIAA CERTIFICATION: Gold

> 1. Working Man 2. Fly by Night 3. 2112: Overture / The
> Temples of Syrinx 4. Closer to the Heart 5. The Trees 6.
> The Spirit of Radio 7. Freewill 8. Limelight 9. Tom Sawyer
> 10. Red Barchetta 11. New World Man 12. Subdivisions

13. Distant Early Warning 14. The Big Money 15. Force Ten 16. Time Stand Still

NOTES: A limited edition of this compilation included "Mystic Rhythms" as a bonus track plus DVD versions of "Closer to the Heart," "Tom Sawyer," "Subdivisions" and "The Big Money." Also included were the lyrics to each of the 16 audio tracks.

Gold
(Mercury B0006322-02, April 25, 2006)
PEAK U.S. CHART POSITION: n/a
U.S. RIAA CERTIFICATION: n/a
NOTES: *Gold* is essentially a repackage of *Retrospective I* and *Retrospective II*, swapping out "Something for Nothing" for "Working Man."

Retrospective III: 1989–2008
(Atlantic 515813-2, March 3, 2009)
PEAK U.S. CHART POSITION: #160
U.S. RIAA CERTIFICATION: n/a

1. One Little Victory (remix) 2. Dreamline 3. Workin' Them Angels 4. Presto 5. Bravado 6. Driven 7. The Pass 8. Animate 9. Roll the Bones 10. Ghost of a Chance (live) 11. Nobody's Hero 12. Leave That Thing Alone 13. Earthshine (remix) 14. Far Cry

NOTES: A deluxe version was also issued, which included a DVD. Tracks are 1. Stick It Out 2. Nobody's Hero 3. Half the World 4. Driven 5. Roll the Bones 6. Show Don't Tell 7. The Pass 8. Superconductor 9. Far Cry 10. Malignant Narcissism 11. The Seeker (live) 12. Secret Touch 13. Resist (live), plus a bonus interview and Tom Sawyer live.

Working Men

(Atlantic 7567895641, November 17, 2009)

PEAK U.S. CHART POSITION: n/a

U.S. RIAA CERTIFICATION: n/a

> 1. Limelight 2. The Spirit of Radio 3. 2112 4. Freewill 5. Dreamline 6. Far Cry 7. Subdivisions 8. One Little Victory 9. Closer to the Heart 10. Tom Sawyer 11. Working Man 12. YYZ

NOTES: *Working Men* was issued in CD and DVD formats and is essentially a compilation culled from *Rock in Rio*, *R30* and *Snakes & Arrows Live*. Only "One Little Victory" is previously unreleased.

Icon

(Mercury B0014654-12, August 31, 2010)

PEAK U.S. CHART POSITION: n/a

U.S. RIAA CERTIFICATION: n/a

> 1. Working Man 2. Fly by Night 3. The Necromancer 4. The Twilight Zone 5. Closer to the Heart 6. Circumstances 7. Freewill 8. Limelight 9. The Analog Kid 10. Red Sector A 11. Marathon 12. Force Ten

Icon 2

(Mercury B0015674-02, July 29, 2011)

PEAK U.S. CHART POSITION: n/a

U.S. RIAA CERTIFICATION: n/a

CD1: 1. Working Man 2. Fly by Night 3. The Necromancer 4. The Twilight Zone 5. Closer to the Heart 6. Circumstances 7. Freewill 8. Limelight 9. The Analog Kid 10. Red Sector A 11. Marathon 12. Force Ten

CD2: 1. Bastille Day 2. 2112 3. The Spirit of Radio 4. Tom Sawyer 5. La Villa Strangiato 6. Closer to the Heart 7. New World

Man 8. Vital Signs 9. The Big Money 10. Mystic Rhythms
11. Time Stand Still

NOTES: CD1 is the original *Icon* from the previous year; CD2 consists of live tracks.

D: SELECTED SINGLES

Singles is perhaps the department where it most bears reminding that this is a U.S. discography. Also, given that this is the CD age, it switches over to promos exclusively, as the commercial CD single format in North America was rarely exploited (and not at all by Rush) versus, say, the U.K. and the EU with their funny slimline EPs. I figured it was still a useful exercise, however, because it demonstrates the tracks that were being pushed at radio. Again, I've excluded a few that seemed repetitious or in the slight variation category, as well as CDRs.

7″ Vinyl Singles
Caravan / BU2B (527398-7) limited edition; white vinyl

Cassette Singles
Ghost of a Chance / Where's My Thing?, interview (4-87498)
Nobody's Hero / Stick It Out (4-87267)

CD Singles
Dreamline (PRCD 4120 2)
Where's My Thing? (PRCD 4126 2)
Roll the Bones (PRCD 4260 2)
Ghost of a Chance (edit), Ghost of a Chance (PRCD 4458 2)
Bravado (PRCD 4580 2)
Stick It Out (PRCD 5314 2)

Nobody's Hero (PRCD 5430 2)

Double Agent (PRCD 5431 2)

Nobody's Hero (edit) (PRCD 5497 2)

Test for Echo (PRCD 6853 2)

Test for Echo (edit), Test for Echo (PRCD 6885 2)

Half the World (PRCD 6930 2)

Driven (PRCD 8009)

Virtuality (edit), Virtuality (PRCD 8139)

The Spirit of Radio, 2112 (PRCD 8690)

Closer to the Heart (PRCD 8804)

One Little Victory (PRCD 300749-2)

Secret Touch (PRCD 300863)

One Little Victory, Earthshine (PRCD 300857)

Sweet Miracle (PRCD 300930)

Rush in Rio Sampler (PRCD 301227) digipak

Resist (acoustic) (P1ZOE 1279P)

Summertime Blues (PRCD 301512)

Tom Sawyer, R30 Overture, Working Man (011431082-9 PSI-01)

Far Cry (edit), Far Cry (PRCD 133692)

Spindrift (edit), Spindrift (PRCD 260476)

The Larger Bowl (PRCD 294844)

Workin' Them Angels (edit), Workin' Them Angels (live), Workin'
    Them Angels (PRCD 454780)

E: VIDEOGRAPHY

Chronicles
(Polygram PMV 082 765-3, 1990)
U.S. RIAA CERTIFICATION: Platinum
> 1. Closer to the Heart 2. The Trees 3. Limelight 4. Tom
> Sawyer (live) 5. Red Barchetta (live) 6. Subdivisions

7. Distant Early Warning 8. Red Sector A (live) 9. The Big Money 10. Mystic Rhythms 11. Time Stand Still 12. Lock and Key

NOTES: Also issued on LaserDisc (CDV 082 765-1) at the same time and on DVD (827659) in May of 2001. Running time: 63 minutes. The DVD version includes two extra tracks: "The Enemy Within" and "Afterimage." The LaserDisc omits "Red Sector A."

Rush in Rio
(Rounder 66825 1099 9, October 21, 2003)
U.S. RIAA CERTIFICATION: 7 x Platinum
NOTES: Same as CD issue except DVD omits "Between Sun & Moon" and "Vital Signs" while adding "The Documentary: The Boys in Brazil," a film by Andrew MacNaughtan, MX Multiangle of "YYZ," "O Baterista" and "La Villa Strangiato" plus Easter eggs ("By-Tor" movie and "Anthem").

R30: 30th Anniversary World Tour
(Rounder 01143-1083-9, November 22, 2005)
U.S. RIAA CERTIFICATION: 5 x Platinum
DVD1: 1. R30 Overture: Finding My Way / Anthem / Bastille Day / A Passage to Bangkok / Cygnus X-1 / Hemispheres 2. The Spirit of Radio 3. Force Ten 4. Animate 5. Subdivisions 6. Earthshine 7. Red Barchetta 8. Roll the Bones 9. The Seeker 10. Tom Sawyer 11. Dreamline 12. Between the Wheels 13. Mystic Rhythms 14. Der Trommler 15. Resist 16. Heart Full of Soul 17. 2112 / Xanadu / Working Man 18. Summertime Blues 19. Crossroads 20. Limelight
DVD2: Interviews 1. 1979: Hamilton, Ivor Wynne Stadium 2. 1981: Le Studio, Quebec 3. 1990: Artist of the Decade

Interviews 4. 1994: Juno Hall of Fame Induction 5. 2002: Vapor Trails Tour Interview, the Anthem Vault 6. Fly by Night 7. Finding My Way (mpeg1 from Rock Concert) 8. In the Mood (mpeg1 from Rock Concert) 9. Circumstances 10. La Villa Strangiato 11. A Farewell to Kings 12. Xanadu 13. The Spirit of Radio (Sound Check — 1979 Ivor Wynne Stadium) 14. Freewill (from Toronto Rocks — 2003) 15. Closer to the Heart (from Canada for Asia — 2005)

CD1/2:   Same track list as DVD1

NOTES: Issued four years later on Blu-ray (01143-1132-9).

Replay X 3
(Mercury B0006649-50, June 13, 2006)
U.S. RIAA CERTIFICATION: 2 x Platinum
NOTES: *Replay X 3* is a repackage of the concert videos *Exit . . . Stage Left*, *Grace Under Pressure Tour* and *A Show of Hands*, presented with a 5.1 surround sound remix. Also included is an audio version of the *Grace Under Pressure* set. A limited edition of *Replay X 3* sold exclusively by Best Buy contained four bonus audio tracks, added to the *Grace Under Pressure Tour* audio CD: "Limelight," "Closer To the Heart," The Spirit of Radio" and "Tom Sawyer."

Snakes & Arrows Live
(Rounder 01143-1124-9, November 24, 2008)
U.S. RIAA CERTIFICATION: 5 x Platinum
NOTES: Same as CD issue with additions. On DVD1: What's That Smell featuring Jerry Stiller, 2007 Tour Outtakes, What's That Smell outtakes, Far Cry — Alternate Cut featuring Rear Screen Footage, The Way the Wind Blows — Alternate Cut featuring Rear Screen Footage,

Red Sector A from the R30 tour. On DVD3: Oh, Atlanta! The Authorized Bootlegs. Ghost of a Chance, Red Barchetta, The Trees, 2112 / The Temples of Syrinx.

Working Men
(Rounder 01143-1135-9, November 17, 2009)
U.S. RIAA CERTIFICATION: n/a
NOTES: Same as CD version.

Time Machine: Live in Cleveland 2011
(Roadrunner 01143-1156-9, November 8, 2011)
U.S. RIAA CERTIFICATION: n/a
NOTES: Same as CD version, but with the following bonus material: 1. Outtakes from History of Rush, Episodes 2 & 17 2. Tom Sawyer featuring the cast of History of Rush, Episode 17 3. Need Some Love Live from Laura Secord Secondary School 4. Anthem Live from Passaic New Jersey.

Clockwork Angels Tour
(Anthem/Zoe Vision 01143-1153-9, November 19, 2013)
NOTES: Same as CD version, but with the following bonus material: "Can't Stop Thinking Big" tour documentary film, Behind the Scenes (featuring Jay Baruchel), Intro/post-show video outtakes, Interview with Dwush, Family Goy, Family Sawyer, The Watchmaker (video intro for the second set), Office of the Watchmaker (post-show video).

R40 Live
(Anthem/Zoe 01143-38256-02, November 20, 2015)
NOTES: Same as CD version, less the final four "bonus tracks": "Clockwork Angels," "The Wreckers," "The Camera Eye"

and "Losing It." Video adds non-songs "No Country for Old Hens" and "Exit Stage Left."

F: SELECTED SOLO ALBUMS

Victor — *Victor*
(Atlantic 82852-2, January 9, 1996)
PEAK U.S. CHART POSITION: #99
U.S. RIAA CERTIFICATION: n/a
PRODUCED BY: Alex Lifeson

1. Don't Care 4:04; 2. Promise 5:44; 3. Start Today 3:48; 4. Mr. X 2:21; 5. At the End 6:07; 6. Sending Out a Warning 4:11; 7. Shut Up Shuttin' Up 4:02; 8. Strip and Go Naked 3:57; 9. The Big Dance 4:14; 10. Victor 6:25; 11. I Am the Spirit 5:31

NOTES: Alex Lifeson solo project. Also issued on cassette. This album also generated three CD promo singles.

Geddy Lee — *My Favorite Headache*
(Atlantic 83384-2, November 14, 2000)
PEAK U.S. CHART POSITION: #52
U.S. RIAA CERTIFICATION: n/a
PRODUCED BY: Geddy Lee, Ben Mink, David Leonard

1. My Favorite Headache 4:45; 2. The Present Tense 3:25; 3. Window to the World 3:02; 4. Working at Perfekt 5:00; 5. Runaway Train 4:30; 6. The Angels' Share 4:33; 7. Moving to Bohemia 4:25; 8. Home on the Strange 3:46; 9. Slipping 5:06; 10. Still 4:30; 11. Grace to Grace 4:59

NOTES: Also issued on cassette. This album also generated three CD promo singles.

G: MISCELLANEOUS

Feedback
(Atlantic 83728-2, June 29, 2004)
PEAK U.S. CHART POSITION: #19
US. RIAA CERTIFICATION: n/a
PRODUCED BY: David Leonard and Rush
    1. Summertime Blues 3:52; 2. Heart Full of Soul 2:52; 3. For What It's Worth 3:30; 4. The Seeker 3:27; 5. Mr. Soul 3:51; 6. Seven and Seven Is 2:53; 7. Shapes of Things 3:16; 8. Crossroads 3:27

Note: This covers EP was also issued in the U.S. on vinyl (83728-1).

CREDITS

INTERVIEWS WITH THE AUTHOR

Tony Geranios, Geddy Lee, Alex Lifeson, Neil Peart, Howard Ungerleider, Steven Wilson

INTERVIEWS WITH SAM DUNN AND SCOT MCFADYEN

Liam Birt, Les Claypool, Peter Collins, Ray Danniels, Donna Halper, Rupert Hine, Geddy Lee, Alex Lifeson, Ben Mink, Glen Peart, Neil Peart, Kevin Shirley, Howard Ungerleider

ADDITIONAL SOURCES

Allstar online music magazine. Interview with Geddy Lee and Alex Lifeson by Greg Edwards. October 31, 1996.

Bass Guitar. "Working, Man!" by J.D. Considine. August/September 2004.

Bass Guitar. "Back to Basics" by J.D. Considine. July 2007.

Bass Player. "Track by Track: Geddy Lee on Rush's *Vapor Trails*" by Karl Coryat. July 2002.

Bass Player. "Full Steam Ahead: Geddy Lee & Rush Transcend Time on *Clockwork Angels*" by Chris Jisi. August 2012.

Brave Words & Bloody Knuckles. "Sweet Miracles!" by Tim Henderson. July 2002.

Canadian Musician. "The Whole Is Greater Than the Sum of Its Parts: An Interview with Neil Peart" by Peter Hamilton. February 1994.

Canadian Musician. "Rush Put Themselves to the 'Test' (And End Up Even Closer to the Heart)" by Paul Myers. December 1996.

Classic Rock. "Following the Arrows" by Philip Wilding. July 2007.

Classic Rock Revisited. Interview with Alex Lifeson by Jeb Wright. 2012.

Clockwork Angels tourbook. "The Future as Seen From the Past (Or: 'Yesterday's Tomorrowland')" by Neil Peart. 2012.

Counterparts tourbook. "Reflections in a Wilderness of Mirrors" by Neil Peart. 1993.

Drumhead. "A Conversation with Neil Peart" by Jonathan Mover. September/October 2007.

Drumhead. "Neil Peart Reflects on 50 Years of Hitting Things with Sticks" by Neil Peart. December 2015.

Fireworks. "Rush: Working Like Clockwork — An Interview with Geddy Lee" by Phil Ashcroft. July/August 2012.

FYE.com. "Geddy Lee Discusses *Feedback*, the 30th Anniversary Tour and More!" by Brad Parmerter. July 9, 2004.

Guitar for the Practicing Musician. "Alex Lifeson's Attitude Adjustment" by Jon Chappell. February 1994.

Guitar One. "Alex Lifeson: Rock's Gold Standard" by Mac Randall. June 2007.

Guitar School. "Back to the Future: Alex Lifeson and Geddy Lee Return to Their Roots with *Counterparts*, Rush's Nineteenth Album" by Matt Resnicoff. March 1994.

Guitar World. "Vital Signs" by Joe Bosso. August 2007.

Jam! Showbiz. "Ready to Test Echo on the Road" by John Sakamoto. October 16, 1996.

Las Vegas Review-Journal. "New Album of Covers, and Covers of Covers, Celebrates Band's 30th Anniversary" by Doug Elfman. July 16, 2004.

M Music & Musicians. "Full Steam" by Chris Neal. June 2012.

Maclean's. "Neil Peart on Introverts, Learning to Improvise and Why People Should Be Nicer to One Another" by Mike Doherty. August 13, 2012.

MediaAmerica Radio. "Rush: Up Close," a three-hour radio interview/music profile by Dan Neer. January/February 1994.

Metal Express Radio. Alex Lifeson interview by Mick Burgess. May 21, 2012.

Modern Drummer. "Neil Peart: In Search of the Right Feel" by William F. Miller. February 1994.

Modern Drummer. "The Drums of *Snakes & Arrows*: What Went Into What Came Out" by Neil Peart. August 2007.

Modern Drummer. "An Interview with Neil Peart" by Ilya Stemkovsky. 40th Anniversary Issue. January 2016.

MusicRadar.com. "Producer Nick Raskulinecz on Rush's *Clockwork Angels*" by Joe Bosso. June 11, 2012.

Needle. "Getting in Gear" by Philip Wilding. June 2012.

NYDailyNews.com. "It's Rush Hour Again" by Phil Roura. July 9, 2007.

Powerkick: The Rock Drummer's Quarterly. "Rush's Neil Peart." Vol. 2, No. 3. Summer 1992.

Powerplay. "Rush: Groovy New Album *Clockwork Angels* Is a Revelation" by Mik Gaffney. #144. July 2012.

Prog. "Angelic Upstarts" by Jerry Ewing. #26. June 2012.

Rocky Mountain News. "Rush for Cover" by Michael Mehle. June 28, 2004.

Roll the Bones radio special promo CD; interview by John Derringer. 1991.

Roll the Bones tourbook by Neil Peart. 1991.

SI. "'Just a Few Years Ago We Were a Pariah, an Outcast Dinosaur, a Bunch of Weirdos'" by Willebrord Elsing. June 1992.

Snakes & Arrows tourbook. "The Games of Snakes and Arrows: Prize Every Time" by Neil Peart. 2007.

SoundSpike.com. "Interview: Neil Peart of Rush by Don Zulaica." July 30, 2004.

St. Louis Post-Dispatch. "Trio Rolled the Dice and Came Up a Winner" by Roger Catlin. June 11, 1992.

Toronto Sun. "'I Miss My Buddies:' Geddy Lee Reflects on Rush and His Love of Bass" by Jane Stevenson. May 21, 2019.

Total Guitar. "Track by Track: Rush *Clockwork Angels*" by Joe Bosso. August 2012.

Vapor Trails tourbook. "Behind the Fire – The Making of *Vapor Trails*" by Neil Peart. 2002.

WKSC-FM. *Test for Echo* world premiere. Interview with Rush by Jill Robinson. September 5, 1996.

WNEW. *Roll the Bones* CD launch: Geddy Lee and Alex Lifeson interview by Dan Neer. August 29, 1991.

World album premiere of *Counterparts* by Steve Warden. October 14, 1993.

ABOUT THE AUTHOR

M artin Popoff has unofficially written more record reviews
— approximately 7,900 — than anybody in the history of
music, writing across all genres. Additionally, Martin has
penned eighty-five books on hard rock, heavy metal, classic rock
and record collecting. He was editor in chief of the now retired
Brave Words & Bloody Knuckles, Canada's foremost metal publication, for fourteen years and has also contributed to *Revolver*,
Guitar World, *Goldmine*, *Record Collector*, bravewords.com, lolli-
popmagazine.com and hardradio.com, with many record label
band bios and liner notes to his credit as well. Furthermore,
Martin has been a regular contractor to Banger Films and worked
for two years as researcher on the award-winning documentary
Rush: Beyond the Lighted Stage, on the writing and research team
for the eleven-episode *Metal Evolution* and on the ten-episode
Rock Icons, both for VH1 Classic. Moreover, Martin is the writer
of the original metal genre chart used in *Metal: A Headbanger's*

Journey and throughout the *Metal Evolution* episodes. Martin currently resides in Toronto and can be reached through martinp@inforamp.net or martinpopoff.com.

MARTIN POPOFF –
A COMPLETE BIBLIOGRAPHY

Driven: Rush in the '90s and "In the End" (2021)

The Fortune: On the Rocks with Angel (2020)

Van Halen: A Visual Biography (2020)

Limelight: Rush in the '80s (2020)

Thin Lizzy: A Visual Biography (2020)

Empire of the Clouds: Iron Maiden in the 2000s (2020)

Blue Öyster Cult: A Visual Biography (2020)

Anthem: Rush in the '70s (2020)

Denim and Leather: Saxon's First Ten Years (2020)

Black Funeral: Into the Coven with Mercyful Fate (2020)

Satisfaction: 10 Albums That Changed My Life (2019)

Holy Smoke: Iron Maiden in the '90s (2019)

Sensitive to Light: The Rainbow Story (2019)

Where Eagles Dare: Iron Maiden in the '80s (2019)

Aces High: The Top 250 Heavy Metal Songs of the '80s (2019)

Lettin' Go: UFO in the Eighties and Nineties (2019)

Judas Priest: Turbo 'til Now (2019)

Born Again! Black Sabbath in the Eighties and Nineties (2019)

Riff Raff: The Top 250 Heavy Metal Songs of the '70s (2018)

Unchained: A Van Halen User Manual (2018)

Queen: Album by Album (2018)

Iron Maiden: Album by Album (2018)

Welcome to My Nightmare: 50 Years of Alice Cooper (2018)

Sabotage! Black Sabbath in the Seventies (2018)

Judas Priest: Decade of Domination (2018)

Popoff Archive — 6: American Power Metal (2018)

Popoff Archive — 5: European Power Metal (2018)

The Sun Goes Down: Thin Lizzy 1977–83 (2018)

The Clash: All the Albums, All the Songs (2018)

Led Zeppelin: All the Albums, All the Songs (2017)

AC/DC: Album by Album (2017)

Lights Out: Surviving the '70s with UFO (2017)

Tornado of Souls: Thrash's Titanic Clash (2017)

Caught in a Mosh: The Golden Era of Thrash (2017)

Rush: Album by Album (2017)

Beer Drinkers and Hell Raisers: The Rise of Motörhead (2017)

Metal Collector: Gathered Tales from Headbangers (2017)

Hit the Lights: The Birth of Thrash (2017)

Popoff Archive — 4: Classic Rock (2017)

Popoff Archive — 3: Hair Metal (2017)

From Dublin to Jailbreak: Thin Lizzy 1969–76 (2016)

Popoff Archive — 2: Progressive Rock (2016)

Popoff Archive — 1: Doom Metal (2016)

Rock the Nation: Montrose, Gamma and Ronnie Redefined (2016)

Punk Tees: The Punk Revolution in 125 T-Shirts (2016)

Metal Heart: Aiming High with Accept (2016)

Ramones at 40 (2016)

Time and a Word: The Yes Story (2016)

Kickstart My Heart: A Mötley Crüe Day-by-Day (2015)

This Means War: The Sunset Years of the NWOBHM (2015)

Wheels of Steel: The Explosive Early Years of the NWOBHM (2015)

Swords and Tequila: Riot's Classic First Decade (2015)

Who Invented Heavy Metal? (2015)

Sail Away: Whitesnake's Fantastic Voyage (2015)

Live Magnetic Air: The Unlikely Saga of the Superlative Max Webster (2014)

Steal Away the Night: An Ozzy Osbourne Day-by-Day (2014)

The Big Book of Hair Metal (2014)

Sweating Bullets: The Deth and Rebirth of Megadeth (2014)

Smokin' Valves: A Headbanger's Guide to 900 NWOBHM Records (2014)

The Art of Metal (co-edit with Malcolm Dome; 2013)

2 Minutes to Midnight: An Iron Maiden Day-by-Day (2013)

Metallica: The Complete Illustrated History (2013); update and reissue (2016)

Rush: The Illustrated History (2013); update and reissue (2016)

Ye Olde Metal: 1979 (2013)

Scorpions: Top of the Bill (2013); updated and reissued as *Wind of Change: The Scorpions Story* (2016)

Epic Ted Nugent (2012); updated and reissued as *Motor City Madhouse: Going Gonzo with Ted Nugent* (2017)

Fade to Black: Hard Rock Cover Art of the Vinyl Age (2012)

It's Getting Dangerous: Thin Lizzy 81–12 (2012)

We Will Be Strong: Thin Lizzy 76–81 (2012)

Fighting My Way Back: Thin Lizzy 69–76 (2011)

The Deep Purple Royal Family: Chain of Events '80–'11 (2011); reissued as *The Deep Purple Family Year by Year Volume Two (1980–2011)* (2018)

The Deep Purple Royal Family: Chain of Events Through '79 (2011); reissued as *The Deep Purple Family Year by Year (to 1979)* (2016)

Black Sabbath FAQ (2011)

The Collector's Guide to Heavy Metal: Volume 4: The '00s (2011; co-authored with David Perri)

Goldmine Standard Catalog of American Records 1948–1991, 7th Edition (2010)

Goldmine Record Album Price Guide, 6th Edition (2009)

Goldmine 45 RPM Price Guide, 7th Edition (2009)

A Castle Full of Rascals: Deep Purple '83–'09 (2009)

Worlds Away: Voivod and the Art of Michel Langevin (2009)

Ye Olde Metal: 1978 (2009)

Gettin' Tighter: Deep Purple '68–'76 (2008)

All Access: The Art of the Backstage Pass (2008)

Ye Olde Metal: 1977 (2008)

Ye Olde Metal: 1976 (2008)

Judas Priest: Heavy Metal Painkillers (2007)

Ye Olde Metal: 1973 to 1975 (2007)

The Collector's Guide to Heavy Metal: Volume 3: The Nineties (2007)

Ye Olde Metal: 1968 to 1972 (2007)

Run For Cover: The Art of Derek Riggs (2006)

Black Sabbath: Doom Let Loose (2006)

Dio: Light Beyond the Black (2006)

The Collector's Guide to Heavy Metal: Volume 2: The Eighties (2005)

Rainbow: English Castle Magic (2005)

UFO: Shoot Out the Lights (2005)

The New Wave of British Heavy Metal Singles (2005)

Blue Öyster Cult: Secrets Revealed! (2004); update and reissue (2009); updated and reissued as *Agents of Fortune: The Blue Öyster Cult Story* (2016)

Contents Under Pressure: 30 Years of Rush at Home & Away (2004)

The Top 500 Heavy Metal Albums of All Time (2004)

The Collector's Guide to Heavy Metal: Volume 1: The Seventies (2003)

The Top 500 Heavy Metal Songs of All Time (2003)

Southern Rock Review (2001)
Heavy Metal: 20th Century Rock and Roll (2000)
The Goldmine Price Guide to Heavy Metal Records (2000)
The Collector's Guide to Heavy Metal (1997)
Riff Kills Man! 25 Years of Recorded Hard Rock & Heavy Metal (1993)

See martinpopoff.com for complete details
and ordering information.